P9-EBY-595

# Society
## and the
# Environment

# Society
# and the
# Environment

· · · · · · · · · · · · · · · · · · · · · · · · ·

## Pragmatic Solutions
## to Ecological Issues

· · · · · · · · · · · · · · · · · · · · · · · · ·

### SECOND EDITION

# Michael
# Carolan

Colorado State University

WESTVIEW
PRESS

Westview Press was founded in 1975 in Boulder, Colorado, by notable publisher and intellectual Fred Praeger. Westview Press continues to publish scholarly titles and high-quality undergraduate- and graduate-level textbooks in core social science disciplines. With books developed, written, and edited with the needs of serious nonfiction readers, professors, and students in mind, Westview Press honors its long history of publishing books that matter.

Copyright © 2017 by Westview Press
Published by Westview Press,
An imprint of Perseus Books
A Hachette Book Group company
2465 Central Avenue
Boulder, CO 80301
www.westviewpress.com

All rights reserved. Printed in the United States of America. No part of this book may be reproduced in any manner whatsoever without written permission except in the case of brief quotations embodied in critical articles and reviews.

Every effort has been made to secure required permissions for all text, images, maps, and other art reprinted in this volume.

Westview Press books are available at special discounts for bulk purchases in the United States by corporations, institutions, and other organizations. For more information, please contact the Special Markets Department at the Perseus Books Group, 2300 Chestnut Street, Suite 200, Philadelphia, PA 19103, or call (800) 810-4145, ext. 5000, or e-mail special.markets@perseusbooks.com.

A CIP catalog record for the print version of this book is available from the Library of Congress
PB ISBN: 978-0-8133-5000-4
EBOOK ISBN: 978-0-8133-5045-5
10 9 8 7 6 5 4 3 2 1

*For Nora, Elena, and Joey*

# Brief Table of Contents

*Preface to the Second Edition xix*
*Acknowledgments xxiii*

1. Introduction: Individuals, Societies, and Pragmatic Environmentalism 1

## Part I: Living in a Material World

2. Greenhouse Gases: Warmer Isn't Better 19
3. Waste: Our Sinks Are Almost Sunk 44
4. Biodiversity: Society Wouldn't Exist Without It 67
5. Water: There's No Substitute 88

## Part II: At the Intersection of Ecology and Society

6. Population: A Problem of Quantity or Quality? 113
7. Transportation: Beyond Air Pollution 135
8. Food: From Farm to Fork 159
9. Energy Production: Our Sun-ny Prospects 183

## Part III: Organizing a Sustainable Society

10. Political Economy: Making Markets Fair and Sustainable 207
11. Governance: Biases and Blind Spots 229
12. Inequality and Growth: Prosperity for All 247

## Part IV: Shifting the Focus to Results

13. From Our Beliefs to Our Behaviors: Pragmatic Environmentalism in Action 275

*Glossary 299*
*References 304*
*Index 329*

# Expanded Table of Contents

*Preface to the Second Edition xix*
*Acknowledgments xxiii*

**Chapter 1. Introduction: Individuals, Societies, and Pragmatic Environmentalism  1**
    Individualism: Too Much and Not Enough  2
    The Contribution of the Social Sciences  4
    Material Things Have Momentum  7
    The Messy Relationship Between Behaviors and Attitudes  10
    The Journey Ahead  12
    Important Concepts  13
    Discussion Questions  14
    Suggested Additional Readings  14
    Relevant Internet Links  14
    Suggested Videos  14

       **ECONNECTION 1.1.** Some of Those Deep Sociological Drivers  8

## Part I: Living in a Material World

**Chapter 2. Greenhouse Gases: Warmer Isn't Better  19**
    Fast Facts  19
    Implications  21
        Urban Areas  21
        Food Security  25
        Children, Women, and the Elderly  26
        Climate Change Refugees  29
    Solutions  32
        Environmental Movements Matter  32
        Seventeen Pragmatic Behavioral Changes  33

Stabilization Triangle and Wedges 34

Green Building 36

Geoengineering 38

Carbon Markets and Offsets 40

Important Concepts 42

Discussion Questions 42

Suggested Additional Readings 42

Relevant Internet Links 43

Suggested Videos 43

ECONNECTION 2.1. The US Public's Knowledge of Climate Change 20

ETHICAL QUESTION 2.1. The Most Threatened Are the Least Responsible 22

ECONNECTION 2.2. Climate Change Linked to Food-Related Vulnerabilities for Certain Populations 26

CASE STUDY 2.1. Climate Change and the Wine Industry 27

ECONNECTION 2.3. Testimony from Satou Diouf, Gadiag Village, Senegal 29

CASE STUDY 2.2. Climate Refugees from Indonesia and Bangladesh 30

MOVEMENT MATTERS 2.1. Beyond Coal and Its Unusual Bedfellows 33

ECONNECTION 2.4. Examples of Geoengineering, Mitigation, and Adaptation 39

ECONNECTION 2.5. Biochar 41

Chapter 3. Waste: Our Sinks Are Almost Sunk 44

Fast Facts 44

Implications 48

Energy Waste and the Life-Cycle Analysis 49

Recycling 51

Food Waste 54

Waste and Public Health 58

E-Waste 60

Solutions 62

MSW Management Alternatives from Around the World 62

Extended Producer Responsibility 63

Important Concepts 65

Discussion Questions 65

Suggested Additional Readings 65

Relevant Internet Links 66

Suggested Videos 66

CASE STUDY 3.1. The Great Pacific Garbage Patch 46

ETHICAL QUESTION 3.1. What Ought to Be Most Valued? 51

CASE STUDY 3.2. The Close Loop Fund and Recent Recycling
    Trends 53

ECONNECTION 3.1. The Recycling Loophole 54

ETHICAL QUESTION 3.2. Public Health and Value Judgments 60

ECONNECTION 3.2. E-Waste and Public Health 61

MOVEMENT MATTERS 3.1. The Real Junk Food Project 63

**Chapter 4. Biodiversity: Society Wouldn't Exist Without It 67**

Fast Facts 68

Implications 68

  Changing Definitions of Biodiversity 72

  Biodiversity: The Fuel Driving Ecosystem Services 75

  Biocultural Diversity 76

  Biopiracy 77

Solutions 79

  Community Conservation 80

  Agrobiodiversity Conservation 83

Important Concepts 86

Discussion Questions 86

Suggested Additional Readings 86

Relevant Internet Links 87

Suggested Videos 87

ECONNECTION 4.1. Thinking About Ecosystem Services
    Conceptually 69

ETHICAL QUESTION 4.1. Sophie's Choice: What If We Can't Save
    Them All? 70

ECONNECTION 4.2. The Tragedy of the Commodity 72

ETHICAL QUESTION 4.2. The Power of Conservation Maps 74

ECONNECTION 4.3. The Irreplaceable Bee 75

ETHICAL QUESTION 4.3. Sustainability: For Whom and Toward
    What End? 80

ECONNECTION 4.4. Socioecological Benefits Known to Arise from
    Community Conservation 82

CASE STUDY 4.1. Participatory Forest Management in Kenya 83

MOVEMENT MATTERS 4.1. Open Source Seed 84

CASE STUDY 4.2. The Seed Bank That Makes Memories 85

**Chapter 5. Water: There's No Substitute 88**

Fast Facts 88

Implications 91

  Bottled Water 93

  Privatizing Water 95

  Agriculture 99

  Climate Change 100

Surface Water  102

Groundwater  102

Hydrologic Extremes  102

Water Quality  102

Water Demand  102

Solutions  102

Water as a Human Right at the Right Value  103

Water Governance  106

Important Concepts  108

Discussion Questions  108

Suggested Additional Readings  109

Relevant Internet Links  109

Suggested Videos  109

CASE STUDY 5.1. China's Water Woes  91

ECONNECTION 5.1. The IMF and the World Bank  96

ECONNECTION 5.2. US Bureau of Reclamation  97

CASE STUDY 5.2. Neoliberalism and Water Privatization: The Case of India  98

CASE STUDY 5.3. Desalinization in California  103

MOVEMENT MATTERS 5.1. Grassroots Organizations Take on Nestlé Waters Canada  106

CASE STUDY 5.4. Micro-Watershed Councils in Mexico and Guatemala  107

# Part II. At the Intersection of Ecology and Society

Chapter 6. Population: A Problem of Quantity or Quality?  113

Fast Facts  114

Implications  115

Greenhouse Gases  115

Urban Sprawl  116

Food  117

Feeding a Growing Nonhuman Animal Population  121

Feeding a Growing Automobile Population  121

Solutions  122

Socioeconomic Development  124

The Future Role of Cities  128

The Case for a Population Explosion  131

"Up Rather Than Out": If It Works for Cities, Can It Work for Farms?  132

Important Concepts  133

Discussion Questions  133

Suggested Additional Readings  133

Relevant Internet Links  134

Suggested Videos  134

**ECONNECTION 6.1.** From IPAT to STIRPAT 116

**ETHICAL QUESTION 6.1.** Do Countries Have a Right to Their Fair Share of $CO_2$ Emissions? 118

**CASE STUDY 6.1.** Japan: A Rapidly Shrinking Country 124

**CASE STUDY 6.2.** Socioeconomic Development in Kerala, India 126

**ETHICAL QUESTION 6.2.** Whose Behaviors Should Change? 127

**CASE STUDY 6.3.** Family Planning in Ethiopia 128

**CASE STUDY 6.4.** Urban Density: A Tale of Two Cities (Within the Same City) 130

**Chapter 7. Transportation: Beyond Air Pollution 135**

Fast Facts 137

Implications 138

Pollution and Public Health 138

Habitat and Biodiversity 142

Community 144

Solutions 146

Dense, Livable, Intermodal Cities 146

From Street Hierarchy to Interconnectivity 151

Disincentivizing the Car 154

Important Concepts 157

Discussion Questions 157

Suggested Additional Readings 157

Relevant Internet Links 158

Suggested Videos 158

**ECONNECTION 7.1.** Effective Speed 139

**CASE STUDY 7.1.** China's Pollution Problem 143

**ECONNECTION 7.2.** Social Capital 145

**ECONNECTION 7.3.** Community Severance 146

**CASE STUDY 7.2.** The Rise of Bike-Share Programs 149

**ETHICAL QUESTION 7.1.** Value Judgments Embedded in Transportation Policy 150

**ECONNECTION 7.4.** High-Occupancy Vehicle Lanes 151

**CASE STUDY 7.3.** "Daylighting" the Cheonggyecheon Stream in South Korea 152

**CASE STUDY 7.4.** Breaking Through the Street Hierarchy 153

**ECONNECTION 7.5.** Have Cars Reached Their Peak? 155

**MOVEMENT MATTERS 7.1.** The Rise of Public Transit Movements 156

**CASE STUDY 7.5.** The London Congestion Charge 156

**Chapter 8. Food: From Farm to Fork 159**

Fast Facts 160

Implications 163

    Environmental Impacts 163

    Community Impacts 166

    Malnutrition and the Green Revolution 168

    The "Treadmills" of Agriculture 171

Solutions 173

    Agroecology 173

    La Via Campesina and Other Peasant-Based Movements 175

    Urban Gardens 179

Important Concepts 180

Discussion Questions 180

Suggested Additional Readings 181

Relevant Internet Links 181

Suggested Videos 181

    **CASE STUDY 8.1.** Mobile Bay Jubilee 165

    **ECONNECTION 8.1.** Fish In Fish Out (FIFO) Ratio 165

    **ECONNECTION 8.2.** Negative Impacts of Industrialized Farms 167

    **ECONNECTION 8.3.** Yes! We Have No Bananas 172

    **ECONNECTION 8.4.** Agroecology: Growing More Than Food and Fiber 174

    **CASE STUDY 8.2.** Landless Workers' Movement (MST) 176

    **MOVEMENT MATTERS 8.1.** Food Sovereignty Movement Scores Victory in Ecuador 177

**Chapter 9. Energy Production: Our Sun-ny Prospects 183**

Fast Facts 184

Implications 186

    "Clean" Coal 186

    Hydraulic Fracturing (aka Fracking) 187

    Nuclear Power 191

Solutions 193

    Efficiency and Curtailment 194

    Renewables 197

    Incentivizing Renewables and Household Efficiency 199

Important Concepts 201

Discussion Questions 201

Suggested Additional Readings 201

Relevant Internet Links 202

Suggested Videos 202

    **CASE STUDY 9.1.** Three Gorges Dam 184

    **CASE STUDY 9.2.** Experimenting with Carbon Capture in West Virginia 187

ECONNECTION 9.1. Mountaintop Removal Mining 188

ECONNECTION 9.2. Floating on a Cloud . . . of Fossil Fuel Emissions 189

ECONNECTION 9.3. More Cheap Fracking Plastic 191

MOVEMENT MATTERS 9.1. The Fight Over Local Control 192

CASE STUDY 9.3. Fukushima Nuclear Disaster as "Normal Accident" 194

ECONNECTION 9.4. Windmills and Bird Fatalities 198

ECONNECTION 9.5. Social Norms and Behavior 200

## Part III. Organizing a Sustainable Society

Chapter 10. Political Economy: Making Markets Fair and Sustainable 207

Fast Facts 210

Implications 211

    The Growth Imperative 211

    The Treadmill of Production 212

    Internal Contradictions 213

    Metabolic Rift 213

    Another Contradiction of Capitalism 214

    Globalization of Environmental Goods and Bads 216

    Critiquing the Environmental Kuznets Curve 216

    World-Systems Framework 218

Solutions 220

    Total Cost Accounting 220

    Fair Versus Free Trade 223

Important Concepts 227

Discussion Questions 227

Suggested Additional Readings 227

Relevant Internet Links 228

Suggested Videos 228

CASE STUDY 10.1. Compact Fluorescent Bulbs: Jevons Paradox or Rebound Effect? 208

ECONNECTION 10.1. Treadmill/Metabolic Rift: Declining Global Fish Stocks 215

ECONNECTION 10.2. Capital Shaping Humans in Its Image: A Third Contradiction? 217

ECONNECTION 10.3. Forest Transition Theory 219

ECONNECTION 10.4. "Apolitical Ecologies" and Foucauldian Governance 223

ECONNECTION 10.5. Fair Trade 224

MOVEMENT MATTERS 10.1. Italy's Gruppi di Aquisto Soledale (GAS): Solidarity Purchasing Groups 226

**Chapter 11. Governance: Biases and Blind Spots  229**

    Fast Facts  229

    Implications  230

        Welfare Economics and Cost-Benefit Analyses  230

        Tyranny of the Present: Discounting  233

        The Self-Interested Straw Person  235

    Solutions  237

        From Tragedy to Drama  237

        Absolute Sustainability  240

        The Precautionary Principle  243

    Important Concepts  245

    Discussion Questions  245

    Suggested Additional Readings  246

    Relevant Internet Links  246

    Suggested Videos  246

        **ETHICAL QUESTION 11.1.** Unpacking "Science"  231

        **ECONNECTION 11.1.** Discounting and Forest Management  234

        **MOVEMENT MATTERS 11.1.** Dams: Making Changes to How Things Are Counted  236

        **CASE STUDY 11.1.** Central Government, Privatization, or Common-Property Regime?  238

        **CASE STUDY 11.2.** Reducing Emissions from Deforestation and Forest Degradation  241

**Chapter 12. Inequality and Growth: Prosperity for All  247**

    Fast Facts  248

    Implications  248

        Rethinking Growth  249

        The Sociology of Consumption  254

        Environmental Justice  256

    Solutions  260

        A Postgrowth Society  261

        Development as Freedom, Justice, and Empowerment  266

    Important Concepts  269

    Discussion Questions  270

    Suggested Additional Readings  270

    Relevant Internet Links  270

    Suggested Videos  270

        **ECONNECTION 12.1.** Freedom Isn't Free, and Apparently Best in Moderation  251

        **ECONNECTION 12.2.** The Plight of Native Americans  259

        **CASE STUDY 12.1.** Environmental Racism in Cape Town, South Africa  260

ETHICAL QUESTION 12.1. Is There a Right Level of Inequality? 261

CASE STUDY 12.2. Kellogg's Six-Hour Day 263

ECONNECTION 12.3. Community Capitals Framework 267

MOVEMENT MATTERS 12.1. The Metales Plant in Tijuana, Mexico 269

# Part IV. Shifting the Focus to Results

Chapter 13. From Our Beliefs to Our Behaviors: Pragmatic Environmentalism in Action 275

Fast Facts 275

Implications 277

   Knowledge and Worldviews 277

   Denial, Ambivalence, and Apathy 279

   Consumerism, Advertising, and Status Attainment 283

Solutions 284

   Advertisements, Freedom, and the Public Good 284

   Collaborative Consumption 285

   Globalization of Environmental Concern 288

   Pro-Environmental Behavior 292

   Social Movements 293

   Pragmatic Environmentalism 295

Important Concepts 296

Discussion Questions 296

Suggested Additional Readings 297

Relevant Internet Links 297

Suggested Videos 297

ECONNECTION 13.1. The Growing Scourge of Social Distance 276

ETHICAL QUESTION 13.1. Is Pollution Natural? 278

ECONNECTION 13.2. Every Cloud Has a Silver Lining: From "Waste" to "Untapped Idling Capacity" 287

ECONNECTION 13.3. Collaboration Might Build Trust but It Also Needs It to Work 288

CASE STUDY 13.1. The Carrotmob (aka Buycott) 289

ECONNECTION 13.4. The New Environmental Paradigm (NEP) 290

*Glossary 299*

*References 304*

*Index 329*

# Preface to the Second Edition

*Society and the Environment: Pragmatic Solutions to Ecological Issues* was born of my personal frustration as an educator. In my department at Colorado State University, we have an undergraduate concentration in environmental sociology; I teach the introductory-level course in that concentration, called Global Environmental Issues. Every semester in this class, I engage with roughly 130 students about the environmental state of affairs, while also going to great lengths to explain how sociology can inform our understanding of how we've arrived at this state. It's an incredibly fun class to teach, not only because it deals with subject matter that's close to my heart, but because the students tend to be really interested in the material as well. But when I first taught the class, over the course of the term my students' early excitement changed to something cooler. They were becoming, to put it in a word, depressed.

Sociology students talk frequently about their desire to make the world a better place.

Yet in our environment classes, day after day, we focused on all that was wrong with the world. I was feeding my students a steady diet of pessimism—about how they can't really make it better—yet still asking them to take individual responsibility for our environmental future. No wonder they were getting indigestion. When I realized this— when the CFL went on over my head—I began to make *solutions* a central component of my class. My students still occasionally feel disheartened or upset, but these days I rarely see a true cloud of depression settle over them.

I talk about solutions in two ways. Think of the first like a steady drumbeat: problem/ solutions, problems/solutions. . . . Each chapter, following this arrangement, begins by stating environmental issues and their implications for society. At each chapter's midpoint, the discussion becomes solution oriented, tackling the possible solutions to the problem immediately at hand. Yet in the end, solutions—*real* solutions—to our environmental ills come not from fiddling around at the margins but from deep systemic change; we need to also come up with solutions that take us *in other directions*. The second way I therefore talk about solutions takes the form of an argumentative arch that builds throughout the entire book. Think of it as a complementary drumbeat that slowly crescendos until the cymbals crash in Parts III and IV, where attention centers on collectively reorganizing a sustainable society.

I have found this two-part technique for talking about solutions to be particularly useful in the classroom. Sociologists have long been suspect of bolt-on solutions; after all, we are trained to see the root causes of problems—sometimes to a fault. But I would argue that small changes to behavior (such as turning down the temperature on one's hot water heater) and technological fixes (like compact fluorescent bulbs) have their place as long as they are met with an equal zest to create deeper structural change. At the same time, I realize such short-term fixes risk creating short-term apathy, which can derail attempts to solve today's environmental problems at their root. To those reading and assigning this book, I recommend a critical reflection on the solutions proposed in each of the following chapters. Ask yourself: What do they fix and what do they miss?

Much of the material that populates the book comes from my Global Environmental Issues class, so you could say it has, from a student's perspective, been truly *peer* reviewed. It is loaded with figures, tables, and images as well as a variety of text boxes: the Case Study, to briefly highlight case studies; the Ethical Question, to highlight the value disputes that underlie environmental conflicts; the ECOnnection, which allows me to interject additional information into a subject; and the Movement Matters, new in this edition, which offer vignettes on grassroots movements that have affected legislation. I also include at the end of every chapter, which I again draw right from class material, suggested additional readings, discussion questions, relevant online sources, and suggested videos. Finally, I take time at the end of every chapter to highlight particularly important concepts. Definitions of these terms and of all the terms appearing in boldface are then provided in the glossary located near the end of the book.

Talking, thinking, and learning about environmental issues in a pragmatic way may also require going beyond the pages of the book in your hands. With that in mind, I have posted a number of "beyond the book" resources online at www.westviewpress.com/carolan. These resources will link you to the social web by way of video clips, podcasts, and interesting, informative blogs and websites. Slides of the figures, tables, and images as well as a variety of slides expanding on issues raised in the boxes are available to help bring the subject matter alive during lectures. Sample quiz questions are available for use as a study guide to give to students or as a starting place for crafting your own exams. Additionally, the website provides a selection of exercises, scenarios, and games (such as an adaptation of the "wedges" game developed by the Carbon Mitigation Initiative at Princeton University), all of which are designed specifically to promote active learning in the classroom. If you have suggestions for additional resources, please feel free to share them with me via the website.

Before you dig into the book, I want to say a few words about my intentional use of the term *pragmatic* in the book's subtitle (indeed, originally the plan was to call this book *Pragmatic Environmentalism*). As with solutions, my understanding of *pragmatic* operates at two levels. At one level, the term is meant to evoke a very commonsense understanding, relating to practical matters of fact where results are of greater importance than philosophical debates. Yet as is also made clear in the chapters that follow, the world is not that black and white. Matters of fact, for example, particularly when dealing with environmental issues, are rarely self-evident. Philosophical and ethical questions are often embedded within debates around what ought to constitute a fact. I would therefore caution anyone from operating solely according to this understanding of the term as they search for answers to the environmental problems that plague us. Yet you could say this book is *pragmatic* insofar as short-term solutions go.

This brings me to the second interpretation of *pragmatic*: as *pragmatism*. For those unfamiliar with this term, it references a distinct philosophical tradition, whose relevance for environmental sociology I delve into in Chapter 13. At the moment, I will say only that I appreciate the pragmatist approach, for it offers an alternative to overt structuralism, on the one hand, and methodological individualism, on the other. The way it does this, I should also add, makes it inherently *hopeful,* as the changes it seeks are deep and therefore lasting. But you'll have to read the rest of the book to find out how this optimistic story ends.

Finally, a few words about the revisions and changes made, as this book represents a second generation: *Society and the Environment 2.0.* I am often disheartened to see new editions of texts come out with only cosmetic changes—updated citations and statistics but little else. Don't get me wrong; any good text needs to be current. But I also believe authors have a responsibility to update text in additional ways. Fields change, or at least they better—you shouldn't be taking a class on a subject if it isn't! And authors don't always get everything right the first time. I certainly didn't. After the release of the first edition I realized there were areas of literature that deserved greater attention. I don't claim the second edition gets everything right either. But it represents an honest attempt to improve on the range of literature offered in the first edition.

Having surveyed current instructors who have adopted my book, the consensus was *not* to add additional chapters. Rather, they were of the opinion that my energies would be better spent adding material within the existing chapter format. That is what I have done. Some of those substantive additions include the following (in no particular order):

- expanded discussion on fracking
- expanded discussion on the sociological dimension of environmental problems—linking ecological concepts to sociological concepts and more emphasis on the institutions of society, their interrelationships, and how they socially and culturally define nature, resources, and environment
- greater attention to health consequences
- addition of new text boxes called "Movement Matters," which provide vignettes on a grassroots movement that has effected change
- more visual elements—photos, figures, and tables
- expanded ancillaries, offered on the instructor website
- expanded discussion on social movements

# Acknowledgments

How does one begin to acknowledge people when one's career is filled with supportive relationships and enlightening encounters? From my graduate student days, when I was lucky enough to have Michael Bell as my PhD adviser, to today, when I have the good fortune of being chair of a sociology department full of faculty and students interested in issues related to environment sustainability and justice, my experience with scholarship has been inherently collective, and this book is a reflection of this fact. So I'll focus on naming those with a presence more directly felt. First, Evan Carver, the original acquisitions editor at Westview Press who talked me into taking this project on. Without you there would be no book. Period. I also owe a debt of gratitude to the various editors and assistants at Westview Press who have helped immensely over the years—Brooke Maddaford, Leanne Silverman, Krista Anderson, James Sherman, and Grace Fujimoto.

I leaned on a number of colleagues for images and articles and in a couple cases used some as sounding boards for ideas and arguments. Those colleagues include Brett Clark, Maurie Cohen, Jennifer Cross, Riley Dunlap, Cornelia Flora, Jan Flora, Lori Hunter, Colin Khoury, Jack Kloppenburg, Aaron McCright, Kari Norgaard, Thomas Rudel, and Richard York. A heartfelt note of thanks must also be extended to these scholars who provided constructive comments and criticisms of the book: Dr. Shaunna L. Scott (University of Kentucky), Dr. Krista E. Paulsen (University of North Florida), Dr. Manuel Vallee (University of Auckland), Dr. Kooros Mohit Mahmoudi (University of Northern Arizona), Dr. Jesse T. Weiss (University of the Ozarks), Dr. Susan G. Clark (Yale University), and Dr. Christopher Oliver (University of Kentucky).

The original book proposal and final manuscript were extensively reviewed by a list of scholars known only to me as "Reviewer 1, 2, 3, . . . " Thanks too to all those anonymous (at least to me) instructors who adopted my book and were kind enough to provide the publisher and myself with constructive feedback on how the first edition could be improved. A lot of you sacrificed a great deal of time to anonymously involve yourselves in this project. Your comments were invaluable. Thank you.

I am also grateful to all those students whom I have had the good fortune of learning from each semester in my Global Environmental Issues class (the introductory class for our environmental sociology concentration at Colorado State University). This book is the culmination of a lot of trial and error in that class as I sought to make the material interesting, relevant, and, importantly, hopeful in tone. This work was supported in part by the following grant: Social Science Korea (SSK), National Research Foundation of Korea (grant number NRF-2013S1A3A2055243).

Finally: to Nora. Thanks to you I am assured that my days will be full of nonmaterial contentment, while in our children, Elena and Joey, I find hope that the future will be in good hands.

# Introduction: Individuals, Societies, and Pragmatic Environmentalism

Why must books on the environment be so gloomy? Chapter after chapter detail what's wrong, followed by, if you're lucky, a chapter or two on what could be done to turn things around. No wonder my students express bewilderment and, in a few cases, something akin to borderline clinical depression when, during the first week of my Global Environmental Issues class, I ask about their thoughts on the ecological state of the world. A quick query on Amazon.com brings up 66,351 books when the words *environmental problems* are typed into the search bar. A search of the term *environmental solutions*, conversely, brought up 14,062 books. Sex, apparently, isn't the only thing that sells books. We can add apocalyptic ecological predictions to that list.

I understand why, historically, all this attention has been paid to environmental problems. People are not much interested in reading about solutions until they've been convinced that there's a problem in need of solving. More than fifty years have passed since the publication of Rachel Carson's *Silent Spring*. Since then we have been exposed to a steady diet of problem talk, with measurable effect. A 2015 poll found that roughly half of Americans have heard about the ongoing drought in the western United States (Ipsos/Reuters 2015). (As I write this in the summer of 2015, Californians are facing "historic water rationing plans" [Boxall and Stevens 2015].) A 2015 Ipsos poll of eighth graders across the United States offers the following encouraging news: not only are kids widely aware of the terms *global warming* and *climate change*, but they nearly universally agree (94 percent) that climate change is real, while 85 percent agree that human activity significantly contributes to climate change (Ipsos 2015). Even friends of mine who would rather lose a limb than be called *environmentalists* acknowledge the problematic ecological conditions that surround us. (Granted, they might still be in denial about climate change, but not much else.) Who is left to convince? Isn't it time to turn the corner and talk about—and even celebrate—instances of positive socioecological change?

This book is a bit of both: a bit about problems, a little bit more about solutions. By focusing on ecological solutions—rather than entirely on problems—I am striving to make this book hopeful, recognizing that if we can't at least think and talk about and point to sustainable alternatives, we really are in trouble. But I am a realistic dreamer, as indicated by my evoking the term *pragmatic* in the book's subtitle. Although it never hurts to be imaginative about what could be, we must be realistic about the possibilities. Too often we confuse criticism, to the point of focusing only on what is bad and wrong, with gritty realism. That kind of negative approach is not realism but pessimism.

Pragmatism decries grand narratives—those totalizing theoretical views of the world that claim to explain human mind, body, and society since the beginning of time. As someone who finds social theory interesting, I admit that it is fun to try to "scoop up" the world in one all-encompassing conceptual framework. Grand narratives are like flying at thirty thousand feet: they are great for discussing the big picture—things like global capitalism and world political and economic systems. When the time comes to roll up one's sleeves and talk about practical policy solutions, however, I find these approaches less helpful, especially when issues revolve around sustainability. (I realize grand narratives have their solutions too, but they are often unrealistic, nebulous, and even polemical. In a word, they're not pragmatic.) Theoretical grand narratives aside, the nontheoretical sustainability literature is equally rife with overly simplistic, one-size-fits-all solutions. Single-handed praise for such phenomena as vertical farming (Despommier 2010), climate engineering (Keith 2013), algae-based biofuels (Demirbas and Demirbas 2010), and edible insects (as "the last great hope to save the planet," Martin 2014) generates considerable interest in and excitement around a topic. As a professional sociologist, however, I cannot help but cringe when the pilots of these tomes spend the majority of their time at cruising altitude. Fine-grain details matter; often they determine whether a solution will work in a particular space. A pragmatic environmentalist enjoys big pictures like anyone else. But he or she also realizes that there is no substitute to having one's feet planted firmly on the ground for establishing what works—and what's sustainable—for any given situation.

## Individualism: Too Much and Not Enough

The pragmatic value of many environmental books is further limited by the problem of individualism. That is, they place either too much or not enough emphasis on individual action. In the former case we're reduced to selfish, autonomous actors—for instance, sovereign consumers—while in the latter case human behavior isn't even factored into the equation. Both of these extremes miss the *collective* nature of social life. As for ascribing too much weight to individual action, the standard argument goes something like this: saving the environment starts with each of us "doing our part"—so go plant a tree, buy organic food, ride a bike, install solar panels on your house, recycle, and so on. You don't have to be a sociologist to know that our actions, every one of them, are shaped by a whole host of factors. Evidence of this is all around. Most people, for example, already have a good basic understanding of how they can reduce their ecological footprint—who hasn't heard of the three Rs of reduce, reuse, recycle, for example? Yet people's actions seemingly belie this knowledge. I see this all the time in my students: they recognize the negative ecological impacts of many of their actions yet still do them. (I am certainly just as guilty of this.) While we act in ways that reflect our wants and interests, those very wants and interests are heavily shaped by existing structures—cultural, technological, infrastructural, political, organizational, legal, and so forth. It is not that individual action has no value when it comes to creating meaningful socioecological change. Individual action devoid of collective mobilization—think shopping—however, will never produce the same level of change as, for example, a well-organized social movement.

Too much focus on the individual can also create dangerous blind spots that risk making circumstances worse for some people. We see this occasionally in the "sacrifice talk" that abounds in the environmental literature—downshift, buy less, give up your car, stop shopping, and so forth. For one thing, I have found this sacrifice talk to be somewhat demoralizing among people genuinely concerned about the environment. Focusing on what one can't do, rather than on what one can, contributes to the malaise described by many of my students. Moreover, not everyone can afford to sacrifice. To give up something requires you to have something to give up. But not everyone wants to sacrifice, or they are willing to sacrifice only so much for the environment. And in some cases, even wanting to sacrifice may still not be enough to elicit a particular behavior—I know someone, for example, who despises driving his car, yet when the temperature drops below freezing, he makes the choice to drive his child to day care to avoid exposure to the elements. This is why environmental education, as a strategy to change behaviors, can take us only so far: because behaviors do not occur in a vacuum. In order for people to make a "greener" choice, they must have viable greener choices to choose from. And to have those choices often requires collective (not just individual) action.

I think I can speak for all sociologists when I encourage readers to resist the temptation to inject individualist thinking into causal explanations of inequality. To put things plainly, don't blame individuals for a systemic problem. As you'll soon see, rising rates of inequality cannot be chalked up to the failings of specific individuals. Inequality is a *sociological* phenomenon. You will also be hard-pressed to find a greater risk factor for suffering from environmental problems than being poor, which is why issues of global environmental justice are increasingly being discussed in classrooms, courtrooms, and political arenas the world over. Poor people are the least responsible for our environmental ills and yet most affected by them. How is that fair? If we hope to ever make things right, we have to grasp the roots of poverty, which means we have to get over blaming poor people for their lot in life and begin thinking sociologically about how and why we have organized society in such a way that allocates "goods" and "bads" so inefficiently and unjustly. And then we must ask how we can do better, while being clear about what "better" means. The pages that follow are intended to spur on that conversation.

Then there's the other extreme: the world-without-people perspective. I encounter this often in material written by specialists who obviously know a lot more about technoscientific matters than they do about human behavior and social change. These are the books, essays, and research papers that tout impressive technological solutions to a variety of our social and ecological ills, like the one declaring the need for a "rooftop revolution" and promising to explain to readers "how solar power can save our economy—and our planet—from dirty energy" (Kennedy 2012). Don't misunderstand my critique; I enjoy reading these materials. Moreover, they contain just the type of outside-the-box thinking that we need. Nor do I doubt the technological feasibility of many of the solutions proposed; indeed, the authors usually go to great lengths to convince us of their long-term practicality. Yet just because something is technologically *possible* does not automatically mean it is socially, economically, politically, and organizationally *probable*. Too often the two are conflated, leaving the reader guessing as to how to take something that works in a lab or on paper and scale it up to the level of city, state, nation, or entire world.

## The Contribution of the Social Sciences

One explanation for why books with an environmental focus tend to concentrate on problems, and superficially on what ought to be done to change things, is the nature of how expertise has historically been attached to the subject. They are called *environmental* problems, after all. The discussion is therefore dominated by natural or environmental scientists and engineers. All are very competent to tell us *what* the state of things is (though even so-called objective facts, as is made clear in later chapters, are mediated and conditioned by social variables and are often premised on the making of subtle value judgments). Yet by nature of their training, they lack a strong grasp of *why* we got ourselves into this mess and *how* we might be able to get ourselves out of it. These "why" and "how" questions inevitably require a firm working knowledge of social, political, economic, and cultural variables, which makes these questions better suited for social scientists. Feelings of doom and gloom arise when too much focus is placed on the "what" and not enough on the "why" and "how." To be fair, the social sciences share some blame in this. They spent a good part of the twentieth century turning away from the material world, preferring instead to focus almost exclusively on phenomena such as language, nonmaterial culture, and, later, **social constructivism**, an approach that focuses entirely on the sociologically dependent knowledge of a phenomenon rather than on any inherent qualities that the thing possesses (Catton and Dunlap 1978; Carolan 2005a, 2005b). For much of the last century the "worlds" studied by the social and natural sciences had been distinct—indeed, to some degree, even mutually exclusive.

Of my various professional identities, one is "environmental sociologist." Although I am proud to identify myself with this subfield of sociology, I admit to being tired of answering the question, "What does sociology have to do with the environment?" Much of this, I realize, stems from a general misunderstanding of how the so-called social and natural worlds interact. The very fact that we separate the social from the natural sciences at universities underscores the pervasiveness of this misunderstanding. Yet the longer I study the world, the blurrier this division becomes for me. What does sociology have to do with the environment? More than most realize.

Sociology has a long history of sidestepping environmental variables, phenomena historically understood as under the purview of the natural sciences. It is important to remember that early social thought was developed, at least in part, as a reaction to social Darwinism, which sought to explain much of social life by way of biology. To avoid a repeat of this dark chapter in sociology's history, social thinkers found safer territory studying phenomena they took to be largely decoupled from the natural world. The problem with environmental issues, however, is that they make a terrible mess of this historically rooted division of labor between the "social" and the "natural" sciences. I

**FIGURE 1.1** Operational Space for the Social Sciences

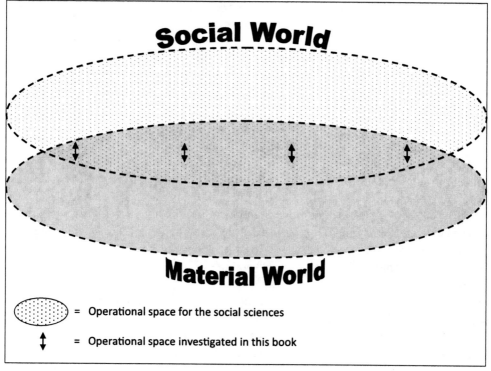

do not want to say much more about this now, as the remainder of the book details ways that the social sciences can contribute to discussions about today's most pressing environmental issues. I will, however, add this: I cannot think of a single environmental problem today that does not touch, in some way, human society. All environmental controversies are the result of social action, and none can be resolved without social action.

Figure 1.1 gives us a way to visualize this interrelationship while marking the terrain that is comfortably within the realm of what social scientists study. As the figure illustrates, environmental sociologists are *equally* as interested in material (or ecological) and social variables. Although acknowledging the fallibility of all knowledge claims, the "emphasis [among environmental sociologists] tends to be on analyzing linkages between the symbolic, social-structural and material realms" (Dunlap 2010, 23).

One could argue that the **sociological imagination**—a way of thinking that involves making connections over time and across scales between the particular and the general—knows no limits, as evidenced by the fact that sociologists have studied such seemingly "natural" phenomena as quarks (Pickering 1999) and genes (Carolan 2010a). I will leave it to someone else to determine exactly where the boundaries of the sociological imagination lie. That said, for students wondering if something falls within what the figure refers to as the "operational space for the social sciences," they need only ask themselves: Has human society ever been of consequence to the phenomenon's existence?

Let's take, for example, the sun. Whereas our *understanding* of the sun is an entirely relevant subject for sociological analysis, I would argue that the sun *itself* is not (since the existence of human society has been of no consequence to the sun's life cycle). While we are shaped by the sun daily, there is no evidence that the relationship is symmetrical. So-called natural ecological processes and phenomena, on the other hand, are very much shaped by our presence and us by them, making them prime candidates for a thorough sociological treatment. Thus, as Richard York (2006) has astutely noted, sociologists who study, for example, environmental controversies or the framing or discursive construction of environmental problems—rather than the interactions between the social and material worlds—might best be described as practicing "sociology of environmental issues."

The double-headed arrows in Figure 1.1 are a key component of the image. Although on paper they may appear insignificant, they represent the figure's conceptual heart. If you want to understand—*really* understand—environmental problems, with the hope of devising practical solutions, then you have to understand how these two realms interact with each other. And I am not just talking about understanding how society affects ecological conditions (which implies a unidirectional arrow). We are shaped as much by the material world as the material world is shaped by us. Shying away from this basic fact will only distract us from what's really going on.

More recently, I, along with my colleague Diana Stuart, have elaborated upon this figure (Carolan and Stuart 2016). Today, a growing number of social scientists are openly talking and writing as if nature, from an analytical, conceptual, and causal standpoint, matters. And yet, while the social sciences seem to be coming around to the fact that the biophysical matters, we still have some way to go in forcefully articulating how sociological variables equally matter—that they too can have force much like so-called laws of ecology and therefore constitute "real" events in the causally efficacious sense. I hear this critique all too often about the social sciences: that the phenomena we interrogate and the processes we hold up as being consequential are not really real—not, that is, like the phenomena that the natural sciences encounter.

The specifics of this argument get fairly theoretical, bordering on the metatheoretical. This is not the place to delve into such a discussion. Cutting right to the chase: Stuart and I overlaid my original figure with a three-part framework that allows us to talk about deep sociological drivers in realist terms, as illustrated in Figure 1.2. The importance of this framework lies in how it further legitimizes the social sciences—and social theory—by pointing to the unique insights these disciplines provide into *all* of the issues that grip us today, from climate change to consumerism, inequality, and hunger and malnutrition. The revised figure now points to three levels: empirical, actual, and real. We use the example of climate change to flesh these levels out. Generally speaking, most of the social scientific literature on the subject can be located within at least one of these analytic boxes: the empirical, those looking at attitudes and knowledge claims toward climate change; the actual, those looking at surface-level drivers contributing to it (for example, food waste, population, transportation, over-consumption; and the real, those looking at deep drivers, where the root causes of it lie (this is where social theory comes into play). Social theories, especially those we take as espousing grand narratives, are trying to point to real things that cannot be easily pointed to. (You cannot point to, for example, the treadmill of production the way you can point to a polluted river; see ECOnnection 1.1.) I try to convey in this book, especially in the later chapters, the nature of those deep drivers: the sociological forces underlying today's environmental

FIGURE 1.2 Socioecological Operational Space for the Social Sciences

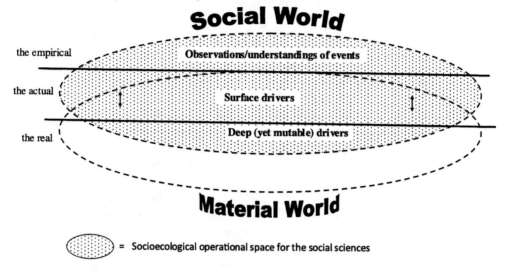

# Social World

the empirical — Observations/understandings of events

the actual — Surface drivers

the real — Deep (yet mutable) drivers

# Material World

⬭ = Socioecological operational space for the social sciences

Source: Adapted from Carolan (2016).

ills—drivers that also must be addressed as we envision more sustainable, just futures. As the book progresses, I drill further down in an attempt to better grasp the really real—the phenomena driving these debates.

## Material Things Have Momentum

Environmental controversies are never just about any one thing. The above discussion ought to have made this clear. Context matters.

It is important to remember, however, that this context also changes over time, a point that is particularly salient when discussion turns to behavioral, and ultimately socioecological, change. Structures—social, economic, political, legal, and even techno-logical—can gather what could be thought of as *sociological momentum* over time. I am drawing here on the term *technological momentum*, which was coined and developed by the famed historian of technology Thomas Hughes (1969).

According to Hughes, society has the greatest control over a technology when it is first introduced. As a technology matures, however, and becomes embedded within society—and society becomes further intertwined with the technology—it becomes increasingly difficult to change paths. Today's gas-powered automobile, for example, would be of considerably less effect were it not for oil, roads, automotive engineers, gas stations, car companies, government taxes on fuel, pro-automobile cultural impera-tives, and the like. The now classic movie *Back to the Future, Part III* (1990) illustrates this perfectly. Marty McFly (played by Michael J. Fox) finds himself in 1885 with a gasoline-powered DeLorean, and his "futuristic" vehicle is worthless: cars are nothing more than processed raw materials when abstracted from the system out of which they emerged. Even understandings of *fuel* are conditioned by these contextual conditions. Nothing is inherently fuel. *Fuel* is simply a term for a carrier of energy. A system must

ECOnnection 1.1

# Some of Those Deep Sociological Drivers

The literature is full of frameworks designed to help us grasp why institutions, groups, and cultures treat the environment in the manner they do. Three such approaches, among many, include the treadmill of production, metabolic rift, and the privileging worldview.

## TREADMILL OF PRODUCTION (SEE ALSO CHAPTER 10):

Modern capitalistic societies are driven by a never-ending commitment to growth—a treadmill. With the support of government and a complicit public, industrial production is allowed to expand, which in turn places still further demands on nature while creating growing amounts of waste (which in turn overload waste sinks, like the Earth's ability to absorb carbon dioxide). The process contains the following paradox: economic growth is privileged, yet the environmental destruction that follows disrupts and severely threatens the system's ability to ensure long-term economic expansion (Schnaiberg 1980).

## METABOLIC RIFT (SEE ALSO CHAPTER 10):

A metabolic rift exists in the exchange between social systems and natural systems, which is hypothesized to lead to ecological crisis (Foster 1999). The origins of the concept lie in the writings of Karl Marx, referring to the crisis in soil fertility generated by urbanization—nutrients from the soil were exported to cities in the form of agricultural products but not returned to the land, causing a disruption in the aforementioned exchange. Over time the process created an ecological crisis, namely, in the case of London, a human-waste-filled River Thames and depleted soil in the countryside. Similar rifts have been shown to exist in the Earth's carbon cycle and the oceans' fisheries.

## PRIVILEGING WORLDVIEW (SEE ALSO CHAPTER 13):

This is an especially diverse literature, encompassing how philosophers since the time of Plato separated nature from society (and mind from body) as well as the historical tendency to feminize nature and the hypermasculine language tied to civilization's need to dominate and tame "her." One especially influential tradition has its roots in a 1967 article by Lynn White Jr. published in the magazine *Science*. The essay, "The Historical Roots of Our Ecologic Crisis," argues that in order to understand environmental problems we must first examine and critique our attitudes toward nature. According to White, prevailing attitudes toward nature are rooted in religious beliefs. As White wrote, "What people do about their ecology depends on what they think about themselves in relation to things around them. Human ecology is deeply conditioned by beliefs about our nature and destiny—that is, by religion" (White 1967, 1206). White focused his analysis on Western Christianity (both Protestantism and Roman Catholicism). He asserted that Western Christianity is "the most anthropocentric religion the world has seen" (1205) and that it encourages and legitimizes a dangerous indifference to the integrity of ecological systems. White argued that within Christian theology, "nature has no reason for existence save to serve" (1207) humanity and thus "bears a huge burden of guilt" (1206) for the environmental mess we are in.

be in place that utilizes a particular carrier of energy if said carrier is to be called fuel. Even oil. Before society organized around it, thereby giving it the designation of *fuel*, oil was once viewed "with indifference or annoyance" (Bolles 1878, 772).

When thought of in abstract isolation, technological artifacts—indeed, all "things"— appear innocuous and open to change. In reality, however, as contexts change, and as society organizes itself around particular ways of doing things, these artifacts can gather momentum. What I like about the metaphor *momentum* is that it keeps us from reducing these discussions to a focus on unembedded things.

I frequently come across comparisons between the truly impressive public transportation systems in Western Europe and Japan and the truly abysmal system found in the United States. Pointing to the widespread use of mass and individual (e.g., biking) transit in parts of Europe, a number of people have told me, "There's no reason we can't duplicate that system here." True enough; there is no reason we can't duplicate that system in the United States. But there are a lot of reasons we have not.

Before World War II, US cities arguably had the best public transportation systems in the world. Following the war, the nation found itself at a crossroads: should those systems be rebuilt and updated (as was being done throughout Europe), or should another transportation model be adopted, namely, the car? We all know the outcome of that decision. And since then, over the course of more than a half century, the country as a whole has slowly organized itself around the automobile. In doing this, the United States has sunk literally trillions of dollars of capital into this transportation model, virtually guaranteeing that the car will remain a central fixture in our lives for decades to come. Here are some examples of how we have stacked the deck in favor of the "choice" to drive a car over other methods of transportation: building parking lots and by making space for cars to park on taxpayer-funded streets; government funding of an extensive infrastructure of roads and bridges that in many cases can be used only by automobiles; restaurants like Starbucks and McDonalds incorporating the automobile into their architectural plans by offering drive-through lanes; and the proliferation of urban sprawl, which simultaneously was made possible because of the car while further making ownership of one a necessity. This level of organization—this *momentum*—makes using the car quite attractive. On the other hand, policy decisions make public transportation, the bike, and walking less convenient and therefore less attractive. This is especially apparent when comparing the United States to other countries, where the decision was made long ago to structurally organize around multiple modes of transportation, which explains why in the Netherlands 27 percent of all trips are by bike versus less than 1 percent in the United States (L. Brown 2009, 153).

Sociological structures, however, refer to more than bricks, concrete, and rails. Another reason why the Dutch use their bikes more than Americans is because the former are less pressed for time. A recent study out of University of California, Los Angeles, highlights three important differences between the two countries that produce these asymmetries in available time (Smart et al. 2014). First, family-friendly labor policies like flex time and paternity leave allow Dutch families to divide child care responsibilities more evenly than American families. Second, workweeks in the Netherlands are shorter. Lastly, Dutch parents do less chauffeuring of children than American parents. Walkable neighborhoods and a high-quality bike infrastructure in the Netherlands make it easy and safe for children to walk or bike to school (see Image 1.1).

**IMAGE 1.1** Human-Power Mobility on Display in the Netherlands

Cyclists bike over a railway in Amsterdam, the Netherlands. In this city there are many alternatives—bike, walking, tram, and bus—to the car. Source: lornet/Shutterstock.com.

In short, the automobile, as the dominant mode of transportation in the United States, has a significant amount of momentum behind it. This is not to suggest that our hands are tied, that we cannot move away from the car and replicate a transportation system more like what's found in, say, the Netherlands. Rather, it is an acknowledgment that change of such magnitude comes with significant transaction costs. The question is: Are we willing to pay them? And a related question: Should all members of society pay these costs equally?

## The Messy Relationship Between Behaviors and Attitudes

In the small rural Iowa town where I grew up, my parents carefully separate their recyclables from the other rubbish that ends up in the garbage truck. They also have to dutifully study every plastic container and verify its number (only certain numbers, and very few numbers at that, can be recycled). Finally, they have to haul their recycle bins to the nearest pickup site, which, fortunately for them because they live in town, is only about three-quarters of a mile away. It would be so much easier if my parents just threw everything away. But they don't. They put up with the "cost" of recycling. I know many in my hometown, and especially those living in the surrounding countryside, however, who do not. For them, all household waste ends up in either the landfill or the burn pile.

Once, one of my more ecologically passionate friends, after hearing this story, looked at me with disbelief, unable to accept that people choose not to recycle. He asked me,

"Why do they do this? Don't they care about the environment?" I think his questions missed the mark. These divergent behaviors seem not to reflect vast differences in attitudes. For example, one individual from my hometown who does not recycle, a lifelong friend, has been a card-carrying member of the Sierra Club for as long as I can remember. He has a hard time walking, lives far from town, and prefers not to drive, which makes the practice of recycling very difficult. Similarly, I know some people in the town where I now live, Fort Collins, Colorado, who admit to having very little interest in reducing their impact on the environment but still diligently recycle.

Fort Collins has a mixed-recycling program. In other words, if it is recyclable—and, unlike in my parents' town, every piece of plastic is recyclable—it goes into a massive blue bin that is wheeled out with the trash to be picked up. That's it. Easy. Moreover, unlike my parents, whose garbage fee allows them to set out as many trash bags as they wish, there is an economic incentive in Fort Collins to divert waste into the recycle stream; namely, you pay more for larger trash cans. To put it in cost-and-benefit terms: whereas it costs my parents to recycle—in terms of time, hassle, and braving the elements (Iowa winters can be brutal)—it costs residents of Fort Collins *not* to.

This goes back to a point I made earlier about the need to contextualize social behavior. I supervised a visiting student from Russia for six months who wanted to learn more about the field of environmental sociology. One of the things that interested her was how attitudes toward the environment in the United States differed from those in Russia. Coming across a statistic about the amount of solid waste that Colorado State University—my employer—recycles (something like 56 percent), she assumed this behavior was evidence of deep attitudinal affinities toward the environment. After noting how comparatively little her Russian university recycles, she asked, "What do they do here to develop these green attitudes?" Holding up a ubiquitous recycle bin and pointing to the words *mixed recycling*, I proceeded to tell her about how socio-organizational changes now make recycling as easy as throwing things away (if not easier, as rubbish bins are notoriously difficult to find in certain university buildings).

The moral of these two stories: structural changes go a long way toward changing behavior. And many times, these changes go further than attitudinal changes alone. As my nonrecycling but otherwise environmentally minded friend from my hometown reminds us, having the "right" attitudes does not do anyone (or the environment) any good if society fails to provide cost-effective ways to act on those beliefs.

I realize that the idea of changing behaviors *prior to* attitudes is somewhat counterintuitive. Yet, for some people at least, perhaps that is what we ought to be shooting for. Just to be clear: I am not talking about making people do something that they don't want to do. In fact, I am saying just the opposite. Recognizing that sacrifice is not for everyone, we should strive to reorganize society in such a way that individuals choose a more sustainable path—like those I know who recoil at the thought of being labeled an "environmentalist" but still diligently recycle. Sacrifice is a rather uninspired solution, and my experience has been that the message tends to turn people off, especially those with exceedingly large ecological footprints. How can we have people want to *act* like an environmentalist even if they don't want to be called it?

I lay no claim to having the answers about what ought to be done. That is a question best left for us all, collectively, to decide. But I do know we will never be able to answer it comprehensively until we have a grasp of the level of complexity involved. The road ahead is not going to be easy, but, as the following chapters explain, there are viable ways forward.

## The Journey Ahead

Some readers (and colleagues) might wonder why, as a professionally trained environmental sociologist, I did not include the term *environmental sociology* in the book's title. You might say it was a pragmatic move to select a title that does not tie me to any one particular disciplinary narrative. Citing my own earlier plea (see Carolan 2005b) to social scientists to expand their sociological imaginations and see the explanatory power of nontraditional sociological variables, Riley Dunlap calls for the *"pragmatic employment of environmental indicators in empirical research investigating linkages between social and biophysical phenomena"* (2010, 23; emphasis added). This book takes this pragmatic call to heart. The conceptual and analytic approaches discussed in the forthcoming chapters come from many disciplines: sociology, to be sure, but also anthropology, geography, political science, science and technology studies, and economics, among others. As I tell my students, there are many ways to make sense of today's ecological state. Undoubtedly, there will be those who find fault with how I go about discussing a particular environmental issue, thinking I should have used "theory X" or "analytic device Y." I accept such criticism. I make no claims that the analyses that follow are the only ways—or even the best ways—to make sense of the environmental issues discussed. Space constraints limit the amount of detail that can be conveyed about any particular topic. But that's okay. The chapters are meant to *start* discussions, not stifle them by claiming to be the last word on any given subject. I urge you to critique, elaborate, and refine the theories and arguments in this book.

The following chapters are problem *and* solution focused. In addition to describing what is wrong (and why), they also discuss alternative institutional, cultural, technological, ethical, and political forms that seek to facilitate more sustainable outcomes. Each chapter follows a similar organizational structure: a brief overview on the current state of the issue, an overview of some of the ways social scientists have explored it, followed by a sociological (and thus still critical) discussion of solutions.

Although each chapter is written to stand alone, the full pragmatic force of the text is best felt when it is read cover to cover. The reason for this is simple: the most sustainable solutions (in other words, the *real* solutions) rarely apply to just one problem. In fact, if we dig deep enough, we would discover that many of today's environmental problems have related causes. Having already cautioned readers to thinking only in terms of grand narratives, it should not come as a surprise that I reject the view that environmental problems are the result of any one thing. Yet I do not symmetrically assign fault, either. The problems we face may not be entirely the product of any one thing, but some things certainly deserve their fair share of the blame. Thus, as the book progresses from "Living in a Material World" (Part I) to "At the Intersection of Ecology and Society" (Part II) to "Organizing a Sustainable Society" (Part III) and, finally, to "Shifting the Focus to Results" (Part IV), critiques sharpen, and proposed solutions become more complete, as the discussion moves closer to those notably culpable sociological artifacts, which I zero in on in the later chapters. As noted earlier, with each section I attempt to drill further down to uncover the really real social dynamics on which considerable blame can be laid and which, once changed, point to opportunities for true sustainability.

Thus, if the solutions proposed early in the text seem shallow, they are. This does not lessen their importance: when you're sick, you need to treat the symptoms as much as the cause. Yet the pragmatist in me wants more; after all, pragmatic solutions need to not only be realistic but also resolve that which ails us.

The first part focuses on issues related to certain environmental phenomena. Specifically, time is taken in this part of the book to examine problems and solutions linked to greenhouse gases (Chapter 2), waste (Chapter 3), biodiversity (Chapter 4), and water (Chapter 5). One of the themes of Part I is that the social sciences have plenty to say about artifacts often assumed to be within the exclusive purview of natural scientists and engineers. Part II adjusts its investigation slightly to discuss phenomena that explicitly weave the "social" and "natural" realms together in complex and fascinating ways. The problems and solutions discussed here revolve around issues relating to population (Chapter 6), transportation (Chapter 7), food (Chapter 8), and energy production (Chapter 9). Part III offers the most pointed response to the question, What does sociology have to do with today's environmental problems? To put it plainly: everything. By highlighting the phenomena driving today's environmental problems—those phenomena located in the realm of "the real" in Figure 1.2—my wish is to approach the closing chapter on a sincerely hopeful note. Only by naming the root dynamics of today's environmental ills—from the political economy (Chapter 10) to issues of governance (Chapter 11) and inequality and growth (Chapter 12)—can we expect to have a real chance of naming truly sustainable solutions. Part IV concludes our journey. Whereas a considerable amount of attention is given throughout the book to structural phenomena (like the aforementioned sociological momentum), the book concludes by elaborating on how social change ultimately hinges on people behaving and thinking in particular ways (Chapter 13). Change must start with us. Lest we forget, although social forces act on us as if independent from us, they are products of our making. This fact is perhaps the most hopeful message of all.

The reader will also find a number of features provided in the forthcoming chapters. In addition to many figures, tables, and images, a variety of text boxes are interspersed throughout to add either further detail or an illustrative case study to bolster a point, concept, or theme in the main text. These take four forms: Case Studies, which briefly highlight case studies relevant to points made throughout the text; Ethical Questions, to highlight the value judgments that lurk everywhere when talking about environmental phenomena; ECOnnections, which I use to interject additional information into the text with minimal disruption to the flow of the main narrative; and Movement Matters, which offer vignettes on grassroots movements that have affected legislation. Finally, suggestions for additional readings are provided at the end of every chapter, as are questions to help spur further thought and discussion on the subject matter. Also at the end of each chapter are Important Concepts, Relevant Internet Links, and Suggested Videos (many of the videos are available for free online).

---

## IMPORTANT CONCEPTS

- ecological complexity
- environmental sociology
- sociological drivers

- sociological imagination
- sociological momentum
- technologically possible versus sociologically probable

## DISCUSSION QUESTIONS

1. How can sociology inform our understanding of environmental problems and solutions?
2. In your experience do people, books, and professors and instructors seem more interested in talking about environmental problems than solutions? If so, why do you think this is?
3. Do old distinctions between the social and natural sciences still hold when facing today's environmental problems? What about disciplines? Do we still need them? Why or why not?
4. What actions of yours clearly cost the environment? Why do you still do them? What would it take for those behaviors to change?

## SUGGESTED ADDITIONAL READINGS

Harris, P., and G. Lang. 2015. "East Asia and the Environment: A Thematic Instruction." In *Routledge Handbook of Environment and Society in Asia*, edited by P. Harris and G. Lang, 3–18. New York: Routledge.

Jackson, T. 2014. "Sustainable Consumption." In *Handbook of Sustainable Development*, 2nd ed., edited by G. Atkinson, S. Dietz, E. Neumayer, and M. Agarwala, 279–290. Northampton, MA: Edward Elgar.

Lidskog, R., Arthur M., and P. Oosterveer. 2015. "Towards a Global Environmental Sociology? Legacies, Trends, and Future Directions." *Current Sociology* 63(3): 339–368.

## RELEVANT INTERNET LINKS

- envirosoc.org. The Environment and Technology subsection of the American Sociological Association. This is an excellent resource for anyone interested in environmental sociology.
- vimeo.com/channels/186979. Videos of the late William "Bill" Freudenburg describing a host of environmental sociological phenomena—anything from "the history of modern environmental theory" to "the 'nature' of sprawl."

## SUGGESTED VIDEOS

- *All Things Are Connected* (2012). While our ethical traditions know how to deal with homicide and even genocide, these traditions collapse entirely when confronted with ecocide and biocide.
- *Disruption* (2014). Shot during the hundred days prior to the People's Climate March held September 21, 2014, in New York City, the film serves as a cautionary countdown intended to motivate viewers to take action on the issue of climate change.
- *Earth Days* (2009). A documentary about the rise of the environmental movement in the United States and the first Earth Day in 1970.

- *Earth on Fire* (2014). A one-hour, Australian special that focuses on mega fires and fires in general as they relate to forests and the ecosystem.
- *Living Downstream* (2010). After being diagnosed with cancer, acclaimed ecologist and author Sandra Steingraber investigates the links between cancer and environmental toxins.

Part I

# LIVING IN A MATERIAL WORLD

# Greenhouse Gases: Warmer Isn't Better

A friend once told me that you know when a person, catchphrase, or subject has become part of our collective consciousness when it has been immortalized on a bumper sticker. Well, I once saw a bumper sticker that read, **"Greenhouse gases:** proof that you can have too much of a good thing." (Greenhouse gases are any gases in the atmosphere that absorb and emit radiation within the thermal infrared range.) True to my friend's words, the topic of human-induced **climate change**—a change in climate patterns that results from human activity like burning fossil fuels—has become unavoidable. (The terms *climate change* and *global warming* are used interchangeably throughout the book.)

Contrary to what certain politicians and media personalities might be saying, scientific debate around climate change is coming to a close. To be sure, there still is a climate change debate within the peer-reviewed literature. Yet that debate is ultimately around questions such as "What are we to do about climate change?" and "Do we all bear equal responsibility for it, or do some individuals and nations deserve a greater share of the blame?" rather than "Is climate change happening?" Interestingly, whereas the peer-reviewed scientific literature is nearly unanimous in its support of the thesis that climate change is occurring and that it is *anthropogenic* (aka human induced) (Cook et al. 2013), the general public holds a greater diversity of views (see ECOnnection 2.1).

So we are left with sociological questions. Some of these include, for example, What might account for the aforementioned discrepancy between the views held among climate scientists and the general public? How did we get ourselves into this mess? and Why is it proving so hard to change course? A thorough treatment of these questions will have to wait for later sections of the book, when we talk about pressures and drivers. In this chapter I address various societal impacts that we can expect from climate change—there are, unfortunately, many—and suggest potential solutions.

## Fast Facts

- A portion of the sun's short-wave radiation that enters the atmosphere is absorbed by the earth's surfaces, where it is then transferred into long-wave radiation (namely, heat)

## ECOnnection 2.1
# The US Public's Knowledge of Climate Change

The Yale Project on Climate Change Communication (with funding help from the National Science Foundation) conducted a national survey on the public's understanding of climate change (Leiserowitz et al. 2015). The survey, published in March 2015, sought to measure general public understanding in the United States about how the climate system works and the causes of, impacts of, and potential solutions to global warming. The study found that 63 percent of Americans believe that climate change is occurring and only 18 percent think it is not happening. Below are some of the findings contained in this extensive report.

- One in three Americans is either "extremely" or "very" sure global warming is happening (37 percent). One in ten Americans is "extremely" or "very sure" global warming is not happening (9 percent).

- Roughly half of Americans (52 percent) think that global warming, if it is happening, is mostly human caused. Three in ten (32 percent) say they believe it is due mostly to natural changes in the environment.
- Approximately one in ten Americans understands that well over 90 percent of climate scientists think human-caused global warming is happening.
- About half of Americans (52 percent) say they are at least "somewhat worried" about global warming; only 11 percent say they are "very worried" about it.
- Only about one in three Americans (32 percent) believes they are being harmed "right now" by global warming.

The full report can be accessed at environment.yale.edu/climate-communication /files/Global-Warming-CCAM-March-2015 .pdf.

and reradiated back into space. Some of this energy, however, is absorbed by the planet's atmosphere, thanks to greenhouse gases like carbon dioxide ($CO_2$), a process known as the **greenhouse effect**. (Other major greenhouse gases are methane and nitrous oxide.)
- Not only are atmospheric levels of greenhouse gases rising, but the *rate of increase is growing*. In the 1970s and 1980s, global emissions of $CO_2$ from burning fossil fuels increased at a rate of 2 percent annually. Since 2000 the annual rate of increase of the world's $CO_2$ emissions is now 3 percent. At this rate of increase, global $CO_2$ emissions will *double* every twenty-five years (Hamilton 2010, 4).
- Present levels of atmospheric $CO_2$ have never been higher in the past 420,000 years (Kirkham 2011).
- Humans emit more than 35 billion tons of $CO_2$ into the atmosphere annually, while natural emissions (coming from plants breathing out $CO_2$ and outgassing from the ocean) equal about 776 billion tons of $CO_2$ per year (Olivier et al. 2014). Natural sources, however, absorb *more* than they emit—roughly 788 billion tons annually. Yet this difference is not enough to compensate for all that humans pump into the atmosphere.
- A comparison between satellite data from 1970 to 1996 found a steady decline in the amount of energy escaping to space at the wavelengths that greenhouse gases absorb.

Since there was no indication that there was less solar energy coming in, this is *direct experimental evidence* for a significant increase in the earth's greenhouse effect (Harries et al. 2001). This evidence has since been independently corroborated by other studies (e.g., Chen et al. 2007; Ohring et al. 2014).

- More than 80 percent of the trapped energy that is the result of the increased greenhouse effect goes into warming the oceans (which isn't terribly surprising, given that oceans cover 71 percent of the earth's surface). The world's oceans, like its land and atmosphere, have been steadily warming over the past half century. For an example of this differential heating of oceans and land, recall the last time you walked on a dry beach on a sunny day. The sand gets warmer faster than the ocean. That is because water is a slow conductor of heat and thus needs to absorb more energy than the sand (or land) for its temperature to increase. Similarly, once warmed, water takes longer to lose its heat than sand (or land).

- Three billion years ago, the earth's atmosphere contained very low levels of oxygen but a great deal of $CO_2$. At the time, the world was teeming with bacteria, many of which survived by breaking down sugars and chemicals present in their environment—a process known as fermentation. These fermenting bacteria produced methane and $CO_2$—two greenhouse gases—as waste products. Over time these bacteria evolved to use sunlight to split the strong bonds of hydrogen and oxygen found in water. The waste produced was oxygen, which over many millions of years began accumulating and changed the composition of the earth's atmosphere (which today contains roughly 78 percent nitrogen, 20 percent oxygen, 1 percent argon, around 1 percent water vapor, and 0.039 percent $CO_2$). This atmosphere killed off many species ill adapted to an oxygen-rich environment. But it also led to the emergence of new life forms, such as, eventually, humans. In sum, the history of life *itself* is an intricate story of the coevolution between life, the earth, and the atmosphere (see Clark and York 2005).

## Implications

While changing ecological conditions affect all life, some species are clearly more threatened than others. We are still learning how climate change affects human societies. Yet although the image emerging lacks high resolution, it is clear that climate change is going to be of major sociological consequence. The forthcoming discussion is organized around the following themes to speak of some of these consequences: urban areas; food security; children, women, and the elderly; and climate change refugees.

### Urban Areas

As the number of people living in cities continues to grow—more than half of the world's population now resides in an urban area—so too will the number of urban residents vulnerable to climate change (see Ethical Question 2.1). Climate change–related risks affecting those residing in urban centers are a function not only of actual events but also of the capacity (or lack thereof) of organizations, social networks, and governments (local and national) to respond to and withstand environmental threats. For example, the quality of housing and infrastructure-based services (like water and sewage), which are typically taken for granted in affluent nations, will considerably shape a society's ability to withstand certain hazards.

# The Most Threatened Are the Least Responsible

Many of the urban centers that face the largest increase in threats from climate change—and with the least capacity to deal with these threats—are in nations least responsible for global warming, as their national greenhouse gas emissions per capita are among the lowest in the world. As illustrated in Figure 2.1, whereas countries in Western Europe, North America, the United Kingdom, and the Mediterranean, along with Australia, Japan, and New Zealand, account for only 19.7 percent of the world's population, they are far and away the leading contributors of total global greenhouse gas emissions, with a national average of 16.1 tons of $CO_2$ equivalent per capita. The term *CO2 equivalent* is used to reduce different greenhouse gases to a common unit. For any quantity and type of greenhouse gas, this signifies the amount of $CO_2$ that would have the equivalent global warming impact.

The rest of the world, meanwhile, as a result of being less affluent, has less capacity to adequately respond to the hazards of climate change. Is this fair? Since they bear a significant share of blame, do affluent nations have a responsibility to help the rest of the world adapt to climate change?

**FIGURE 2.1** Regional Per Capita Greenhouse Gas Emissions Relative to Population

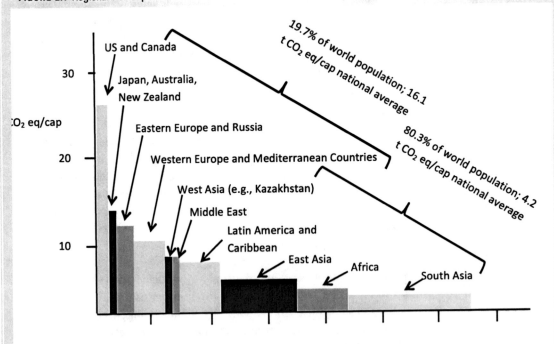

t $CO_2$ eq/cap: tons of $CO_2$ equivalent per capita. Source: Adapted from IPCC (2014).

**IMAGE 2.1** Urban Heat Island Effect

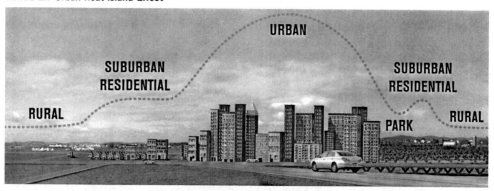

The dotted line represents the mean late-afternoon summer temperatures for the average city (with at least one million inhabitants) and surrounding landscapes. Research indicates that cities are between 1.8 and 5.4° Fahrenheit (1–3° Celsius) warmer than the countryside immediately surrounding them, while temperature increases recorded in suburban residential districts show a slightly less pronounced heat island effect. Source: NASA.

Within **informal settlements** (unplanned housing constructed on land illegally or not in compliance with current building regulations, or both), residential structures rarely comply with official safety standards and are often crowded and poorly maintained, making for a deadly witch's brew of sorts in a future where drastic weather swings become increasingly the norm. There is also very little planning between neighbors when building these structures and altering the landscape, which increases the entire neighborhood's vulnerability to climate change. Homes in the low-lying outskirts of many cities in lower-income countries are thus frequently built in an uncoordinated fashion, as many of these neighborhoods are made up of newly arrived residents who have yet to develop a sense of community among themselves. Some of these homes are elevated. And throughout the settlement, soil has been moved without any thought given to drainage. When it rains, some homes are hit particularly hard either because they are low-lying or as a result of landscape alterations that place them in the path of most of the runoff (Tschakert 2014).

The vast majority of the world's poor also live without air-conditioning or adequate insulation, making heat waves lethal to the very young and old and the ill (Di Ruocco, Gasparini, and Weets 2015). Exacerbating matters further is the fact that in many cities in low-income countries, a sizable proportion of the poor live in tenements and central districts with excessively high densities, precisely where the urban **heat island effect** is at its most pronounced. This effect describes the well-documented phenomenon of how built-up areas are warmer than nearby rural areas. Because concrete, tarmac, and other common construction materials absorb heat readily, the annual average air temperature of a city with at least one million people is between 1.8 and 5.4° Fahrenheit (1–3° Celsius) warmer than the area outside of the city. In the evening, as this solar energy is released back into the atmosphere, the difference in temperature between city and countryside can be as high as 22° Fahrenheit (12° Celsius) (see Image 2.1). (My ninety-four-year-old grandmother has told me stories of going to bed as a child in the winter with a heated

**TABLE 2.1** Urban and Health Impacts of Climate Change

| CHANGE | URBAN IMPACTS | HEALTH IMPACTS |
|---|---|---|
| Temperature | Increased energy demand for heating/cooling; worsening of air quality | Increased vulnerability to respiratory diseases; young and elderly particularly at risk |
| Precipitation | Increased risk of flooding; increased risk of landslides; distress migration | Increase in waterborne and water-washed diseases; food shortages and malnutrition |
| Sea-level rise | Coastal flooding; salinization of water sources | Loss of land and property; health problems from salinated water (especially for children) |
| Extreme rainfall/tropical cyclones | More intense flooding; higher risk of landslides; disruption to livelihoods and city economies | Higher levels of mortality and morbidity; loss of income and assets |
| Drought | Water shortages; higher food prices; disruption of hydroelectricity | Higher prevalence of waterborne and water-washed diseases; food shortages |
| Heat or cold waves | Short-term changes in energy demand | Mortality from extreme heat or cold |
| Abrupt climate change | Rapid and extreme sea-level rise; rapid and extreme temperature change | Significant effects on morbidity and mortality (especially in most vulnerable groups) |
| Population movements | Movements from stressed rural habitats | Increased population; increased stress on infrastructure and resources |
| Biological changes | Extended vector habitats | Increased risk of diseases such as malaria and dengue |

Source: Adapted from Bartlett et al. (2009).

brick under the covers. It's the same principle.) Heat islands increase summertime peak energy demands, air-conditioning costs, greenhouse gas emissions, and heat-related illness and mortality. And as the mean atmospheric temperature continues to rise, the effect will become only more pronounced in the years ahead.

Countries with adequate resources and institutions, infrastructure, services, and regulations in place to protect public health will be able to adapt rapidly to a changing climate. There are many measures implemented in affluent nations that—often unknowingly—enhance a city's adaptive capabilities to climate change: integrated health-care services with emergency services; sufficient sewer and drainage capacity to serve not only daily requirements but also less frequent (yet high-capacity) storm events; structures that conform to building codes and health and safety regulations and that are serviced by piped water, sewers, all-weather roads, and electricity twenty-four hours a day; and institutions that can respond rapidly to high-impact weather events, from utility companies to repair downed power lines to the National Guard (as in the United States) for the more severe events. A summary of some urban and associated health impacts linked to climate change confronting populations within low-income nations can be found in Table 2.1.

A growing proportion of the world's population is also residing in what are known as **low-elevation coastal zones** (LECZ), a trend occurring most rapidly in least-developed countries. This refers to areas within ten meters of mean sea level—about 2 percent of the world's land mass. The coastal cities most at risk are in low-income countries, as fifteen of them contain over 90 percent of the world's LECZ rural poor (Barbier 2015). The country with the greatest proportion of its population living in an LECZ is the Bahamas, where 88 percent of the country lives within ten meters of sea level (McGranahan, Balk, and Anderson 2007).

Some of the fastest urban expansion in low-income nations is also taking place in floodplains, along mountain slopes, and in other zones prone to flooding, sea surges, or other weather-related hazards. Typically, individuals living in these risky sites are poor, as those with means can afford to live someplace safer. Consequently, not only are the sites themselves not well suited for settlement, but the houses are also often structurally deficient and thus do not provide adequate protection from more intense and frequent weather-related threats.

## Food Security

According to the Food and Agriculture Organization of the United Nations, the world's poor will likely be (if not already) the first affected by global warming, as they are food insecure to begin with. Future climate changes will only exacerbate this vulnerability through an increased risk of crop failure, new patterns of pests and diseases, lack of appropriate seeds and planting material for the changing micro and macro climates, and through the loss of livestock (HLPE 2012; see also ECOnnection 2.2). It is worth noting, so it can be immediately set aside, the claim that $CO_2$ emissions are good for humanity because they will turn the world into a lush oasis—$CO_2$, after all, is "plant food." Let's remember that plants rely on more than just $CO_2$ to survive. Any so-called $CO_2$ fertilizer effect will therefore be limited, as ecosystems become increasingly overwhelmed by the negative effects of heat damage and drought. To put it simply: plants can't metabolize $CO_2$ when stressed by a lack of water and excessive heat. Or to put it more simply still: they can't grow when they're dying.

With models used in the analyses that informed the *Fourth Assessment Report* by the **Intergovernmental Panel on Climate Change** (IPCC), Battisti and Naylor (2009) conclude there is a greater than 90 percent chance that average growing-season temperatures by this century's end will exceed any single growing-season average recorded between 1900 and 2006 for most of the tropics and subtropics (see Case Study 2.1). (The IPCC was established by two UN organizations, the United Nations Environment

ECOnnection 2.2

# Climate Change Linked to Food-Related Vulnerabilities for Certain Populations

The Food and Agriculture Organization of the United Nations has highlighted certain populations that warrant special attention because of their heightened food-related vulnerabilities attributable to climate change. These populations include

- low-income groups in drought- and flood-prone areas with poor food-distribution infrastructure and limited access to emergency response
- low- to middle-income groups in flood-prone areas that may lose homes, stored food, personal possessions, and means of obtaining an income
- farmers whose land risks becoming submerged or damaged due to sea-level rise or saltwater intrusions
- farmers who lack capital to adjust to changing temperature and rainfall conditions
- farmers at risk from high winds

- low-income livestock keepers in drylands where changes in rainfall patterns will affect forage availability and quality
- low-income livestock keepers who, because of heat waves, will lose animals from excessive heat
- fishers whose infrastructure for fishing activities (e.g., port, landing, and storage facilities; fish ponds; and processing areas) becomes submerged or damaged by sea-level rise, flooding, or other extreme weather events
- fishing communities whose livelihoods depend on the presence of healthy coral reefs for food and protection from natural disasters
- fishers and aqua farmers whose catch suffers from shifts in fish distribution and the productivity of aquatic ecosystems as a result of changes in ocean currents and temperatures, increased discharge of freshwater into oceans, or both

*Adapted from HLPE (2012).*

Programme and the World Meteorological Organization, in 1988 to provide scientific assessments on issues relating to climate change. With the IPCC as the internationally accepted authority on the subject, the world's governments look to it as the official advisory body on climate change.) More than three billion people currently live at these latitudes, and undoubtedly this number will increase in the decades ahead. Many of them live in **abject poverty** (a severe state of poverty) and depend on agriculture for their survival. While the wealthiest of the world's farmers will have the resources to adopt new technologies and techniques suited for future agroecological conditions, those living at a subsistence level likely will not. The biggest losers from climate change could well be those who depend most on agriculture, aquaculture, and pastoral animal husbandry and who have the least alternative sources of income—namely, the poor.

**CASE STUDY 2.1**

# Climate Change and the Wine Industry

Few crops are as vulnerable to temperature and extreme weather events as wine grapes. And with the prime agroecological conditions go the spoils: for example, there was a fifteen-fold price difference in 2006 between caber-net sauvignon grapes grown in Napa Valley ($4,100 per ton), California, and those raised in California's warmer Central Valley ($260 per ton). The difference in average temper-ature between the regions: 5° Fahrenheit (or roughly 2.8° Celsius) (Hertsgaard 2010).

In France there is worry that the famed Champagne region will become too hot to produce premium-quality champagne. In another prime wine-growing area in south-eastern France, the prized white soil, once cherished for its ability to hold heat, may be-come the region's downfall.

Thanks to climate change, the premium wine grape production area in the United States could shrink by as much as 81 percent by this century's end. In California, warming temperatures coupled with the state's water crisis have many worried that this could re-sult in an enormous loss of land suitable for premium grape production, especially in Napa and Santa Barbara Counties, where land loss could be near 50 percent of present levels (Mozell and Thach 2014). The real killer for the industry is not so much the rise in aver-age temperatures as an increased frequency of excessively hot days, which could "eliminate wine grape production in many areas of the United States" (White et al. 2006, 11217).

## Children, Women, and the Elderly

The roles of women in less developed countries are as diverse as they are important. A classic piece from 1991 on women's work in tribal India highlights the following major areas of work in poor rural areas that are overwhelmingly performed by women: food procurement, such as food gathering and production; the protection of life and property, including the procurement of water, energy (e.g., firewood, charcoal), and fodder; and childbearing and rearing, including the maintenance of health standards for the household, like securing clean water and collecting medicinal plants (Menon 1991). Note how climate change has the ability to touch on all these areas. Floods, droughts, wildfires, and higher or colder than average temperatures all affect the lives of those responsible for the well-being of the household, which, especially in less affluent nations, continues to be women (see Figure 2.2). It is again one more case of climate change having a disproportional impact on a population that is neither to blame for its existence nor capable of responding to its effects because of a lack of resources (see ECOnnection 2.3).

During extreme events like flooding, high winds, landslides, and tsunamis in poor countries, the loss of life is disproportionately higher among children, women, and the elderly (Zhou et al. 2014). A study of a severe flood in 1993 that devastated the Sarlahi district in Nepal found the death rate for children ages two to nine to be more than twice that of adult men (among preschool girls the rate was five times greater). When

**FIGURE 2.2** Women's Vulnerability to Climate Change in Less Developed Countries

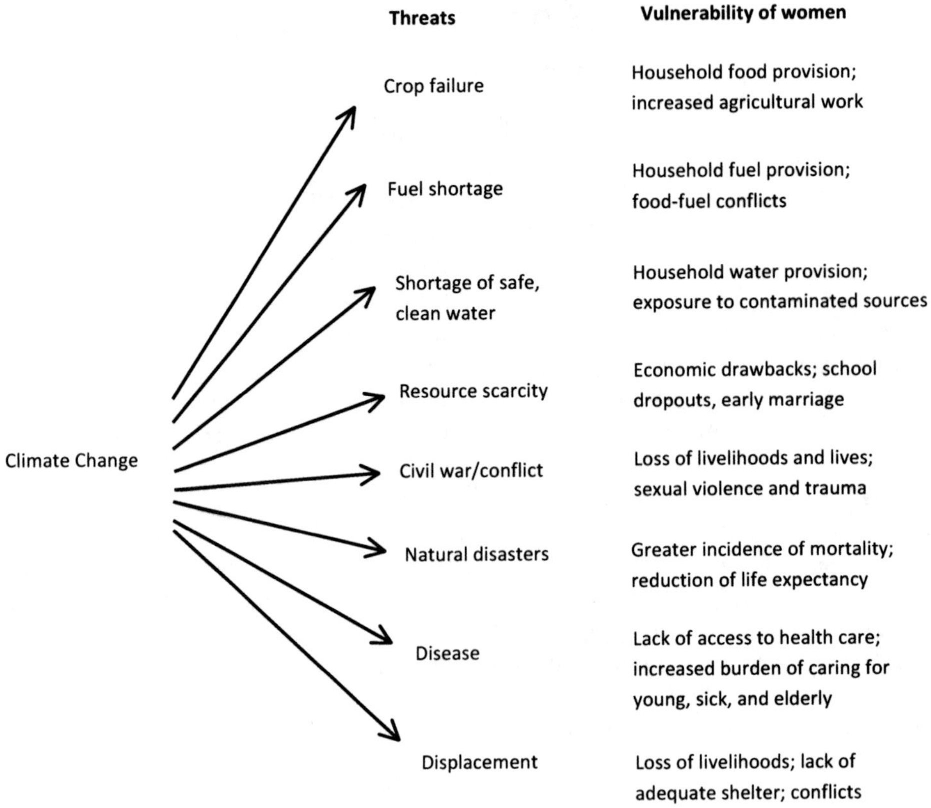

| Threats | Vulnerability of women |
|---|---|
| Crop failure | Household food provision; increased agricultural work |
| Fuel shortage | Household fuel provision; food-fuel conflicts |
| Shortage of safe, clean water | Household water provision; exposure to contaminated sources |
| Resource scarcity | Economic drawbacks; school dropouts, early marriage |
| Civil war/conflict | Loss of livelihoods and lives; sexual violence and trauma |
| Natural disasters | Greater incidence of mortality; reduction of life expectancy |
| Disease | Lack of access to health care; increased burden of caring for young, sick, and elderly |
| Displacement | Loss of livelihoods; lack of adequate shelter; conflicts |

(Climate Change → Threats)

Source: Adapted from WEDO (2008).

aggregated according to class, death rates among poorer households were found to be six times more than those of higher-income households (Pradhan et al. 2007). Rising temperatures are also expanding the range of tropical diseases, with children the most susceptible to the illnesses. Diseases like malaria increase the severity of other maladies, in some cases more than doubling the overall mortality of young children (Bartlett et al. 2009). Climate change is ultimately about greater fluctuations in weather extremes, which include both very hot and very cold temperatures. Hence the U-shaped relationship between temperature and mortality: deaths occur when temperatures spike and when they drop. A recent study examining the temperature-mortality relationship in four subtropical Chinese cities shows that in these areas accustomed to hot temperatures "the cold effect was more durable and pronounced than the hot effect" among elderly populations (Wu et al. 2013, 355). The authors of the study speculate that while these areas have adapted to hotter temperatures, they are woefully maladapted to low temperature extremes, thus making their effects all the more dangerous.

## Climate Change Refugees

Climate change will fundamentally alter the lives of millions who will eventually be forced in years ahead to leave their villages and cities in search of refuge, fresh water,

ECOnnection 2.3

# Testimony from Satou Diouf, Gadiag Village, Senegal

We the women are responsible for feeding our families. The bush has now become a desert shrub in my area and there is nowhere to go to fetch wood. It is prohibited to cut acacia trees. If caught, one has to pay a fine. Every morning, we go to the bush with our bassinette to fetch cow dung for cooking. Unfortunately, during the dry season, it is rare to find foraging livestock. Therefore, we don't have a choice but to go against the Department of Water and Forests and cut acacia trees. One day, unable to find enough wood after a long search, I used some branches to cook. Since the wood was not enough, I cut my plastic bassinette in pieces to fuel the fire. My bassinette was gone before I finished cooking. Then I took the wooden bench where I was seated and cut it to feed the fire. That was not enough. I also had to use my bed sheet for the fire so the food could cook. After serving the food, my mother-in-law refused to eat. She said she didn't think food cooked with plastic bassinette and bed sheet was edible. I told her that if she doesn't eat, the children would eat her portion. Still, she refused. Since that day, I have been crying whenever I think of that incident. My children who don't understand why my eyes are always watery keep asking me why I cry, and I tell them that I am not crying; that's the way my eyes have become!

*Quoted in WEDO (2008, 26).*

food, employment, and the like. The **climate change refugees** crisis is expected to surpass all known refugee crises in terms of the number of people affected. (The term *climate change refugees* refers to populations that have been displaced as a result of climate change.) The problem will likely be most pronounced in poorer countries, where the adaptive capacity of people, cities, and nations to the effects of climate change is low (see Case Study 2.2). In more affluent countries, a refugee crisis may be largely avoided through successful steps at adapting to climate change, like fortified coastal protections or changes in agricultural production and water-supply management (and by having the capability to tightly patrol and effectively close one's borders). The term **adaptation** is useful here, as it refers to actions taken to adjust socioecological systems in response to existing or predicted climatic effects in order to reduce harmful effects. It is worth wondering, however, how many of these displaced people in the future will be seeking refuge in countries like the United States and whether they will be granted access.

At present, the developing world hosts the vast majority of the world's refugees. According to the United Nations (2014), at the beginning of 2014 an estimated 51.2 million people worldwide had been forcibly displaced as a result of persecution, conflict, generalized violence, or human rights violations, the majority of them concentrated in climate change hotspots (places particularly vulnerable to its effects) around the world. As for climate change refugee estimates, the United Nations notes in some of its publications that up to 250 million people could be displaced by climate change by the year 2050 (United Nations 2014).

CASE STUDY 2.2

# Climate Refugees from Indonesia and Bangladesh

Two countries viewed as prime candidates for climate change–induced migration are Indonesia and Bangladesh.

- Indonesia: Roughly 85 percent of this island nation of about 300 million people live within just a few miles of the coast. The steep inland terrain makes much of the noncoastal parts of the country poorly suited for large-scale resettlements. Some of the population could move inland temporarily to escape tidal surges and tropical storms. The more likely scenario, however, has a sizable population leaving the island entirely as sea levels rise.

- Bangladesh: This is a country of 160 million people living essentially at sea level. It has already been hit by serious storms (see Image 2.2). Hurricane Sidr, for example, devastated the nation in 2007, killing, officially, 3,447 people, though some estimates place the death toll closer to 10,000. These storms are expected to increase in both intensity and frequency in the future. This development, coupled with even a modest sea-level rise, risks making much of the country potentially uninhabitable. From Bangladesh alone, the world could see an additional 100 million refugees.

*Based on Climate Refugees (2010).*

In addition to having few financial resources, refugees are also usually poorly integrated into the community and lack connections to influential people, institutions, and organizations, having left behind all their social networks when they moved (Elliott and Yusuf 2014). In most cases, it takes years for refugees to insert themselves into local communities, at which point they may begin to participate in community organizations and local government. Research also indicates that climate change–induced population displacement is not gender neutral, especially when it comes to factors driving migration (Hunter and David 2011). For instance, research looking at migration from West African nations because of climate stress suggests that the deaths of young male migrants trying to reach Europe by boat is in part due to gendered cultural variables (Terry 2009). As the main economic providers for their households, many of these men felt compelled to seek out incomes for their families, even if that meant placing themselves in harm's way by migrating by small boats to other countries. Environmental "push" factors have also been shown to affect women. In Nepal's Chitwan Valley, for example, outmigration among women has been linked to environmental deterioration. Specifically, as collection times increase for fodder and firewood for the Chitwan Valley's women residents, so too increases their likelihood of migration (Bohra-Mishra and Massey 2011).

Population displacement resulting from climate change has also been linked to conflict (Gemenne et al. 2014). Some contributing factors to climate change–induced conflict include the following:

**IMAGE 2.2** Hurricanes Surround Hawaii

Hurricane Kilo is located approximately 1,220 miles west of Honolulu, Hurricane Ignacio is located around 315 miles east of Hilo, and Hurricane Jimena is located around 1,425 miles east of Hilo. Climate modelers predict greater atmospheric activity, phenomena that can include tropical storms, as a result of climate change (see, e.g., Sarthi, Agrawal, and Rana 2015). Image taken August 31, 2015. Source: NOAA.

- Competition: The arrival of climate change refugees in an area can increase the competition over already scarce resources, especially in nations where property rights are underdeveloped.
- Ethnic tension: When climate migrants and residents belong to different ethnic groups, climate-induced migration may promote tension. This will be a particular problem in regions and countries with long-standing ethnic disputes between migrants and residents.
- Fault lines: Conflict may also follow previously established socioeconomic fault lines, such as between migrant pastoralists and resident farmers competing over land or migrants and residents competing over jobs.
- Weak states: Political instability and civil strife in receiving countries will also increase the likelihood of conflict, as weak states are less capable of keeping the peace if tensions arise between migrants and residents for any of the above reasons.

## Solutions

Let's say we lived on a planet whose sun was expanding and consequently warming at an alarming rate. If nothing were done, future generations would experience wildly different climate patterns. Under this scenario I am willing to bet—just as if an asteroid were on a collision course with the Earth—there would be considerable social and political will to take action. That action would likely include not only adapting to post–tipping point climate patterns but also **mitigation** strategies—that is, lessening our greenhouse gas footprint—knowing the role emissions play in contributing to the greenhouse effect.

(As opposed to adaptation, mitigation refers to making reductions in the concentration of greenhouse gases by reducing their sources, increasing absorption capacity, or both.) My point is that we know the earth's atmospheric temperature is rising, and we know these warming trends are going to have devastating social effects. Does it really matter who—or what—we assign blame to for all of this? With that in mind, let's turn to some solutions to the problems of greenhouse gas emissions and climate change more generally.

## Environmental Movements Matter

A recent study examines the extent to which politics and collective action mitigate the effects of economic and demographic factors on environmental outcomes (Dietz et al. 2015). Examining variation in $CO_2$ emissions across and within US states, the team found that the impacts of well-known drivers of anthropocentric climate change—namely, growth in both an economic and a demographic sense—can in part be offset by a local and regional political climate supportive of the environment. Thus, while the authors warn that a do-nothing attitude toward climate change will "substantially increase anthropogenic environmental stress," they add that "the effect of environmentalism is a potentially powerful mediating factor" (4). As they explain, "even as efforts to establish a national policy to limit emissions have yet to be implemented, at the state level, it appears that a strong and broadly accepted environmental movement does produce a mix of shifts in policy, consumption patterns, and production practices that slows emissions" (4). It is important to qualify these findings by noting how trade can greatly obscure what's really going on at local and state levels. That is to say, effective social movements do occasionally merely move environmental pressures into someone else's backyard, improving conditions in one spot but doing little to reduce overall impacts. While this pattern can be difficult to track, there is compelling research documenting how international trade allows affluent countries to export a good chunk of their ecological footprint to lower-income nations, resulting in the latter's incurring the ecological costs of the former's affluence by having goods and food produced in their backyards (Weinzettel et al. 2013). Fortunately, there are plenty of examples supporting the conclusions of the study by Dietz and colleagues, where the environmental movement played a clear role in reducing overall impacts of known greenhouse gas contributors (see Movement Matters 2.1).

## Seventeen Pragmatic Behavioral Changes

Energy consumed by households accounts for roughly 38 percent of all $CO_2$ emissions in the United States (or approximately 8 percent of global emissions). A study by Thomas Dietz and others (2009) explored ways in which those emissions can be reduced through behavioral changes. Their findings are encouraging, explaining that a 20 percent emissions reduction can be achieved in the US household sector within ten years through some well-targeted policies aimed at changing behaviors. To put this into some perspective, the reduction that Dietz and colleagues are expecting is slightly *larger* than the total national emissions of France and *greater* than cutting to zero all emissions in the United States from the pollution-intensive sectors of petroleum refining and iron, steel, and aluminum manufacturing.

MOVEMENT MATTERS 2.1

## Beyond Coal and Its Unusual Bedfellows

King Coal might soon be demoted to a prince, or perhaps even to a baron. While coal today generates close to 40 percent of US power, that's down from the more than 50 percent figure I would have cited a decade ago. More stunning still, practically every watt of new generating capacity is not coming from coal but from natural gas, wind, or solar. Coal now employs fewer workers than the solar industry—the very industry coal proponents laughed at for decades as being just another fad (Grunwald 2015). The Sierra Club's Beyond Coal campaign, which has brought together grassroots activists, lawyers, manufacturers, and other business interests, has been responsible for a good share of coal's fall from grace. There were 523 coal-fired power plants in the United States when Beyond Coal began targeting them a little more than a decade ago. Early in 2015, the campaign cele-

brated its 190th "retirement" (another way of saying "coal plant closing").

Coal used to produce cheap electricity—not anymore. Now that it has to internalize some of the costs it used to externalize, the electricity it produces is becoming more expensive, and the costs of gas, wind, and solar are dropping. That's why businesses are lining up alongside environmentalists, because coal is bad for their bottom line: it means higher electricity bills. An analysis found that at least 40 percent of recent coal retirements in the United States could not have happened without Beyond Coal's advocacy (Grunwald 2015). It's an example of how collective action can often result in strange bedfellows—unconventional alignments that may be necessary to create sufficient leverage to overpower even the most powerful actors.

To get to this level of household-emissions reduction, the authors analyzed seventeen types of household activities that rely upon existing technology, are low in cost or bring attractive returns on investment, and do not require appreciable changes to one's lifestyle. They then estimated the potential emissions reduction (PER) in terms of $CO_2$ after ten years from each action—in other words, the total reduction that would be achieved if every household in the United States adopted it. Next they estimated plasticity into their study, which, according to the authors, "introduces a behavioral realism" (18453). This represents an assessment of the percentage of current nonadapters who could be enticed to make the behavioral change. Table 2.2 shows the seventeen behavioral changes along with their associated PER, behavioral plasticity, adjusted PER after accounting for behavioral plasticity (aka "reasonably achievable emissions reduction," or RAER), and RAER as a percentage of total US household-sector emissions. As illustrated in the table, the four lowest-hanging fruits are (1) the adoption of fuel-efficient vehicles, (2) weatherization, (3) the adoption of high-efficiency appliances, and (4) the use of more efficient home heating and cooling systems. Combined, these four steps are estimated to result in a 12 percent reduction in $CO_2$ emissions in the United States.

**TABLE 2.2** Achievable Carbon Emission Reductions Resulting from Household Actions

| BEHAVIORAL CHANGE | PER (MTC) | BEHAVIORAL PLASTICITY (%) | RAER (MTC) | RAER AS PERCENTAGE OF TOTAL US HOUSEHOLD SECTOR EMISSIONS |
|---|---|---|---|---|
| Weatherization | 25.2 | 90 | 21.2 | 3.39 |
| HVAC (central heating, ventilation, and air-conditioning systems) and equipment | 12.2 | 80 | 10.7 | 1.72 |
| Low-flow showerheads | 1.4 | 80 | 1.1 | 0.18 |
| Efficient water heater | 6.7 | 80 | 5.4 | 0.86 |
| Appliances | 14.7 | 80 | 11.7 | 1.87 |
| Low rolling resistance tires | 7.4 | 80 | 6.5 | 1.05 |
| Fuel-efficient vehicle | 56.3 | 50 | 31.4 | 5.02 |
| Laundry temperature | 0.5 | 35 | 0.2 | 0.04 |
| Water heater temperature | 2.9 | 35 | 1.0 | 0.17 |
| Standby electricity | 9.2 | 35 | 3.2 | 0.52 |
| Thermostat setbacks | 10.1 | 35 | 4.5 | 0.71 |
| Line drying | 6.0 | 35 | 2.2 | 0.35 |
| Change HVAC air filters | 8.7 | 30 | 3.7 | 0.59 |
| Tune up air conditioner | 3.0 | 30 | 1.4 | 0.22 |
| Routine auto maintenance | 8.6 | 30 | 4.1 | 0.66 |
| Driving behavior | 24.1 | 25 | 7.7 | 1.23 |
| Carpooling | 36.1 | 15 | 6.4 | 1.02 |
| **Totals** | 233 | -- | 123 | 20 |

PER: potential emissions reduction; MTC: million tonnes of carbon; RAER: reasonably achievable emissions reduction. Source: Adapted from Dietz et al. (2009).

**FIGURE 2.3** Stabilization Triangle

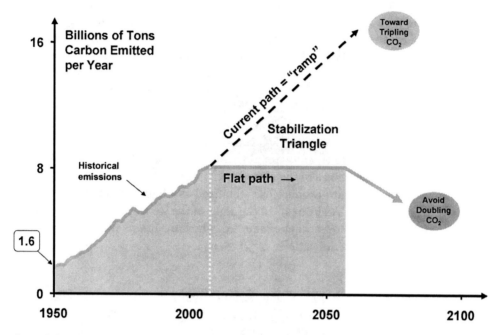

The stabilization triangle refers to the total carbon savings that must be achieved to hold $CO_2$ emissions at a constant level and avoid the predicted tripling of output by 2060. Source: Remik Ziemlinski, The Carbon Mitigation Initiative, Princeton University.

## Stabilization Triangle and Wedges

Carbon emissions from the burning of fossil fuels are projected to double in the next fifty years. This business-as-usual scenario will lead to a tripling of atmospheric $CO_2$ from preindustrial levels. But let's say we wanted to keep emissions essentially flat over the next fifty years, followed by a decrease in $CO_2$ emissions as technologies improve and become cheaper (see Figure 2.3). In the United States, such a strategy would require cutting the projected carbon output by some 9 billion tons per year by 2060; globally, 225 billion tons might need to be cut annually. The amount that would need to be cut to level off $CO_2$ emissions has been called the "stabilization triangle" (Pacala and Socolow 2004). The triangle is made up of large units of $CO_2$ emissions that would no longer be produced with the right policies and incentives; these units are referred to as *wedges*. Let's say, then, that a unit of one billion tons of $CO_2$ avoided is represented by one wedge. (At the global level, each wedge represents 25 billion tons, as the entire stabilization triangle involves cutting $CO_2$ output by some 225 billion tons per year by 2060.) Nine wedges like this in the United States would stabilize $CO_2$ output, and nine at 25 billion tons a piece would stabilize levels worldwide. So the question is: Can we do it? It looks as if we can.

Wedges can take different forms. The behavioral changes outlined in the study by Dietz and colleagues (2009) could certainly represent one such wedge. Another wedge or two could involve zero-emission technologies like wind and solar power. Still other wedges might come from building carbon-storage capacity of **sinks**: natural or artificial reservoirs—like a forest—that hold and store greenhouse gases for an indefinite period, thus preventing their accumulation in the atmosphere. There may also be a wedge by moving toward carbon capture and storage coal plants, though this technology, as discussed further in Chapter 9, is still in its infancy (Carbon Mitigation Initiative 2011). One thing is certain: we cannot afford to wait. Robert Socolow, Princeton University professor and codirector of the Carbon Mitigation Initiative Robert Socolow, noted that in 2011 nine wedges were required to fill the stabilization triangle (Socolow 2011). Yet only *seven* would have been needed if we had acted when the stabilization triangle was first introduced back in 2004 (see Figure 2.4). Our collective unwillingness to take climate change seriously also means we could expect an extra half degree Celsius rise in the average surface temperature of the planet even if we were to come up with all nine wedges today because the atmosphere has stabilized at a higher total emissions level (indicated in Figure 2.4 by "Additional" to the right of the wedges). And if we wait still longer to act, even more wedges will be required, which means an even higher average surface temperature after stabilization.

## Green Building

The energy consumed in the US building sector constitutes about half (48 percent) of all energy used in the country. Globally, that percentage is even higher—76 percent. In light of these figures, any serious attempt to reduce greenhouse gas emissions must include changes to the building sector. Yet buildings are not as flexible as, say, behaviors. Whereas I could conceivably be enticed to drastically change my ways in an attempt to radically reduce my $CO_2$ footprint, it is often not as easy (or cost-effective in the short term) to turn an old, poorly insulated, leaky building into a paragon of ecoefficiency. Yet when building new, there is now little excuse not to go green. The cost to build highly efficient buildings increases total costs between 0 and 2 percent. Yet this investment yields a total life-cycle savings of 20 percent (Lovins and Cohen 2011, 99).

There are still other ways it pays to go green when it comes to our buildings, beyond the obvious saving in energy costs. Green building, to put it bluntly, also makes people happy. In buildings that optimize the use of daylight, students perform better (Earthman 2014), while employees express greater satisfaction and display greater productivity (Whitehead et al. 2010). Consumers have also been shown to buy more in stores using natural lighting, a fact that business owners may like to hear but one that has obvious broader ecological consequences. As employers on average pay one hundred times more for people as they do for energy, a "mere" 1 percent increase in productivity would go a long way toward offsetting the costs of green building (Lovins and Cohen 2011, 100).

Taking a step back, let's talk briefly about the built urban environment. Cities are now home to more than half of the world's population. Cities consume about 75 percent of the world's energy and emit between 50 and 60 percent of its total greenhouse gases, though this figure rises to roughly 80 percent when the indirect emissions generated by urban inhabitants are included (United Nations 2015a). If New York worked to reduce its carbon emissions by 30 percent over the next twenty years, the city would see

**FIGURE 2.4** Stabilization Triangle, Now Versus Then

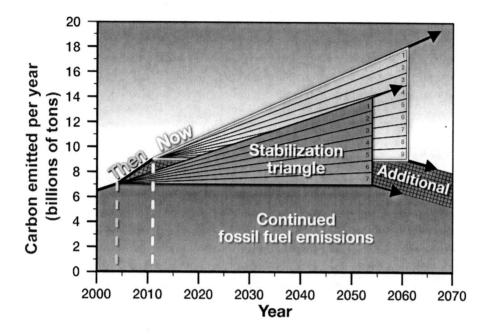

If we had acted in 2004, when the stabilization triangle was first introduced, we would have only needed seven wedges. But in 2011, nine wedges were required to fill the stabilization triangle. The effect is compounding. Source: Remik Ziemlinski, the Carbon Mitigation Initiative, Princeton University.

substantial savings from this effort in terms of energy consumed and emissions released into the atmosphere. Perhaps less recognized, however, are benefits to the labor market that would follow as tens of thousands of new jobs would be created to retrofit, caulk, seal, and insulate the city's buildings (Lovins and Cohen 2011, 118).

More than 80 percent of all commercial buildings in the United States are greater than ten years old and therefore represent a considerable opportunity for energy savings and reducing carbon emissions. It has been calculated that if all commercial space built as of 2010 were included in a ten-year retrofit program, the savings in energy expenses could exceed $41.1 billion annually (Bayani 2010). The cost to carry out such a plan: $22.5 billion for each year of the ten-year period. Not only does that represent a sound investment—after all, taxpayers would be getting almost twice as much as what they put in—but that $22.5 billion spent annually to retrofit the nation's commercial buildings would create a lot of good-paying jobs. For roughly the same price it costs the United States to air-condition its military bases and embassies in Iraq and Afghanistan annually ($20.2 billion) (NPR 2011), it could work toward green-retrofitting every commercial building in the United States.

In June 2011, the Carbon Disclosure Project, a UK-based organization that publicizes the greenhouse gas emissions of major corporations, released its first-ever global report on city governments. The report details how many of the world's largest urban centers are tackling greenhouse gas emissions. For example, some 57 percent of reporting cities claim to have adopted citywide greenhouse gas reduction targets. The most commonly mentioned reduction activities are subsidies and other financial incentives to improve building efficiencies. Some cities are supporting renewable energy initiatives and engaging in major infrastructure overhauls that involve making improvements in public transportation, cycling lanes and paths, and pedestrian areas. London, for example, hopes to have one hundred thousand electric vehicles on its streets by 2020. Seoul, South Korea, hopes to retrofit ten thousand buildings by 2030. And Austin, the capital of Texas, is aiming for zero waste by 2040 (Riffle 2011).

## Geoengineering

*Geoengineering* (also known as climate engineering) is a term often used "to describe activities specifically and deliberately designed to effect a change in the global climate with the aim of minimizing or reversing anthropogenic climate change" (House of Commons 2010, 11). In discussions about societal responses to global warming, geoengineering increasingly accompanies mitigation (strategies seeking to reduce our collective greenhouse gas footprint) and adaptation (strategies seeking to make communities, regions, and nations more resilient to the effects of climate change). Methods typically involve either $CO_2$ removal from the atmosphere or solar-radiation management, whereby the amount of solar energy that penetrates the earth's atmosphere is reduced (see ECOnnection 2.4). The idea of literally engineering the climate is nothing new, as scientists have been seriously discussing the possibility for well over a decade. What has changed in recent years, however, is that it is no longer just scientists who are talking about it. A watershed moment occurred in 2006 with an editorial essay by Nobel Prize–winning atmospheric scientist Paul Crutzen (2006). In this essay, Crutzen calls for serious consideration of geoengineering. With the idea now out in the open—as evidenced by the very fact that I am mentioning it here—talk of climate engineering has expanded beyond the scientific community, becoming a popular focal point of discussion and sometimes heated debate.

Late in 2010, during its meeting of the **Convention on Biological Diversity** (CBD) in Nagoya, Japan, the United Nations voted to impose a moratorium on geoengineering projects and experiments. (The Convention on Biological Diversity—an international legally binding treaty that entered into force in 1993—has three main goals: conservation of biological diversity, sustainable use of biological resources, and fair and equitable sharing of benefits arising from genetic resources.) The moratorium means all signatories to the CBD—a group of nations that, it is worth noting, does not include the United States—must ensure that climate-engineering projects do not take place until risks to the environment as well as social, cultural, and economic impacts have been properly assessed. This builds on a UN moratorium on ocean fertilization adopted in 2008. As noted, the United States is not a signatory, which was why many were concerned when the prestigious National Academy of Sciences released two studies in February 2015 that assessed the potential impacts, benefits, and costs of two different proposed classes of climate intervention: (1) carbon dioxide removal and (2) albedo modification (reflecting sunlight). In the words of one such critic, "the report is balanced in its assessment of the science. Yet by bringing geoengineering from the fringes of the climate debate into the mainstream, it legitimizes a dangerous approach" (Hamilton 2015).

ECOnnection 2.4

# Examples of Geoengineering, Mitigation, and Adaptation

### CO2 REMOVAL (GEOENGINEERING)

*Ocean fertilization:* Iron filings would be dumped into the ocean to spur phytoplankton blooms that draw $CO_2$ from the atmosphere, a saltwater version of forestation. Some downsides: we do not know what this would do to ocean life (it could likely have a negative effect), and blooms could release methane—another greenhouse gas.

### SOLAR-RADIATION MANAGEMENT (GEOENGINEERING)

*Space mirrors:* Hundreds of thousands of thin reflective disks fired into low earth orbit could lower the amount of solar energy that enters the earth's atmosphere. Some downsides: cost aside, the rocket fuel burned to place these little mirrors in orbit would inject massive quantities of black soot into the atmosphere, which would absorb sunlight, trap heat, and thus exacerbate global warming.

### MITIGATION

*Carbon tax:* Impose a tax on carbon emissions, and therefore reward green behavior at both the industry and the household levels. Some downsides: energy-efficient technologies— from hybrid cars to high-efficiency furnaces— are more likely to be adopted by high-income households, meaning such a tax could fall disproportionately on those least able to afford it.

### ADAPTATION

*Genetically engineered (GE) food:* Crops are currently being engineered to withstand changes to climate (e.g., drought tolerance). Some downsides: these seeds would likely be patented, meaning those most vulnerable— the poor—would likely not have access to these technologies; these plants may require additional inputs like fertilizer, which has its own significant $CO_2$ footprint, that could push the cost of production even higher; and there is always the risk that the crops will cross-breed with conventional or traditional (non-GE) plant varieties.

The question arises, then: Does geoengineering really *solve* anything, or do these "solutions" better represent temporary technological Band-Aids? By totally ignoring the root cause(s) of climate change, what's to stop unrestrained emissions from rearing their ugly head again sometime in the future when we can no longer engineer away the warming effects of an atmosphere dense with greenhouse gases? I also worry that these strategies will make us complacent about the impact our actions have on the environment. Geoengineering, it could be argued, merely reinforces the unfounded belief that technology will always ride in at the eleventh hour and save us.

## *Carbon Markets and Offsets*

**Cap and trade** programs seek to halt (the "cap"), and eventually reduce, greenhouse gas emissions that result from human activity. Cap and trade systems are regulatory programs that cap harmful greenhouse gas emissions by limiting them through a per-mitting system and distribute the allotted emissions (what are known as allowances, permits, or credits) to different participants, who then trade them. The goal of the "cap" is to prevent further increases in net emissions. Cap and trade systems in principle therefore seek absolute rather than just relative emissions efficiency. Those businesses that find it most economical to reduce emissions can do so. The resulting **carbon credits** can then be sold to those who cannot yet modify operations to achieve emission reductions. Being market based, cap and trade schemes have found a receptive global audience, especially in comparison to more top-down approaches that spell out specif-ically what businesses can and cannot emit. Under cap and trade, companies still have a choice to pollute at higher levels. But to do so they will need to purchase allowances. Polluters therefore have an incentive to eventually clean up their acts.

Let's say, for example, that for a given year Company X has ten carbon allowances, representing one thousand metric tons of greenhouse gas. Yet thanks to recently adopt-ing certain greener technologies, they are able to reduce their annual greenhouse gas emissions to seven hundred metric tons. This company will therefore have three emis-sions allowances, representing three hundred metric tons of greenhouse gas, which it can sell on the market.

The **Kyoto Protocol**—a UN treaty signed in 1997 that requires its signatories to reduce greenhouse gas emissions—is perhaps the most famous cap and trade scheme. But it's not the only one. Although refusing to sign onto Kyoto, the United States does house examples of successful cap and trade programs, as individuals, companies, and states are voluntarily making agreements to reduce emissions or purchase credits (or both) from others who have done so successfully. One example is the Regional Greenhouse Gas Initiative (RGGI). According to RGGI's website, this initiative "is a cooperative effort among the states of Connecticut, Delaware, Maine, Maryland, Mas-sachusetts, New Hampshire, New York, Rhode Island, and Vermont to cap and re-duce $CO_2$ emissions from the power sector" (www.rggi.org). But like all cap and trade schemes, RGGI's journey has not been free of controversy. Take the 2011 announce-ment, by Republican governor Chris Christie, that New Jersey will be leaving the RGGI. According to Governor Christie, "RGGI does nothing more than tax electricity, tax our citizens, tax our businesses—with no discernible or measurable impact on our envi-ronment" (quoted in Newman 2011). For others, cap and trade programs like the RGGI don't go far enough. The argument goes something like this: We can't fix a problem using the same business-as-usual, market-driven mentality that caused global warming in the first place.

What is RGGI's record thus far? $CO_2$ emissions from power plants in participating states have fallen considerably, from 188 million tons in 2005 to 91 million tons in 2013. It is difficult to say, however, how much that has to do with RGGI and how much it has to do with the recession, as well as the wave of old-technology coal plant retirements sweeping the country. Power plant emissions in the Northeast have actually fallen much faster than the cap requires, which explains why RGGI announced in 2013 that it was lowering the cap to match current levels. It would then decline 2.5 percent each year from 2015 to 2020.

Different from cap and trade, though still a market approach to climate change mit-igation, **carbon offsets** are also gaining in popularity. Carbon offsetting is just as it

ECOnnection 2.5

# Biochar

The standard approach to removing carbon from the atmosphere is to grow plants (typically trees) that sequester $CO_2$ in their biomass or in soil. **Sequestering CO2**—the act of removing $CO_2$ from the atmosphere and holding it in a sink—through reforestation is in fact one of the more popular ways to offset carbon emissions. This sequestration can be taken a step further by heating the plant biomass without oxygen, producing biomass-derived charcoal, or **biochar**. Biochar is another name for charcoal derived from a thermochemical decomposition of organic material at heightened temperatures in the absence of oxygen. In some places, it has long been used to improve soil fertility and sequester carbon. Biochar oil and gas by-products can also be used as biofuels.

Fossil fuels are known as carbon positive, which is to say they add more carbon to the atmosphere. Sequestering carbon through typical biomass systems is, over the long term, largely carbon neutral, as much of the carbon captured will eventually be returned to the atmosphere when plants are burned for energy or through the inevitable process of decomposition. Biochar systems, however, can be carbon *negative* because they retain a substantial portion of the carbon fixed by plants. The precise length of time that the carbon remains locked up in biochar is still under debate, with claims ranging from millennia to "only" centuries. Calculations indicate that emission reductions can be greater than 90 percent if biochar is put back into the soil instead of being burned to offset fossil-fuel use; burning, of course, would release some of the sequestered carbon into the atmosphere (Verheijen et al. 2013). Mixing it into the soil also reduces the need for fertilizer, leading to reduced emissions from fertilizer production, while increasing soil microbial life, which in turn leads to still greater carbon-storage capacity in the soil (Lehmann 2007).

sounds: individuals and organizations buying carbon credits to offset some of their own carbon footprint (see ECOnnection 2.5). One popular offset organization is Carbonfund, a not-for-profit organization based in Silver Spring, Maryland, that provides carbon offsetting options to individuals, businesses, and organizations. Clicking on the "carbon calculator" on its website, I find that I can offset the one-year carbon footprint of my four-person household by paying Carbonfund $222.16. Carbonfund claims to allow consumers to live a "carbon-neutral" lifestyle, or even a carbon-*negative* lifestyle if one purchased sufficient offsets.

Carbon offsets have also had a mixed reception. On its face, sequestering (also referred to as *retiring*) carbon from the carbon cycle—that is, fixing it out of the atmosphere and storing it for long periods of time—seems an admirable goal. Yet rarely do carbon offsets challenge the underlying factors responsible for climate change. In fact, many contend they have just the opposite effect, by providing "moral cover" for consumers of fossil fuels (Bachram 2004). Irrespective of their claims of actually retiring carbon, carbon offsets also raise serious social justice issues. For example, corporations from industrialized countries are enclosing land areas in less developed nations and forcibly evicting local residents. This was famously the case in Uganda, where a Norwegian company leased lands for a carbon-offset project that led to the eviction of eight thousand people in thirteen villages (Bachram 2004). Unfortunately, residents of African nations have faced injustices like this more than once; see, for example, Leach and Scoones (2015).

## IMPORTANT CONCEPTS

- adaptation and mitigation
- climate change refugees
- costs of action versus inaction
- human-induced climate change
- stabilization triangle
- vulnerable populations

## DISCUSSION QUESTIONS

1. Why do some Americans continue to deny the existence of anthropogenic climate change? (This question is investigated further in Chapter 13.)
2. What are your thoughts on geoengineering? Can we effectively engineer ourselves out of this mess and thus avoid making any substantial changes to the status quo?
3. How is climate change a social justice issue?
4. What are some of the more pronounced impacts of climate change for those in low-income countries? And for those residing in high-income countries?

## SUGGESTED ADDITIONAL READINGS

Carolan, M., and D. Stuart. 2016. "Get Real: Climate Change and All That 'It' Entails." *Sociologia Ruralis* 56(1): 74–95.

Dunlap, R., and R. Brulle, eds. 2015. *Climate Change and Society: Sociological Perspectives.* New York: Oxford University Press.

Zehr, S. 2015. "The Sociology of Global Climate Change." *Wiley Interdisciplinary Reviews: Climate Change* 6(2): 129–150.

## RELEVANT INTERNET LINKS

- www.aaas.org/news/global-climate-change-resources. Global climate change resources from the American Association for the Advancement of Science (AAAS).
- climate.nasa.gov/resources/education. Listings of student and educator resources related to global climate change, including NASA products.
- www.nature.org/greenliving/carboncalculator/index.htm. Calculate your carbon footprint.
- www.skepticalscience.com. Excellent resource for debunking climate change skeptics.

- www.skepticalscience.com/docs/Debunking_Handbook.pdf. Free download of *The Debunking Handbook* (2011), a guide for debunking misinformation, including misinformation about global warming.

## SUGGESTED VIDEOS

- *The Burning Question* (2010). A look at what ordinary people think about climate change in relation to what scientists are trying to convey and how the media has portrayed this story.
- *Climate Refugees* (2010). Investigates the global mass migrations caused by climate change.
- *Do the Math* (2013). We need to do something about our greenhouse gas emissions before it's too late.
- *Meet the Climate Sceptics* (2011). A journey into the heart of climate skepticism to examine the key arguments against human-made global warming and to try to understand the people who are making them.
- *Our Rising Oceans* (2015). Investigates the science behind climate change and the doubters that remain, even when faced with seeming indisputable evidence.
- *Sun Come Up* (2011). Academy Award–nominated film that follows the relocation of the Carteret Islanders, who live on a remote island chain in the South Pacific Ocean—some of the world's first climate change refugees.
- *Years of Living Dangerously* (2014). A nine-part documentary concentrating on climate alteration. James Cameron, Jerry Weintraub, and Arnold Schwarzenegger are executive producers. The episodes promote celebrity "detectives" who travel to regions around the world hit by global warming to consult professionals and ordinary people about the effects of climate change.

# Waste: Our Sinks Are Almost Sunk

The trash can is a remarkable artifact, sociologically speaking. To begin, it's the "rabbit hole"—to draw momentarily on one of my daughter's favorite stories (*Alice in Wonderland*)—into the postconsumer world we all know exists but that few from the middle class and above have actually experienced. Whether the rubbish cans in your classroom, the Dumpster next to your friend's apartment complex, or the sixty-gallon waste bin in the alley behind your parents' house: stuff goes in, and . . . That's just it; it goes in and then "poof"—gone!

We moderns really want our waste to just disappear. The trash can, toilet, and kitchen sink are all designed to get our waste out of sight almost as quickly as we're able to generate it. Of course, it wasn't always this way. For our ancestors, there was no hidden world when it came to waste. As recently as a century ago, waste for many of the world's urban dwellers was largely a household issue. As evidenced in Image 3.1, showing a New York sanitation worker in 1907 disposing of municipal waste by burning it right on the street, it wasn't until well into the twentieth century that the **municipal solid waste** (MSW) rabbit hole as we know it today started taking shape. (MSW, generally speaking, refers to all solid waste originating from homes, industries, businesses, demolition, land clearing, and construction.)

Yet the rabbit hole is filling up (see Case Study 3.1). This is a problem. And like all environmental problems, there are multiple entry points into the subject. Importantly, I do not see waste as just a problem of *management*. If "merely" a management issue, the problem of waste would disappear once we figured out how to utilize resources more efficiently during the production process and improve our disposal techniques. I don't buy that it's just a management issue, for reasons discussed shortly.

## Fast Facts

- MSW consists of items like product packaging, grass clippings, furniture, clothing, bottles, food scraps, newspapers, appliances, and batteries. Not included in this category are materials that may also end up in **landfills**, such as construction and demolition materials, municipal wastewater treatment sludge, and nonhazardous industrial wastes.

**IMAGE 3.1** Garbage Burning at East Broadway and Gouverneur Street, New York City, 1907

Source: Library of Congress.

A decade ago there were 2.9 billion urban residents who generated about 0.64 kilograms of MSW per person per day (0.68 billion tons per year). Those amounts have increased to about 3 billion residents generating 1.2 kilograms per person per day (1.3 billion tons per year). By 2025, these figures are estimated to increase to 4.3 billion urban residents generating about 1.42 kilograms per capita per day of municipal solid waste (2.2 billion tons per year) (World Bank 2012; see Table 3.1).

- MSW management varies widely by country. Germany, for instance, imposed a ban on traditional landfills in 2005. This country of eighty-three million inhabitants operates with fewer than three hundred landfills, and the only thing they accept is waste after recycling and incinerating. (By comparison, Canada has a population of thirty-four million and more than ten thousand landfills.) By 2020, all of Germany's landfills are expected to be out of operation, as the country plans to make use of all garbage and the energy produced by it. So, for example, in 2001 Germany recycled about 48 percent of its municipal waste, approximately 25 percent was landfilled, and 22 percent was incinerated. In 2010, the level of recycling had increased to 62 percent, landfilling was practically 0 percent, and incineration had increased to 37 percent (EEA 2013). At the other extreme in the European Union is Bulgaria, which landfills almost all of its MSW (see Figure 3.1).

## CASE STUDY 3.1
# The Great Pacific Garbage Patch

"It's a giant trash island, as big as Texas!": I frequently hear this about the massive floating field of waste trapped by the North Pacific Gyre. (The North Pacific Gyre, located in the northern Pacific Ocean, is one of five major oceanic gyres, which are large systems of rotating ocean currents caused by the Coriolis Effect.) This is where a lot of the renegade plastic goes after having escaped the municipal waste stream. When people hear that plastic hangs around for hundreds of years, they assume that means in its present form. After all, plastic is not biodegradable. But plastic does break down—which is part of the problem. As opposed to being consumed by microorganisms and transformed into compounds found in nature, plastic is broken down into ever smaller pieces as sunlight photodegrades the bonds in its polymers. Plastic never goes away. The pieces just break down and thus multiply in number, making it easier for plastic to find a pathway into organisms and the food chain. And that is precisely what is happening. Plastic pieces now outweigh surface zooplankton in the Great Pacific Garbage Patch by a factor of six to one. Further compounding matters is the fact that plastics take even longer to break down in seawater than on land, as cool seawater and ultraviolet-ray-blocking seaweed act as preservatives. Thus, except for what is picked up manually during sea-cleaning expeditions, every piece of plastic to find its way into the ocean over the last half century is still there (Carolan 2014). And it's not confined to the North Pacific Gyre. According to recent estimates, there are 5.25 trillion pieces of plastic debris in the world's oceans. Approximately one-quarter of a million tons float on the surface, leaving some four billion pieces per square kilometer littering the deep sea (Parker 2015).

- The average nuclear power plant generates approximately 20 metric tons of used nuclear fuel annually. Worldwide, the nuclear industry produces a total of about 8,800 metric tons of used fuel per year. If all the world's used fuel assemblies were stacked end to end and side by side, they would cover a football field roughly a yard deep. (Depending on reactor type, a fuel assembly may contain up to 264 fuel rods and have dimensions of five to nine inches square by about twelve feet long.)

- A 2012 study estimates the total value of food loss at the retail and consumer levels (thus *not including* losses further up the commodity chain) in the United States to be $165.6 billion (Buzby and Hyman 2012). The top three food groups in terms of the value of food loss are meat, poultry, and fish (41 percent); vegetables (17 percent); and dairy products (14 percent). This loss translates into a per capita annual loss of approximately 124 kilograms (273 pounds) at an estimated retail price of $390 per capita per year. The study's authors estimate that the annual value of food loss is almost 10 percent of the average amount spent on food per consumer, or more than 1 percent of average disposable income. These losses translate into over 0.3 kilogram (0.7 pound) of food per capita per day valued at $1.07 a day.

- The number of computers in use in the world topped two billion in 2015. If we are to believe industry estimates, which place the average life expectancy of a computer at

**TABLE 3.1** Solid Waste Generation (in Metric Tons) by Region and Globally, Selected Years

| REGION | 1972 | 1980 | 1990 | 2009 | 2013 |
|---|---|---|---|---|---|
| East Asia | 25 | 45 | 100 | 170 | 190 |
| Europe | 150 | 125 | 170 | 202 | 218 |
| Latin America | 35 | 50 | 72 | 110 | 135 |
| Middle East | 5 | 25 | 45 | 75 | 90 |
| North Africa | 2 | | 5 | 20 | 25 |
| North America | 110 | 125 | 165 | 243 | 254 |
| Pacific Rim | 40 | 50 | 52 | 74 | 79 |
| Sub-Sahara | 5 | 10 | 20 | 50 | 52 |
| Southeast Asia | 10 | 17 | 28 | 52 | 63 |
| World | 400 | 500 | 660 | 1,001 | 1,111 |

Source: Adapted from Defra (2011) and EEA (2013).

between three and four years and global recycling rates for computers at less than 10 percent, then most of those two billion computers will be landfilled by 2020. And that is just computers. There are more than four billion mobile phone users worldwide—a number that is growing annually. The materiality of these devices might last forever, as they are largely nonbiodegradable, but for the average mobile phone owner "forever" is ephemeral, as ownership barely extends beyond a year.

- Waste has multiple links to climate change. First, everything we discard is **embodied energy** and thus already-emitted greenhouse gases. (Embodied energy refers to the sum total of the energy utilized throughout an entire product life cycle.) When we discard, say, a chair or an uneaten apple, we are therefore wasting more than just a chair or an apple but everything that went into making and transporting that object. Landfilling, the most common waste-management practice, also contributes to climate change. The trucks used to haul waste to landfills emit greenhouse gases (though the same can be said for vehicles that haul material for recycling). Landfills also release significant quantities of methane ($CH_4$) into the atmosphere from the **anaerobic decomposition** (the breaking down of biodegradable material by microorganisms in an oxygen-free environment) of organic materials—a process known as fermentation. (And $CH_4$ is twenty-one times more potent at trapping heat in the atmosphere than $CO_2$.) Landfills are the third-largest human source of $CH_4$ emissions in the United States. Encouragingly, this "landfill methane" is beginning to be harnessed in some countries for energy generation—what's known as biogas production. Landfills also act as carbon sinks. Lacking oxygen, organisms that feed on waste and respire $CO_2$ are not present a few meters below a landfill's surface. Items such as grass clippings, then, which drew in carbon from the atmosphere to grow, will have their carbon sequestered when buried in a landfill. The carbon sequestering potential of landfills, however, does not offset its methane emissions (EPA 2011).

**FIGURE 3.1** Municipal Solid Waste Management in the European Union, 2013

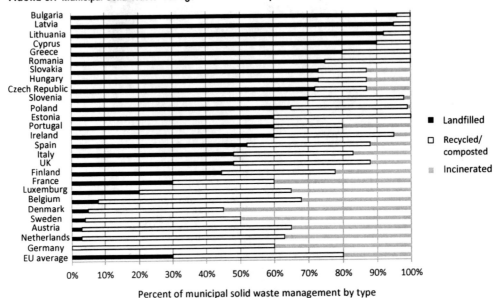

How waste is managed in the European Union varies tremendously, with some countries landfilling almost all of their waste (e.g., Bulgaria) while others (e.g., Germany) landfill practically nothing. Source: Adapted from EEA (2013).

## Implications

The very concept of waste is a social construction. There is no waste in the so-called natural world; everything released, emitted, secreted, and discarded is *food* for something else. *Waste* refers to what we (read: humans) have no use for. Thompson, in his book *Rubbish Theory* (1979), points out the fluidity of the term *rubbish*. Even something once deemed "waste" can regain societal value. Take *scrap*, a term that reclassifies objects of waste as having real economic (and thus societal) value. *Collector's item* is another term that varies considerably over time and can rescue an object from being identified as trash.

*Pollution* is another interesting term, referring to a specific type of waste. Pollution is, quite simply, matter that is out of place. Or, to be still more specific, it refers to waste that is out of place. A while back, I examined societal understandings of odor pollution as they related to large-scale hog farms in Iowa (Carolan 2008c). To do this, I interviewed people working in and living near hog confined animal-feeding operations. One thing I found was that the odors emanating from these facilities were not in and of themselves defined as "pollution" by those I spoke to. Only when "out of place" were the odors classified as such. Thus, for example, no one said the inside of the highly odorous hog facilities was "polluted," as everyone expected the place to smell terrible. There the odors were "in place." Conversely, when *those same odors* were detected in a neighbor's kitchen while eating breakfast, they were classified as pollution, where they were viewed as clearly out of place. Extending this thinking, we tend not to see a landfill as polluted, as the space by definition is meant to be filled with trash. The same holds for, say, sewage treatment plants, even though they are spaces where human excrement concentrates. Yet take those same artifacts—trash and human fecal matter—and put them where they are out of place, and presto: pollution! There are, in short, many ways to talk about waste sociologically. Rather than aim to be comprehensive, the goal of this section is to give the reader a sense of this diversity.

## Energy Waste and the Life-Cycle Analysis

Traditional approaches to environmental impacts have tended to focus on a single business or link in the **commodity chain** (a term that refers to the collective networks encompassing the beginning and end of a product's life cycle) and on one or two pollutants. Doing this, however, can lead to **footprint shifting**, where ecological efficiencies might be achieved at one stage of a product's life cycle only to increase environmental impacts in another. Examining the entire life cycle of a product also allows hotspots—links where impacts are high and where reductions can be achieved at minimal cost and effort—to be identified. The life-cycle analysis (LCA) is a useful tool when attempting to assess overall ecological footprints of practices, like landfilling and recycling, and competing commodities, such as disposable versus reusable coffee cups. By doing this, though, much to the chagrin of my students, we frequently learn that what's best from the perspective of environmental sustainability is rarely black and white.

Take the disposable-paper versus reusable-ceramic versus disposable-foam coffee cup debate. The winner is obvious: the reusable ceramic coffee cup, right? It depends. In fact, under certain circumstances, either disposable cup may well be the "greener" choice (at least in terms of energy consumption) over the ceramic mug. Confused? Let me explain.

Everything, obviously, takes energy and resources to be made. Reusable cups, as they have to be made to be reusable (and thus withstand the abuses of dishwashing, drying, and so on), consume more energy than disposable varieties when being produced— quite a bit more, in fact. The average ceramic mug requires, at least according to one LCA (Institute for Lifecycle Energy Analysis 2002), 25.5 times more energy to make than the average paper cup—14 megajoules (MJ) versus 0.55 MJ per cup. The embedded energy disparity is even greater with foam cups, 14 MJ compared to 0.20 MJ per cup—a difference of 700 percent. Does that therefore mean it takes roughly twenty-six use cycles for the ceramic mug to reach its break-even point with the paper cup and seven hundred use cycles before it matches the embedded energy of a foam mug? Not quite. Remember, those reusable ceramic mugs need to be washed.

This is where the calculations get a little more uncertain, as washing techniques and frequencies vary considerably from case to case. Dishwashers generally require less energy than hand washing, as the newest models are made to make particularly efficient use of hot water and hot water usage is the most energy-intensive part of washing dishes. Moreover, not all households run their dishwasher using the "hot water" or "high temperature" setting. The same, however, cannot be said of commercial settings. Industrial-grade dishwashers (like those found at Starbucks) always use hot water to guarantee their dishes and mugs are fully sanitized. Factoring in for dishwashing after each ceramic mug use, its actual break-even point was calculated at 39 uses when compared to the paper cup and 1,006 uses when compared to the foam cup (see Figure 3.2).

**FIGURE 3.2** Uses of Ceramic Cup to Reach Energy-Breakeven Point Relative to Alternatives

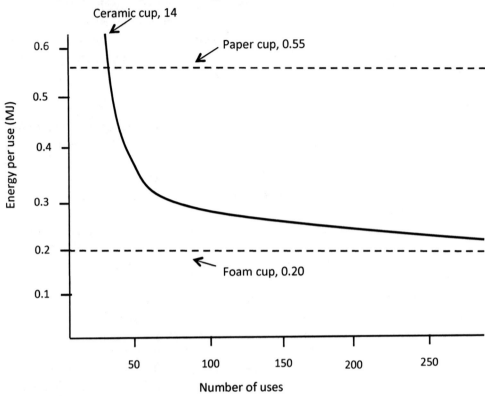

Ceramic cups require on average 14 megajoules (MJ) to produce (and additional energy to clean after every use). For paper and foam cups those figures are 0.55 and 0.20 MJ, respectively. Recognizing this, it is important to maximize one's reuse of a ceramic cup before disposing it for a new one. Those prone to losing or breaking reusable mugs might want to rethink how they transport coffee. Source: Adapted from Institute for Lifecycle Energy Analysis (2002).

There are a couple of take-home points to be derived from such analyses. First, if we choose to go with a reusable mug, we had better make sure we are going to reuse it. I know someone, for example, who buys a new ceramic mug monthly. From an energy conservation standpoint, that's a bad move. Similarly, we need to ask whether the setting will allow a reusable ceramic mug to survive for a couple dozen (or 1,006!) uses. Friends who work in coffee shops have confirmed my suspicions: ceramic mugs do not stand up nearly as well in commercial applications as they do at home, where they tend to be better cared for. If a ceramic mug at your local coffee shop survives, say, only twenty use cycles, you might be better off, from an energy-saving perspective, never using them. There are also clear energy (not to mention water) savings if we can avoid washing our reusable mugs after each use. Or, if you really want to cut energy waste, try reusing disposable paper cups.

That's just energy use. Air pollution and landfill impacts tell a somewhat different story. Clearly, while 1,006 foam coffee cups might be "equal," in terms of energy consumed, to 1,006 ceramic-mug use cycles, those foam cups will have a significantly greater landfill footprint than a single ceramic mug used 1,006 times. That's what I

ETHICAL QUESTION 3.1

# What Ought to Be Most Valued?

LCAs show that being an informed, green consumer is less about being able to choose between "good" and "evil" products than it is about choosing between, say, the lesser of the two (or three, four, or more) evils. All products come with some environmental footprint. And if it comes down to deciding between affecting, for instance, water, air, soil, or energy resources, the consumer must somehow rank these resources when deciding which product ought to be purchased. Then there are all the other *social* variables missed in LCAs, which insert into the equation an even more diverse array of ethical questions. For example, when striving for both social justice and ecological sustainability, should we select bananas grown by smaller farmers in cooperatives in the Caribbean or those grown on plantations in Central America but by unionized and politically empowered workers? Should we place ecological concerns above social ones when forced to privilege one set of concerns over others, which is something we often have to do as consumers? If you're having a problem answering these questions, you should. That's my point.

meant earlier when I said LCAs rarely cast the world in black-and-white terms. We have to ultimately choose for ourselves what to value (see Ethical Question 3.1). What's worse: landfill impacts, air pollution, water consumption, energy use? . . .

## Recycling

Judging by increasing recycling rates from around the world, the practice of recycling appears to be catching on. Nevertheless, these rates continue to vary tremendously across regions (as detailed earlier in Figure 3.1) as well as within countries. And, interestingly, a nation's level of affluence seems at best marginally correlated with recycling levels. San Francisco and Adelaide, Australia, for example, each report recycling rates of around 80 percent. In Rotterdam, Netherlands, citizens recycle at a rate of 30 percent, whereas in Houston only 2.6 percent of the city's MSW is recycled. These rates are comparable to what you would find in less affluent nations. Nairobi and Delhi report recycling rates of 24 and 34 percent, respectively. At the higher end, with rates equal to or surpassing those found in San Francisco, Quezon City, Philippines, and Bamako, Mali, recycle 67 percent and 85 percent of their MSW, respectively (Pouchard 2014; United Nations 2010).

LCAs have been very helpful in providing empirical support to what most environmentalists have been saying for decades: that recycling, to put it plainly, is good for the environment. These LCAs calculate the energy consumed from the moment the recycling trucks stop at your place of residence until this "waste" is processed into brand-new products. This figure is then compared with the amount of energy required to send the same goods to landfills or incinerators and to make new consumer goods from scratch. We find, for example, that aluminum requires 96 percent less energy to make from recycled cans than when processed using bauxite. Recycled plastic bottles use 76 percent less energy, newsprint about 45 percent less, and recycled glass about 21 percent less than when processed from raw (unrecycled) materials. Across the board, recycled goods come out on top, as the energy used to extract and process raw materials is an order of magnitude higher than what is used to recover the same material through recycling (Brogaard et al. 2014; Morris 2005).

An additional point to keep in mind when assessing the economics of recycling: the revenue generated from recycling need not actually surpass its costs to be a good investment for a city. This might at first sound counterintuitive—after all, how could a money-losing venture be a good investment? You must keep in mind that landfilling costs money too. Let's say it costs $175 a ton to collect and process mixed recyclables—a figure not too far off from what a lot of US cities pay. Let's further suppose that those recyclables can be sold on the open market for $120 a ton, which represents still another sensible assumption. This does not necessarily mean, however, that recycling is a money loser. What matters is the cost of taking that material to a landfill. If it is more than $50 a ton, then a recycling program is still a good investment. Looking toward the future, the price of mixed recyclables is expected to climb. This will be due, in large part, to the rising cost of energy, which is increasing the price of raw materials, recognizing that the extraction and processing of these materials is energy intensive. Another variable driving up the price of recyclables is the growing demand of consumer goods in places like China, though the recent economic slump in that country has dampened this a bit. Nevertheless, more municipalities ought to find value in recycling (see Case Study 3.2).

Yet at what—or more specifically, *whose*—expense? That is a question asked by those not yet ready to embrace recycling unconditionally. A body of compelling evidence indicates that, in some instances at least, the ecological gains of recycling may be coming at the expense of social justice (Vallance, Perkins, and Dixon 2011). To enhance efficiencies, a number of cities mix rubbish with recyclables during pickup. The rationale: to cut expenses by eliminating what are perceived as unnecessary redundancies—like two trucks making separate trips to each house—when handling MSW. The contents of each garbage and recycling truck are then sorted. This is bringing workers—those responsible for manually sorting through everything set out for residential pickup—into closer contact with environmental hazards, like **biohazards** (environmental threats resulting from biological agents or conditions, like used needles) and other toxic substances (United Nations 2010).

Once separated, recycled waste itself can be hazardous. Plastic waste, for instance, often contains residues from its original contents, like toxic cleaners, pesticides, and herbicides. And in recycling operations in less affluent nations especially, workers may not be given protective clothing to safeguard against exposure to these potentially toxic chemicals. Yet the problems are not limited to the developing world. Tens of millions of pounds of electronic waste (televisions, computers, and the like) in the United States get funneled annually into its prison system for recycling. The prisoners break the components down (which, according to some reports, involves smashing with hammers) and then pack them up for shipment to processors (Conrad 2011). The organization responsible for overseeing this program, Federal Prison Industries (a government-owned corporation created in 1934 that produces goods and services from the labor of inmates),

# The Close Loop Fund and Recent Recycling Trends

Consumers and stockholders are asking companies to do more to reduce waste, and those businesses, in turn, are responding by promising to use more recycled materials in their products. But there's a problem: not enough high-grade recycled material exists to meet their need. Coca-Cola, for example, pledged to use at least 25 percent recycled plastic in its containers by 2015 but has since revised that percentage downward because of a lack of supply. Walmart is also having a hard time sourcing sufficient material to meet its goal to use three billion pounds of recycled plastic in its packaging and products by 2020 (E. B. 2015). As a result, companies—including Walmart, Coca-Cola, Kuerig, Johnson & Johnson, PepsiCo, and Goldman Sachs—have aligned with the Close Loop Fund, a multistakeholder program that looks to invest $100 million in recycling programs. The fund offers zero-interest loans to municipalities so that they can develop new recycling programs. The fund will also provide below-market loans to private companies so they can develop new local recycling infrastructures (Kaye 2015).

Let's leave aside the fact that analysts estimate that $1.25 billion is needed to fully modernize America's recycling infrastructure (E. B. 2015). As the old saying goes, "junk in, junk out." When municipalities, in an attempt to make recycling easier, began moving toward single-stream (also known as "fully commingled") recycling, they began seeing their streams contaminated with residue at greater rates. The problem has only increased since cities began increasing the size of their bins, assuming bigger was better for keeping material from landfills. Consumers have been using those bigger bins, but often in ways that *increase* the waste going to landfills thanks to that aforementioned contamination. *What* we consume has also changed since recycling plants were built ten to fifteen years ago. Back then, newspaper, thick plastic bottles, and aluminum were king. Now newspapers have all but disappeared, plastic bottles have gotten thinner to cut down on transportation costs, and aluminum cans have been replaced with vacuum-packed plastic with little recycling value (Davis 2015).

was the focus of a four-year-long US Justice Department investigation for exposing prisoners to unnecessary health risks. The findings of that investigation were released in 2010, noting that inmates and employees at ten federal prisons were exposed to toxic metals and other hazardous substances while processing electronic waste for recycling (Kauman 2010).

Let's go back for a moment to the ecological gains associated with recycling. While proponents of recycling proudly tout the practice as green, the more critically minded should be asking in response, "Relative to what?" The empirical evidence is indisputable: recycling is clearly a win for the environment relative to landfilling (at least when recycling streams are not contaminated and the materials actually get recycled). But what if we were comparing recycling to the act of not consuming the item in the first place? Recycling is a big ecological loser in this head-to-head comparison. Remember

ECOnnection 3.1
# The Recycling Loophole

Technically speaking, the recycling symbol (and accompanying number) only identifies the plastic resin used in the making of the article in question, never mind that the chasing arrows that prominently envelope the resin code are the internationally recognized symbol used to designate recyclable materials. The recycling rates of each resin code vary greatly from one recycling facility to another (see Table 3.2). And even when a facility is capable of recycling a particular resin, a whole host of other variables enter into the picture that could cause it to still be landfilled.

The following recycling rates represent averages for the United States as a whole. Number 1 plastic, also known as polyethylene terephthalate (PET or PETE), the resin most likely to be recycled, has a recycling rate of 13 percent. Number 2, high density polyethylene (HDPE), has a recycling rate of 8 percent; number 3, polyvinyl chloride (PVC), less than 1 percent; number 4, low density polyethylene (LDPE), 6 percent; number 5, polypropylene (PP), less than 1 percent; and number 6, polystyrene (PS), less than 1 percent. Finally, number 7, the enigmatic category called simply "other," has a US average recycling rate of 7.5 percent (Carolan 2014).

Recycling facilities are also in the business—lest we forget they are businesses too—of making money. And they are paid by the quality of the bales they produce. Not surprisingly, the less contaminated bales are typically worth more. Recycling facilities therefore tend to focus on those plastics sure to capture a price premium: namely, clear narrow-neck (e.g., soda and water) bottles made with PET/PETE (aka number 1 plastic). As Luke Vernon (2011) of Eco-Products explains, recyclers "have come to trust [that these plastics are most likely to be contaminate-free] as nearly fact which also means their buyers of bales also trust it as fact." And since it is relatively easy to spot bales composed of alternative-shaped plastic objects, many facilities ignore those containers entirely so as not to risk obtaining a lower market price, even those made with PET/PETE. The risk for buyers is twofold: odd-shaped containers have a higher likelihood of not only being made of an alternative resin, which cannot be easily recycled, but also being contaminated. Ever wonder how that empty laundry detergent container gets clean enough to have its resin reclaimed? The answer is simple: it doesn't.

the so-called three Rs of environmentalism: reduce, reuse, and recycle. Recycling is last in this hierarchy for good reason (see ECOnnection 3.1).

## Food Waste

A study by the FAO reports that 33 percent of all food produced for human consumption is lost or wasted globally. That constitutes roughly 1.2 billion metric tons of food annually (Gustavsson, Otterdijk, and Meybeck 2011). A 2013 study by the Institution of Mechanical Engineers paints an even more depressing picture, estimating that as much as 2 billion metric tons of food are wasted annually (Fox 2013). The House of Lords in the United Kingdom conducted a study looking at the cost of food waste across the European Union. It concluded that an estimated 89 metric tons of food are wasted every year in the European Union and projected that figure to rise to around 126 metric tons by 2020 if no action is taken (House of Lords 2014). In light of these trends, France's

**TABLE 3.2** Plastic Packaging Resin

| RESIN CODES/ DESCRIPTIONS | PRODUCT APPLICATIONS | PRODUCTS THAT COULD BE MADE WITH RECYCLED CONTENT |
|---|---|---|
| 1 / Polyethylene terephthalate (PET/PETE) | Plastic bottles for soft drinks, water, juice, sports drinks, beer, mouthwash, catsup, and salad dressing. Food jars for peanut butter, jelly, jam, and pickles. Microwavable food trays. | Fiber for carpet, fleece jackets, comforter fill, and tote bags. Containers for food, beverages (bottles), and nonfood items. |
| 2 / High density polyethylene (HDPE) | Bottles for milk, water, juice, cosmetics, shampoo, dish and laundry detergents, and household cleaners. Bags for groceries and retail purchases. Cereal box liners. | Bottles for nonfood items, such as shampoo, conditioner, liquid laundry detergent, household cleaners, motor oil, and antifreeze. Plastic lumber for outdoor decking, fencing, and picnic tables. Pipe, floor tiles, buckets, crates, flower pots, garden edging, film and sheet, and recycling bins. |
| 3 / Polyvinyl chloride (PVC) | Rigid packaging applications include blister packs and clamshells. Rigid applications such as pipes, siding, window frames, fencing, decking, and railings. Flexible applications include medical products such as blood bags and medical tubing, wire and cable insulation, carpet backing, and flooring. | Pipes, decking, fencing, paneling, gutters, carpet backing, floor tiles and mats, resilient flooring, mud flaps, cassette trays, electrical boxes, cables, traffic cones, garden hoses, and mobile home skirting. Packaging, film and sheet, and loose-leaf binders. |
| 4 / Low density polyethylene (LDPE) | Bags for dry cleaning, newspapers, bread, frozen foods, fresh produce, and household garbage. Shrink wrap and stretch film. Coatings for paper milk cartons and hot and cold beverage cups. Container lids. Toys. Squeezable bottles (e.g., honey and mustard). | Shipping envelopes, garbage can liners, floor tile, paneling, furniture, film and sheet, compost bins, trash cans, landscape timber, and outdoor lumber. |
| 5 / Polypropylene (PP) | Containers for yogurt, margarine, takeout meals, and deli foods. Medicine bottles. Bottles for catsup and syrup. | Automobile applications, such as battery cases, signal lights, battery cables, brooms and brushes, ice scrapers, oil funnels, and bicycle racks. Garden rakes, storage bins, shipping pallets, sheeting, trays. |
| 6 / Polystyrene (PS) | Food service items, such as cups, plates, bowls, cutlery, hinged takeout containers (clamshells), meat and poultry trays, and rigid food containers (e.g., yogurt). Protective foam packaging for furniture, electronics, and other delicate items. Compact disc cases and aspirin bottles. | Thermal insulation, thermometers, light switch plates, vents, desk trays, rulers, and license plate frames. Cameras or video cassette casings. |
| 7 / Other | Three- and five-gallon reusable water bottles, and citrus juice and catsup bottles. Oven-baking bags, barrier layers, and custom packaging. | Containers and plastic lumber. |

Source: Adapted from the American Chemistry Council.

**FIGURE 3.3** Per Capita Food Lost/Wasted (Kilograms per Year), at Consumption and Preconsumption Stages, for Select Regions

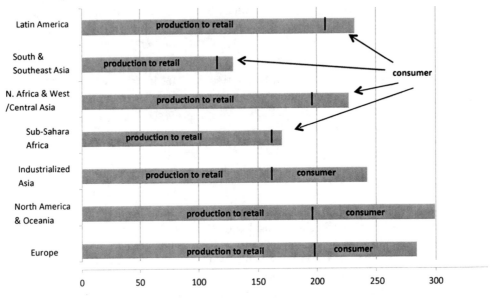

Total per capita food lost/wasted (kg per year)

Source: Gustavsson, Otterdijk, and Meybeck (2011).

parliament announced in 2015 measures to reduce food waste: it passed legislation banning supermarkets from landfilling unsold food and requiring them to pass the food on to charities or put it to other uses, such as using it for animal feed (Chrisafis 2015). But according to the House of Lords study (2014), the future of food waste lies in the hands of households, as the report estimates that 42 percent of all food wasted (by weight) occurs in the home (39 percent food/drink manufacturing, 14 percent food service/hospitality, and 5 percent retail/wholesale). As a percentage of their total food, lower-income countries do not fare much better in terms of wasting food. What varies is *where* in the food system losses occur. As illustrated in Figure 3.3, whereas high-income regions incur considerable losses at the consumer end, most of the food lost in lower-income regions occurs prior to its arrival in people's homes.

One way to think about food waste sociologically is through the concept of **waste regimes**, developed by environmental sociologist Zsuzsa Gille (2007). Gille points out that institutions, regulations, policy initiatives, and social conventions determine not only what is waste but also how waste is valued. In other words, a number of factors are responsible for all this food waste. Some might be classified as cultural. The Chinese have a long-held practice of providing more than their guests can eat, as hosts seek to "gain face" (Smil 2004, 107). Rising costs for waste disposal caused one Shanghai branch of the roast-duck restaurant Quanjude to offer its customers a 10 percent discount if they would finish their food, as many of its customers were eating less than half of what they ordered (Smil 2004). Another variable is aesthetics, or what could be referred to as the cultural expectations about how we think particular foods ought to look. The state

**IMAGE 3.2** From What Was Then Called the US Food Administration (1917)

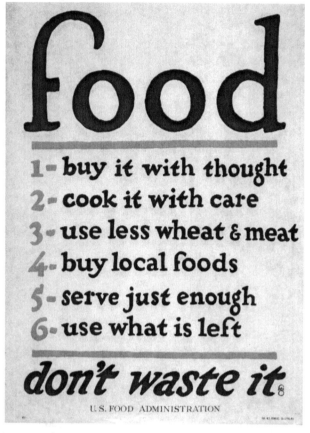

# food

1. buy it with thought
2. cook it with care
3. use less wheat & meat
4. buy local foods
5. serve just enough
6. use what is left

## don't waste it

U.S. FOOD ADMINISTRATION

Can you imagine the US government encouraging the American public to do some of these things today? Granted, it could happen. But not without incredibly forceful pushback from certain powerful food players. Source: Library of Congress, LC-USZC4-9739.

of Queensland, Australia, disposes of more than a hundred thousand tons of bananas annually because the fruits fail to meet national cosmetic retail standards (Hurst 2010). A particularly memorable story came from Bristol, England, involving a fruit seller who was breaking the law by selling kiwi that were two grams below the sixty-two-gram minimum prescribed by EU law (*Daily Mail* Reporter 2008). Fortunately, after the story broke, EU officials decided to clear the law from the books.

Tristram Stuart (2009, 103–111) tells a story of a large British carrot farmer who supplies the supermarket chain Asda. Annually, 25 to 30 percent of his crop fails to meet the chain's aesthetic standards. "Asda insists," the farmer explains, "that all carrots should be straight so the consumer can peel the full length in one easy stroke" (104). Any—and only—oversized carrots go to food processors, which account for about a third of those unwanted by Asda. Small carrots require too much labor to handle, so food processors usually avoid using them. What's left, the remaining two-thirds of that originally rejected by Asda, is fed to livestock (see Image 3.2).

The power wielded by food processors and supermarkets through **market concentration** (the dominance of a particular market by a few large corporations) in these sectors also encourages food waste. Supermarkets in particular have considerable lever-age over those operating earlier in the food chain. This leverage comes from **buyer power**—an effect that results when a market has numerous sellers but only one buyer or a few. Buyer power means that whereas supermarkets or processors can select from a range of farmers to work with, the inverse is less often the case, giving the former tremendous leverage over the latter when it comes to setting the terms of the contract. In some cases, farmers supply only one processor, which effectively allows the buyer (the processor) to write the terms of the contract. This allows companies like Birds Eye, for example, to contractually forbid their growers from selling their peas to anyone else, even those rejected by the company for not meeting certain standards. In such a scenario, growers are left with no choice but either to feed their surplus to livestock or to recycle the vegetables back into the soil (Stuart 2009, 117). In this case, the cost of waste is pushed onto farmers.

As already noted, consumers waste a lot of food. Yet in some instances, it's not en-tirely their fault, thanks to a nifty little marketing strategy by supermarkets called the buy-one-get-one (BOGO) free promotion. Grocers often reserve these campaigns for items on the brink of expiring, items that they would lose money on if they held onto them just a day or two longer. These schemes might be a great deal if you actually use the "free" one. The research indicates, however, that most do not (Gooch, Felfel, and Marenick 2010). In Britain, in light of the aforementioned House of Lords (2014) study, the government is now urging supermarkets to end BOGO offers in an effort to stop the amount of food being wasted by customers (Cox 2014). In the United States, conversely, BOGO schemes remain very popular. It is also worth noting that "sell by," "best by," and "use by" dates go largely unregulated around the world. In the case of the United States, for instance, the federal government regulates such statements only when they apply to infant formula. That means companies decide on these dates. Yet they have an incentive to make those freshness windows unduly short, which further encourages food waste.

## Waste and Public Health

All waste represents a potential health hazard (see ECOnnection 3.2). Those of us liv-ing in affluent countries often do not think about waste in the context of public health. Although all societies put their waste somewhere, the characteristics of this location can vary considerably from nation to nation. In countries like Australia, Japan, and the United States, "somewhere" is often a combination of landfills, incinerators, and recycling facilities. In less affluent nations with poor waste-management practices it's usually a lot closer, like in nearby rivers, lakes, or parks; along public roadways; or in huge heaps in the middle of the street, creating a toxic playground of sorts for neighborhood children (World Bank 2012). **Collective coverage**, as it's called in the waste-management community, is the proportion of an area serviced by the municipal waste stream, and it varies widely not only between developing nations but also within nations. This is particularly noticeable when "slum" and "nonslum" households are sep-arated. As Table 3.3 details, some nations (like Colombia) have quite high coverage rates for all of their inhabitants. Many, however, have a long way to go.

Uncollected waste is a scourge for everyone involved. It clogs drains and sewers, causing flooding and thus the spread of infectious disease. Stagnant water—from, for

**TABLE 3.3** Collective Coverage for Nonslum and Slum Households for Select Countries in Africa and the Middle East and Latin America and the Caribbean

| COUNTRY | PERCENT OF HOUSEHOLDS WITH A COLLECTION SERVICE | |
|---|---|---|
| | Nonslum/incorporated | Slum/unincorporated |
| **Region: Africa and the Middle East** | | |
| Benin | 50 | 11 |
| Egypt | 90 | 65 |
| Ethiopia | 61 | 32 |
| Ghana | 46 | 28 |
| Kenya | 46 | 12 |
| Senegal | 75 | 50 |
| **Region: Latin America and the Caribbean** | | |
| Bolivia | 93 | 65 |
| Colombia | 100 | 91 |
| Dominica | 84 | 66 |
| Guatemala | 75 | 19 |
| Nicaragua | 89 | 48 |
| Peru | 92 | 54 |

Collective coverage among select low- and middle-income countries varies considerably. Some countries, like Colombia, have been quite successful at providing collection services to all strata of society, while others, like Benin, have had considerably less success. Source: Adapted from United Nations (2010).

example, backed-up storm drains—offers prime breeding habitat for mosquitoes and rodents, which can also lead to the spread of disease. Uncollected waste can make it more difficult to attract businesses and tourists. It can also disrupt a country's ability to provide basic utilities. In Costa Rica, for example, an electric utility company has problems maintaining power to their grid from a hydroelectric plant because plastic litter repeatedly clogs its turbines (United Nations 2010).

Even after it is collected, waste represents a potential public health hazard. One review looked at the health risks associated with domestic waste-composting facilities and their product (Domingo and Nadal 2009). Since MSW contains a number of chemical and biological agents, compost was found to be a potential biohazard. The contaminants were cited for creating varying levels of risk to plant workers at composting facilities as well as to the consumers of vegetable products grown in soils treated with the adulterated compost. Other studies point to the public health risk of living next to waste management facilities and solid waste incinerators (e.g., Domingo et al. 2015). There is also tentative evidence linking certain negative health effects to living

## ETHICAL QUESTION 3.2
# Public Health and Value Judgments

As members of a social network—with its own norms, identity structures, and social conventions—epidemiologists' understanding of "evidence" often differs from those embedded within different social networks (e.g., community activists). Among professional epidemiologists, social norms strongly discourage the making of false positives—that is, concluding that there is a causal link between contaminant X and a cancer cluster when there isn't one (also known as a **Type I error**). This explains why higher confidence limits—of typically 90 percent or higher—are usually the norm within this professional field. Scientists have a reputation to uphold as a result of their membership in a larger professional community, which could be severely undermined if they were to proclaim a causal link when none exists. Such Type I errors could be not only embarrassing but potentially damaging to one's membership within the community and resources therein embedded (e.g., access to grants). If such errors occurred with great frequency, it could in fact undermine the legitimacy of the entire profession.

On the other hand, community activists, as a result of their different network connections and interests, have equally compelling reasons to avoid false negatives (known as **Type II errors**). For them, erring on the side of caution, if it means saving their lives and the lives of loved ones, is well worth making a false negative occasionally. This in part explains why proponents of what has been called **popular epidemiology** (a type of citizen science that involves laypeople) prefer a much lower confidence limit when examining causal relationships between pollutants and cancer clusters.

near landfill sites, like low birth weight, birth defects, and certain types of cancers (Ashworth, Elliott, and Toledano 2014; see also Ethical Question 3.2).

### E-Waste

Those of us in affluent nations throw away an awful lot of electronic waste, or what is becoming commonly known as e-waste. How often do you get a new cell phone? Every year? Perhaps every two? My service provider currently incentivizes getting a new phone every year, offering a hefty new phone credit after owning the device for only twelve months. And what about your computer? How often do you replace it?

This e-waste—discarded computers, printers, mobile phones, pagers, digital photo and music devices, refrigerators, toys, and televisions—is expected to rise sharply in the decades ahead with the growth in sales of electronics in countries like China and India. A 2011 report from one Ghana-based organization found, remarkably, that of 215,000 tons of electronic waste imported into the country annually, 30 percent was *brand new* but deemed "obsolete" (Green Advocacy Ghana 2011). According to the United Nations Environment Programme, by 2020 e-waste from computers will increase by 500 percent from 2007 levels in India and by 400 and 200 percent in China and South Africa,

ECOnnection 3.2

# E-Waste and Public Health

A systematic review of five electronic databases (PubMed, Embase, Web of Science, PsycNET, and CINAHL) summarized what the peer reviewed literature has to say about e-waste's impact on public health (Grant et al. 2013). Some of the findings highlighted include the following:

- Outcomes associated with exposure to e-waste include changes in thyroid function, changes in cellular expression and function, adverse neonatal outcomes, changes in temperament and behavior, and decreased lung function.
- Children living in e-waste recycling towns had a lower forced vital capacity than did those living in a control town. (A forced vital capacity is the volume change of the lung between a full inspiration to total lung capacity and a maximal expiration to residual volume.)
- Findings from most studies showed increases in spontaneous abortions, stillbirths, and premature births, and reduced birth weights and birth lengths associated with exposure to e-waste.
- People living or working in e-waste recycling towns had evidence of greater DNA damage than did those living in control towns.
- One study related exposure to e-waste and waste electrical and electronic equipment to lower educational outcomes.

respectively. They also predict e-waste from cell phones, over the same time period, to rise 700 percent in China and 1,800 percent in India. By 2020, e-waste from televisions will be 1.5 and 2 times higher in China and India, respectively, while in India e-waste from discarded refrigerators will double or triple (UNEP 2009).

The majority of e-waste in developed countries is exported to less affluent nations to be recycled. China currently receives the largest share of the world's e-waste: roughly 70 percent of the world's discarded gadgets, a strange twist given that most were also manufactured there (Watson 2013). Recycling in China takes many hazardous forms, such as incinerating materials over an open flame in order to recover valuable metals like gold. These practices release toxic gases while yielding very low metal recovery rates, especially compared to modern industrial facilities. Some of the toxic materials found in e-waste include barium, cadmium, lead, lithium, mercury, nickel, palladium, rhodium, and silver. Exposure to these materials has been linked to, among other things, birth defects and organ, nervous system, and skeletal system damage (e.g., Feldt et al. 2014).

There is hope, however, that with the establishment of ambitious regulations and oversight, the processes for collecting and recycling e-waste in developing nations can be improved and produce a net gain for the people of these nations as well as for the environment. The result would be steady employment while cutting greenhouse gas emissions and recovering a wide assortment of valuable metals, including silver, gold, palladium, copper, and indium, without negative impact on public health (UNEP 2009). In truth, something like this *must* happen. In the United States, the average home has slightly less than three televisions (and 2.62 persons to watch them). The average US family owns four mobile devices; among young adults, 84 percent admit to using another device, a smartphone or tablet, when watching TV (Atkinson 2014). Once other populations—like the roughly three billion people who live in India and China—begin emulating this type of consumption for electronic goods, we will be swimming in a sea of e-waste unless a just, sustainable recycling system is put into place.

## Solutions

I have noticed when discussing the subject of waste in the classroom that the conversation inevitably turns to individuals. "We need to stop wasting so much!" a student told me when asked how we solve the problem of waste. Yes, we do waste too much. But why do we? Are we the only ones to blame for this? Solutions to waste must reflect the multifaceted nature of the problem, or, as I told my student, "Working only to change what we as consumers do to produce waste will not effectively solve much."

### *MSW Management Alternatives from Around the World*

There is a tendency to think that what works in affluent countries when it comes to MSW management will work equally well for less affluent countries. Unfortunately, to quote from a UN document on the subject, "Nothing could be further from the truth" (2010, 93). The average inhabitant of a developing nation generates a fraction of what their counterpart in an affluent nation generates. Thus, the twenty-five-ton garbage trucks that seem so necessary to MSW planners in countries like the United States are a needless expense in countries that do not generate sufficient waste; these vehicles can cost more than $130,000 new. And let's not forget: many roads and bridges in low-income nations just can't handle trucks of that size.

A popular trend, which started in China and has since spread outside of Asia to the Middle East, Africa, and Latin America, is a hybrid approach to waste transfer. This system involves setting up small, local transfer stations around the city to which people bring their trash. As labor costs in low- and middle-income countries are relatively low, this can be accomplished far more cost-effectively using handcarts and the like than with expensive trucks. The transfer stations also facilitate small-scale entrepreneurialism, as people are employed to collect and deposit trash from the neighborhood at these sites for those who choose not to or are unable to do it themselves. Once at the transfer station, the city takes over and hauls the waste away. Once concentrated at one site, capital-intensive technologies like large trucks become more cost-effective. In countries using this plan, the waste is collected daily and the transfer stations washed down to minimize odor and prevent rodent problems (Pariatamby and Tanaka 2014).

And what about all the food waste? (See Movement Matters 3.1.) Some commentators have argued that if food were more expensive—if its retail price more accurately reflected the actual costs that went into producing, processing, and transporting it—we would likely not waste so much of it (Stuart 2009). Perhaps. Yet there are other ways to disincentivize the act of wasting food, such as by charging people who do it. That's exactly what South Korea does. In 2005 they made it illegal to send food to the landfill; you won't actually go to jail for breaking this law, but you will be fined. South Koreans now

### MOVEMENT MATTERS 3.1
## The Real Junk Food Project

The Real Junk Food Project is a UK-based scheme started by Adam Smith, Sam Joseph, and Conor Walsh. These three entrepreneurs have opened what they call Pay As You Feel (PAYF) cafés that ask customers to pay what they believe a fair price would be for food past its "sell by" and "best by" dates, which often have little to do with food safety and everything to do with appearance and taste. (It is important for manufacturers to have their foods consumed within a specific window to establish consumer loyalty and to ensure flavor and texture consistency.) The first café opened in the city of Leeds in December 2013. There are now more than forty PAYF cafés selling surplus food. In 2014, the original café in Leeds diverted more than twenty tons of food from the landfill and fed ten thousand people (Mellino 2015).

must separate all food waste and place it in a special 100 percent compostable bag. The policy has been incredibly successful. The country has managed to remove more than 98 percent of food waste from its MSW stream, just the opposite of the United States, where just 2.6 percent of food waste is composted (Thyberg, Tonjes, and Gurevitch 2015).

Food waste can also be fed to livestock. Poultry and pigs thrive on organic waste. Under European laws, however, feeding food waste to pigs is banned. Conversely, in Japan, South Korea, and Taiwan, a percentage of the nation's food waste must be diverted to livestock. Japan disposes of roughly 20 million tons of food waste a year—five times the amount that it gives annually as food aid to the world's poor. As prices for animal feed and fertilizers reached record highs in 2008, there was heightened demand for food pellets for pigs and poultry made from recycled leftovers. During this period, recycled feed was half the price of regular feed. Although only 1 percent of feedstock comes from recycled food, this percentage is growing. The majority of the food waste that is recycled into feed comes from convenience stores and restaurants, where strict health laws require food to be thrown away after one day (itself a problematic policy, as it accelerates the wasting of food). The discarded food is first taken to a plant, where it is sorted to remove skewers, plastic trays, and plastic wrap. From there it is turned into two kinds of dry feed—one high in fat and protein and another that is rich in carbohydrates—and a liquid feed made from pasteurized drinks and leftover vegetables.

### Extended Producer Responsibility

"Waste isn't the fault of consumers—it's a design flaw," I once had a friend tell me. Although she was perhaps overstating matters a bit—clearly, as consumers we can do better when it comes to reducing our waste—I appreciate her point. As long as consumers continue to need (or think they need) the things supplied by the market, they have little choice but to waste. I realize that many consumers confuse "wants" for "needs," so the problem of waste must also be addressed from the angle of consumption (which is discussed in Part III of this book). But sometimes these needs are legitimate; for example, when someone's job requires the purchase of a computer and printer. And even when those needs are not legitimate, the pragmatist in me realizes that people are going to continue to buy stuff, at least for the foreseeable future. So why not buy stuff that can be recycled and reused?

That's what my friend meant when she said waste is a design flaw. We're currently not making things that can be easily reused and recycled. This is where the concept of **extended producer responsibility** (EPR) comes in. Under EPR, manufacturers are held responsible for a product beyond the time of sale, thereby relieving consumers, governments, future generations, and the environment from the costs associated with landfilling and recycling hazardous materials. EPR is an attempt to internalize some of the costs of a product that have previously been externalized (not included in the retail price) onto society, taxpayers, the environment, and future generations. This cost externalization model not only is terribly unfair—by forcing people to pay for the consequences of actions not of their own doing—but also creates completely unsustainable actions and business models. Think about it in the context of waste. When, for example, companies manufacture computers, most are currently responsible for the product only from the moment it was manufactured through the life of its warranty. And not surprisingly, their design reflects these parameters. Consequently, they have no interest in designing products that can be either disposed of safely (e.g., that are not full of hazardous materials) or recycled and reused. Computer manufacturers currently don't care what the consumer does with their product when it reaches the end of its life. And why should they? Similarly, when the consumer disposes of their computer (and it is sent off to the landfill or to be recycled), they may pay a nominal disposal fee, but it is society, taxpayers, future generations, and the environment that are paying the real costs for this action. How is that fair?

EPR extends the producer's responsibility for a product throughout its life cycle, from cradle to grave. The concept was first used and defined in a report by Thomas Lindhqvist for the Swedish Ministry of the Environmental and Natural Resources in 1990 (see Lindhqvist and Lidgren 1990). EPR seeks to prioritize preventative measures (by asking questions like "How do we make things better so they don't become waste?") over end-of-pipe approaches (which involve such questions as "What should we do with the waste?"). EPR makes producers the primary actors responsible for the entire life cycle of their products. The logic behind this is simple: making producers responsible for having to recycle and reuse what they manufacture will lead them to redesign products for this end. When products are not designed to be recycled, they often are not. We often mistake **down-cycling** (converting waste into new materials or products of lesser quality and decreased functionality) for recycling. Carpet, for example, not designed to be recycled is typically down-cycled to, for example, carpet padding.

Maine was the first state in the United States to pass an EPR e-waste law in 2004, requiring manufacturers to be financially responsible for recycling specific electronics. Under this law, while cities still ensure that collection sites are available and consumers must bring their e-waste to these sites, the manufacturers pay for all recycling costs. Since 2004 twenty-four states have enacted similar legislation. EPR has an even longer track record in Europe, where the problem of landfill shortage is particularly acute.

We also need to create incentives that entice businesses—and electronics companies in particular in light of what was just said about e-waste—to make products that can be repaired. It's often cheaper to buy a new appliance or piece of electronic equipment than it is to get that old one repaired because it's not designed with that aim in mind, making repair expensive. I find it curious how much we as a society focus on the recycling aspect of the equation—on, in other words, the *end* of the life cycle. We talk about expanding recycling markets and improving recycling technology, which we hope will bring down its costs and help keep countries like the United States from shipping its e-waste overseas, where labor is cheap and where environmental and labor laws are weak. But if goods are not designed and manufactured to be recycled, what good does any of this do? And lest we forget: designing products that could actually be repaired or upgraded would effectively render this entire discussion about recycling moot. If we could just focus a fraction of those moneys and political energies on encouraging and regulating businesses to make electronic products that can be refurbished, recycled, reused, and easily repaired, just think how far that would go toward reducing e-waste and stopping the types of recycling practices currently used in developing countries that are placing the health of individuals and the environment at risk.

## IMPORTANT CONCEPTS

- e-waste
- extended producer responsibility (EPR)
- food waste
- life-cycle analysis (LCA)
- three Rs of environmentalism
- waste and public health
- waste regimes

## DISCUSSION QUESTIONS

1. It is often said that we've become a throwaway society. Why do you think this is?
2. When something of yours breaks, rips, or simply stops working, how often do you first try to get it repaired? What are some of the barriers to repair and reuse?
3. Do corporations bear any responsibility for waste, or is it a problem best addressed among consumers and through better municipal waste management practices?
4. Is necessity the mother of invention, to repeat an old and familiar saying, or is invention the mother of necessity?

## SUGGESTED ADDITIONAL READINGS

Evans, D., H. Campbell, and A. Murcott, eds. 2013. *Waste Matters: New Perspectives on Food and Society*. New York: Wiley.

Foote, S., and E. Mazzolini, eds. 2012. *Histories of the Dustheap: Waste, Material Cultures, Social Justice*. Cambridge, MA: MIT Press.

McAllister, L., A. Magee, and B. Hale. 2014. "Women, E-Waste, and Technological Solutions to Climate Change." *Health and Human Rights* 16(1).

## RELEVANT INTERNET LINKS

- www.footprintnetwork.org/en/index.php/GFN/page/calculators. An ecological footprint calculator. Find out how large your footprint is.
- www.lovefoodhatewaste.com. A useful resource for learning more about food waste and how you can cut down on the amount you produce.
- ngm.nationalgeographic.com/2008/01/high-tech-trash/trash-quiz-interactive. Take this quiz, and learn your e-waste IQ.
- www.youtube.com/watch?v=IKG8xRTFktg. An instructional video on how to practice backyard composting.

## SUGGESTED VIDEOS

- *Bag It!* (2011). A film that examines our love affair with plastic.
- *Inside the Garbage of the World* (2014). A look at how we're trashing our world and what we can do to turn things around.
- *The Plastic Cow* (2012). An examination of the impact of our almost complete dependence on plastic bags, which we use and discard carelessly every day, often to dispose of our garbage and kitchen waste.
- *Plasticized* (2012). A journey through the center of the South Atlantic Ocean aboard the *Sea Dragon* with the 5 Gyres Institute on the very first scientific expedition focused on plastic waste.
- *Unwasted: The Future of Business on Earth* (2011). There is no waste in nature; humans are in fact the only animals on the planet to create waste that nature cannot process. Can we create an economy that uses waste rather than makes it?
- *Waste Land* (2010). Follows renowned artist Vik Muniz as he journeys from Brooklyn to his native Brazil and the world's largest garbage dump located just outside Rio de Janeiro. There he chronicles the lives of *catadores*—trash scavengers.
- *Waste Wars* (2011). vimeo.com/32400188. Documents a battle over access to and control over garbage, as waste pickers and recyclers in Delhi fight attempts to privatize trash collection.

# Biodiversity: Society Wouldn't Exist Without It

It has been my experience that while everyone seems to believe biodiversity ought to be preserved, few can articulate the reasons we value it to the level we do. I discuss the subject every semester in my Global Environmental Issues class. And every semester, when I ask why we ought to preserve biodiversity, I receive in return . . . silence. Sure, after an awkward stillness I hear from a few in the audience, but the silence always quickly reappears. It then becomes my turn to speak. I usually begin by making some grand statement pertaining to the value of biodiversity to society, talking about its links to quality of life, therapeutic applications, ability to limit infectious disease, and its role in maintaining "services." In short, biodiversity supports a number of things that lead to happier and healthier humans. Human *health*, as the term is defined here, and as the World Health Organization (WHO) has defined it since 1948, is "a state of complete physical, mental, and social well-being and not merely the absence of disease or infirmity" (WHO 2012c). I will touch briefly on each of the four benefits mentioned above.

*Quality of life* can be enhanced innumerably by biodiversity, as it boosts mental and spiritual health, provides opportunities for recreation, and enriches human knowledge.

Biodiversity is also responsible for supplying *therapeutic applications*, thanks to medicinal and genetic resources coming from plants and other organisms. The United Nations, for example, recently valued anticancer agents from marine organisms at roughly $1 billion a year, while the global value of herbal medicine has been estimated to be worth more than $80 billion annually (Booker, Johnston, and Heinrich 2015).

Biodiversity places *limits on infectious disease* through biological controls that rein in **disease vectors** (an organism, such as a mosquito or tick, that carries disease-causing microorganisms from one host to another). For instance, when an ecosystem is biologically diverse, predation throughout the food chain is likely to keep populations of all species under control, including those linked to the spread of infectious disease.

The benefits of biodiversity-dependent *services* is incalculable, as many of these values cannot (and should not) be reduced to a monetary figure. This is not to say some haven't tried. Take the concept of **ecosystem services**: the processes by which the environment produces resources that we often take for granted but need for our survival, such as clean air and water, timber, habitat for fisheries, and pollination of native and agricultural plants. A 1997 article published in *Nature* placed the value of seventeen ecosystem services at approximately $33 trillion per year, compared to a gross world product at the time of around $18 trillion (Costanza et al. 1997). More recently, a revised estimate involving updated data was published in 2011 and valued global ecosystem services at between $125 trillion and $145 trillion per year, compared to a gross world product at the time of around $72 trillion (Costanza et al. 2014). From this estimated range, the study's authors calculate the loss of eco-services from 1997 to 2011 as a result of land use change at $4.3 trillion to $20.2 trillion annually. Land use changes include anything from, for example, decreases in coral reef area to deforestation and the draining of wetlands. Yet we can't—nor would we want to—put a price tag on everything that's provided by ecosystems. Right? (See ECOnnection 4.1.)

## Fast Facts

- Approximately 1.2 million species (excluding bacteria) have already been cataloged—just a fraction of the 8.7 million species estimated to exist (Mora et al. 2011).
- We are losing species at an alarming rate, many before even being discovered. Famed biologist Edward O. Wilson ([1992] 1999) has estimated the current rate of species extinction at roughly 27,000 annually, or 74 per day (see Ethical Question 4.1). A study published in *Science* estimates that current extinction rates are up to a thousand times higher than they would be if we humans were not around (Pimm et al. 2014; see Image 4.1).
- A recent analysis of ninety-four studies comparing biodiversity under organic and conventional farming methods found that, on average, organic agriculture *increased* species richness by about 30 percent relative to biodiversity levels on conventionally farmed land (Tuck et al. 2014).
- From the more than 1.2 billion hectares of tropical rain forest habitat that originally existed, less than 400 million remain (Spilsbury 2010).

## Implications

As detailed in Table 4.1, a great number of events and activities (most of which are human induced) threaten biodiversity. And these threats will only grow in the decades ahead, especially as the world becomes warmer (thanks to climate change), more crowded (as a result of population growth and urbanization trends), and more affluent (particularly in Southeast Asia). Complicating matters further are the ways in which pressures upon biodiversity can act at different temporal and spatial scales. For instance, sediments from deforestation in the headwaters of the Orinoco River along the Venezuelan/Brazilian border negatively affect marine life in the Caribbean more than a thousand miles away by altering the nutrient availability and clarity of the waters (UNEP 2008).

The reasons for biodiversity decline will come up again later, as many of the pressures and drivers discussed in Table 4.1 are subjects of later chapters. What I am most

# Thinking About Ecosystem Services Conceptually

Ecosystems cannot provide any benefits to humanity without the presence of skilled people (human capital), their communities and social networks (social capital), and their built environment (built capital). This interaction, articulated by Costanza and colleagues (2014), is illustrated in Figure 4.1. (Seven types of capital are highlighted in Chapter 12, which go well beyond the four presented here.) The challenge for policies aimed at sustainable development involves understanding how this interaction plays out in enhancing well-being and then taking steps to appropriately enhance all capitals to maximize outcomes.

One thing I appreciate about this figure is that it contextualizes value. Values are not plucked out of thin air. What we value and the degree to which something is valued cannot be abstracted from social context. This is plainly evident in debates over the value of ecosystem services. The $125 trillion to $145 trillion range calculated by Costanza and colleagues (2014) is a lot—an order of magnitude larger than what the global economy produces in a year. And yet our actions indicate that we don't actually value global ecosystem services that much, or anywhere even close to that much (otherwise we wouldn't be trashing them). Why is that? What is it about our political systems, cultures, markets, and social norms and routines that cause us to undervalue ecosystem services to the degree we do?

**FIGURE 4.1**

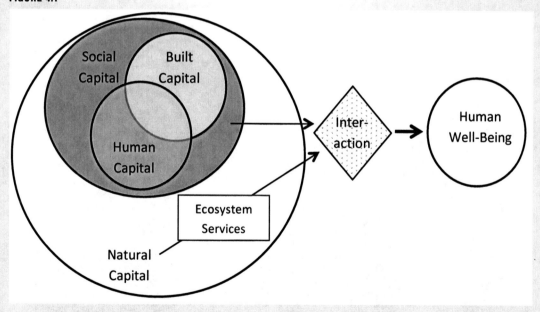

*Source: Adapted from Costanza et al. (2014).*

# Sophie's Choice: What If We Can't Save Them All?

Some twenty thousand species are on the cusp of extinction (Dell'Amore 2013). If we had endless resources to commit to saving them all, we wouldn't have to choose which to save. But that's not reality. Ecologists have long argued that how we choose which species live or die is often unscientific, skewed heavily toward preserving cute and fuzzy animals even if those species do little to keep the planet humming by contributing to ecosystem functions (and those ever-important services). For example, ants play a foundational role in most ecosystems: distributing seeds, aerating soils, eating other insects, and providing food for other species. And yet, for every child with a poster of ants in their bedroom there are tens of thousands with posters of pandas, elephants, and polar bears. In the words of Marc Bekoff, an ethologist at the University of Colorado, Boulder, "if we're going to save pandas rather than ants, we need a good reason, and being cute is not a good reason" (Dell'Amore 2013).

Something else to think about: cost. Should the cost of conservation play into our calculations? If so, those charismatic megafauna come with a pretty hefty price tag—managing the world's tiger reserves costs more than $82 million annually (N. L. 2010). Then again, how can you place a price tag on the existence of a species, when once it is gone, it is gone for good? But if we do not take into consideration the annual cost of saving each individual animal of a given species—what some conservationists call ROI (return on investment)—what variables *should* we use?

**IMAGE 4.1**

Photograph from the mid-1870s of a pile of American buffalo skulls waiting to be ground for fertilizer. Source: Courtesy of the Burton Historical Collection, Detroit Public Library.

**TABLE 4.1** Threats to Biodiversity

| | |
|---|---|
| **Residential & Commercial Development** <br> • Housing & Urban Areas <br> • Commercial & Industrial Areas <br> • Tourism & Recreation Areas | **Agriculture & Aquaculture** <br> • Annual & Perennial Non-Timber Crops <br> • Wood & Pulp Plantations <br> • Livestock Farming & Ranching <br> • Marine & Freshwater Aquaculture |
| **Energy Production & Mining** <br> • Oil & Gas Drilling <br> • Mining & Quarrying <br> • Renewable Energy | **Transportation & Service Corridors** <br> • Roads & Railroads <br> • Utility & Service Lines <br> • Shipping Lanes <br> • Flight Paths <br> • Air and Space Transport |
| **Biological Resource Use** <br> • Hunting & Collecting Terrestrial Animals <br> • Gathering Terrestrial Plants <br> • Logging & Wood Harvesting <br> • Fishing & Harvesting Aquatic Resources | **Human Intrusions & Disturbance** <br> • Recreational Activities <br> • War, Civil Unrest & Military Exercises <br> • Work & Other Activities |
| **Natural System Modifications** <br> • Fire & Fire Suppression <br> • Dams & Water Management/Use <br> • Other Ecosystem Modifications | **Invasive & Problematic Species & Genes** <br> • Invasive Non-Native/Alien Species <br> • Problematic Native Species <br> • Introduced Genetic Material |
| **Pollution** <br> • Household Sewage & Urban Waste Water <br> • Industrial & Military Effluents <br> • Agricultural & Forestry Effluents <br> • Garbage & Solid Waste <br> • Airborne Pollutants <br> • Excess Heat, Sound, or Light That Disturbs Wildlife and/or Ecosystems | **Geological Events** <br> • Volcanoes <br> • Earthquakes/Tsunamis <br> • Avalanches/Landslides |
| **Climate Change & Severe Weather** <br> • Habitat Shifting & Alteration <br> • Droughts <br> • Temperature Extremes <br> • Storms & Flooding | |

Source: Adapted from Conservation Measures Partnership.

## ECOnnection 4.2
# The Tragedy of the Commodity

In Chapter 11 you will learn about the theory of the tragedy of the commons—the belief that species extinction (and environmental ruin more generally) is exacerbated in those instances where natural capital has yet to be privatized. Rebecca Clausen and Stefano Longo (along with, more recently, Brett Clark) turn this thinking on its head, arguing for what they call the **tragedy of the commodity** thesis (e.g., Clausen and Longo 2012; Longo et al. 2015). Accordingly, rather than being our ecological savior, "commodification is a primary *contributor* to decline as well as an underlying *cause* for the failure of environmental policy prescriptions" to protect biodiversity (Clausen and Longo 2012, 231; emphasis in original). As the authors of this argument explain, "once

the precedent has been set to view the value of a resource through the lens of a commodity, government regulations to help 'solve' the ecological problem will prioritize market-based solutions that accommodate capitalist needs for growth and accumulation" (232). As evidence of their thesis, they point to the AquAdvantage Salmon—selected by *Time* magazine as one of "The Best Inventions in 2010" (Clausen and Longo 2012). Here's a "solution" of salmon recovery and conservation that allows the status quo to continue, a technological fix that at least in the short term allows the treadmill of production to not miss a beat. In the long run, however, it is allowing biologically diverse natural salmon stocks to literally be gobbled up, along with their habitat.

interested in detailing at the moment are impacts. (Even so, those "deep" sociological drivers discussed in Chapter 1 should never be far from our minds; see ECOnnection 4.2.) Yet before we look at impacts, there is one small conceptual problem that requires our attention: What precisely does *biodiversity* even mean? Only after working our way through this question can we begin having a conversation about the various consequences associated with biodiversity loss.

### Changing Definitions of Biodiversity

Early definitions of biodiversity tended to focus almost entirely on species diversity, in which case biodiversity was simply another way of saying "species richness" (see, for example, Lovejoy 1980). More recently, the definition of the term has expanded to include, along with species richness, genetic diversity (within and across species) and ecological diversity (which includes ecosystem services and habitat) (see, for example, Hunter and Gibbs 2007). Yet the problem doesn't lie just in deciding which criteria to include in our definition. It also stems from the inherent ambiguity of the criteria themselves. Take the concept—or, I should say, *concepts*—of species.

A review of the modern biological literature roughly two decades ago found at least twenty-four different species concepts (Mayden 1997), a figure that has no doubt increased in recent years, given the expanding literature on the subject. The **species problem**, as it has come to be known, refers to the inherent ambiguity surrounding the use and definition of the species concept. The three more widely utilized contemporary species concepts include the biological species concept (centering on the property of reproductive isolation), the ecological species concept (emphasizing speciation through ecological selection), and the phylogenetic species concept (focusing on the property of common descent). This all matters tremendously from a conservation standpoint, for ultimately which species concept we adopt affects the number of species we find.

It has been argued, for instance, that the biological species concept tends to over-emphasize gene flow between populations and thus aggregates species together, while the phylogenetic species concept often splits such populations into distinct and thus potentially new species (Meijaard and Nijman 2003). This inflation and deflation of biodiversity levels based on which species concept is ultimately employed have been well documented. A team of researchers reanalyzed organisms utilizing a phylogenetic species concept that were earlier classified according to other species definitions (Agapow et al. 2004). The reanalysis yielded a species *increase* of 121 percent. Focusing on avian endemism in Mexico (birds that are found only in Mexico), another team applied two alternative species concepts: the phylogenetic species concept and the biological species concept (Peterson and Navarro-Siguenza 1999). Their findings indicate not only divergent levels of biodiversity based on which species concept was used but also divergent **biodiversity hotspots** (a biogeographic region with a significant reservoir of biodiversity that is under threat from humans), signifying where endemism is particularly concentrated. When the biological species concept was used, 101 bird species were found to be endemic to Mexico, with populations concentrated in the mountains of the western and southern portions of the country. Using the phylogenetic species concept, the endemic species total rose to 249, with population concentrations in the mountains and lowlands of western Mexico.

Equally problematic is the concept of "ecosystem"—a phenomenon, as mentioned previously, recently folded into biodiversity definitions. Maps of biologically diverse hotspots typically include tropical rain forests, for reasons related not only to species richness but also to the important ecosystem services, such as climate regulation and nutrient cycling, they provide. Wetlands and marshes, however, are typically ignored in these maps, even though they provide equally essential ecosystem services, such as nutrient cycling, erosion control, water purification, and storm protection. (See Ethical Question 4.2.)

And what about humans? Are we not a species who create and alter ecosystems? Shouldn't *we* factor into measures of biodiversity, other than being viewed as yet another thing that negatively affects it?

The Bombay Natural History Society noticed in the late 1970s that bird populations were on the decline in the Bharatpur Bird Sanctuary (what is today known as Keoladeo National Park) in Rajasthan, India. An accusatory finger was eventually pointed at cattle and buffalo, which were entering the preserve in sufficient quantities and disrupting what was believed to be an otherwise balanced ecosystem. In an attempt to correct the problem of decreasing bird populations, Bharatpur was declared a national park in 1981. This act was quickly followed by a ban on all grazing activities within the park. (Nine people were killed in the resulting riots that ensued as the park was cleared of its earlier human inhabitants.)

By the mid-1980s, something was amiss. Studies were beginning to indicate the seemingly impossible: bird diversity within the park had *declined further* since the ban

ETHICAL QUESTION 4.2

# The Power of Conservation Maps

A wealth of literature has emerged in the past thirty years examining the power embedded within maps (e.g., Edney 1997; Harley 1989; Wood 1993). For example, modern maps embody the commercial and political interests of Western European and North American nation-states. Most world maps place north at the top, have zero degrees longitude running through Greenwich, England, and are centered on either Western Europe, North America, or the North Atlantic. Maps can also reflect societal preferences for certain landscapes and ecosystems. For example, forests are far more frequently mapped than grasslands (Hazen and Anthamatten 2004). Yet even what's defined as *forest* is hotly contested. A mapped, legally defined *forest* may in fact not contain a single tree (Vandergeest 1996).

Similar to how world maps give readers the sense that political boundaries are natural and objectively given, conservation maps also tend to naturalize a static view of ecological and social systems. In other words, while the socioecological space being represented in conservation images is inherently fluid, once mapped these spaces take on a near timeless, permanent quality. Maps also tend to minimize differences across geophysical space. Harris and Hazen (2006), for instance, examined a widely distributed map created by the UN Environment Programme that visually depicts the spatial distribution of internationally recognized "protected" areas. Such global perspectives, however, risk endorsing the view that conservation spaces are comparable across what are in reality widely divergent areas. They point out how places of conservation in the United States and United Kingdom are often appreciably different. For example, as a result of divergent historical trajectories, national parks in the United States reflect the wilderness ideal (an image of nature devoid of human presence), while in the United Kingdom they are often populated agricultural landscapes. Although such spaces are radically different on the ground, these differences are washed away when viewed at the level of a global map. As argued in an article on the power of ecosystem service maps, "designing maps is thus a means of exercising power" (Hauck et al. 2013, 28). The authors go on to note that "the designer makes decisions on what to include and which scales are to be chosen" (28). One strategy then to avoid these pitfalls is to incorporate "a high degree of transparency with regard to the specific reasons for mapping" (28).

on grazing (Vijayan 1987). By the early 1990s, it was irrefutable: biodiversity not only had declined since the grazing ban but was diving downward at an alarming rate. The absence of grazing animals, it turns out, had a disastrous effect on the ecology of the park. Weed species were taking over wetlands and choking canals, thereby reducing fish populations. As the open wetland habitat—a habitat that once attracted a tremendous mix of birds—was being overrun by a handful of fast-growing opportunistic plant species, avian species went elsewhere in search of more suitable places to nest. In 1991, in a stunning course reversal, the Bombay Natural History Society—originally the most vocal opponent on grazing in the park—concluded that, to avoid further weed takeover, grazing animals needed to be brought back. A report announcing this policy reversal

## ECOnnection 4.3
# The Irreplaceable Bee

Pollinators—honey and native bees in addition to certain birds, bats, and butterflies—not only provide a critical ecosystem service but are also an essential component to food security. Honey bees alone enable the production of at least ninety commercially grown crops in North America. Pollinators make possible the "growing" of 35 percent of the world's food and contribute more than $24 billion to the US economy (White House 2014). The number of managed bee colonies in the US has dropped over the past sixty years, from 6 million colonies in 1947 to just 2.5 million today. Crops like almonds are almost exclusively pollinated by honey bees. California's almond industry, which supplies 80 percent of the world's almonds, requires the pollination services of roughly 1.4 million beehives annually—that's 60 percent of all beehives in the United States (White House 2014). Unable to discern insect friend from insect foe, pesticides have had a major impact on all insect pollinators and are suspected of playing a significant role in what is known as colony collapse disorder (Chensheng, Warchol, and Callahan 2014; Doublet et al. 2015).

admitted the shortsightedness of conservation policies that place humans apart from—rather than as a part of—biologically diverse ecosystems: "In the case of most wetlands in this country, [human] interaction with them has become almost inseparable and hence, [humans have] to actively manage them" (Vijayan 1991, 1).

## Biodiversity: The Fuel Driving Ecosystem Services

Biodiversity loss is our loss. Biodiversity may not make the world go around, but it certainly makes the planet inhabitable. Here I speak in a little more detail about some of the services provided by biodiversity.

### AGRICULTURE

No amount of technology and innovation could substitute for the ecosystem services provided by biodiversity in the production of food and fiber production (see ECOnnection 4.3). Biodiversity makes soil habitable for plant growth, as it is central to the breakdown and recycling of nutrients within this life-giving medium. Biodiversity also makes pollination possible and is essential for pest control, without which productivity losses would be even greater. Biodiversity may well also hold the key to future food security in light of climate change, as plant breeders will have to look increasingly into the gene pool to come up with varieties suitable to withstand and ideally thrive under a variety of agroecological conditions.

### FORESTS

As with agriculture, commercial forestry depends on biodiversity for nutrient recycling and pest control. Some forests also generate revenue from hunting, the collection of wild food (e.g., berries and fungi), the collection of firewood, and bird watchers and nature photographers. Forests also offer spaces for recreation, itself a major revenue-generating activity. Last, there is an incalculable intrinsic value associated with these spaces, as they not only serve as sources of creativity and inspiration but also hold religious and cultural significance for populations around the world.

## FISHERIES

Waterways provide a provisioning ecosystem service in the form of fish catch. The fish catch, however, is heavily dependent on a functioning biologically diverse ecosystem that supplies nutrients, prey species, habitats, and a desirable water quality (Bullock 2008). There is also an intensely cultural component to fishing, as many societies have deep historical roots in this practice.

## WATER

Biodiversity performs an irreplaceable service in terms of both recycling nutrients and ensuring desirable water quality for agricultural use, fisheries, and human consumption. A significant amount of research has emerged in recent years documenting that species-rich aquatic ecosystems are more efficient at removing excess nutrients and even some pollutants from water than those with fewer species (Carnicer et al. 2015).

## ATMOSPHERIC REGULATION

Forests and other vegetation—and to a lesser extent all organisms—modify climate (though humans look to be the most influential organism). Plants and trees affect solar reflection, water-vapor release, wind patterns, and moisture loss. Forests help maintain a humid environment, as evidenced by the fact that half of all rainfall in the Amazon basin is produced locally by the forest-atmosphere cycle (Kozloff 2010).

### *Biocultural Diversity*

As acknowledged by the United Nations Environment Programme, "biodiversity also incorporates human cultural diversity, which can be affected by the same drivers as biodiversity, and which has impacts on the diversity of genes, other species, and ecosystems" (UNEP 2007, 160). The term **biocultural diversity** speaks to an unmistakable and increasingly well-documented empirical fact: that cultural diversity does not merely parallel biological diversity but is profoundly interrelated with it (Maffi and Woodley 2010).

There is a subtle but noticeable disdain toward humans in many environmental texts in their noting only the ways in which humans threaten biodiversity. It is unquestionably true that we are the greatest threat to the earth's biodiversity. But this shouldn't lead to the conclusion that humans somehow represent an *inherent* risk to biological diversity. Granted, it's far easier to see the various ways in which we are mucking things up, as we read routinely about the latest species threatened or lost entirely at our own hands. Yet growing evidence points to how humans are also positively contributing to ecosystems and biodiversity levels.

There are two general approaches to biological conservation: **ex situ** and **in situ**. Ex situ conservation involves the sampling, transferring, and storage of a species in a place other than the original location in which it was found, like a zoo or seed bank. The other option is in situ conservation, which involves the management of a species at the location of discovery. The ex situ model is often what comes to mind (at least for most in the developed world) when people think of biodiversity conservation, which is understandable in light of the more than fourteen hundred seed and gene banks and more than one thousand zoos worldwide.

The popularity of the in situ model, however, has grown considerably among conservationists in recent decades. Proponents of the in situ approach argue that it provides a more complete form of conservation, in that it makes room for, unlike ex situ approaches, socioecological dynamics. It is no coincidence that most of the world's biologically diverse hotspots are also its **cultural hotspots**—biogeographic regions with a significant reservoir of cultural diversity that are under threat of extinction (Stepp et al. 2004). Research looking at indigenous populations in North America consistently notes a correlation between measures of biodiversity within a given region and its levels of cultural and linguistic diversity (Smith 2001; Stephenson et al. 2014).

Virginia Nazarea has extensively studied sweet potato farmers in the Philippines. At one site they were beginning the processes of commercializing production, while at another they remained firmly at the level of subsistence agriculture. She had hypothesized that commercialization causes a narrowing of genetic and cultural diversity among sweet potatoes raised. Her hypothesis was confirmed. Yet she also observed something unexpected. There was a large disparity between the two sites in terms of the number of varieties known or remembered, compared to the biodiversity that actually existed. At the commercial site, farmers had knowledge about a far lower percentage of sweet potato varieties than at the other site, having forgotten many that still existed and were being planted elsewhere in the country. This suggests a faster erosion of cultural knowledge than genetic diversity itself. Reflecting on this research, Nazarea writes how this finding signified that "in the context of agricultural development and market integration, knowledge may actually be the first to go" (2005, 62).

Sociologists MacKenzie and Spinardi (1995) argued a while back that nuclear weapons are becoming "uninvented" as a result of global nuclear disarmament trends and nuclear test–ban treaties. It is their contention that "if design ceases, and if there is no new generation of designers to whom that tacit knowledge can be passed, then in an important (though qualified) sense nuclear weapons will have been uninvented" (44). They are pointing, to put it simply, to the importance of putting knowledge to work. A lot of knowledge has to be acted out—literally *practiced*—for it to exist and be passed along to others. Try, for example, teaching someone to ride a bike with words alone—it just doesn't work. The same principle applies to our knowledge of biodiversity. This is why the term *biocultural diversity* is so apt, because the cultural knowledge tied to traditional crops is very much rooted in practice. Many traditional cultures are oral, meaning that much of this folk knowledge is not physically recorded (written down) anywhere. Once lost, there is a good chance this knowledge—and with it a piece of biocultural diversity—is gone forever.

## Biopiracy

Although we often think about biological loss in the context of, say, extinction, this is not the only way it is experienced. In some cases, while the object of concern still exists (perhaps even thrives), the loss felt is the result of the misappropriation of biocultural knowledge. Enter **biopiracy**: essentially the loss of biocultural diversity through legal and sometimes illegal means.

It is estimated that developing nations would be owed $5 billion per year if they received royalties of 2 percent for their contributions to pharmaceutical research and another $302 million annually for royalties from agricultural products (see, e.g., Ramon 2011). Biopiracy—or what's called *bioprospecting* by those doing it—occurs when folk knowledge and biological artifacts are conjointly exploited for commercial gain without just compensation to those responsible for discovering or originating it. Although it's easy to chalk biopiracy up to the greedy actions of powerful multinational corporations seeking to exploit the knowledge and resources of indigenous populations, it is important to understand certain sociolegal realities that make such activities possible in the first place.

To begin with, patent law makes it exceedingly difficult for indigenous populations to call biocultural knowledge their own. According to patent law, no patent can be issued where prior art exists because of the statutory requirement that patents are to be granted only for new inventions on the basis of novelty and nonobviousness. An invention is generally not regarded as new if it was patented or described in a printed publication. **Indigenous knowledge**—or local knowledge, which is knowledge unique to a given community, culture, or society—however, has tended to be an oral and embodied effect, acquired through years of literally *doing* and applying that knowledge. As such, it is rarely ever written down. Its transmission occurs through storytelling, not book reading. The knowledge of these indigenous societies can thus often be freely plundered for private gain, as evidenced by corporations patenting and claiming as their own knowledge what had for centuries been part of the (indigenous) public domain.

One way indigenous groups are responding to this legal reality is by publishing their biocultural knowledge in large digital libraries, what are commonly known as Traditional Knowledge Data Libraries (TKDLs). Transforming this age-old embodied and oral knowledge into a written form turns it into something that patent law recognizes and that therefore constitutes prior art. Many countries—such as South Korea, Thailand, Mongolia, Cambodia, South Africa, Nigeria, Pakistan, Nepal, Sri Lanka, and Bangladesh—are following in the footsteps of India, which developed one of the first TKDLs in the late 1990s.

To what extent is biopiracy occurring? That's not easy to say, as a number of national laws, international agreements, and legally binding treaties make biopiracy illegal. So whatever is occurring is taking place under the radar. The most consequential legal structure to emerge to reduce biopiracy is the Convention of Biological Diversity (CBD), which was adopted at the Earth Summit of Rio de Janeiro in 1992. Its objectives are threefold: the conservation of biodiversity, the sustainable use of biodiversity, and the equitable sharing of benefits arising from the use of genetic resources.

Agreements reached through the CBD, however, do not apply to materials collected before 1992. Thus, any material in a gene or seed bank before 1992 can still be exploited for commercial ends without any money going back to the source country as compensation. Take the case involving a disease-resistant peanut from Brazil. The peanut was first picked in 1952 by Alan Beetle. It was not until 1987, however, that Beetle's sample would be used for commercial ends. In 1987 the tomato spotted wilt virus (TSWV) was first detected in US peanuts. This virus severely injures or kills any peanut plant that it infects. It quickly spread throughout Georgia, Florida, Alabama, and South Carolina, seriously threatening the US peanut industry. Beetle's sample peanut was known to be resistant to TSWV and was quickly sought out for this trait by breeders. A number of peanut varieties have since been bred to be resistant to TSWV using this nut from Brazil. In fact, the germplasm from this nut was estimated roughly a decade ago to add at least $200 million annually to the US economy (Edmonds Institute 2006). Brazil, conversely, receives nothing. Nevertheless, as a recent report on the subject adds, "no laws were transgressed." Rather, this example speaks to a perfectly legal case of "pre-CBD biopiracy" (ibid., 3).

Even with CBD, however, biopiracy remains a problem. Let's look briefly at two recent well-publicized cases of biopiracy, involving Bt brinjal from India and herbal teas from South Africa.

Bt brinjal is a genetically modified strain of brinjal (eggplant) created by India's largest seed company, Mahyco, which also happens to be a subsidiary of the multinational company Monsanto. Bt brinjal has been engineered to be resistant to lepidopteran insects, particularly the brinjal fruit and shoot borer. According to the National Biodiversity Authority (NBA) of India, the development of Bt brinjal is a case of biopiracy, which means Monsanto and Mahyco could face criminal proceedings. The NBA charges these alleged biopirates with accessing nine Indian varieties of brinjal to develop their genetically modified eggplant without prior permission from the NBA or relevant national and local boards. This is a violation of the country's 2002 Biological Diversity Act, which provides for the conservation of biological diversity and calls for fair and equitable sharing of the benefits that arise out of the use of biocultural resources. (It is also illegal under the CBD.) By using the local brinjal varieties without permission, Monsanto and Mahyco weakened India's sovereign control over its resources while denying economic and social benefits to local communities under the benefit-sharing requirements of the Biological Diversity Act (Jebaraj 2011).

Example two: biopirated tea. Global food giant Nestlé is facing allegations of biopiracy after applying for patents based on two South African plants used in the making of herbal teas without first receiving permission from the South African government. This puts Nestlé in direct violation of South African law as well as the CBD. The controversy centers on two South African plants, rooibos and honeybush, commonly used to make herbal teas with well-known—and long-known—medicinal benefits. A Nestlé subsidiary has filed five international patent applications seeking to claim ownership over some of those medicinal benefits, such as using the plants to treat hair and skin conditions and for anti-inflammatory treatments. At issue is benefit sharing: namely, Nestlé believes it does not need to share any future profits that might be derived from these patents. Yet according to the 2004 South African Biodiversity Act, businesses must obtain a permit from the government if they intend to use the country's genetic resources for research or patenting. And these permits can be obtained *only* in exchange for a benefit-sharing agreement (ICTSD 2010).

## Solutions

As biodiversity is threatened by multiple practices, pressures, and events, solutions directed at the problem of biodiversity loss must be equally multiple and diverse. I offer here two strategies that have had some success at enhancing biodiversity levels. In the space that remains, I discuss the practice of community conservation and

ETHICAL QUESTION 4.3

# Sustainability: For Whom and Toward What End?

The term *sustainability* reminds me a lot of the term *nature*: we seem to talk endlessly about both but struggle when forced to offer a clear definition of either. *Social sustainability*, *environmental sustainability*, and *economic sustainability* are hotly contested terms. What they mean depends on whom you ask. For example, when we talk about social sustainability, do we mean improving social justice or reducing inequality or something else entirely? Or environmental sustainability: Do we mean zeroing out all ecological impact or just minimizing impact? If it is the latter, is everyone expected to reduce equally, or might those with the largest ecological footprints be asked to reduce more? Or economic sustainability: Does this mean simply that households and businesses need to be profitable, or does it also suggest a desire to reduce, for example, economic inequality?

What do you think about when you hear the term *sustainability*? If you're anything like my students, ecological sustainability likely comes to mind before social sustainability (and this is even among sociology students). Can you think of instances where an ecologically sustainable practice might not be socially sustainable?

---

agrobiodiversity conservation. These are not our only two solutions. Later chapters examine many of the other drivers of biodiversity loss and their potential solutions.

## Community Conservation

The modern conservation movement emerged in Europe in the nineteenth century. The wilderness model, around which so many of the world's national parks are built, came shortly thereafter out of the United States. Although these top-down—which is to say they are typically implemented and overseen by the state—conservation methods have had their successes, they are not without their problems.

For one thing, conservation has historically been viewed as separate from development. Indeed, in some camps they are antithetical to each other. The social costs of these conventional models of conservation have been great. Removing, sometimes forcibly, indigenous populations—like Native Americans in the United States and Parakuyo and Massai pastoralists in Tanzania—from lands they have lived on for centuries for purposes of "saving nature" is morally repugnant. But also, looking beyond the morality of these acts, the science refutes the ecological soundness of such policies. As the earlier case involving the Bharatpur Bird Sanctuary in India shows us, there may be better ways of conserving biodiversity than by removing people from the equation.

A paradigm shift of sorts is taking place in conservation and developmental circles. On the one hand, it is becoming clear that developmental policies that overlook conservation are unsustainable in the long run and ultimately offer no relief from threats to biodiversity. On the other hand, conservationists are beginning to understand that they can no longer afford to ignore the impoverishment they may be causing when they exclude human populations from habitats they are seeking to conserve. In fact, what

**TABLE 4.2** Citizen Involvement in Conservation Decision Making

| | Low (full control by agency in charge) | | High (full control by stakeholders) | |
|---|---|---|---|---|
| **PROCESS** | **Information Sharing:** Builds awareness by telling people what is planned | **Consultation:** Identifies problems, offers solutions, and obtains feedback to broaden knowledge base allowing for better top-down decisions | **Co-Directed:** Involves and actively engages stakeholders to contribute ideas and opinions when deciding best way to move forward | **Independent Community Initiatives:** Groups are enabled to act, in terms of process as well as outcome |
| **ACTIVITY OF CITIZEN GROUP** | **Passive:** Receptors of information | **Marginally Engaged:** Pre-determined phase is devoted to seeking public input | **Equal Players:** Involvement throughout entire processes | **Directing:** Groups set agenda and determine direction and outcome of project |
| **OUTCOME** | **Information Dissemination** | **Weak Participation** | **Strong Participation** | **Determination** |

Citizen involvement can take many different forms. Some options offer little more than a façade of "involvement" (as illustrated by the "low" end toward the left of the table), while others (far right or "high" end of the table) put communities firmly in the driver's seat. Source: Forgie, Horsley, and Johnston (2001) and Trotman (2008).

we've learned is that those indigenous populations that conservationists have been so busy evicting over the past century may hold the key to truly sustainable development (see, e.g., Garcia, Rice, and Charles 2014; see also Ethical Question 4.3).

This is where community conservation comes into the picture (see ECOnnection 4.4). As generally practiced, community conservation is place-based and highly participatory. There are different "flavors" of community conservation, as there are many different ways to define community involvement when it comes to conservation. This variability is captured in Table 4.2. As illustrated in the table, levels of community involvement can run the spectrum: from low, where an agency is in charge, to high, where independent community-centered groups develop their own initiatives as a result of a crisis or problem.

Arguably the most publicized community conservation success story comes out of Tanzania. It involves two woodland reserves, both of which were being poorly conserved under previous management regimes. In 1994 and 1995, communities located near the edge of the forests secured the return of control over woodlands they had previously informally managed for generations.

As one of the few remaining tracts of the Miombo woodlands in the Babati District, the Duru-Haitemba woodlands were targeted to be turned into a forest reserve as early as 1985. (The Miombo woodlands stretch in a broad belt across south-central Africa, extending from Angola to Tanzania.) The intention was to protect the forest against further deforestation by deploying government forest guards to prevent expanding human settlements. By taking control, local governments were promised a steady source of revenue through the issuing of licenses for timber and pole-wood extraction, which would be granted to people living adjacent to the forest (Wily 1999).

The plan met significant opposition among local people whose livelihood was dependent on that tract of forest. There were also concerns about the plan's feasibility. As experience has shown, it is unrealistic to expect low-paid forest guards (many of whom are recruited from the same rural areas they are expected to police) to monitor the forest's border from villagers in need of forest products for basic subsistence. By the early

---

ECOnnection 4.4

# Socioecological Benefits Known to Arise from Community Conservation

## FIRST BENEFIT: STRENGTHENS COMMUNITIES

- builds local skills, interests, and capacities
- builds a sense of stewardship and community capacity for environmental problem solving that will remain with the community
- builds community cohesion
- increases the likelihood that the community will be able to solve future problems on their own

## SECOND BENEFIT: APPROACHES ARE TAILORED TO LOCAL NEEDS

- As opposed to top-down approaches, which tend to serve nonlocal interests, community conservation can be highly responsive to unique community and environmental needs by incorporating local knowledge, and strategies and solutions will likely be well suited to local socioecological dynamics.

## THIRD BENEFIT: POSITIVE OUTCOMES FOR INDIVIDUALS

- Knowledge of and relationship with surrounding ecosystems are enhanced.

- Working with others can have therapeutic benefits.
- Building social ties with others enhances individual well-being.

## FOURTH BENEFIT: INCREASED LIKELIHOOD OF LOCAL ACCEPTANCE AND SUSTAINABLE OUTCOMES

- There is an increased likelihood of successful implementation when actions and decisions are viewed by those involved as responsible and appropriate.
- As local populations rely on having a healthy surrounding ecosystem, they have an incentive to be sure they get conservation strategies right.

## FIFTH BENEFIT: EFFICIENT USE OF RESOURCES

- Enforcement and monitoring are often done cost-effectively, as informal social norms, trust, and a shared commitment to success are linked positively to compliance.

*Adapted from Trotman (2008) and Wily (1999).*

1990s, an agreement was reached to find a more acceptable management strategy. The solution ultimately involved allowing and assisting each of the eight villages that border the woodlands to take full rights and responsibility for its conservation.

The results have been unmistakable. The forests show visible signs of gain, as most of the earlier unregulated in-forest settlement, charcoal burning, and illicit timber harvesting have ceased. The size of the woodland has actually increased. In the Duru-Haitemba Forest, which had previously suffered the most damage, the return of understory shrubbery, grasses, and bees points to improved forest health. In other parts of the forest, increases in wildlife biodiversity are being recorded. Hundreds of young village men have volunteered to patrol the protected areas, at zero cost to the government, out of a vested interest in the health of the forest (see, e.g., Lupala et al. 2015; see also Case Study 4.1).

## Agrobiodiversity Conservation

**Agrobiodiversity**—all forms of life directly relevant to agriculture, including crops and livestock but also many other organisms, such as soil fauna, weeds, pests, and predators—is the result of natural and human selection processes, involving farmers, herders, and fishers over millennia. The future of food security, it is widely believed (Cairns 2015), hinges on agrobiodiversity. Agrobiodiversity gives us options when responding to whatever threats to food production we can expect to face in the future. Phenomena that can fall under the category of agrobiodiversity include harvested crop varieties, livestock breeds, fish species, and nondomesticated (wild) animals used for food; nonharvested species in production ecosystems that support food provision (like soil microbiota, pollinators, and other organisms such as earthworms); and nonharvested

---

**CASE STUDY 4.1**

# Participatory Forest Management in Kenya

Kenya has widely embraced participatory forest management, a variation of community conservation. Because of its track record, it is believed that this approach not only effectively achieves sustainable forest management goals but also simultaneously involves stakeholders whose livelihoods depend on the forest (Mbuvi et al. 2015). Participatory forest management is supported under the Forest Act of 2005. This act provides for the establishment, development, and sustainable management of forest resources for the socioeconomic development of the country. The avenues through which Kenyans in general, and Kenyan forest communities in particular, can directly or indirectly participate in the management and monitoring of their forests include the following: as members of community forest associations, as representatives appointed to the forest conservation committees, as representatives appointed to the Board of the Kenya Forest Service, and as individuals. The Forest Act of 2005 also allows forest communities to constitute up to 50 percent of the representation in the forest conservation committee that oversees the management of a recognized forest. The law further provides for community representation on the board of the Kenya Forest Service.

# Open Source Seed

On April 17, 2014, on the campus of the University of Wisconsin, Madison, the Open Source Seed Initiative (OSSI) released twenty-nine seed varieties under an open source pledge printed on all OSSI-distributed seed packets. It reads as follows:

> This Open Source Seed Pledge is intended to ensure your freedom to use the seed contained herein in any way you choose, and to make sure those freedoms are enjoyed by all subsequent users. By opening this packet, you pledge that you will not restrict others' use of these seeds and their derivatives by patents, licenses, or any other means. You pledge that if you transfer these seeds or their derivatives you will acknowledge the source of these seeds and accompany your transfer with this pledge. (quoted in Kloppenburg 2014)

In other words, any future plant that's derived from these **open source seeds** must be freely available. They cannot be patented, licensed, or commodified in any way, even in those instances where they have been bred or genetically modified into something new.

Irwin Goldman, professor of horticulture at the University of Wisconsin, Madison, was one of the organizers of the event. For him, OSSI is about restoring the practice of sharing that was once the rule among plant breeders around the world. In his own words, "If other breeders asked for our materials, we would send them a packet of seed, and they would do the same for us." Regrettably, he further notes that because of intellectual property rights "that way of working is no longer with us" (quoted in Charles 2014). For other members of the movement, the rationale of open source goes even deeper. For Jack Kloppenburg, professor of sociology at the University of Wisconsin, Madison, open source is a way

to reshape our very food system: "The problem is concentration, and the narrow set of uses to which the technology and the breeding are being put" (quoted in Charles 2014). Within the first month after its launch, OSSI had received over two hundred orders from eight countries (Shemkus 2014). June 2015, after a three-day meeting near Hyderabad, India, saw the birth of Apna Beej (Hindi for "Our Seeds"): OSSI now has a sister organization, Open Source Seed System India (OSSSI). (See Image 4.2.)

**IMAGE 4.2**

Pictured above is Indian attorney and prominent intellectual property rights activist Shahlini Butani. Six months prior to this picture being taken in June 2015, she was skeptical of open source seeds. She is now a vocal advocate, believing open source seeds encourage innovation and enhance biodiversity while respecting farmer livelihoods. Source: Jack Kloppenburg and Shahlini Butani.

## CASE STUDY 4.2

# The Seed Bank That Makes Memories

The Seed Savers Exchange (SSE) is a US-based heritage seed bank in northeastern Iowa (see www.seedsavers.org). Founded in 1975, the SSE is a nonprofit organization that both saves and sells heirloom fruit, vegetable, and flower seeds. On this 890-acre farm, called the Heritage Farm, there are twenty-four thousand rare vegetable varieties, including about four thousand traditional varieties from eastern Europe and Russia; approximately seven hundred pre-1900 varieties of apples, which represent nearly every remaining pre-1900 variety left in existence out of the eight thousand that once existed; and a herd of the rare Ancient White Park cattle, which currently have an estimated global population below two thousand.

Although in part a gene and seed bank, the SSE is much more. Visitors can learn about the seeds being saved, including their history and how to cultivate the seeds and cook and prepare their harvest. If it's the right time of year, they can even experience how the fruits and vegetables taste. Indeed, calling SSE a memory bank doesn't go far enough, as many visitors find the organization also responsible for memory *making*. An example of this occurs at their heirloom tomato tasting workshop. During this event, participants get to not only taste more than forty different kinds of tomatoes but actively learn how to save the seeds of their favorite varieties for future planting (Carolan 2011a).

species in the wider environment that support food production ecosystems (such as species in a waterway that encourage the process of water purification).

Agrobiodiversity is not only viewed as representing one of the keys to future food security but also widely seen as central to any sustainable model of food production. There is compelling evidence that, through the implementation of agroecology farming techniques, an approach relying heavily on ecological principles rather than commercial inputs (see Chapter 8), agrobiodiversity can help increase crop productivity—potentially even outproducing conventional agriculture. Agrobiodiversity is also a key ingredient to the effective control of disease and pest outbreaks without the use of harmful chemical inputs (Gliessman 2015).

The promotion of agrobiodiversity can take many forms. Simply allowing farmers to save seed from one year to be planted the next is a good place to start, particularly since patents and other controls like so-called **terminator technology** (genetically engineered seeds that produce sterile plants) are making this increasingly difficult (Carolan 2010a; see Movement Matters 4.1). **Memory banks**, spaces that preserve not only genetic material but the skills to grow and save seeds and prepare the fruits of those labors, also help promote agrobiodiversity by ensuring that future generations have a working knowledge of this species diversity (see Case Study 4.2).

Agrobiodiversity (or more specifically agrobiocultural diversity) can also be promoted and enhanced through activities related to urban agriculture, whether those gardens are located in, for example, Denver (Carolan and Hale 2016); Chicago (Taylor and Lovell 2015); Moshi, Tanzania (Schlesinger, Munishi, and Drescher 2015); or Rio Negro, Brazil (Emperaire and Eloy 2015). One study examining urban agriculture in migrant neighborhoods in Chicago found their gardens to be quite diverse, though the level of biodiversity varied by ethnicity group. African American gardens demonstrated the highest food plant richness (with an average of 16.3 food crops per garden), followed by Chinese-origin gardens (14.4) and Mexican-origin gardens (8.6) (Taylor and Lovell 2015). Cultural tastes and household-specific ethnic cuisine preferences also often compel urban gardeners to grow and thus preserve certain species not easily acquired at grocery stores and food markets (Carolan and Hale 2016). More than just a source of affordable food, these gardens also supply households with ingredients necessary for the making of certain cultural dishes, thus helping ensure both plant species and cultural survival.

Although humans pose the gravest threat to biodiversity, at the moment we are also its greatest potential ally. Once we accept our rightful identity as being part of nature, rather than seeing ourselves independent of it, new possibilities open up. These links are particularly conspicuous between agricultural systems and ecological ones, given the former's grounding (pun intended) in the latter. Agriculture, when done ecologically—*agroecology*—can go a long way toward preserving the ecological integrity of systems while helping to safeguard biological as well as cultural diversity and enhancing long-term food security.

## IMPORTANT CONCEPTS

- agrobiodiversity
- biocultural diversity
- biopiracy
- community conservation
- ex situ and in situ conservation
- memory banking
- open source seeds
- participatory forest management
- tragedy of the commodity

## DISCUSSION QUESTIONS

1. What are the links between cultural and biological diversity?
2. Conventional agriculture has become a monoculture within a monoculture, where fields are populated by not just one crop but one variety of a single crop. What are some of the forces driving this specialization?
3. Can we rely entirely on zoos and gene banks when it comes to preserving our biological heritage?
4. Why isn't community conservation more popular in a country like the United States?

## SUGGESTED ADDITIONAL READINGS

Cocks, M., and F. Wiersum. 2014. "Reappraising the Concept of Biocultural Diversity: A Perspective from South Africa." *Human Ecology* 42(5): 727–737.

Dickman, A., P. Johnson, F. van Kesteren, and D. Macdonald. 2015. "The Moral Basis for Conservation: How Is It Affected by Culture?" *Frontiers in Ecology and the Environment* 13(6): 325–331.

Lynch, M., M. Long, and P. Stretesky. 2015. "Anthropogenic Development Drives Species to Be Endangered: Capitalism and the Decline of Species." In *Green Harms and Crimes: Critical Criminology in a Changing World*, edited by R. A. Sollund, 117–146. Critical Criminological Perspectives. Hampshire, UK: Palgrave Macmillan.

## RELEVANT INTERNET LINKS

- www.biocultural.iied.org/about-biocultural-heritage. Resource seeking to promote "resilient farming systems and local economies" through a biocultural diversity lens.
- www.conservation.org/how/pages/hotspots.aspx. Excellent resource to learn more about biodiversity hotspots.
- www.gaiafoundation.org. The Gaia Foundation is committed to regenerating cultural and biocultural diversity and their website is rich in resources for those interested in the subject.
- www.ted.com/talks/lang/en/e_o_wilson_on_saving_life_on_earth.html. Video of well-known biologist E. O. Wilson talking about biodiversity and conservation.

## SUGGESTED VIDEOS

- *Drop in the Ocean?* (2015). In less than fifty years, ocean life as we know it could be completely done for. This not only means dead oceans, but a dead ecosystem, and mass deaths of all who depend on it.
- *The End of the Line* (2010). Examines the subject of overfishing, suggesting the possibility of nearly fishless oceans by 2048 if sustainable fishing practices are not implemented soon.
- *The Fight for Amazonia* (2012). From the heart of the Amazon jungle comes a three-part series examining the strides being made to save the world's most endangered rain forest.
- *Queen of the Sun* (2010). A film on the honeybee crisis and colony collapse disorder.
- *Rachel Carson's "Silent Spring"* (1993). Though more than twenty years old, this production from the PBS series *The American Experience* offers an excellent historical lesson for anyone not familiar with this landmark book and its pioneering author.
- *Salmon Confidential* (2013). What's killing British Columbia's wild salmon? Watch this video and find out.

# Water: There's No Substitute

Economists, until recently, were fond of discussing what's known as the "water and diamonds paradox." The paradox, as summarized in an economics textbook from the 1990s, goes something like this: Why is it that "water, which has so much value in use, has no value in exchange, while diamonds, which have practically no value in use, are exchanged at high prices" (Ekelund and Hébert 1997, 294)? This is clearly less the case today, as in some instances people are willing to pay more for a liter of bottled water than they are for a comparable amount of gasoline. Indeed, the paradox now is why are some willing to pay so much for this commodity when they can just as easily get it for free? The reason water seems to defy economic reasoning is that its value cannot be expressed in exclusively monetary terms. In this chapter, I explore some of the consequences associated with humanity's growing need for this life-giving resource and, later, articulate some potential responses to ensure that this need never exceeds supply.

## Fast Facts

- The water cycle does not favor continents equally. Six countries—Brazil, Canada, China, Colombia, Indonesia, and Russia—account for half of the world's renewable freshwater (Sterling and Vintinner 2012).
- Approximately 70 percent of all the freshwater used by humans goes to agriculture, industry uses 22 percent, and the remaining 8 percent is used by municipalities and households (Sterling and Vintinner 2012).
- A per capita freshwater supply of below 1,700 cubic meters places countries in the category of being "water stressed." When annual water supplies drop below 1,000 cubic meters per person, the population faces "water scarcity." And when below 500 cubic meters, it is facing "absolute scarcity." As documented in Table 5.1, a number of countries currently fall well within, or dangerously close to, this category. One word describes the situation for many countries: *thirsty* (see Case Study 5.1).
- The **water footprint** of countries, as illustrated in Table 5.2, varies wildly. (A water footprint is an indicator of freshwater use that looks at both direct and indirect water use by a consumer or producer.) The annual water footprint per capita in the United States,

IMAGE 5.1

Photo taken in downtown Sacramento, CA, in August 2014. Source: "CalPERS and the Drought" by Kevin Cortopassi (flickr.com/kevincortopassi) is licensed copyright © 2014 under CC BY-ND 2.0.

for example, is 7,800 liters per day, compared to, say, China, which is 2,900 liters daily. China's population, however, is more than four times that of the United States, making its total water footprint much larger, despite its lower per capita use.

- **Virtual water** refers to water used during the growing, making, or manufacturing of a given commodity. Commodity water footprints are increasingly broken down into the green, blue, and grey water that go into their making. The *green water footprint* refers to the use of water resources (such as rainwater that does not become runoff) for growing crops. A *blue water footprint* denotes the use of water resources—surface and groundwater—along the supply chain of a product. And the *grey water footprint* represents the volume of freshwater required to assimilate and adequately dilute the load of pollutants that results from the production and processing of commodities. As shown in Table 5.3, a lot of (virtual) water goes into the making of common commodities.

- Dams, as solutions to water-starved areas, are not without their problems. In addition to changing the ecology of a watershed and potentially negatively affecting human communities (when they are displaced to make space for a reservoir), dams are often responsible for losing the very thing they are charged with storing: water. They can lose multiple meters of depth per year as a result of evaporation, especially in hot, dry climates (see, e.g., Vervoort 2014). The Aswan Dam on the Nile River, for instance, loses roughly 2.7 meters in depth annually, or 11 percent of the reservoir's capacity (Toulmin 2009). Or take Lake Mead, roughly thirty miles southeast of Las Vegas, Nevada, which formed behind Hoover Dam and is the largest reservoir in the United States. According to the US Bureau of Reclamation (2015), this body of water is at 37 percent capacity and dropping rapidly.

- As of 2015, some 3,700 large hydroelectric dams were either being built or on the verge of being built around the world, most located in South America, Southeast Asia, and

**TABLE 5.1** Renewable Water Resources Per Capita for Select Countries, 2013

| COUNTRY | CUBIC METERS PER YEAR | COUNTRY | CUBIC METERS PER YEAR |
|---|---|---|---|
| Kuwait | 0 | Algeria | 287 |
| Bahrain | 3 | Pakistan | 302 |
| United Arab Emirates | 16 | Oman | 385 |
|  |  | Kenya | 467 |
| Egypt | 22 | Somalia | 572 |
| Bahamas | 53 | Hungary | 606 |
| Saudi Arabia | 83 | Rwanda | 807 |
| Yemen | 86 | South Africa | 843 |
| Israel | 93 | Morocco | 879 |
| Jordan | 106 | Lebanon | 1,074 |
| Singapore | 111 | Ethiopia | 1,296 |
| Libya | 113 | Poland | 1,409 |
| Niger | 196 |  |  |

Source: Adapted from World Bank (2015c).

Africa. The number of free-flowing river systems worldwide will decrease by 21 percent if all these structures are built (Zarfl et al. 2015). This brings up a good question: What are we to make of the costs of these projects? A 2014 study examining the costs and benefits of 245 large dams built between 1934 and 2007 found that construction costs alone were on average nearly double their projections and that construction took 44 percent longer than originally promised (Ansar et al. 2014). The authors go on to warn, "Forecasts of costs of large dams today are likely to be as wrong as they were between 1934 and 2007," concluding that "the actual construction costs of large dams are too high to yield a positive return" (44).

- Climate change is expected to drastically alter the water cycle. As mean atmospheric temperature rises, the water-holding capacity of the air increases exponentially. In the future we can therefore expect an atmosphere saturated with moisture, which will only serve to intensify storms and other weather events. A higher atmospheric temperature also means more energy to drive intense weather events. More water, falling at greater rates of intensity, means more floods and soil erosion for some regions. Elsewhere rain will become an increasingly rare event, which, coupled with increased temperatures, will hasten the drying up of rivers, lakes, and reservoirs.

- People living in the slums often pay five to ten times more per liter of water than those residing in affluent neighborhoods in the same city (Frérot 2011). This statistic is particularly sad, given the impressive returns on investment that can be realized when a country invests in its water infrastructure. According to the United Nations (2009), safe drinking water, proper sanitation, and efficient irrigation systems contribute to a country's economic growth while also saving it money. Each $1 spent toward these ends

## CASE STUDY 5.1
# China's Water Woes

In 2011, residents of Hualiba Village in central China's Henan Province were relocated ten kilometers away (roughly six miles). Between their new homes and where they used to live and the fields they cultivated is a massive new concrete water canal. The canal started moving water from China's water-rich south to its water-poor north in 2014—the biggest water diversion project in the world. (The north of China holds a fifth of the country's freshwater while possessing two-thirds of its farmland.) Eleven of China's thirty-one provinces fall below the World Bank's definition of "water scarce," with less than 1,000 cubic meters of freshwater per person per year (Xichuan 2014). To put that figure into perspective: the US per capita water footprint, which is the highest in the world, is 2,842 cubic meters per year; meat consumption accounts for 30 percent of this figure, and sugar consumption another 15 percent (Fischetti 2012). And let's not forget that not all freshwater is equal. Polluted freshwater can be as useless as saltwater in many applications. The Chinese government admits that half the water in its seven main rivers is unfit for human consumption.

The transfer is expected to ease the water stress experienced by Beijing (also located in the north), supplying the city with about a third of its annual demand. And of course it will help nourish farmland in the north. There is concern, however, that this project will actually make China's water situation worse in the long run. By reducing water stress in the short term, it incentivizes water-intensive practices—urbanization, conventional agriculture, and so forth—that will likely speed the country toward the peak water cliff. Huge social disruptions have also been caused by this project. Some estimates place the number of people displaced at more than half a million. Then there are the potential public health costs, like those associated with the spread of disease common in the south—such as schistosomiasis, a devastating snail-borne disease (Xichuan 2014).

returns somewhere between $3 and $34—a return of between 300 and 3,400 percent—depending on the region and technology that is being invested in (ibid.).

- As watersheds are developed and become blanketed with impervious surfaces (streets, parking lots, tennis courts, rooftops, and so on), they lose their ability to absorb rainwater, resulting in more being lost to runoff. With increased runoff comes a heightened chance of flooding, soil erosion, and the overall disruption of a watershed's water cycle (see Table 5.4).

## Implications

It is a bit surprising that sociologists have not been more interested in water. So much of our lives is touched, in some way, by this precious compound. Cities, nations, and entire civilizations all need water to survive, though not too much, either, as I am reminded of a small town in Iowa near where I grew up that was relocated after the so-called Great Flood of 1993. (Sadly, there have been two other "Great Floods" in the state since

**TABLE 5.2** Composition of Water Footprint (WF) for Select Countries

| COUNTRY | POPULATION | WF, TOTAL (BILLION CUBIC METERS PER YEAR) | WF, PER CAPITA (LITERS PER CAPITA PER YEAR) |
|---|---|---|---|
| Australia | 19,300,000 | 45 | 6,300 |
| Bangladesh | 142,000,000 | 110 | 2,100 |
| Brazil | 175,000,000 | 360 | 5,600 |
| Canada | 30,900,000 | 72 | 6,400 |
| China | 1,280,000,000 | 1,400 | 2,900 |
| Egypt | 71,000,000 | 95 | 3,700 |
| France | 59,400,000 | 110 | 4,900 |
| Germany | 82,100,000 | 120 | 3,900 |
| India | 1,050,000,000 | 1,100 | 3,000 |
| Indonesia | 207,000,000 | 230 | 3,100 |
| Italy | 57,500,000 | 130 | 6,300 |
| Japan | 127,000,000 | 8.3 | 3,800 |
| Jordan | 4,960,000 | 6.27 | 4,600 |
| Mexico | 99,800,000 | 200 | 5,400 |
| Netherlands | 15,900,000 | 23 | 4,000 |
| Pakistan | 150,000,000 | 200 | 3,600 |
| Russia | 146,000,000 | 270 | 5,100 |
| South Africa | 45,200,000 | 57 | 3,400 |
| Sudan | 35,200,000 | 61 | 4,800 |
| United Kingdom | 59,300,000 | 75 | 3,400 |
| United States | 289,000,000 | 820 | 7,800 |
| Zambia | 10,600,000 | 9.7 | 2,500 |

Source: Adapted from Hoekstra and Mekonnen (2012).

then.) Water also resonates with us culturally. Take the case of the Klamath people in Northern California and southern Oregon, who were deemed, in the landmark legal decision *United States of America and the Klamath Indian Tribe v. Ben Adair* (1983), to have rights to water on reservation lands dating back to "time immemorial" (the distant past beyond memory) to protect culturally essential activities like hunting and fishing.

This chapter aims to give the reader a taste of how water affects our world. It has repeatedly been said that water promises to be to the twenty-first century what oil was to the twentieth century. If so, sociologists (and the social sciences more generally) ought to play as central a role in its study in this century as petroleum geologists did for oil in the last.

**TABLE 5.3** Global Per Unit Average of Virtual Water Content for Select Commodities

| COMMODITY | VIRTUAL WATER (LITERS PER KILOGRAM) | GREEN (%) | BLUE (%) | GREY (%) |
|---|---|---|---|---|
| chocolate | 17,195 | 98 | 1 | 1 |
| 1 tomato (70 grams) | 214 | 50 | 30 | 20 |
| 1 potato (100 grams) | 287 | 66 | 11 | 22 |
| margarita pizza | 1,259 | 76 | 14 | 10 |
| powdered milk | 4,745 | 85 | 8 | 7 |
| 1 orange (100 grams) | 560 | 72 | 20 | 9 |
| 1 apple (100 grams) | 822 | 68 | 16 | 15 |
| leather (bovine) | 17,093 | 93 | 4 | 3 |
| dates | 2,277 | 41 | 55 | 4 |
| cotton | 2,495 | 54 | 33 | 13 |

Source: Based on Mekonnen and Hoekstra (2011).

**TABLE 5.4** Runoff Versus Soil Infiltration for Every Three Inches of Rainfall on Select Surface

| SURFACE TYPE | RUNOFF (INCHES) | INFILTRATION (INCHES) |
|---|---|---|
| Forest | 0.6 | 2.4 |
| Meadow | 0.6 | 2.4 |
| Cultivated agricultural field | 1.0 | 2.0 |
| Residential lawn | 1.6 | 1.4 |
| Parking lot, street, sidewalk | 3.0 | 0.0 |

Source: Adapted from Marinelli (2011).

## Bottled Water

Have you had bottled water in the past twelve months? Chances are good you have. Estimates predict that the global bottled water market will grow from $157.27 billion in 2013 to $279.65 billion by 2020 (Transparency Market Research 2015). While campaigns against bottled water continue to affect the industry, they have not drastically damaged sales. In the United States, for instance, where bottled water bans have been adopted in some cities, national parks, and college campuses, sales continue to increase; sales in the so-called functional water—water formulated with micronutrients—market are increasing rapidly. Mexico has the world's highest per capita consumption rate of bottled water among countries, as noted in Table 5.5, though perhaps for not long

**TABLE 5.5** Top Global Consumers of Bottled Water, 2009 and 2014 (Gallons Per Capita)

| COUNTRY | 2009 | 2014 |
|---|---|---|
| Mexico | 59.2 | 69.8 |
| Thailand | 26.3 | 69.8 |
| Italy | 49.0 | 65.1 |
| United Arab Emirates | 25.0 | 41.6 |
| Belgium/Luxembourg | 35.5 | 39.4 |
| Germany | 34.7 | 39.2 |
| France | 34.4 | 37.4 |
| United States | 27.6 | 34.0 |
| Hong Kong | 22.2 | 32.7 |
| Spain | 27.7 | 32.1 |
| Lebanon | 30.1 | 28.2 |

Source: Adapted from Statista (2015).

(Statista 2015). China might appear conspicuously absent from the table. Remember, however, that this is a per capita breakdown. With a population of 1.4 billion, it would take *a lot* of sales for China to make the list. In terms of volume, however, it dominates. China has 7 percent of the world's freshwater supplies but 20 percent of its population, and its intake of bottled water has doubled from 2010 to 2015, from 19 billion to 37 billion liters. In 2013, China overtook the United States as the biggest market for bottled water by volume ("Spring Tide" 2015).

As water sources become more polluted, the growing middle class in China is looking to bottled water as the safe alternative. But the safety of this product is in question; after all, the most popular bottles sell at around 1 yuan (16 cents), and it's not possible to use sophisticated filtration technology and sell the product that cheaply ("Spring Tide" 2015). The tests carried out by national health inspectors on tap water are far more comprehensive than on bottled water; for example, the government does not monitor levels of mercury, silver, or acidity in bottled water. Bottlers do not need to specify their source. And more worrisome still, those companies extracting from groundwater reserves are allowed by law to bypass treating their product altogether (ibid.).

Bottled water also risks contributing to political apathy, as Andrew Szasz argues in his important book *Shopping Our Way to Safety* (2007). Szasz develops a term for the type of individualized consumer "solutions" that things like bottled water are meant to represent. Szasz argues these consumer-focused solutions create an "inverted quarantine." Similar to a conventional quarantine, the inverted quarantine seeks to provide protection from a threat. Unlike a traditional quarantine, which works by isolating threats to a particular area, the inverted quarantine works by isolating the consumer in "a personal commodity bubble" (97) from the threats, which are ubiquitous. As the title of the book aptly proclaims, we try to shop our way to safety by, among other things, purchasing organic food, bottled water, and air purifiers for our homes.

But there are problems with this strategy. For one, all consumer-based solutions are biased toward those who can afford them. From the perspective of the working poor, this strategy might better be called "shopping *their* way to safety." In addition, in buying safety for themselves and their loved ones, the middle and upper class risk becoming politically indifferent to attempts at larger social change that could solve the problem for *all* segments of society. If, for example, bottled water were not available and the world's middle class and above had to drink from their tap, I wonder if greater willingness would be expressed for public investment in clean and affordable water.

## Privatizing Water

Another way society is affected by water is through recent attempts to privatize public water utilities under the guise of **neoliberalism**. According to David Harvey, "neoliberalism is in the first instance a theory of political economic practices that proposes that human well-being can best be advanced by liberating individual entrepreneurial freedoms and skills within an institutional framework characterized by strong private property rights, free markets, and free trade" (2005, 2). (Neoliberalism is discussed further in Chapter 10). As opposed to liberalism, which prioritizes individual liberties, neoliberalism elevates free enterprise above all else, even if that means grossly impinging on those allegedly sacred individual liberties. Neoliberalism is also said to transform the state. The neoliberalization of the state results in an erosion of government commitment in areas such as education and health while the power of private sector actors increases. The rise of neoliberalism on the world economic stage can be seen in recent decades with the rapid push to hollow out the state by eliminating regulations and privatizing anything and everything, even water.

There is also an environmental argument, some contend, for privatizing water. **Market environmentalism**—emphasizing markets as a solution to environmental problems—is a way of packaging neoliberalism in green wrapping. The thinking goes something like this: by strengthening and expanding private property rights to things like water and relying more on markets for the allocation of resources, environmental goods will be more efficiently used, leading ultimately to less environmental degradation and a more sustainable use of resources.

Two influential international bodies heavily pushing **water privatization** are the World Bank and the International Monetary Fund (IMF) (see ECOnnection 5.1). Put simply, water privatization means treating water like any other commodity and leaving questions of access and sanitation to market mechanisms. Yet doing this risks creating two water worlds: affluent nations that still overwhelmingly rely on publicly funded water services (and that would never dream of handing control of them over to profit-seeking corporations) and the rest of the world, which may have no choice but to get its water from a private water company. Beyond obvious access questions—for example, what about slums and other areas where a profit could not be made by supplying its people with water?—the two-world scenario advantages affluent nations. We can see this occurring, for example, in the farming sector. The amount of money recovered by the US Bureau of Reclamation from irrigation projects averages at around 10 to 20 percent; the remaining 90 to 80 percent comes out of taxpayers' pockets (Peterson 2009; see ECOnnection 5.2). US farmers, under the above scenario, would benefit

## ECOnnection 5.1

# The IMF and the World Bank

The World Bank and the International Monetary Fund (IMF) are known collectively as the Bretton Woods Institutions, after the small community in rural New Hampshire where they were founded in July 1944. Each is charged, in different ways, with directing and supporting the structure of the world's economic and financial order. The World Bank's first loans were granted following World War II to help finance the reconstruction of Western Europe. As these nations recovered, the bank turned increasingly to the world's poorer countries to, in part, help them "develop" by folding them into the world economy and thus lure them away from communism; this was at the height of the Cold War. The World Bank's stated mission is to promote economic and social progress in developing countries—though the bank believes the latter comes only *after* the former.

Whereas the World Bank is primarily a lending institution, the IMF's main role is to keep the international monetary system running smoothly. It does this by monitoring the world's currencies, making sure the unpredictable variations that helped to trigger (and unduly extended) the Great Depression in the 1930s do not happen again. Thus, although the IMF does provide loans, it is more than just a bank. Both institutions wield considerable power over international affairs, as their loans come with substantial conditions. Some of the strings attached to the loans have required countries to privatize their municipal water systems.

tremendously if many of their global competitors had to get their water from a corporation seeking full-cost recovery plus a little more (the profit). It would give them a significant market advantage if they could obtain this valuable input for a fraction of the price it costs their competitors overseas.

In 1990 approximately fifty million people globally received their water from private water companies. In 2013, that number surpassed one billion for the first time (see Case Study 5.2). To ensure this shift toward water privatization, developing countries are now unable to borrow from the World Bank or IMF without having in place a domestic water-privatization policy. It's fair to say that the majority of public-utility privatization deals that have occurred in the past decade in lower-income countries are the result of the direct participation of these global monetary institutions.

Unfortunately, the societal cost of privatization has been great. No profit-seeking company can expect to expand their services to populations that cannot pay. So the water situation for the poor remains deplorable in many countries that were promised to be saved by these privatization schemes. It is estimated that 75 percent of the costs of running a water utility are for infrastructure alone (Lappé 2014). Corporations are interested in cutting costs in order to maximize profits, which is precisely what you see happening among private water entities—cuts to spending on infrastructure. While the World Bank continues to promote water privatization, its own data reveal deep problems with the approach. According to its Private Participation in Infrastructure

ECOnnection 5.2

# US Bureau of Reclamation

The US Bureau of Reclamation, the largest public purveyor of irrigation water in the American West, develops projects and delivers water to locally organized irrigation districts that provide water service to farmers. Congress directed the bureau to allow repayment without interest and to determine repayment schedules based on farmers' ability to pay and other special circumstances. The law that created the bureau allows farmers to receive three types of water subsidies:

1. interest-free repayment of a project's construction costs
2. reduced repayments based on ability to pay
3. reduced repayments under special circumstances (The federal government can cancel some or all of farmers' repayment obligation in the case of special circumstances, such as economic hardship, settlement of Native American water rights claims, unproductive lands, or drought.)

The cumulative values of such subsidies can be substantial. One example: the Tualatin irrigation project in Oregon. Its total construction cost was $58.7 million. Yet when water became available to farmers in 1976, the government determined that they could not repay the full amount. Instead, they repaid roughly 3 percent of total construction costs, shifting the remaining balance to other beneficiaries, namely, commercial users of electricity generated by the project (Wichelns 2010).

Database, there was a 34 percent failure rate for all private water and sewerage contracts entered into between 2000 and 2010, compared to a failure rate of 7 percent for transportation, 6 percent for energy, and 3 percent for telecommunications during the same period.

Evidence that water companies are failing in their contractual commitments to provide water for all can be seen by how some corporations are vigorously redefining the language of their contracts. In the city of La Paz, Bolivia, for example, to connect a large slum to the water system the privately owned utility argued that "connection" meant not only a "piped connection" but also "access to a standpipe or tanker." What's particularly distressing about this expanded definition is that it perpetuates the very conditions that water companies earlier used to make the case for water privatization, as developing countries were previously criticized for their inadequate water infrastructure that in some cases involved bringing temporary water tankers into neighborhoods (Goldman 2007). Back then, water tankers in slums were pointed to and used by proponents of neoliberalism to justify water privatization. Now, water tankers are used by private water corporations because that's the only way those companies can earn a profit in some neighborhoods. And the water supplied is often sold at a higher price than when provided by a public municipality in order to ensure profitability.

In fairness to advocates of privatization, whatever we did in the twentieth century to deliver clean water to the world's poor didn't work either, or at least didn't work

## CASE STUDY 5.2

# Neoliberalism and Water Privatization: The Case of India

While the Indian government once viewed water as a social good that ought to be left to local communities to use, value, and regulate, it now increasingly grasps water as a commodity whose value ought to be determined by the market. For example, the government's Eighth Plan explains, "Water has to be managed as a commodity in exactly the same way as any other resource; supply of water to consumers should normally be based on the principle of effective demand which should broadly correspond to the standard of service, that the users are willing to maintain, operate and finance" (Eighth Plan 14.12.2). In its Ninth Plan, it is noted that water "should be managed as an economic asset" (Ninth Plan 3.7.38). As Subramaniam (2014, 401) argues, "the increased use of economic terms in the Plans, such as 'supply and demand,' 'scarcity,' 'consumers,' and the aforementioned 'stakeholders,' serves as evidence of a major shift in the understanding of water and water relations, distinct from the ways in which local communities perceive this resource." This movement toward privatized water occurred in India in two interrelated ways: contracting water harvesting and delivery to private enterprises and enticing private companies via tax breaks, lax environmental regulations, and so forth to take over water provisioning under the guise of economic development. The 2002 National Water Policy clearly articulates how the private sector should be involved in water delivery:

> Private sector participation should be encouraged in planning, development and management of water resources projects for diverse uses, wherever feasible. Private sector participation may help in introducing innovative ideas, generating financial resources and introducing corporate management and improving service efficiency and accountability to users. Depending upon the specific situations, various combinations of private sector participation, in building, operating, leasing, and transferring of water resources facilities, may be considered. (quoted in Subramaniam 2014, 401)

as well as many had hoped. Clearly, a new approach is needed, as we know for a fact that improving access to clean water can help eradicate extreme hunger and poverty. Among other things, access to water has direct positive effects on education and gender equity. Severe and repeated cases of diarrhea, often the result of water-related diseases, contribute to malnutrition by reducing the body's ability to retain essential micro- and macronutrients, which impairs short- and long-term cognitive and physical development among children. Moreover, sick kids are more likely to miss school, thus further reducing their ability to take advantage of opportunities that could improve their lives. Because water is so difficult to access in some parts of the world—most notably many nations in Africa—millions of women and children must walk long distances daily just to obtain this needed resource for their families. There are countless reports of women and children in some African nations spending hours every day fetching water (see

**TABLE 5.6** Total Estimated Environmental and Social Costs from Pesticides in the United States

| TYPE OF IMPACT | COSTS (IN MILLIONS OF DOLLARS) |
| --- | --- |
| Public health | 1,140 |
| Domestic animal deaths and contaminations | 30 |
| Loss of natural enemies | 520 |
| Pesticide resistance | 1,500 |
| Honeybee and pollination losses | 334 |
| Crop losses | 1,391 |
| Fishery losses | 100 |
| Bird losses | 2,160 |
| Groundwater contamination | 2,000 |
| Government regulations to prevent damage | 470 |
| **Total** | **9,645** |

Source: Adapted from Pimentel and Burgess (2014).

thewaterproject.org). All this time walking for water is time that could be spent, for example, in school.

## Agriculture

For a variety of reasons, it does not make sense to import large quantities of water for purposes of raising water-intensive agricultural commodities, especially given that the commodities themselves can be imported. A sizable portion of a country's virtual water footprint (or embedded water) thus comes in the form of the agricultural commodities it imports. The United States is the largest virtual water exporter, followed by China, India, and Brazil. You might be surprised to learn that the United States is also the largest virtual water importer, though this only offsets 75 percent of exports leaving the country with one of the largest virtual water trade deficits. Other major net exporters include Canada, Australia, India, Argentina, and Brazil. The world's largest net importers are North African, Middle Eastern, and European countries, in addition to Mexico, Japan, and as mentioned, the US (Hoekstra and Mekonnen 2012).

One thing that is as surprising and counterintuitive as it is disturbing is that a country's virtual water trade is not determined by its water situation. Virtual water, instead, often flows out of water-poor, land-rich countries into land-poor, water-rich countries. The evidence suggests that many countries import food not because they lack water but because they lack sufficient arable land that can be put to cultivation. In other words, water is not the limiting agricultural factor; fertile land is.

It would be careless of me to talk about water in the context of agriculture and not at least mention how agricultural practices can negatively affect water quality and human health. Take the case of pesticides. (More agriculture-related impacts on water supplies are discussed in Chapter 8.) One analysis places the cost of pesticides in the United States, after factoring in issues related to public and environmental health, at $9.645

billion dollars annually (Pimentel and Burgess 2014; see Table 5.6). Recent research shows that tobacco farmers in Brazil have high rates of cellular damage at the genetic level from the pesticides they regularly use and come into contact with (Kahl et al. 2016). Among agricultural workers in Sri Lanka, Costa Rica, and Nicaragua, 7.5 percent, 4.5 percent, and 6.3 percent, respectively, experience occupation pesticide poisoning annually (van der Hoek et al. 1998; Wesseling, Castillo, and Elinder 1993; Garming and Waibel 2009). The total number of pesticide poisonings annually in the United States is believed to be around three hundred thousand (Pimentel 2005). When broken down according to ethnicity, US poisoning rates disproportionately affect Latinos (Liu and Apollon 2011). A survey of epidemiological literature indicates that the incidence of cancer in the US population related to pesticides ranges from about ten thousand to fifteen thousand cases per year (Pimentel 2005).

Whereas agriculture continues to be a major water stakeholder—after all, approximately 70 percent of all the water used by humans globally goes to agriculture (Sterling and Vintinner 2012)—it is not the only one. As the demands from other interests increase, like the growing thirst of cities, water conflicts will arise and will not always be solved to the satisfaction of all stakeholders.

As revealed in Table 5.7, not all foods are equal when assessed according to their respective water footprints. The relative thirstiness of ground beef ("bovine meat" in the table) is due in large part to the beef cow's consumption of grains. Even after factoring in for nutritional value, the global average confined beef cow requires 10.16 liters of water for every kilocalorie produced. As a protein source, it fares better than only nuts and fruits on a liter per gram of protein basis (Hoekstra 2015). Nuts also require copious amounts of water. Compared to other products listed in the table, they are especially large users of blue water.

More than 75 percent of the population of developed countries resides in urban areas. This percentage is expected to increase to well over 80 percent by 2030. In less affluent nations, roughly 50 percent of the population lives in urban areas. Of this, more than 70 percent—or approximately 1 billion people—reside in slum-like conditions. By 2030 the urban population of poorer nations is expected to increase to just below 60 percent as a proportion of their total population. Meanwhile, the number of **megacities**, that is, cities with more than ten million residents, is expected to rise globally from forty-six to sixty-one between 2015 and 2030. The majority of these new megacities will be located in and around the Asian continent. Balancing the competing water demands of the city and the countryside, along with those of industry and wildlife—and let's not forget that all these people have to eat—promises to be a truly monumental task of the twenty-first century.

## Climate Change

Freshwater systems are repeatedly cited as among the most vulnerable sectors to climate change. I will now briefly review, drawing from multiple sources (Kernan, Battarbee, and Moss 2010; Martin-Ortega et al. 2015), the impact of climate change on important components of the earth's freshwater systems. Even though our future water woes are not insurmountable, aggressively pursuing policies to combat climate change would go a long way toward making those woes a little less daunting.

**TABLE 5.7** The Global Average Water Footprint of Crop and Animal Products in Relation to Their Nutritional Value

| FOOD ITEM | WATER FOOTPRINT PER UNIT OF WEIGHT (L/KG) | | | | NUTRITIONAL CONTENT | | | WATER FOOTPRINT PER UNIT OF NUTRITIONAL VALUE | | |
|---|---|---|---|---|---|---|---|---|---|---|
| | GREEN | BLUE | GREY | TOTAL | CALORIE (KCAL/KG) | PROTEIN (G/KG) | FAT (G/KG) | CALORIE (L/KCAL) | PROTEIN (L/G PROTEIN) | FAT (L/G FAT) |
| Sugar crops | 130 | 52 | 15 | 197 | 285 | 0 | 0 | 0.69 | 0 | 0 |
| Vegetables | 194 | 43 | 85 | 322 | 240 | 12 | 2.1 | 1.34 | 26 | 154 |
| Starchy roots | 327 | 16 | 43 | 387 | 827 | 13 | 1.7 | 0.47 | 31 | 226 |
| Fruits | 726 | 147 | 89 | 962 | 460 | 5.3 | 2.8 | 2.09 | 180 | 348 |
| Cereals | 1,232 | 228 | 184 | 1,644 | 3,208 | 80 | 15 | 0.51 | 21 | 112 |
| Oil crops | 2,023 | 220 | 121 | 2,364 | 2,908 | 149 | 209 | 0.81 | 16 | 11 |
| Pulses | 3,180 | 141 | 734 | 4,055 | 3,412 | 215 | 23 | 1.19 | 19 | 180 |
| Nuts | 7,016 | 1,367 | 680 | 9,063 | 2,500 | 65 | 193 | 3.63 | 139 | 47 |
| Milk | 863 | 86 | 72 | 1,020 | 560 | 33 | 31 | 1.82 | 31 | 33 |
| Eggs | 2,592 | 244 | 429 | 3,265 | 1,425 | 111 | 100 | 2.29 | 29 | 33 |
| Chicken meat | 3,545 | 313 | 467 | 4,325 | 1,440 | 127 | 100 | 3 | 34 | 43 |
| Butter | 4,695 | 465 | 393 | 5,553 | 7,692 | 0 | 872 | 0.72 | 0 | 6.4 |
| Pig meat | 4,907 | 459 | 622 | 5,988 | 2,786 | 105 | 259 | 2.15 | 57 | 23 |
| Sheep/goat meat | 8,253 | 457 | 53 | 8,763 | 2,059 | 139 | 163 | 4.25 | 63 | 54 |
| Bovine meat | 14,414 | 550 | 451 | 15,415 | 1,513 | 138 | 101 | 10.19 | 112 | 153 |

L: liter; kg: kilogram; kcal: kilocalorie; g: gram. Source: Hoekstra (2015).

### Surface Water

There is a remarkable similarity among climate models when it comes to predicting greater runoff in the tropics and higher latitudes and reduced runoff in many already dry, midlatitude regions such as the Mediterranean, South Africa, and the southwestern United States and northwestern Mexico. In regions with significant snowmelt, we can expect changes to the timing of runoff and rapidity of spring melt. In regards to the latter, this could lead to an increased risk of floods as that water overloads the capacity of the land to absorb it.

### Groundwater

Demand for groundwater is expected to increase to offset reduced surface flows in some regions. Some sites will also see reductions in the rate at which they recharge, while others will experience increases in recharge rates. Warmer temperatures will also result in higher evaporation rates, which could lead to increasing rates of groundwater **salinization** (the buildup of salt in soil and groundwater). Sea-level rise will also increase the risk of saltwater intrusion in coastal aquifers.

### Hydrologic Extremes

The frequency of intense flooding and drought conditions is expected to increase. Mid-continental regions, for example, are expected to be unusually dry during the summer. In all areas, climate models predict that when it does rain, the chance of an intense event will increase.

### Water Quality

Warmer atmospheric temperatures are expected to result in increases in the temperature of lakes, reservoirs, and rivers, which in turn will increase algal and bacterial blooms and cause dissolved oxygen concentrations in those bodies of water to decrease. More intense weather events could also increase soil-erosion rates and negatively affect water quality. Similarly, significant flooding could increase the amount of pollutants and toxins that get washed into waterways.

### Water Demand

There are a lot of unknowns that make it difficult to speak definitively on the subject of future water demand. Water demand could increase dramatically in the agricultural sector, though if drought-tolerant crops are grown and improvements in irrigation efficiencies achieved, these demands could be tempered. Similarly, demand in urban areas might increase radically as, say, warmer temperatures further stress lawns, gardens, and parks, thus increasing irrigation rates in metropolitan areas. However, if drought-tolerant grasses, bushes, and trees are planted or xeriscape lawns become more culturally accepted, these demands too could be reduced dramatically.

## Solutions

There are so many problems, tensions, and conflicts involving water that I couldn't begin to adequately summarize solutions to every one. Consequently, to make this

## CASE STUDY 5.3
# Desalinization in California

California is in trouble (see Image 5.1). The state needs water, or needs to use less of it—it all depends on how you look at the problem. One idea gaining favor is desalinization: converting seawater into drinking water. Desalinization plants are expensive to build and run. (One plant in Santa Barbara has been idle since the 1990s because of the costs.) Three main environmental considerations represent additional challenges to desalinization proponents: how seawater is brought in, how the drinkable water is separated out, and what happens to the salt afterward.

You can't just suck water in through a pipe, as that would risk trapping and killing sea life. Grates at the end of such a pipe still would allow in larvae and fish eggs. So the goal is to perfect a subsurface intake method: run a pipe hundreds of feet out and hundreds of feet beneath the dunes (whereby the sand acts as a natural filter). But that requires a large amount of energy to pump so much water so far. Once the seawater gets to the plant, it must be pushed through tiny membranes to filter out the salt. This requires immense pressure and thus immense amounts of energy. Finally, only half of the saltwater piped into a desalinization plant is made drinkable. The rest ends up as part of a thick salty soup that has to be disposed of. It can't just be dumped back into the sea—its density would cause the concoction to sink and kill anything in its path. It can't be dumped on land either: terrestrial life likes salt even less than marine life. One suggestion: blending the byproduct back into the ocean with sprayers that run thousands of feet out to sea (with small holes spaced roughly ten feet apart). This act too would require considerable energy (Potter 2015).

discussion manageable, the following text will be broken up into two subsections. In the first, I talk about changing how we think about water. Technological solutions will get us only so far. It is also important to keep in mind that not everyone can afford them. Technological fixes also involve trade-offs—**desalinization** (the removal of salt and other minerals from saline water), for example, is immensely energy intensive (see Case Study 5.3). This is why we need to revisit how we think about water. Specifically, it is worth discussing first whether water is something to which we all have a fundamental human right. I conclude the chapter by discussing citizen engagement around water, also known as water governance.

### Water as a Human Right at the Right Value

There are only two international conventions that explicitly recognize the right to water: the UN Convention on the Rights of the Child of 1989 (article 24) and the UN Convention on the Elimination of All Forms of Discrimination Against Women of 1979 (article 14). Prior to 1979, one must go back to the Geneva Convention of 1949 (article 26) to find any international legal document recognizing a human's right to water, though in this text that right extends only to prisoners of war. More recently, in 2002, General Comment Number 15 to the International Covenant on Economic, Social, and Cultural Rights, a major human rights treaty, was signed by 153 countries and recognizes that "the human right to water is indispensable for leading a life in human dignity" and "is a prerequisite for the realization of other human rights" (United Nations 2002). The treaty also notes the importance of sanitation in the fulfillment of these rights.

According to this document, the human right to water entitles everyone to "sufficient," "safe," "acceptable," "physically accessible," and "affordable" water for personal and domestic uses. Of course, the precise meaning of these terms is up for debate. As a limited resource, we cannot treat the right to clean water the same as, say, the right to clean air. Indeed, precisely so we can ensure access to everyone, we will likely need to impose a *limit* to the right to water, a practice not all that unusual, as we impose limits on rights all the time. Those living in the United States, for example, are protected by strong free-speech rights. Yet they still can't say anything they wish—like *bomb* in a crowded airplane. The scope of humans' right to water is normally limited, as it tends to refer to the fulfillment of basic needs, like those related to drinking, cooking, and other vital domestic needs (such as washing). It has proven very difficult, however, to translate this to a specific volume. Although it is generally agreed that an amount of three to five liters per day of clean water is the absolute minimum to allow for human survival, most understand that we can do better than just provide enough for mere survival. Research suggests that well-being improves significantly when these values increase to around twenty liters per day per person. That added water improves sanitary conditions considerably. For this reason, a number of international organizations, including the United Nations (see un.org/en/globalissues/water), proclaim humans have a right to between fifty and one hundred liters per day per person, which, as noted earlier, must be safe, affordable (water costs should not exceed 3 percent of household income), and physically accessible (the water source has to be within a thousand meters of the home and collection time should not exceed thirty minutes).

To say water is a human right does not mean, however, that it must be delivered for free. When many argue humans have a right to food, they are not arguing that it ought to be provided at no cost. To accept the principle of a human right to water does, however, require that we treat water as a *social* as well as an economic good. This is where that aforementioned change in how we think about water comes into play (see Image 5.2).

No discussion of rights is complete without talk of related responsibilities. Take property rights: if your bull gets out and destroys your neighbor's property and impregnates her cow, you are responsible for the damages incurred, and your neighbor owns the offspring of that encounter. In other words, your right to that bull also implies responsibility, namely, keeping the animal on your property. This legal principle dates back centuries and forms the backbone of common property law as we know it today (Carolan 2010a). So when corporations look to claim property rights over water, they need to be held to the responsibilities that ought to go along with owning that water (see Movement Matters 5.1).

Water doesn't fit into the "economic good" box as easily as other things. For one, the so-called law of supply and demand doesn't exist when talking about water. You can't choose what company's water you want piped into your house. That choice is made for you. Moreover, the price is based on a lot more than just market mechanisms. There

**IMAGE 5.2** Everyone Needs Water

Protests in Detroit in July 2014 over the city's move to shut water off to households delinquent on their water bills. Source: Used with permission of National Nurses United.

are also social and political factors that shape the cost of tap water, most notably subsidies—either for the water itself or for, say, the electricity that pumps the water.

There are two main competing visions about how to think about water as an economic good. The first, supported by traditional economic approaches, explains that water should be priced at whatever the market will bear. The second vision believes value, especially when it comes to water, cannot and should not be left entirely to the free market to decide.

The first approach is problematic because it could—and likely would—disproportionately negatively affect rural populations and the urban poor who cannot "pay to play" in the life-sustaining game of water access. Water does seem to deserve the designation of a special economic good. It must be priced, but when going about establishing that price, we would do well to not let just the market decide. Others have laid out five characteristics of water that they believe justify pricing it with a little more care than other economic goods (see, e.g., Cunha 2009):

1. Water is essential: there is no life, economic production, or environment without it.
2. Water is nonsubstitutable: there is no alternative.
3. Water is finite: the water that currently circulates through the hydrological cycle is all there is.
4. Water is a system: water is part of a complex system and helps make possible innumerable ecosystem services.
5. Water is bulky: water's physical properties make long-distance transportation difficult.

## Grassroots Organizations Take on Nestlé Waters Canada

Wellington Water Watchers, a citizens' group in Wellington County, Ontario, along with Ecojustice and the Council of Canadians, played a key role in getting Nestlé Waters Canada to drop its quest to have drought restrictions removed from one of its water takings in Ontario, Canada. Nestlé is allowed to pump and package 1.13 million liters of groundwater per day in the town of Hillsburgh, approximately eighty kilometers north of Toronto. The company pays only $3.71 (Canadian dollars) for every million liters of water it draws (Kerr 2013). A severe drought in the area, however, led the Ministry of the Environment to place restrictions on how much it could draw. Nestlé shortly thereafter announced it had persuaded the ministry to remove the mandatory reductions. The aforementioned community groups then successfully challenged the agreement through the Environmental Review Tribunal of Ontario. The tribunal ruled that the settlement agreement between Nestlé and the ministry was not in the public interest and that the original appeal should proceed to a full hearing, at which point Nestlé dropped their bid for special treatment.

Would the mere recognition of the human right to water actually improve conditions worldwide? Likely not. My point in talking about expanding our understanding of water as an economic good is a pragmatic realization that the imperatives to meet basic human water needs are more than just moral. They are also rooted in law and markets. We can change how people think about water all we want, but unless we likewise alter the social, economic, and political structures presently standing in the way of universal water access, millions will continue to go to bed at night in an unsanitary environment and thirsty.

## Water Governance

Water resource management underwent a bit of a paradigm shift in the 1990s. Previously, the command-and-control—top-down, government-driven—model had proven modestly successful at regulating **point-source pollution** (pollution with an identifiable source). As recently as the 1970s, rivers were literally catching fire in affluent nations as a result of major pollution releases by industry. With the success of point-source pollution control measures, attention slowly turned to the impact of more diffuse pollution, called **nonpoint-source pollution**. From a governing standpoint, however, this shift complicates things for all but the most Orwellian of societies. The effective monitoring of pollution from nonpoint sources would require a level of government intrusion that most would be uncomfortable with. A new form of water governance has thus emerged: a broad social system of governance that operates at different levels of society while including, but not limiting itself to, the narrower perspective of government as the main decision-making political entity. A number of attributes of effective water governance have been identified (Norman, Cook, and Cohen 2015):

## CASE STUDY 5.4
# Micro-Watershed Councils in Mexico and Guatemala

Deforestation and climate change are increasing the risk of flash flooding in communities located in the high-altitude watersheds near the Tacana volcano in Mexico and Guatemala. The water cycle has become particularly vicious in recent years, as an increase in frequency of flash floods has further eroded the formerly deep soils, which previously had tremendous capacity for water retention, thus further heightening the risk of flash flooding. With support from governmental and nongovernmental organizations, local communities are being empowered to form micro-watershed councils. These councils are leading watershed restoration projects. The projects are designed and implemented by the local councils. In addition to helping provide employment opportunities for community members, and thus also facilitating the meeting of development priorities, the micro-watershed councils are making local watersheds more secure and surrounding communities less vulnerable (IUCN 2010).

- Participation: all water users should have a voice in the decision-making process.
- Transparency: the decision-making process should be transparent and open for scrutiny.
- Equity: all stakeholders should have opportunities to meaningfully participate in the process.
- Accountability: governments, the private sector, and civil society organizations should all be accountable to the public.
- Responsiveness: institutions and processes should serve stakeholders and respond properly to their interests (e.g., if a water source becomes contaminated, steps are immediately taken to address the problem).
- Ethics: effective water governance should be grounded in society's ethical principles (such as the belief that water is a fundamental human right).

These new participatory models are appealing to governments and **nongovernmental organizations** (NGOs) on a number of levels. (An NGO refers to any legally constituted organization that operates independently from any government.) Many governments, especially those in less affluent nations, express a desire for decentralized forms of governance, as they are already overstretched in attempting to deliver and maintain rural services. As for NGOs, many operate by constructing a number of water systems as part of a project but then leave the project area after several months or years to start new projects. Community-rooted governance projects have in some instances became a convenient method for shifting responsibility from the state and corporations to end users. And in light of future threats related to climate change, these locally based models can help bolster watershed resiliency, at least at the micro level, given the level of local expertise involved (see Case Study 5.4).

Most problems with such open models of water governance do not occur immediately. Problems, when they do occur, often appear later, after the initial excitement fades. A review of the literature came up with the following commonly cited reasons for the breakdown of community management systems (Cunha 2009; Norman, Cook, and Cohen 2015):

- Participation often relies on voluntary inputs from community members that can erode over time, as there are often no long-term incentives to keep the activity going.
- Key individuals leave the community or die and are not easily replaced.
- The community organization charged with managing the water supply loses the trust and respect of the general community, perhaps from a lack of transparency and accountability.
- When some community members fail to contribute maintenance fees—whether they are free riders or because they cannot afford to—others become disillusioned.
- If government steps entirely away from the project, community members may feel they have been abandoned and become unmotivated.
- Communities are too poor to replace major capital items when they break down, which can be particularly problematic when or if government abdicates its responsibilities.

Too often public participation is viewed as something just needing to be checked off on a list of steps that are supposed to lead to successful environmental management. Nevertheless, when engaged meaningfully, public participation can produce long-term and sustainable results (OECD 2015b). It takes a lot of work to make community-level governance projects work. Yet given the scope and severity of the problems at hand and the general excitement people tend to display when empowered to be involved in solution-oriented activities (Taylor, Taylor, and Taylor 2012), I have no doubt we can muster the energy and resources toward this end.

## IMPORTANT CONCEPTS

- inverted quarantine
- neoliberalism
- virtual water
- water as a right
- water governance
- water privatization

## DISCUSSION QUESTIONS

1. Do you drink bottled water? If so, why? Other than an outright ban, what policies would need to be implemented for you to stop your bottled-water consumption?
2. Do you believe humans have a fundamental right to water? If so, what's the best way to go about ensuring that right is satisfied: the market, government, community-based governance, or perhaps something else?
3. What are some of the downsides of letting markets allocate water? And some benefits?
4. If you were made more aware of your water footprint, would your consumption patterns change? Why or why not? What are some of the barriers to change, and how could those barriers be overcome?

## SUGGESTED ADDITIONAL READINGS

Chellaney, B. 2015. *Water, Peace, and War: Confronting the Global Water Crisis.* New York: Rowman and Littlefield.

Haglund, L. 2014. "Water Governance and Social Justice in São Paulo, Brazil." *Water Policy* 16:78–96.

Rusca, M., and K. Schwartz. 2014. "'Going with the Grain': Accommodating Local Institutions in Water Governance." *Current Opinion in Environmental Sustainability* 11:34–38.

Sanderson, M., and R. S. Frey. 2015. "Structural Impediments to Sustainable Groundwater Management in the High Plains Aquifer of Western Kansas." *Agriculture and Human Values* 32:401–417.

## RELEVANT INTERNET LINKS

- environment.nationalgeographic.com/environment/freshwater/water-footprint-calculator. A water-footprint calculator.
- waterfootprint.org/en. A comprehensive resource for anything and everything having to do with water footprints.
- waterdata.usgs.gov/nwis. Real-time data from selected surface-water, groundwater, and water-quality sites from around the United States, among other things.
- www.wateruseitwisely.com/kids. A website full of useful information (and even some games) directed at water conservation.

## SUGGESTED VIDEOS

- *Bottled Life: Nestlé's Business with Water* (2012; English version released in 2013). Swiss journalist Res Gehringer investigates the Nestlé water bottling company.
- *DamNation* (2014). Film about the changing attitudes in the United States concerning dams and a critical look at the role they should play in the future.
- *Damocracy* (2013). Debunks the myth of large-scale dams as clean energy and a solution to climate change.
- *The Fight for Water* (2011). On February 28, 2009, near the tiny village of Santa Rosa, Ecuador, an oil pipeline broke inside the Amazon rain forest. An estimated fourteen thousand barrels of crude oil spilled into the Napo and Coca Rivers, both of which are tributaries of the Amazon River. This film tells what happened next.
- *Last Call at the Oasis* (2011). Illuminates the essential role water plays in our lives, exposes the defects in the current system, and shows communities already struggling under the status quo. The film features activist Erin Brockovich; water experts Peter Gleick, Jay Famiglietti, and Robert Glennon; and a variety of social entrepreneurs in search of revolutionary solutions.
- *Tapped* (2010). Documents the push by corporations to privatize water and then sell it back to us in plastic bottles that end up polluting our oceans.

Part II

# AT THE INTERSECTION OF ECOLOGY AND SOCIETY

# 6

# Population: A Problem of Quantity or Quality?

If I had written this book forty years ago, I might have focused entirely on the subject of population growth. This was a period when people spoke of "the population bomb" and "a population explosion," when we were told that earth was like a spaceship with a near maxed-out seating capacity. It was also around this time when a group of scientists commissioned by the Club of Rome—a global think tank founded in 1968 with a history of examining a variety of international issues—looked at **exponential growth** in resource use, population, and economic activity and announced that we should see significant resource scarcities before the new millennium.

Although perhaps this anxiety was a bit misplaced—after all, the global population growth rate has considerably lowered since that time—I understand why the subject grabbed the attention it did. We have to remember that some forty years ago, world population was growing at an unprecedented (and since unprecedented) level. It was, quite frankly, a scary rate of growth, which explains the alarming talk of "bombs" and "explosions" when discussing world population levels.

In the previous century, countries could be fairly easily classified into one of two categories: affluent/developed or less affluent/developing. The former had low population growth rates, the latter high. With **birthrates** (or the ratio of live births per one thousand people per year) now declining in the latter category, including much of Asia, Latin America, and the Middle East, the high population growth rates prevalent forty years ago are today restricted to the countries in sub-Saharan Africa plus a few others (like Liberia, Afghanistan, and the Palestinian territories). A number of less affluent countries in fact have birthrates that, a couple of decades ago, would have been found only in high-income countries. China has infamously slashed its birthrates, thanks in part to its **one-child policy**, by penalizing families that have more than one child. But strides toward lowering birthrates have also been made because of recent socioeconomic attainments. To quote Nobel economist Amartya Sen, "While China gets too much credit for its authoritarian measures, it gets far too little credit for other supportive policies it has followed that have helped to cut down the birth rate" (1994, 22). Some countries that would certainly not be considered affluent yet have fertility rates below that found in the United States (with a rate of 1.87) include Iran (1.85), Uzbekistan (1.8), Thailand (1.5), Slovakia (1.39), Taiwan (1.11), and Singapore (0.8) (CIA 2015).

*How* environmental sociologists talk about population growth, however, tends to be different from how others—such as, say, Paul Ehrlich (author of *The Population Bomb* [1968])—have grappled with the subject. For environmental sociologists, it is not population growth per se that is the central focus of concern but rather the *relationships* between population and resource consumption, use, and waste, recognizing too that these relationships are fundamentally mediated by social structures. Focusing too much on population growth itself also risks sidetracking us from understanding the reasons behind those growth rates. From a pragmatic environmentalist standpoint, what good does it do to bemoan excessive population growth if it means being distracted from uncovering its underlying drivers?

This is not to suggest that population growth itself is not worth talking about. It is important, however, not to rest too much of the blame at the feet of those parts of the world with higher than average fertility rates. Lest we forget, the average US citizen's ecological footprint is 23 acres, whereas the often-demonized China (with its massive population of some 1.35 billion inhabitants) has a per capita ecological footprint of 5.1 acres—a figure that's very close to the estimated per person sustainable budget of 5 acres (Wackernagel 2013). When we talk about population, we need to also have an honest discussion about *which* populations are having the biggest ecological impact, as not all people are equal in this regard. Nevertheless, current growth rates, while down from just a couple of decades ago, are not making things any easier. The stark reality is that the more people there are on earth, the more competition there will be for its already scarce resources, which only complicates matters as we strive to find ways to improve the livelihood of the world's poorest billion, a population who, quite frankly, are *not consuming enough*, as they live at subsistence levels—and some not even at those.

## Fast Facts

- The world's population is just over seven billion; for the latest figure, see www.census.gov/popclock. We are all but certain to see a world population of at least nine billion people by 2050.
- The ecological footprint per capita of high-income countries is approximately five times greater than that of low-income countries. Uganda's population, for example, increased by roughly 400 percent between 1969 and 2015, and yet its per capita footprint remained essentially unchanged. If everyone in the world lived like the average person living in the United Arab Emirates (the country with the world's highest per capita footprint), we would need the equivalent of 6 planets to regenerate resources and absorb $CO_2$ emissions. If everyone lived like the average resident of the United States, we would need the resources and waste sinks of 4.5 planets (WWF 2014).
- The UN median projection for global population growth from 2010 to 2050 estimates the addition of more than 2.5 billion people to our planet. While much of this growth

will occur in lower-income countries, where some are arguably not presently consuming enough (which is to say they are living at absolute poverty levels), this is still the carbon equivalent of adding two United States to the planet (IPCC 2014).

- Exceedingly high national fertility rates are now almost exclusively concentrated in a single part of the world: sub-Saharan Africa. All but one (Afghanistan) of the sixteen countries with estimated total fertility rates at five or higher can be found there. The same can be said for nearly all of the thirty-nine countries with fertility rates of four or greater (CIA 2015).
- Although fertility rates in sub-Saharan Africa tend to be high, the countries of this region also have very high child mortality rates. On the bright side, child mortality in this part of the world has been continuously falling for the last fifty years—one in four children died in the early 1960s, whereas today that figure is less than one in ten. On the not so bright side: that means nearly one child in ten still fails to see adulthood (Roser 2015). Conflict, AIDS/HIV, malaria, and extreme poverty have combined to drastically reduce life expectancy in this part of the world, in some cases close to forty years of age (WHO 2012b).

## Implications

I understand the appeal of placing the responsibility for our ecological ills at the feet of population growth. Reducing environmental problems to demographics—thinking fewer people equals fewer environmental problems—is much easier than trying to deal with the root causes of global environmental impacts. And it's an attractive argument, especially for those living in affluent nations who can employ it to elude any moral responsibility for reducing their ecological footprints. To paraphrase sentiments I hear from those looking to make ecological scapegoats out of rapidly growing lower-income countries: "We can just keep doing what we're doing—no reason to change our actions. *They* are the ones—those in poor countries with the high-fertility rates—who need to change!" Yet this argument fails to hold up to empirical scrutiny. In discussing the impacts of population, this section looks at whether today's environmental ills are primarily the result of population growth per se or a product of a process that's a bit more complex (see ECOnnection 6.1).

### *Greenhouse Gases*

Table 6.1 compares different regions and countries with regard to their share of world population growth and $CO_2$ emissions growth between 1970 and 2010. It is clear from this table that population growth alone cannot account for raising $CO_2$ emissions. We see, for example, that sub-Saharan Africa accounted for very little of the growth in $CO_2$ emissions between 1970 and 2010, while accounting for 19 percent of global population growth during this period. At the other extreme, while accounting for 3.4 percent of population growth, the United States is responsible for 13.6 percent of the growth of $CO_2$ emissions in the same time period. In light of these facts, we need to realize that the actual impact of future fertility rate reductions on greenhouse gas emissions will likely not be proportional, especially if those declines are occurring in countries in sub-Saharan Africa (see Ethical Question 6.1).

ECOnnection 6.1

# From IPAT to STIRPAT

A widely applied accounting model to examine the relationship between human activities and the environment is the IPAT. First proposed in the early 1970s (see, for example, Ehrlich and Holden 1971), the IPAT model specifies that environmental *i*mpacts are the product of *p*opulation size, *a*ffluence (in terms of per capita consumption or production), and *t*echnology (defined as impact per unit of consumption or production). Each variable is assumed to have proportional effects on the environment. When calculating environmental impacts, in other words, IPAT reminds us that we cannot divorce talk about population from variables pertaining to levels of affluence and technology impacts.

Although a valuable accounting equation, the IPAT model remains a relatively crude instrument for social scientists, as it does not allow for the testing of hypotheses (York, Rosa, and Dietz 2003). To overcome this limitation, Dietz and Rosa (1994) advanced a new model, one that allows for the calculation of probabilities and hence an evaluation of competing hypotheses and theories. This alternative model is called STIRPAT: *s*tochastic *i*mpacts by *r*egression on *p*opulation, *a*ffluence, and *t*echnology (Rosa and Dietz 1998). One of the most notable contributions of the STIRPAT program has been its ability to show that basic material conditions like demographic and economic factors shape the size of national-level ecological footprints to a significant degree. In practical policy terms, STIRPAT tells us that there is no "magic bullet" that will solve environmental problems and that we must deal with deeper driving forces, which include population but also things like economic growth. (Thanks to Richard York for helping me distill an otherwise extensive literature into a couple of sentences.)

## Urban Sprawl

**Urban sprawl**—the spreading of urban development into areas adjoining cities—can occur with or without population growth. The causes of urbanization are multiple (Image 6.1). People may migrate from rural to urban areas for employment opportunities or for something as fundamental as food.

More than half of the world's expected nine billion people will live in large urban expanses by 2030; cities and their outskirts will cover an additional 1.2 million square kilometers—a tripling in size from today. For a point of comparison, urban areas increased by just 58,000 square kilometers between 1970 and 2000 (Seto, Guneralp, and Hutyra 2012). It has been estimated that the total population of cities in developing countries will double between 2000 and 2030, yet their built-up areas will triple. This calculation is not surprising, as cities in low-income countries are currently more than four times as densely populated as cities in affluent countries. These cities can't get much more densely concentrated than they already are, meaning for many their only choice is to sprawl out. In high-income nations, urban populations are expected to increase by 20 percent during this time period, their built-up areas will increase two and a half times (Dodman 2009).

**TABLE 6.1** Share of Population and $CO_2$ Emissions Growth for Select Regions/Countries, 1970–2010

| REGION/NATION | SHARE OF POPULATION GROWTH (%) | SHARE OF EMISSIONS GROWTH (%) |
|---|---|---|
| Northern Africa | 2.5 | 2.5 |
| Sub-Saharan Africa | 19.0 | 2.4 |
| China | 15.5 | 43.5 |
| India | 21.5 | 9.9 |
| United States | 3.4 | 13.6 |
| South Korea | 0.5 | 3.7 |
| Japan | 0.5 | 3.6 |

Source: Adapted from IPCC (2014).

Just how big are cities getting? There is a reason the adjective *mega* is used to describe today's largest urban centers. In 1950 there were two cities with 10 million or more inhabitants. By 2005 that number had increased to twenty. In 2015, there were thirty-four cities with 10 million or more residents, with three more being home to between 9 and 10 million individuals (Demographia 2015; see Table 6.2).

Just as there is growth that can be labeled as "smart," there are also forms that seem not so smart, like, for example, urban sprawl. There is now over a decade's worth of research showing that, after controlling for things like age, education, fruit and vegetable consumption, income, race/ethnicity, and smoking status, residents of more compact counties have lower BMIs (body mass indexes) and lower probabilities of obesity and chronic diseases (Ewing et al. 2003; Ewing, Brownson, and Berringan 2006; Ewing et al. 2014). (One possible reason for this: compact urban spaces encourage "active travel" as opposed to using one's car for every trip.) Ecological impacts also vary widely depending on which path of urban development is followed. Studies have shown that metropolitan regions ranking high on a quantitative index of sprawl experience a greater number of ozone exceedances (concentrations that exceed what is allowed by the federal government) than more spatially compact metropolitan regions. Importantly, this relationship held even after controlling for population size, average ozone seasonal temperatures, and regional emissions of nitrogen oxides and **volatile organic compounds** (compounds that evaporate from housekeeping, maintenance, and building products made with organic chemicals) (Kashem, Irawan, and Wilson 2014; Stone 2008). In fact, most of the negative environmental indicators often attributed to urbanization are actually the result of urban sprawl.

## Food

Many have a difficult time divorcing population growth from the subject of food security. It's a fair link to make. Each additional mouth that needs to be fed means additional competition for food. Fortunately, the links between population growth and food security are mediated by a number of social variables, which is cause for hope. But first, let's start with the bad news.

ETHICAL QUESTION 6.1

# Do Countries Have a Right to Their Fair Share of $CO_2$ Emissions?

A sizable proportion of future growth in the world's population will undoubtedly come from low-income people residing in low-income nations, who, unfortunately, will likely remain in a state of poverty for the foreseeable future. For these very poor nations, there will continue to be little connection between future population growth and greenhouse gas emissions. Yet some countries—most notably India and China—will undoubtedly see their standard of living and populations (and thus their $CO_2$ footprint) increase between now and 2050. India's population is expected to surpass China's, currently the most populous country in the world, by 2030, when it becomes home to some 1.53 billion people. For these countries, we can expect to see a positive correlation between population, affluence, and greenhouse gas emissions. Yet this situation calls forth an ethical question: Are countries entitled to a certain fair share of greenhouse gas emissions? And if so, what should that level be? More to the point: If an impoverished country's per capita greenhouse gas emissions levels are drastically less than, say, those of the United States, do they have a right to *increase* those emissions up to a point? Or should we treat emission increases in the developing world the same as we would treat increases occurring in wealthy nations?

According to the United Nations, global agricultural production will need to be at least 60 percent higher in 2050 than 2007 levels (FAO 2012). This is a smaller output increase than the agriculture sector has achieved over the past half century. But before we let out a collective sigh of relief, it is questionable whether these increases can be achieved, let alone achieved sustainably. A 2013 study examined yields of four key staple crops: maize, rice, wheat, and soybeans (Ray et al. 2013). The findings are not encouraging, as it notes that yields are increasing by only about 0.9 percent to 1.6 percent a year. That would lead to an overall yield increase of somewhere between 38 percent (low-end estimate) and 67 percent (high-end estimate) by 2050. In other words, it is actually plausible that there will not be enough food to go around by 2050. Next throw into the equation climate change, which could be a game changer as far as agriculture output is concern (and not in a good way), plus rising demand for biofuels and certain animal proteins, and we have serious cause for concern.

If we cannot increase yields sufficiently to satisfy future demand—and there's plenty of research out there suggesting we can't (Ray et al. 2013)—perhaps we can increase the amount of land under cultivation. To make up for the yield shortfall, we'll need roughly 750 million additional hectares of land by 2050 (Schade and Pimentel 2010). There is an emerging consensus that there are roughly 1.4 billion hectares around the world that could be brought under cultivation (Alexandratos and Bruinsma 2012). Yet we must realize that a lot needs to be accomplished before land can be brought into production: land rights have to be settled, credit must be available to farmers so they can buy necessary inputs (like seed), and an infrastructure and market must be in place. These constraints explain why **arable land** (land that can be cultivated to grow crops) worldwide

**IMAGE 6.1** Suburban Sprawl

View of Salt Lake City from the International Space Station, photographed on June 14, 2003, shows the city and its suburbs nestled between the Wasatch Front and the Great Salt Lake. Source: NASA.

has grown by a net average of 5 million hectares per year over the past two decades, even though there are tremendous pressures to expand faster (Rabobank Group 2010). As the easiest land to convert has already been plowed under, we can expect a slowdown in the annual growth of arable land, recognizing that what remains is increasingly marginal, which means it will require even more fertilizer and other inputs to be productive. Specifically, the annual growth of arable land is expected to slow from 0.30 percent between 1961 and 2005 to 0.10 percent between 2005 and 2050. This calculates out to an average annual net increase of arable area of 2.75 million hectares per year between 2005 and 2050, or a total of 120 million additional hectares (Rabobank Group 2010, 14). This figure is well below the most optimistic estimates that claim we need 200 million additional hectares by mid-century to satisfy global food demand. Furthermore, the estimate ignores the fact that arable land in developed and transitional countries is *declining* (thanks most notably to urban sprawl). For instance, there was an 8 percent drop in the number of acres cultivated in the United States from 1990 to 2012 (EPA 2013).

In 1798 Thomas Malthus published his immensely influential *Essay on Population*. His argument, greatly oversimplified, was that growth in population will always outpace our ability to feed, shelter, and clothe people and that without some controls on population growth, it would ultimately be humanity's undoing. The future, in the eyes of Malthus, was bleak, especially for the poorest class. His view is held to this day by so-called **neo-Malthusians,** who advocate for the control of population growth. Before we declare the statistics cited above a testament to Malthus's foresight, let's look more closely at why there is food scarcity in the world today.

**TABLE 6.2** Cities with 10 Million Inhabitants or More, 1950, 2000, and 2015 (in Millions)

| 1950 | | 2000 | | 2015 | |
|---|---|---|---|---|---|
| CITY | POPULATION | CITY | POPULATION | CITY | POPULATION |
| New York-Newark | 12.3 | Tokyo | 34.4 | Tokyo-Yokohama | 37.843 |
| Tokyo | 11.3 | Mexico City | 18.1 | Jakarta | 30.539 |
| | | New York-Newark | 17.8 | Delhi | 24.998 |
| | | São Paulo | 17.1 | Manila | 24.123 |
| | | Mumbai | 16.1 | Seoul-Incheon | 23.480 |
| | | Shanghai | 13.2 | Shanghai | 23.480 |
| | | Calcutta | 13.1 | Karachi | 22.123 |
| | | Delhi | 12.4 | Beijing | 21.009 |
| | | Buenos Aires | 11.8 | New York-Newark | 20.630 |
| | | Los Angeles-Long Beach-Santa Ana | 11.8 | Guangzhou | 20.597 |
| | | Osaka-Kobe | 11.2 | São Paulo | 20.365 |
| | | Jakarta | 11.1 | Mexico City | 20.063 |
| | | Rio de Janeiro | 10.8 | 22 additional cities with populations between 10 and 20 million | |

Source: Adapted from United Nations (2005) and Demographia (2015).

According to the Nobel Prize–winning economist Amartya Sen (1981), modern food crises are less related to the absence of food as to the inability to buy it. Examining the 1943 Bengal famine, which at its peak claimed the lives of more than fifty thousand Bengalese weekly (Fisher 1943), Sen describes how there was actually plenty of food to go around; he also looked at the 1974 Bangladesh famine and drew similar conclusions. The problem, in other words, was not a lack of food but a lack of *available* food, as those with the means to acquire it were engaging in acts of hoarding, knowing that its price would only go up. Whereas natural disasters may have been the main culprits in the past, extreme food insecurity today is more often than not the result of markets, governments, and civil society failing those at the margins of society.

This brings us to the subject of democracy. Sen argues that democracy creates an important political, social, and civil environment where famine is unlikely. Indeed, as Sen famously wrote, "No famine has ever taken place in the history of the world in a functioning democracy" (1981, 16). Famines tend to affect only the poorest segment of a country's population. In nondemocratic states, those most likely to experience famine are likewise the least likely to have political access. Their famine-related suffering is therefore allowable to elites, as it does little to threaten their grip on power. What democracy provides is a voice to those living on the margins of society who would otherwise lack access to any levers of political influence. In nondemocratic states, famines can also go on without most of the public even being aware of the suffering. A cornerstone of democracy is accountability, which is in part made possible through a free press. Without a free press, citizens have a very difficult time holding politicians accountable for, among other things, failing to act expeditiously when the first signs of calamity arise. As we saw throughout the twentieth century, whether the massive Soviet and Chinese famines of mid-century or the Ethiopian famine of the mid-1980s, food can all too easily be grossly misallocated when governments are not held accountable (Carolan 2013).

## Feeding a Growing Nonhuman Animal Population

When discussing the relationship between population growth and food security, it is also important to be clear about what exactly we mean by the term *population*. When talking about the "mouths" that our food systems feed, we need to be clear that we are not talking just about those of the human variety. We feed a lot more than just humans with the food we produce. If we fed only humans, the task at hand would be considerably easier. According to the Food and Agriculture Organization of the United Nations, world agriculture produces enough food to provide every woman, man, and child with some twenty-seven hundred calories a day. But we don't feed just humans. We also feed livestock, in the form of animal feed, and increasingly cars, in the form of biofuels.

If current trends continue, we are going to have to produce twice as much animal protein by 2050 just to keep up with demand. This means that by 2050, livestock will be consuming enough food to feed 4 billion people (the world's population in the early 1970s). In other words, if the world continues to eat meat at the rates that we are expecting—and since most of the animals that provide that meat are going to have to eat an enormous amount of grain—the world's effective population in 2050 will be 13.5 billion (9.5 billion, the projected human population, plus 4 billion, as that is how many people could be fed with the grain that is expected to be diverted to livestock) (Tudge 2010). Why these trends matter from a food-security perspective is because collectively, cattle, pigs, and poultry in high-income countries already consume around 70 percent of available grains within those nations. Globally, livestock consume at a minimum one-third of the world's cereals, with 40 percent of such feed going to ruminants, chiefly cattle (Eisler at al. 2014). In case you're wondering: if the whole world were to consume meat at the same per capita rate as the average American, total grain output could sustain a global population of roughly only 2.6 billion people (Carolan 2013).

## Feeding a Growing Automobile Population

World ethanol production has increased from roughly 5.5 billion gallons (17 billion liters) in 2000 to 23.5 billion gallons (89 billion liters) in 2013. The production of biodiesel, which is still only a fraction of the world's biofuels, has also grown in the last decade, from less than 2 million metric tons in 2000 to approximately 30 million metric tons in 2014 (Ruitenberg 2014). To meet all the targets set throughout the world, biofuel production is going to have to increase considerably. Mandates for blending biofuels into vehicle fuels have been legislated in at least forty-one states and provinces and twenty-four countries; the laws require blending 10 to 15 percent ethanol with gasoline or 2 to 5 percent biodiesel with diesel fuel. For example, Brazil, Indonesia, and the European Union expect to meet 10 percent of their energy demands by 2020 with biofuels. China hopes to meet 5 percent of their energy demands by 2020 with biofuels. While approaching 4 billion liters—3 in ethanol and 1 in biodiesel—as of early 2015, that is still less than 1 percent of China's liquid fuel production. And its thirst for those liquids is growing with every year. Meanwhile, the United States has its own biofuel aspirations, namely, to produce 36 billion gallons by 2022 (with at least 16 billion gallons from cellulosic biofuels and a cap of 15 billion gallons for corn-starch ethanol).

Of course, we can't separate automobile populations from human ones. After all, someone has to drive all those biofuel automobiles. And while car ownership is down in certain high-income countries (I'll get to why later in the book), it is increasing exponentially in other countries. There were, for instance, 18 passenger cars per thousand Chinese in 2006 and 60 cars per thousand in 2015. In Jordan, during that same period, those figures increased from 87 to 144 cars; in Syria, from 18 to 42; in Bulgaria, from 230 to 362; and in Poland, from 351 to 470 (World Bank 2015a).

## Solutions

It would be wrong to attribute all the world's ecological problems to population growth. Yet as far as long-term sustainability is concerned, it is hard to deny the virtues of a less populated planet, as long as those growth rates are brought down in an ethical, just, and equitable manner. With that, I offer the following piece of encouraging news: there is evidence that population growth rates will come down for countries as their levels of prosperity grow—which is known as the **demographic transition model**.

The demographic transition model illustrates the move from a state of high birthrates and death rates to low birthrates and death rates, the time between representing a period of rapid population growth (see Figure 6.1). A brief summary of the model is in order. Preindustrial (stage 1) countries have high birthrates and death rates and consequentially fairly stable populations. In the earliest stage of industrialization (stage 2), death rates fall with improvements in food supply, sanitation, and health, while birthrates remain high because of lagging **pronatal social norms** (which refers to individual attitudes and societal expectations that promote high fertility rates). In late industrialization (stage 3), death rates continue to fall, while birthrates also begin to drop. Once a certain level of affluence is achieved (stage 4), however, birthrates begin flattening out to match death rates, causing the country's population to stabilize. Children in highly urbanized affluent countries are also more likely to be viewed as a "cost" to families much earlier than they are in rural, low-income nations, where they can help tend livestock and work the fields at a relatively young age. More recently, adding to the original four stages, there is growing discussion about a fifth stage to represent countries that have below-replacement fertility rates (below 2.1 children per woman). As their resident population ages, some European and Asian countries, such as Germany and Japan, actually have higher death rates than birthrates (see Case Study 6.1). More

**FIGURE 6.1** Demographic Transition Model

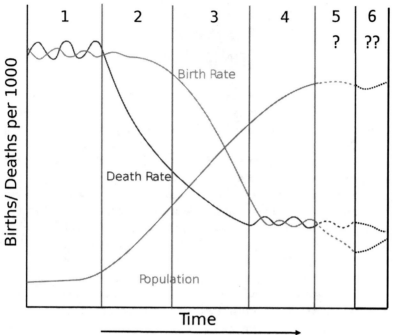

The dashed lines signify recently hypothesized stages.

recent still is the addition of a possible sixth stage. First suggested in a 1999 issue of the journal *Nature* (Myrskyla, Kphler, and Billari 2009), this stage shows that high levels of economic and social development promote (in some countries at least) a rebound in fertility, notable exceptions being Germany and Japan. There is still considerable debate around the existence of this newly suggested stage.

The demographic transition model does not attempt to forecast what will happen. It's simply a statistical representation of what has occurred for countries that have already undergone the transition—countries like the United States, Japan, and those in Western Europe. It is therefore entirely fair to ask, "What makes us so sure those countries in stages 2 and 3 will move to stage 4 (or beyond) anytime in the foreseeable future?" If history is any guide, this demographic transition is anything but guaranteed; after all, many nations on the UN list of least-developed countries (LDCs) have essentially been stuck at their present level of development for decades. (The LDCs constitute about 12 percent of the world population but account for less than 2 percent of the world's gross domestic product and about 1 percent of global trade in goods.)

Another variable that is different today from a century ago is population mobility. This is not to suggest that people didn't move around the world in earlier decades. (I wouldn't be here if that were true, as all my ancestors emigrated from somewhere in Europe in the late 1800s.) There are, however, far more modes to travel great distances today than generations ago. Moreover, there are powerful "push" variables at work, essentially forcing people to relocate: climate change, religious persecution, war, and so on. An irony in a post-9/11 age is that as police and various other security forces

CASE STUDY 6.1

# Japan: A Rapidly Shrinking Country

Japan shrunk by a record 244,000 people in 2013 as a result of fewer babies being born and more people dying. The country's population began falling in 2004 and is now aging faster than any other on Earth. Roughly a quarter of the entire population is sixty-five or older (in the United States that figure is about 15 percent). In response, the government is seriously contemplating a solution that thirty years ago would have been ridiculed by all: mass migration. The figure being discussed is 200,000 new foreigners a year to help stabilize the population. (A United Nations estimate places that figure at closer 650,000 new immigrants every year.) This is a remarkable suggestion when you consider that Japan remains, at least relative to many Western countries, a fairly homogeneous nation. But that wouldn't entirely keep the country from shrinking. The government would also need to raise the fertility rate from its current 1.39 (one of the world's lowest) to 2.07. But to elicit such a change—after all, you can't (or at least shouldn't) force people to procreate—would require radical changes, such as family-friendly labor laws like flex time, longer maternal and paternal leave, and subsidized child care. The population crisis has so alarmed the government that it created a ministerial post in 2005 charged specifically with raising fertility rates. The angst is understandable when you consider that the government has record-breaking budgets every year to pay for the health care and pensions of all its late-in-life residents and fewer and fewer working residents to pay for these benefits. A 2012 government report projected that without policy changes, the number of Japanese could fall in 2110 to 42.9 million—a third of its current population. From a sustainability perspective that might sound appealing. But from a political perspective it is an unacceptable outcome for many Japanese, especially considering its proximity to China, as it also means a drastically diminished economic, political, and military role in not only the world but Asian matters too (D. M. 2014).

battle to keep immigrants at bay in countries across North America and Europe, another (non-terrorist-related) crisis is unfolding in those countries, one demographic in nature. With their low birth rates these countries desperately need more young people to pay taxes, work in their health care sectors, populate their rural areas, and look after their elderly before it's too late. Take Portugal. Unless steps are taken to radically increase birth rates (something very hard to do) or to entice a flood of immigrants over its borders (something very unlikely after the terrorist attacks in Paris in November 2015), its population could drop from roughly 10.4 million to 6.3 million by 2060 (Kassam et al. 2015).

## Socioeconomic Development

Although economic development helps reduce fertility rates, it is not the panacea it was once thought to be. A popular development slogan from the 1970s, which has since been debunked, was "economic development is the best contraceptive." The problem with putting all our eggs in the "economic development" basket is that it misses the fact

**IMAGE 6.2**

Poster from 1986 promoting China's one-child policy. The child in the image appears to be male. Coincidence? Source: "Carry out family planning, implement the basic national policy," Zhou Yuwei, 1986. Image courtesy of the Lansberger Collection, International Institute of Social History (flickr.com/iisg), licensed copyright © 1986 under CC BY 2.0.

that population growth, at least in some countries, is so great that it actually *hinders* the very thing so many are hoping will forestall it: economic growth. That fact alone should be taken as evidence that we cannot rely on pro-growth strategies alone in many of the world's fastest-growing countries to bring down fertility rates. Moreover, while gross domestic product (GDP) per capita is negatively correlated with a country's fertility rate (as the former goes up, the latter goes down), the correlation is not perfect. Quite a few countries, in fact, manage to maintain low fertility rates with GDP per capita levels well below that of, for example, the highly affluent United States, with its 2.01 fertility rate. Some of those countries include Costa Rica (1.91), Vietnam (1.85), Uruguay (1.84), Romania (1.32), and Lithuania (1.29).

While declines in fertility have been facilitated by **family planning** programs—most infamously in China with its one-child policy but also in places like Indonesia and Malaysia—these reductions were equally facilitated by social and economic transformations (see Image 6.2). Family planning refers to educational, social, and medical services that empower individuals to make choices around reproduction. In Brazil sharp declines in fertility rates (it was 1.79 in 2014) have been attributed mainly to larger socioeconomic transformations—including urbanization—that have encouraged people to limit family size. The old paradigm—out of which came the slogan "economic development is the best contraceptive"—was not necessarily wrong, just shortsighted.

CASE STUDY 6.2

# Socioeconomic Development in Kerala, India

Kerala, an Indian state located on the southwest coast of the country, has made remarkable socioeconomic strides over the past couple of decades. Kerala's fertility rate is actually lower than China's, even with the latter's coercive one-child policy. The reason, undoubtedly, is tied to Kerala's impressive strides in areas relating to basic education, health care, and gender equality (see Table 6.3). And it has done this with a mediocre—by global standards—GDP per capita. If it were a country, its GDP per capita would be lower than that of, for instance, Peru, South Africa, and Turkey. When it comes to reducing fertility rates, Kerala's developmental trajectory disputes the need for oppressive population-control policies like forced sterilization or the criminalization of families with multiple children. It should also serve as a reminder of the shortsightedness of approaches that place too much emphasis on economic development to the detriment of social improvements and overall welfare enhancement.

TABLE 6.3 Well-Being Indicators for Indian State of Kerala Compared to the Nation of India

| WELL-BEING INDICATORS | KERALA | INDIA |
|---|---|---|
| Birth rate (per 1,000) | 14.6 | 21.4 |
| Death rate (per 1,000) | 6.6 | 7.4 |
| Infant mortality rate (per 1,000) | 12 | 53 |
| Child mortality rate, 0–4 years (per 1,000) | 3 | 17 |
| Total fertility rate (children per woman) | 1.7 | 2.5 |
| Life expectancy at birth (age at death) | | |
| a) male | 71.4 | 65 |
| b) female | 76.3 | 68 |
| c) total | 74 | 66.2 |
| Literacy rate | | |
| a) male | 94.2% | 82.14% |
| b) female | 87.86% | 65.46% |
| c) total | 90.92% | 74.04% |

Source: Adapted from Ministry of Home Affairs (2013).

## ETHICAL QUESTION 6.2
# Whose Behaviors Should Change?

Are we asking those in the developing world to change their behaviors so those of us in rich nations do not have to change ours? If consumption were not occurring in affluent countries at the rates that they are, we likely would not be having this conversation about population growth. Residents of less affluent countries have told me how the finger wagging of countries like the United States toward poor regions of the world with higher fertility rates seems insincere. Rich countries are far from ecological sainthood, given their rampant consumerism and fertility rates that are actually slightly up since the 1970s. Is it fair—or even empirically justified—to continue framing the population problem as a developing country problem?

What really matters is the *type* of development. A country can have an impressive GDP per capita, but if all that wealth is concentrated in the hands of a few, the average citizen is essentially no better off than if he or she lived in any of the LDCs. What is required is *socio*economic development. This means improvements in literacy and rates of school enrollment, gender equity and women's empowerment, heath care, and social institutions (e.g., education) while also meeting the needs of individuals in terms of sexual and reproductive health. Economic development alone—a point discussed in greater detail in Chapter 12—is insufficient on many levels (see Case Study 6.2).

When talking about "development," the following fact should never be far from our minds: although socioeconomic enhancements tend to motivate people to reduce their fertility rates, they also tend to increase consumption levels. One solution then for reducing consumption and emissions in the short term would be to further reduce fertility rates in affluent countries to compensate for the increased consumption and emissions in other countries as they climb out of poverty. Reducing fertility rates among those whose offspring would have a sizable ecological footprint would clearly go a long way toward reducing the stress that ecosystems are currently being placed under. Yet I also realize this is not a terribly realistic suggestion, as many affluent countries have actually started taking steps to *increase* their birthrates. These pro-fertility policies are grounded in national interests triggered by demographic concerns about shrinking military and consumer might. It is therefore highly unlikely that a groundswell of popular support could be generated for fertility-reduction campaigns in these countries (see Ethical Question 6.2).

We also need to realize that even immediate reductions in fertility in less affluent nations will not rapidly stabilize the world's population. This is where the term **demographic inertia** comes into the picture. This is a term from demography based on the fact that a time lag is to be expected before the full effects of changes to a fertility rate are seen—until the youngest cohort just prior to fertility rates' dropping essentially becomes too old to have children. Take China. Although it reached a below-replacement level of fertility in the early 1990s, the nation will grow by an additional 320 million bodies before its population finally stabilizes and starts to decrease after 2035. In fact, the majority of population growth today is due less to present fertility patterns than to

CASE STUDY 6.3

# Family Planning in Ethiopia

For every 100,000 live births in Ethiopia in 2013, 420 women died from pregnancy-related problems. This figure is known as the **maternal mortality ratio**: the number of women who die from pregnancy-related causes while pregnant or within forty-two days of pregnancy termination per 100,000 live births. (For comparison, in the United States that figure was 28; for Italy, it was 4; and Israel, 2.) As the country is predominantly rural, about 90 percent of women deliver at home. In light of these abysmal figures, the Ethiopian government has restructured its health care system. Particular attention has been given to the problems faced by rural women, as some 80 percent of the population resides outside of cities. The government now trains and has on its payroll approximately thirty thousand health-extension workers, whose job it is to cover the countryside providing health services.

Access to affordable contraception has also become a top priority. In 2005 less than 15 percent of women had access to contraception. Since then the Ethiopian government has implemented a plan for providing free birth control pills or a contraceptive injection with effects that last for three months. Yet these "short-term" birth control methods are still problematic, given that for some women, the nearest health center may be an eight-hour walk from where they reside. In light of such barriers to access, there is a move to make widely and freely available an implant that protects women from pregnancy for three years (Hegarty 2010). While the aforementioned figures are without question unacceptable, they are at least moving in the right direction. Just three years earlier—in 2010—the country's maternal mortality ratio was 500.

past fertility and mortality patterns. Nevertheless, some things can slow demographic inertia, such as if the age at marriage or age at conception of first child were delayed a year or two (see Case Study 6.3).

Figure 6.2 is based on demographic modeling by the United Nations (2015c), which attempts to estimate future world population out to 2100 by offering a range within which future populations will most likely fall (at a 95 percent confidence level). Making such calculations is tricky given the uncertainties involved, as assumptions have to be made about not only fertility rates but also, for instance, infant survivability rates and life expectancies, both of which are predicated on future technological, food production, and sanitation improvements. According to the figure, we can say with a 95 percent degree of confidence that global population will be between 8.8 and 9.3 billion in 2040 and between 9.6 and 13.1 billion in 2100. In other words, global population is all but certain to rise in the short- to medium-term future. Later in the century, global population is still likely to continue to increase, though there is approximately a 23 percent chance that it could stabilize or begin to fall before 2100.

## The Future Role of Cities

If you are like some of my students, you might be thinking, "Cities as a *solution* to our environmental ills? You can't be serious! Didn't we just get done discussing the problems associated with urban sprawl?" For reasons that are largely justified, cities have

**FIGURE 6.2** High and Low Future World Population Estimates (95 Percent Confidence Level)

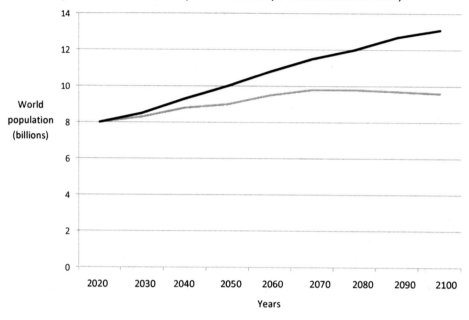

Source: Adapted from United Nations (2015c).

generally been viewed in a noticeably *un*ecological light. Otherwise well-intentioned approaches, like ecological footprint analyses, have further reinforced the idea that cities are fundamentally unsustainable, as they have a tendency to conflate sustainability with self-sufficiency. To be sure, urban areas concentrate people, cars, industries, and the like, which naturally means they concentrate emissions, pollution, noise, and consumption. And historically, this concentration made cities—and continues to make many cities around the world—hazardous places to live. Yet those very things that often caused people to look on urban areas as a "brown" blight on the landscape also give them distinct green ecological advantages.

Urban residents, for example, tend to possess substantially smaller carbon footprints than residents elsewhere in the same country. Per capita greenhouse gas emissions in New York City are less than 30 percent of those for the United States as a whole, those for London roughly half of the British average. The average resident of Rio de Janeiro has a greenhouse gas footprint that's less than a third the size for the average Brazilian, while the per capita greenhouse gas emission in Barcelona is 33.9 percent of that for Spain as a whole (see, e.g., Chester et al. 2014; Dodman 2009). There are many reasons for this phenomenon: The concentration of services and industries lessens the need to travel long distances. Dense cities generally have better public transportation services, in part because the concentration makes building an efficient transportation system more cost-effective. Residents of dense cites also generally live in smaller residential dwellings because of the scarcity and high cost of land.

That said, not all cities possess this ecological profile. Many newly formed megacities in Asia suffer from overcrowding, in which case *reducing* urban density might help meet a number of social, environmental, and developmental needs (Hasan 2014). For example, while the average urban density for cities in the United States, New Zealand, and

CASE STUDY 6.4

## Urban Density: A Tale of Two Cities (Within the Same City)

Urban planners in South Asia are continually advised by North American and European experts about the ecological benefits that come with increased urban population density. The reality faced by planners in South Asia, however, is radically different from what you find in, for instance, American cities. In megacities like Dhaka, Mumbai, and Karachi there are millions of low-income households packed together surpassing all building ordinances and zoning regulations. Karachi, Pakistan's most populous city, has 2,280 people living on each hectare of its land. Yet if you dig into the data you see a marked discrepancy between the rich and the poor. Parts of Karachi's inner city have more than 4,000 people living on each hectare of land, while the city's laws permit a maximum of 1,625 people per hectare. Elsewhere in the city, where the wealthy live, densities are as low as 200 people per hectare. Some in these areas live on plots as large as 0.2 to 0.3 hectares, land that in the city's center would otherwise be occupied by more than 800 people. Or take Mumbai (formerly Bombay), in India: it has 3,230 people per hectare. But in some of its so-called slum areas, density ratios are much higher. In Dharavi, for instance, population density is as high as 44,460 people per hectare in its Chamra Bazar neighborhood (Hasan 2014).

Australia is estimated to be roughly fifteen persons per hectare, the average density for certain Asian cities is in some cases in excess of one thousand persons per hectare (see Case Study 6.4). Then there is the problem with suburbs. According to a recent study by UC Berkeley researchers (Jones and Kammen 2014), while population-dense US cities contribute less greenhouse-gas emissions per person than other areas of the country, their extensive suburbs typically wipe out these carbon benefits. Thanks primarily to emissions from cars, trucks, and other forms of transportation, suburbs account for roughly 50 percent of all household emissions in the United States. (The researchers have made available interactive carbon footprint maps for more than thirty-one thousand US zip codes in all fifty states at coolclimate.berkeley.edu/maps.) So while the average carbon footprint of households living in the center of large, population-dense urban cities is about 50 percent below the US average, households in suburbs are up to twice the average. The research also points to the fact that increasing population density cannot be the sole solution for reducing emissions. A tenfold increase in population density in central cities corresponds to only 25 percent lower greenhouse gas emissions. Increasing population density in suburbs is even more problematic, as population-dense suburbs have significantly higher carbon footprints than less-dense suburbs largely as a result of residents' higher incomes and greater levels of consumption.

Evidence suggests that the number of households in a country has a more direct environmental impact than its population per se (Liu et al. 2003; Marcotullio et al. 2014). Yet the number of households in a country and its population do not grow together. Globally, household formation exceeded population growth from 2007 to 2012. Household numbers increased by 9 percent to 1.9 billion—growth driven largely by China,

India, and the United States, with 434 million, 233 million, and 120 million households, respectively, in 2012. Growth in household numbers would have increased faster during this period were it not for the Great Recession. But even so, despite the need for recession-hit families to combine households to save resources during this period, globally, the overall trend toward single- and two-person households and single-parent households continued to grow at a rapid pace. In developing markets, multigenerational households, which were once the norm, are becoming less common as living standards rise and young people sever ties with families to move to cities in search of work (Euromonitor International 2013). And as the number of households grows, so does the global demand for more stuff.

## The Case for a Population Explosion

Although empirically unsubstantiated, there is the argument out there that the best solution to the problems associated with population growth is . . . *more* population growth. Let me start by offering a more moderate position: that given by Ester Boserup.

Boserup (1965) famously turned Thomas Malthus on his head. Malthus's argument was essentially that agricultural methods (and more specifically the available food supply) determine population size. Boserup, instead, argued population determines agricultural methods and in turn food supply, suggesting that population pressures will sufficiently incentivize ways to feed those additional mouths. To put it simply: given the essential nature of food, people will always find ways to increase agricultural production by increasing their labor (or workforce), machinery, fertilizer applications, and other technologies.

Yet the Boserup effect, as it has come to be known, is also sensitive to certain realities that can dampen the otherwise optimistic scenario painted by its namesake. Having written extensively on the relationship between gender and development (giving us some of the earliest scholarship on the subject), she was well aware of how inequality can limit the impact of the Boserup effect. Making the necessary investments to one's operation to keep agricultural output ahead of population takes money and credit, two things, unfortunately, that are not always available to the millions of small farmers in less developed countries (Carolan 2011b). Boserup was also well aware that the sheer level of population growth that some countries were experiencing—especially in the 1960s, when she was formulating this argument—outstripped the capacity of their governments, economies, and agricultural sectors to keep ahead of growing needs. In sum: a Boserup effect might be discernible in some countries but certainly not all.

I would classify Boserup as a pragmatic optimist; her optimism, after all, was tempered by empirical reality. Another person rather famously takes technological optimism to the extreme. For Julian Simon (1981), people represent, as the title of the book detailing his position states, "the ultimate resource." Hence, the greater the population, the greater the collective brainpower and the faster we'll find answers to all the problems that currently trouble us. An increase of a hundred million, one billion, ten billion . . . : the more, the better. Each birth, Simon reasons, increases our chances of yielding another Einstein or Mozart (he fails to acknowledge that by this reasoning it increases our chances of more Hitlers and Bin Ladens too). Simon's position epitomizes what is known as **cornucopian**. Based on the Greek myth of a horn from a goat that suckled Zeus and became filled with fruit, a cornucopian is someone who believes unending progress, economic growth, and material abundance can be had with advancements in technology.

Yet there is an enormous gap in this reasoning. Had Einstein been born to a poor family in, say, Calcutta, the capital of India during the British Raj until 1911, I doubt we would be speaking of him today. My point is that we already have billions of these underused "resources" available to us today: minds and bodies that, if just given a chance, could do great things. If we only spent more time concentrating on educating, feeding, and generally improving the lives of the more than one billion people living in poverty around the world (Banerjee and Duflo 2011), we would all be better off.

Simon also assumes that our resources are infinitely substitutable, that when we get low on one resource, we'll find, through technology, brainpower, and hard work, something else to use in its stead. That's an awfully big assumption to make, given the stakes involved. If anything shows the folly of this assumption, it is climate change. Simon died in 1998, well before the definitive evidence came out about climate change. It's hard enough to even think about what a substitute for things like clean water and air might look like. But with global climate change, how can we substitute an entire planet?

## "Up Rather Than Out": If It Works for Cities, Can It Work for Farms?

I've already discussed some of the possible ecological benefits that urban density has over urban sprawl. Of course, to make something like this work will take an immense amount of coordination. Urban density is not going to solve anything without a sustainable supporting structure in place, like agriculture. The issue of food production takes center stage in Chapter 8, so I will limit my comments here. But the following question bears asking: How are we going to feed tomorrow's megacities in a way that's ecologically sound? One possibility is to turn agriculture, literally, on its head: **vertical farming**—the practice of farming "up," rather than "out."

Other than the footprint of the facility itself, vertical farms require no land. Contrary to what we think we know about plant physiology, plants do not require soil to survive. Hydroponics—from the Greek words *hydro* (water) and *ponos* (labor)—involves growing plants using mineral nutrient solutions in water, without soil. The practice has been around since the 1930s and is used in nurseries around the world for seed germination. More recent still is what is known as aeroponics, essentially an ultra-efficient version of hydroponics in which tiny nozzles spray a nutrient-rich mist onto the plant's roots (Roberto 2003). NASA and the European Space Agency are at the forefront of aeroponic and hydroponic agriculture, working to make these systems entirely self-contained for long-distance space exploration (see, for example, Finetto, Lobascio, and Rapisarda 2010).

Another misconception about plant physiology: plants also do not need all the energy in sunlight to grow to maximum yield. Light-emitting diodes (LEDs) have recently been engineered just for plants, giving them only the parts of the spectrum of light that they need. On the horizon are organo-light-emitting diodes (OLEDs), which promise to offer an even more narrow spectrum of light, thus further reducing the energy demands of vertical farms (Cox 2009; Despommier 2010). Of course, in those regions of the world where sunlight is plentiful, vertical farms could take advantage of this free and abundant resource. Similarly, buildings could be powered using wind turbines and photovoltaic panels.

Despommier, in his book *The Vertical Farm* (2010), tells the story of a strawberry farmer who replaced his thirty-acre farm after it was destroyed by a hurricane with a one-acre vertical farm utilizing hydro-stackers (a hydroponic vertical gardening system). That single acre now yields as many strawberries as the thirty acres did prior to the hurricane. The farmer also reports that the remaining twenty-nine acres, those not replanted with strawberries, have returned to a more biologically diverse—or "wild"—state.

It is not my suggestion that vertical farms could entirely support tomorrow's megacities. Yet we've got to ask how tomorrow's megacities are going to be fed, particularly in light of the growing interest in concepts like regional food security and resiliency and rising energy prices. The world's largest megacities in 2030 are projected to have populations approaching forty million—not far away from the same population as what lived on the *entire planet* in the year 1000 BCE (roughly fifty million people). To feed them all will require some outside-the-box—perhaps even some vertical—thinking.

---

## IMPORTANT CONCEPTS

- Amartya Sen on famines
- Boserup effect
- demographic transition model
- IPAT
- Julian Simon's ultimate resource
- maternal mortality ratio
- socioeconomic development
- STIRPAT
- Thomas Malthus on population growth

## DISCUSSION QUESTIONS

1. Is it fair to continue framing the population problem as a low-income country problem when the average US citizen's ecological footprint is thirty times greater than that of the average Indian and one hundred times greater than that of the average person in the world's poorest countries?
2. Having large families in low-income nations is perfectly rational for many living in those environments. What are some of the sociological forces underlying high fertility rates in developing countries?
3. Does a person have a fundamental human right to have as many children as he or she chooses?
4. What is the earth's carrying capacity (how many people can it hold)? What factors play into such a calculation?

## SUGGESTED ADDITIONAL READINGS

Arman, M., and K. Davidson. 2014. "A Typology to Position Population Within Sustainability Discourse." *Local Environment* 19(4): 433–448.

Hartmann, B., A. Hendrixson, and J. Sasser. 2016. "Population, Sustainable Development, and Gender Equality." In *Gender Equality and Sustainable Development*, edited by M. Leach, 56–81. New York: Earthscan/Routledge.

Toth, G., and C. Szigeti. 2016. "The Historical Ecological Footprint: From Over-Population to Over-Consumption." *Ecological Indicators* 60:283–291.

Welze, H. 2015. *Climate Wars: What People Will Be Killed For in the 21st Century*. New York: Wiley.

## RELEVANT INTERNET LINKS

- www.census.gov/popclock. US and world population clocks, maintained by the US Census Bureau.
- populationpyramid.net. Population pyramids of the world and for every nation, based on UN data.
- www.prb.org/Journalists/Webcasts/2009/distilleddemographics1.aspx. Link to the Population Reference Bureau's (PRB) *Distilled Demographics* video series. In the first video, *Deciphering Population Pyramids*, the PRB's senior demographer shows how population pyramids give us a snapshot of a country's demographic profile.
- rumkin.com/tools/population. Population statistics for every country.

## SUGGESTED VIDEOS

- *The Dirtiest Place on the Planet* (2012). Linfen, China: a day breathing its air is like smoking three packs of cigarettes. The scary part is that there are a lot of cities in China like this.
- *Don't Panic: The Truth About Population* (2013). BBC documentary about human overpopulation.
- *Earth Days* (2009). A documentary about the rise of the environmental movement in the United States and the first Earth Day in 1970. It also chronicles the late 1960s and 1970s, when talk of a "population bomb" was at its peak.
- *How Many People Can Live on Planet Earth?* (2011). documentaryvideos.org/bbc -documentary-about-earths-population. A BBC-produced six-part series on the Earth's population.
- *Mother: Caring for 7 Billion* (2011). An award-winning film about the controversies surrounding our world of seven billion, and one woman's journey to make sense of it.
- *The Nature of Cities* (2010). A story of the nature in our own backyards as well as that being built into cities of the future. We've got to rethink everything that we do in cities today to make them profoundly more resilient.

# Transportation: Beyond Air Pollution

It is understandable why discussions on transportation in my classes repeatedly veer to pollution, since roughly 27 percent of US greenhouse gas emissions are transportation related (EPA 2015b). Not surprisingly, then, the tone taken toward the subject has grown increasingly critical, as its global shape and character look increasingly like those found in the United States, where the car takes center stage. According to one national survey:

- 25 percent of all trips by automobile are made within a mile of the home;
- 40 percent of all trips by automobile are made within two miles of the home;
- 50 percent of the working population commutes five miles or less to work;
- more than 82 percent of trips five miles or less are made using the car (whereas about half of all car trips in the United Kingdom and Netherlands are less than five miles);
- 60 percent of the pollution created by automobile emissions happens in the first few minutes of operation—before pollution-control devices become fully effective—which means shorter car trips are more polluting on a per-mile basis than longer trips (LAB 2012).

Yet it is more than just its links to pollution that make transportation a fascinating subject for sociologists. We often think about transportation as a response to changes in how society is organized. In this scenario, we drive because our urban environments require us to. Yet the data tell precisely the opposite story. Urban and community patterns, in other words, have taken the shape they have in part because of available transportation systems. The car, for example, made certain patterns of urbanization possible—patterns that, not surprisingly, are found today to be difficult to service under alternative transportation forms. Thus, although many urban environments leave us with little choice but to drive, those very environments place this demand on us only because the car makes their existence possible. Although we often like to think of the car's rise as the outcome of consumer democracy—where you vote with your wallet—a careful analysis reveals the votes have been rigged in its favor. After all, wouldn't you

**FIGURE 7.1** Idealized and Conceptual Diagrams of Traditional, Commuter, and Automobile Cities

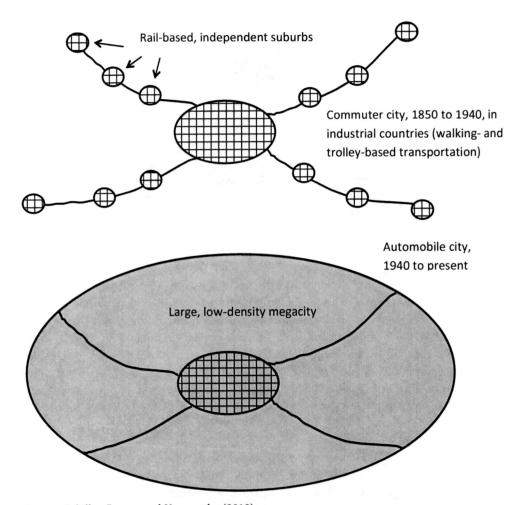

Traditional city, e.g., prior to 1850, in Europe (horse-carriage- and walking-based transportation)

Rail-based, independent suburbs

Commuter city, 1850 to 1940, in industrial countries (walking- and trolley-based transportation)

Automobile city, 1940 to present

Large, low-density megacity

Source: Schiller, Bruun, and Kenworthy (2010).

expect the automobile to win when the question is, "What mode of transportation would you choose in a society that's specifically designed for the automobile?"

Figure 7.1 offers idealized conceptual diagrams of three urban types that are meant to illustrate how the shape and character of cities have changed with available transportation systems. Cities prior to 1850 were highly dense and mixed-use—residential and commercial were mixed together. They reflected the fact that people got around either with their feet or by horse. As rail was established, suburbs began to form along the rail

| AGE | MALE | FEMALE |
|---|---|---|
| 16–19 | 8,206 | 6,873 |
| 20–34 | 17,976 | 12,004 |
| 35–54 | 18,858 | 11,464 |
| 55–64 | 15,859 | 7,780 |
| 65+ | 10,304 | 4,785 |

**TABLE** 7.1 Average Annual Miles per Driver by Age Group and Gender

Source: Adapted from the US Department of Transportation (2015).

line. The city itself, however, while slowly beginning to grow outward, remained moderately to highly dense, as transportation within the city was limited. The car changed everything, ushering in an almost anything-goes model of urban sprawl. Those previously independent suburbs have since spread out, as has the inner city, making for all intents and purposes one large megacity. And without well-thought-out alternative transportation systems (like those discussed in the Solutions section of this chapter), many urban dwellers today have little choice but to take the car, even perhaps when going just a couple of blocks. I have a friend, for example, who must cross an eight-lane intersection when she wishes to walk to a local grocery store that's less than a mile away. How can we expect people to abandon their cars if doing so comes at great risk to life and limb?

## Fast Facts

- More than one billion vehicles populate the world today; we surpassed the one billion mark back in 2010. Some estimates indicate that we will break the two billion mark by 2035 (Voelcker 2014).
- Americans drove more than three trillion miles in 2014 (Doan and Murtaugh 2015). Table 7.1 breaks those miles driven down according to age group and gender.
- Approximately 1.24 million people die each year as a result of road traffic crashes. Road traffic injuries are the leading cause of death among young people ages fifteen to twenty-nine. Ninety-one percent of the world's traffic fatalities occur in low-income and middle-income countries, even though these countries have approximately half of the world's vehicles. Without action, road traffic crashes are predicted to result in the deaths of around 1.9 million people annually by 2020. Only twenty-eight countries, representing 416 million people—7 percent of the world's population—have adequate laws that address all five major risk factors attributed to automobile injuries and deaths: speed, drunk driving, and the lack of helmets (in the case of motorcycles), seat belts, and child restraints (WHO 2015).
- The American Automobile Association estimates the average annual cost to own and operate a car in the United States based on driving fifteen thousand miles per year: for a small sedan, $7,606, or 38.0 cents per mile; for a medium sedan, $9,790, or 49.0 cents per mile; for a minivan, $10,571, or 52.9 cents per mile; for a large sedan, $11,906, or 59.5 cents per mile; and for an SUV, $11,931, or 59.7 cents per mile (AAA 2015). But wait! Americans own an average of 2.28 vehicles per household, and more than 35 percent of households own three or more cars. So the average household—assuming there are two cars in its garage—spends roughly $20,000 a year on its vehicles, more if it owns SUVs, a

little less if the cars are small or medium sedans. And 35 percent spend at least $30,000 annually so they can have the "freedom" that a car allows.

- The Texas Transportation Institute at Texas A&M University released a report that measures the difference in travel time between congested and free-flowing conditions (Lomax et al. 2011). Commuters in Chicago and Washington, DC, see on average seventy hours of their lives eaten up by rush-hour traffic every year, followed by those in Los Angeles (sixty-three hours) and Houston (fifty-eight hours). That's not how much time they spend in a car but the *additional time* spent in a car because of congestion. Nearly three billion gallons of fuel were wasted in 2012 in the United States from traffic congestion (Texas A&M Transportation Institute 2013; see ECOnnection 7.1).

- Greenhouse gas emissions from transport represent approximately 14 percent of the global emissions and 23 percent of $CO_2$ emissions from global fossil fuel combustion. Transport is the sector with the fastest growing consumption of fossil fuels and is also the fastest growing source of $CO_2$ emissions globally. Road transport is responsible for more than 70 percent of $CO_2$ emissions from the transport sector. At current rates, $CO_2$ emissions from transport are on track to double by 2050 (OECD 2015a).

## Implications

This section focuses on the automobile because of its ubiquity and oversize ecological footprint. The following represents a brief overview of some of the socioecological impacts associated primarily with this mode of transportation. Our understanding of *transportation* broadens considerably when solutions are discussed.

### *Pollution and Public Health*

It's ironic that the very technology to win praise a century ago from street cleaners, public health officials, and politicians because it delivered urban dwellers from a major environmental ill at the time—namely, horse manure that blanketed urban streets—would someday be responsible for far more severe public health threats. Although it is difficult to attach a specific dollar amount to transportation-related health outcomes (some have tried; see Table 7.2), the car's deleterious effects to public health are obvious.

If we accept the argument that cars helped create urban conditions that eventually made them a necessity, which by definition discourages human-powered forms of transportation, then it is entirely fair to associate the cost of things like obesity to the automobile, as obesity has been closely linked to automobile-centered urban design (Chiu et al. 2015). The data on this relationship are quite compelling. For example, one study found that each additional kilometer walked per day lowers an individual's likelihood of becoming obese by 4.8 percent, whereas each additional hour spent in a car per day is associated with a 6 percent increase in being obese (Frank, Andresen, and Schmid 2004). A study examining urban sprawl in US metropolitan areas between 1970 and 2000 estimates that had those areas held to their 1970 levels of urban density, their rates of obesity would be 13 percent lower than what they presently are (Zhaoa and Kaestnerb 2010). Another study, looking at three different states, California, Massachusetts, and Pennsylvania, found population density, intersection density (the more the streets connect with each other, the more walkable the city is), and building density

ECOnnection 7.1

# Effective Speed

Effective speed is, in some respects, calculated conventionally: speed equals distance divided by time. The novelty of the concept lies in its aim to consider *all* time costs when comparing transportation forms. For car drivers, a significant—though typically invisible—time cost is the time spent at work to earn the money to pay for all the expenses associated with this costly mode of transportation. Key variables needed to calculate effective speeds for any mode of transportation are average trip speed; the direct and indirect costs of the mode of transportation; the average income of the population, which determines how much time is devoted to earning the money to pay the costs; and any other time devoted to the mode of transportation besides travel, such as time spent filling a vehicle with fuel.

Research has looked at effective speeds of cyclists in different cities, calculating how slow cyclists could travel and still be effectively faster than a car. If only out-of-pocket costs are considered, then the fastest that a cyclist would need to travel, among the cities studied, would be 13.3 miles per hour in Canberra, Australia; the slowest, 1.9 miles per hour, in Nairobi, Kenya. (The car's near-standstill effective speed in Kenya is largely a product of the country's abysmally low average income that makes car ownership a very time-consuming activity.) If external costs are also considered, cyclists in Canberra would need to average only 11.3 miles per hour to be faster than a car driver. In New York, Los Angeles, Tokyo, and Hamburg cyclists would not need to travel faster than 8 miles per hour to outrun an automobile (Tranter 2012).

The idea of effective speed points to a speed paradox of sorts when it comes to the motor vehicle: the faster one tries to go with this mode of transportation, the slower it becomes. Increasing trip speeds has little impact on effective speed because the main time cost is not driving but the time spent earning money to pay for the costs of driving. Indeed, driving faster could further reduce effective speed by causing those costs to go up, such as by reducing gas mileage, increasing the rate of tire wear, and perhaps even resulting in a costly accident. There is also little that governments can do to reduce the car's effective speed. The costs of building wider roads, for instance, more than offset any reductions in travel time. After converting these immense costs to a time measure—costs that are paid for by taxpayers—we find the effective speed of automobiles to be further slowed.

The cumulative cost of traffic congestion in France, the United Kingdom, Germany, and the United States between 2013 and 2030 is projected at $469 billion, $480 billion, $691 billion, and $2.8 trillion, respectively (INRIX 2014). Wasted fuel and time seem to account for the majority of these costs, meaning these estimates are arguably conservative. What about costs to, for example, public health (pollution, the sedentary nature of sitting in a car for hours a day, and so forth) and the environment (greenhouse gas emissions, habitat fragmentation, and so forth)?

**TABLE 7.2** Annual Cost of Transportation-Related Health Outcomes in the United States

| HEALTH OUTCOME | COST (IN $ BILLIONS) | ESTIMATE INCLUDES |
|---|---|---|
| Obesity and overweight | 142 | Health care costs<br>Lost wages due to illness and disability<br>Future earnings lost because of premature death |
| Air pollution from traffic | 50–80 | Health care costs<br>Future earnings lost because of premature death |
| Traffic crashes | 180 | Health care costs<br>Lost wages because of injuries<br>Property damage<br>Travel delay<br>Legal/administrative costs<br>Pain and suffering<br>Loss of quality of life |

Source: Adapted from the American Public Health Association (2010).

to each be positively associated with walking and inversely correlated with overweight/obesity (Troped et al. 2014).

Globally, approximately 24 million people die each year on roads, while another 20 to 50 million suffer nonfatal injuries. The overall global road traffic fatality rate is 18 per 100,000 residents. Middle-income countries have the highest annual road traffic fatality rates, at 20.1 per 100,000, followed by low-income countries with a rate of 18.3, while the rate in high-income countries is 8.7 per 100,000. The risk of dying as a result of a road traffic injury is highest in the African Region (24.1 per 100, 000 population), followed by the Eastern Mediterranean Region (21.3 per 100,000), Western Pacific Region (18.5 per 100,000), Southeast Asian Region (18.5), Regions of the Americas (16.1 per 100,000), and European Region (10.3 per 100,000) (WHO 2013). As Table 7.3 illustrates, road traffic injuries are a major cause of death for people ages five to forty-four, and among those ages fifteen to twenty-nine, it represents the number one cause of death. While road traffic injuries are currently the tenth leading cause of death worldwide, the World Health Organization estimates that by 2030, that ranking will be fifth (WHO 2015).

Who are these people dying and getting injured on the world's roads? That again depends on whether the accidents are occurring in high-income or lower-income countries. In the United States and Canada, for instance, 65 percent of reported road deaths involve vehicle occupants. Conversely, in low-income and middle-income countries of the Western Pacific Region, 70 percent of reported road fatalities are among what are known as **vulnerable road users**. According to the WHO, this population includes pedestrians, cyclists, and users of motorized two-wheel vehicles (WHO 2015).

There is also growing evidence pointing to a positive association between exposure to road traffic and aircraft noise and hypertension (high blood pressure) and ischemic

TABLE 7.3 Worldwide Leading Causes of Death by Age

Source: Adapted from WHO (2013).

| RANK | 0–4 YEARS | 5–14 YEARS | 15–29 YEARS | 30–44 YEARS | 45–69 YEARS | 70 AND ABOVE | AGGREGATE AVERAGE |
|---|---|---|---|---|---|---|---|
| 1 | Perinatal causes | Lower respiratory infections | Road traffic injuries | HIV/AIDS | Ischemic heart disease | Ischemic heart disease | Ischemic heart disease |
| 2 | Lower respiratory infections | Road traffic injuries | HIV/AIDS | Tuberculosis | Cerebrovascular disease | Cerebrovascular disease | Cerebrovascular disease |
| 3 | Diarrhea | Malaria | Tuberculosis | Road traffic injuries | HIV/AIDS | Chronic pulmonary disease | Lower respiratory infections |
| 4 | Malaria | Drowning | Violence | Ischemic heart disease | Tuberculosis | Lower respiratory infections | Perinatal causes |
| 5 | Malaria | Meningitis | Self-inflicted injuries | Self-inflicted injuries | Chronic pulmonary disease | Trachea, bronchus, lung cancers | Chronic pulmonary disease |
| 6 | Congenital anomalies | Diarrhea | Lower respiratory infections | Violence | Trachea, bronchus, lung cancers | Diabetes | Diarrhea |
| 7 | HIV/AIDS | HIV/AIDS | Drowning | Lower respiratory infections | Cirrhosis of the liver | Heart disease | HIV/AIDS |
| 8 | Whooping cough | Tuberculosis | Fire | Cerebrovascular disease | Road traffic injuries | Stomach cancer | Tuberculosis |
| 9 | Meningitis | Protein-energy malnutrition | War and conflict | Cirrhosis of the liver | Lower respiratory infections | Colon and rectum cancers | Trachea, bronchus, lung cancers |
| 10 | Tetanus | Fires | Maternal hemorrhage | Poisonings | Diabetes | Nephritis | Road traffic injuries |
| 11 | Protein-energy malnutrition | Measles | Ischemic heart disease | Maternal hemorrhage | Self-inflicted injuries | Alzheimer and other dementias | Diabetes |
| 12 | Syphilis | Leukemia | Poisonings | Fires | Stomach cancer | Tuberculosis | Malaria |
| 13 | Drowning | Congenital anomalies | Abortion | Nephritis | Liver cancer | Liver cancer | Heart disease |
| 14 | Road traffic injuries | Trypanosomiasis | Leukemia | Drowning | Breast cancer | Esophagus cancer | Self-inflicted injuries |
| 15 | Fires | Falls | Cerebrovascular disease | Breast cancer | Heart disease | Cirrhosis of the liver | Stomach cancer |
| → | → | → | → | → | → | → | → |
| 20 | Epilepsy | Poisonings | Malaria | Trachea, bronchus, lung cancers | Mouth and oropharynx cancers | Road traffic injuries | Violence |

heart disease (reduced blood supply to the heart). Road traffic noise is known to increase the risk of ischemic heart disease, including myocardial infarction (heart attacks). And both road traffic noise and aircraft noise have been shown to increase the risk of high blood pressure (WHO 2011). One WHO report calculated **disability-adjusted life-years** (DALYs) resulting from noise pollution for all of Europe, recognizing that the majority of the noise comes from road traffic and airplanes. The WHO defines DALYs as "the sum of years of potential life lost due to premature mortality and the years of productive life lost due to disability" (WHO, 2012a). It was estimated that DALYs lost in Europe from environmental noise equated to 61,000 years for ischemic heart disease, 45,000 years for cognitive impairment of children, 903,000 years for sleep disturbance, 22,000 years for tinnitus, and 654,000 years for annoyance. In short, more than 1 million healthy life years are lost annually in Europe as a result of auto and airplane noise (WHO 2011; see Case Study 7.1).

## Habitat and Biodiversity

**Habitat fragmentation**—the emergence of discontinuities (or fragmentation) in an organism's preferred environment (or habitat)—is also a concern when looking at impacts associated primarily with the automobile. One of the more well-known examples involves the pygmy possum. The habitat of this threatened marsupial had become highly fragmented thanks to roads and other land-use changes. By constructing tunnels—or what are known in Australia as *talus tunnels* (tunnels of love), as they increase the rate of breeding in an area—to run under roadways, natural movements were restored. In the Netherlands, road mortality in the 1980s accounted for between 20 and 25 percent of total annual badger deaths. The installation of tunnels beneath many of the country's roadways caused national badger populations to increase some 65 percent while simultaneously reducing the animal's road mortality rates to 10 percent. A similar story, but involving panthers, comes from Florida. Roughly half of all panther deaths occurred on roads prior to the 1990s, as the result of collisions. The state has since built a number of underpasses that give animals (panthers included) safe passage beneath the busy four-lane divided interstate highway I-75.

Habitat fragmentation has received a lot of attention over the past two decades. In the early 1990s, a five-year-old alpha female wolf, wearing a radio collar containing a satellite transmitter, began a remarkable two-year journey. She was tracked making an unexpectedly large circle, beginning far north, near Banff National Park in Alberta, Canada, then south into Montana, turning west through Idaho into Washington State, before heading north into British Columbia, finally ending up again near Banff. In other words, this wolf's habitat was literally thousands of times the size of Yellowstone National Park (Fraser 2009).

The term **islandization** is often used to talk about the disastrous effects that transportation systems like multilane roads can have on wildlife. It refers to the "chunking up" of habitats without **wildlife corridors** like underpasses and tunnels between roadways to connect them. Without this connectivity, the isolated plants and wildlife within an "island" risk going extinct. Island populations (an ecological term used to refer to largely isolated populations of species) are also susceptible to disease, overhunting, and major events like floods or fires. With climate change, the issue of connectivity becomes even more significant. As the ecological conditions of habitats change, wildlife will need

## CASE STUDY 7.1
# China's Pollution Problem

China has a pollution problem. Life expectancy in the north has decreased by 5.5 years as a result of the region's disastrous air quality (Xu 2014; see Image 7.1). According to a recent study by researchers at the think tank RAND, health impacts and lost labor productivity costs from pollution are estimated at 6.5 percent of China's gross domestic product (Crane 2015). Applying that figure to China's 2012 GDP of $8.2 trillion implies that reducing air pollution in China to levels considered acceptable by WHO would yield annual benefits of more than $500 billion annually.

In January 2013, Beijing experienced a bout of smog that lasted so long, and of such severity, that citizens began calling it "airpocalypse." Its concentration of hazardous particles was forty times the level deemed safe by the World Health Organization. But December proved the worst month of 2013 for air quality in China, with more than 80 percent of the seventy-four cities with air-monitoring devices failing to meet national standards for at least half the month. Less than 1 percent of China's five hundred largest cities meet the WHO's air quality standards (Xu 2014).

**IMAGE 7.1**

Source: testing/Shutterstock.com.

to migrate in order to remain in optimal environments. Without wildlife corridors to facilitate this movement, the future of many species is at risk.

*How* to connect these islands depends on the situation and the species in question. Some animals, like badgers and possum, are more comfortable using tunnels under roadways. Other animals, such as deer, cross at higher rates when given the opportunity to go over the road, in which case a wildlife overpass may be the preferred option. To enhance their effectiveness, vegetation has proven to be an important component to overpasses, as it reduces noise and creates a visual wall between the animals and traffic (O'Brian 2006).

### Community

There is also compelling evidence pointing to the car's adverse impact on communities. Robert Putnam's famous book *Bowling Alone* (2001) is often cited for single-handedly bringing this link into popular light, through the conceptual lens of "social capital" (see ECOnnection 7.2). Putnam's extensive research led him to conclude that "the car and the commute . . . are demonstrably bad for community life." He continues by noting that "each additional ten minutes in daily commuting time cuts involvement in community affairs by 10 percent—fewer public meetings attended, fewer committees chaired, fewer petitions signed, fewer church services attended, less volunteering, and so on." In sum, though not quite as powerful an influence on civic involvement as education, commuting time "is more important than almost any other demographic factor" (213).

Research generally supports Putnam's conclusions. For example, studies have shown that high dependence on the automobile is positively associated with weakened neighborhood social ties, whether that community is located in the United States (Israel and Frenkel 2015), South Korea (Seo and Chiu 2014), or Colombia (Torres et al. 2013). Other studies suggest that the emotional and intellectual development of children is enhanced in more walkable, mixed-use communities, most likely from a combination of increased opportunities for physical activity, independence, and community cohesion (Litman 2010; Møllegaard and Jæger 2015). Automobile reliance is found to have a strong negative impact on whether an individual visits friends or participates in out-of-home sports and cultural activities, and a positive effect on in-home and potentially asocial amusements such as watching television.

One of the more extensive studies looking at the links between the automobile and community health comes out of Harvard University's Department of Government (see Williamson 2002). Based on some thirty thousand interviews from forty different US geographical settings, this research paints an unflattering picture of the car as a vehicle (pun intended) of civic disengagement. Findings to come out of this research include the following:

- The lower the percentage of solo commuters in one's zip code, the more likely an individual is to belong to a political organization, attend a partisan political meeting, attend a demonstration, sign a petition, or vote.
- Living in a high-density area is a positive predictor of membership in a political organization, attendance at demonstrations, and signing a petition (even after controlling for central-city residence status and an individual's interest in politics).
- Residence in a very high density area is associated with membership in a local reform group.

## ECOnnection 7.2
# Social Capital

Social capital formalizes what we all intuitively know: that who we know matters as much as what we know. A growing literature over the past two decades shows that social capital—social networks and the norms of trust and reciprocity that come with frequent social interaction—is central to community well-being. Norms of trust and reciprocity enhance social interaction much the same way cash enhances trade, namely, by allowing action to be taken without having to separately negotiate the terms of every exchange. But how? "Dense" social networks make it easier for individuals and the community as a whole to discover who should not be trusted. They also create a significant incentive to live up to people's trust expectations, as failing to do so will result in an immediate loss in reputation across the community as a whole. More generally, social capital makes working with others easier, enhances information flow across the community, encourages cooperative behavior, and reduces the likelihood of unproductive "defensive" behaviors, like locking doors, avoiding going out for walks at night, and so forth. Yet social capital can also have a dark side, as it can result in community exclusion, group think, and a general distrust of outsiders if levels of **"bridging" social capital** (networks between groups or weak ties) are not present at concentrations comparable to **"bonding" social capital** forms (networks within groups or strong ties).

- Residents of neighborhoods built before 1950 (which is a strong predictor of being a walkable neighborhood) are significantly more likely to belong to a political organization, attend a partisan political event, attend a march or demonstration, vote in a national election, or attend a public meeting (even after controlling for central-city residence status).
- A long commute is a very strong predictor of a reduced number of friends and attendance at public meetings and a modestly strong predictor of reduced social trust and reduced membership in groups.
- Neighborhood-level (zip code) commuting time is a very strong predictor of reduced social trust and even a stronger predictor than individual commuting time (if your neighbors are stuck in traffic every day, the fact that your commute is short isn't going to do much to increase your social interaction with them).
- Commuting time is inversely associated with an individual's subjective levels of personal happiness as well as their levels of happiness toward their community.

Pointing to these findings, the author of the study explains that "there is good reason, from a civic point of view, to encourage forms of community design that reduce commuting time and to encourage the preservation and increased livability of both our older neighborhoods and our central cities." He goes on to point out that "the biggest payoff, at least from a political participation point of view, appears to be in getting Americans out of their cars" (Williamson 2002, 243).

ECOnnection 7.3

# Community Severance

**Community severance** is an important social impact associated with transportation. It can be defined as a real or perceived barrier to people's movement through an area that is created by the transportation infrastructure (like roads or rails) or traffic. Whereas physical severance is the most obvious type, there are also psychological and social forms. An example of the former might be having a fear of crossing busy roads, whereas an example of the latter could be when one's friendships do not go beyond the barrier in question, thus creating less of a social need to traverse any particular physical structure. Groups most adversely affected by severance include those without cars, those with restricted mobility—most notably disabled and elderly people—and schoolchildren (Markovich and Lucas 2011).

Precisely *how* we do this, however, he does not say. What we do know is that many current urban planning practices tend to reduce community interaction by favoring vehicular mobility over alternative modes such as walking, cycling, and public transit. Traffic engineers generally evaluate transportation systems based on things like vehicle traffic speeds and road capacity, even if this practice degrades the pedestrian environment and reduces community cohesion (Litman 2010; see ECOnnection 7.3).

## Solutions

There is no going back. Having organized society over the past century around the automobile, we cannot pretend that those structures—whether made of concrete and reinforcing steel bars or of long-held habits and routines—are of no sociological consequence (Cohen 2012). There are, however, a number of ways forward that reduce the impacts addressed in the previous section, as I'll now explain.

### Dense, Livable, Intermodal Cities

I've already talked a little about the potential ecological benefits associated with the high-density city, particularly in affluent nations, where the financial resources are available to maximize those benefits. We already know that population density is negatively associated with transportation-related energy consumption at the per capita level (see Figure 7.2). Dense cities come with reduced travel distances for the average inhabitant to things like work and social visits. Urban density also reduces the transaction costs for building a viable public transportation system, as the network can service more people per unit of track than is possible in sprawled-out cities.

One of the ecological benefits associated with mass public transit lies in its vehicle per-passenger fuel efficiencies, especially when maxed to capacity. Table 7.4 documents the energy efficiency of various passenger modes, in terms of miles per gallon (mpg) and per-passenger mpg (for average and maximum capacity). The Toyota Prius's respectable 238 mpg per passenger (when fully loaded up with five occupants) pales in

**FIGURE 7.2** Urban Density and Transport-Related Energy Consumption, Select Cities

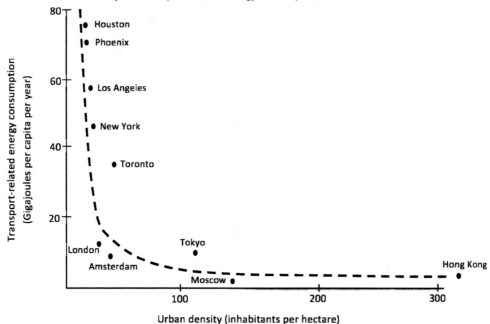

The dotted line represents the regression line when all cities are plotted. (A regression line comes as close to all points as possible through a scatterplot of two variables.) With over 7 million inhabitants packed onto an island of roughly 426 square miles, residents of Hong Kong never have to travel very far to get anywhere—a reality that also makes public transportation highly attractive from an urban planning standpoint. The city of Houston, conversely, spreads 2.1 million inhabitants out over 656 square miles. This lower density means not only that Houstonians have to travel on average farther than residents of Hong Kong but that they do so in most instances using an inefficient mode of transportation: the automobile. This level of urban sprawl makes the car nearly the only option for many of the inhabitants of this iconic Texas city. Source: Twidell and Weir (2015).

comparison to intercity rail, high-speed rail, the London Underground, or light rail, which, when fully loaded with passengers, register 560 mpg per passenger, 767 mpg per passenger, 1,125 mpg per passenger, and 2,460 mpg per passenger, respectively.

There are also social benefits that come when one abandons the solo commute for something less isolating. Recent research indicates that public transportation, for instance, can increase social capital for individuals and neighborhoods as a whole (Mattisson, Håkansson, and Jakobsson 2015). And among those unable to drive, such as elderly and disabled people, having alternatives to the car is crucial to improving their integration within a community as well as to providing access to such life-sustaining phenomena as food and health care (Levasseur et al. 2015).

Yet just having alternatives to the automobile is rarely enough to make people choose to leave their cars in the garage. Multimodality gives individuals choices, but without intermodality—the ability to make efficient connections between modes—those alternative choices are rarely as attractive as the car. For example, if you still have to walk ten blocks after getting off the nearest light-rail stop to get to your friend's house, you'll likely choose to take the automobile more often than not (see Case Study 7.2). Just what those

**TABLE 7.4** Energy Efficiency of Various Passenger Modes (Land, Air, and Water)

| MODE (EXAMPLE) | MPG | AVERAGE NO. PASSENGERS (MPG PER PERSON) | MAXIMUM NO. PASSENGERS (MPG PER PERSON) |
|---|---|---|---|
| Scooter (50cc engine) | 75 | 1 (75) | 2 (150) |
| Medium motorcycle (Suzuki GS500) | 60 | 1 (60) | 2 (120) |
| Hybrid auto (Toyota Prius) | 47.6 | 1.5 (72) | 5 (238) |
| Very small auto, highway (Smart Car) | 41 | 1.5 (62) | 2 (82) |
| Very small auto, city (Smart Car) | 33 | 1.2 (40) | 2 (66) |
| SUV, highway (Ford Explorer, V8) | 21.6 | 2 (43) | 7 (151) |
| SUV, city (Ford Explorer, V8) | 14.1 | 1.2 (17) | 7 (98) |
| 40-foot diesel transit bus | 3.1 | 25 (78) | 90 (279) |
| 40-foot trolley bus | 9.77 | 30 (293) | 77 (752) |
| Light rail | 13.6 | 65 (887) | 180 (2,460) |
| London Underground | 7.4 | 19 (141) | 152 (1,125) |
| Intercity rail (Swedish Railways Regina) | 3.35 | 34 (114) | 167 (560) |
| High-speed rail (LGV Atlantique; runs from Paris to western France) | 1.58 | 291 (460) | 485 (767) |
| Private small airplane (Cessna 172) | 12.6 | 1 (12.6) | 4 (50.4) |
| Regional turboprop (DHC 8-300) | 1.19 | 35 (41.7) | 137 (58.9) |
| Short/medium-range airliner (Boeing 737; average flight, 607 miles) | 0.43 | 96 (41.3) | 137 (58.9) |
| Medium/long-range airliner (Airbus 320, average flight, 1,358 miles) | 0.447 | 109 (48.7) | 156 (69.7) |
| Very-long-distance airliner (Boeing 777-200ER, average flight, 6,818 miles) | 0.252 | 211 (53.1) | 301 (75.8) |
| Passenger-only ferry (Vancouver SeaBus) | 0.25 | 140 (35) | 400 (100) |
| Passenger and car ferry (BC Ferries Spirit Class) | 0.0246 | 1,000 (24.6) | 2,100 (51.7) |
| Transoceanic luxury ship (Queen Mary 2, 25 knots) | 0.00753 | 2,000 (15) | 3,090 (23.2) |

Vehicles are typically designed to carry more than just one passenger. Indeed, some—like transoceanic luxury ships—can accommodate thousands. It is therefore inaccurate (and unfair) to compare modes of transportation by their miles per gallon without also factoring in the number of people each can accommodate at any given time or on average. Table 7.4 shows the miles per gallon if only one person rode each mode of transportation in addition to the miles per gallon per person according to both average capacity and maximum capacity per mode. Source: Adapted from Schiller, Bruun, and Kenworthy (2010).

## CASE STUDY 7.2
## The Rise of
## Bike-Share Programs

Elliot Fishman (2015), director of the Institute for Sensible Transport, examined data and studies on large bike-sharing systems worldwide and found convenience to be a universal driving factor in whether people use them. For instance, Washington, DC's Capital Bikeshare surveyed more than 11,100 members and found that 69 percent of respondents said getting where they need to go fast was "very important" in encouraging them to use the program (Stein 2015). The distance between a rider's home and the nearest docking station also proved to be a central motivational variable in determining whether a person would pay for a membership. For example, residents of Montreal, Canada, living within three-tenths of a mile of a docking station were about three times more likely than the average resident to have used that city's bikeshare program. In general, those using bikeshare programs are more likely affluent and better educated than the general population (Fishman 2015). However, this appears to be changing, as these sharing systems are extending into lower-income neighborhoods. (Sadly, stereotypes still dog some programs as organizers worry about bike theft in lower-income neighborhoods.) In London, the majority of early bike-share users were affluent. Yet the percentage of low-income residents using the system doubled from 6 to 12 percent between 2010 and 2013 (Stein 2015).

connections will involve will vary from community to community, depending on what those communities value (see Ethical Question 7.1). The overarching goal, however, is the same: to make alternative modes as attractive as—or ideally, more attractive than—the car.

We are presently doing a lot to incentivize driving. For example, many federal, state, and local government tax policies prioritize motor vehicle use. Fuel is exempt from general taxes in many jurisdictions. Land devoted to public roads and parking facilities is exempt from rent and taxes. And oil companies are given significant tax exemptions and subsidies (Litman 2011). Large taxpayer-funded roads represent a significant portion of land that cannot be taxed, while being of benefit primarily to private motorists. Similarly, private lands are typically taxed at a lower rate when paved over to make a parking lot (ibid.).

Let's talk more about free parking. If it were not in such abundance (especially in the United States), do you think we would have as much of an incentive to drive? And who pays for that "free" parking? We all do, as taxpayers, regardless of whether we use it. Many current zoning codes also favor automobile-oriented land-use patterns, which include things like density restrictions, single-use zoning, and, yes, minimum parking requirements. An ambitious calculation was attempted by Mark Delucchi while employed by the Institute of Transportation Studies at University of California, Davis. (Unfortunately, given its ambitious nature, studies like this are not done routinely.) Using an extensive data set from the early 1990s, Delucchi calculated that the total cost of the automobile for Americans at the time was as high as $3.3 trillion—the equivalent of roughly $5.1 trillion in today's dollars, or one-third of the country's entire GDP (Delucchi 2004). There were only 188 million registered vehicles on the road in the

## ETHICAL QUESTION 7.1
# Value Judgments Embedded in Transportation Policy

Value judgments are unavoidable in transportation policy. You can't value all transportation forms equally. If we decide we want dense, walkable cities, for example, we will need to stop giving priority to the automobile, recognizing that it creates an urban scale much too expansive (e.g., sprawl) for our feet. Below are some of the thorny questions embedded in any comprehensive transportation policy:

- Whose trips do we prioritize—individual citizens or freight interests?
- Which trips do we prioritize—work commutes, long-distance freight, local goods distribution, or leisure?

- Which transportation services—whether entire modes (e.g., light rail) or components of specific modes (e.g., free parking)—should be supported with public funding, and which should be left to individuals and private-sector interests?
- Should mobility be thought of as a right, recognizing that those unable to drive—most notably elderly and disabled people—can be dangerously isolated in communities where the car is the only transportation option?

*Source: Adapted from Schiller, Bruun, and Kenworthy (2010).*

United States in 1991. Today, the figure exceeds 250 million, which means that the $5.1 trillion figure is undoubtedly too low to accurately reflect present costs. If you think that number is absurdly high, there is also a more recent analysis by Todd Litman, founder and executive director of the Victoria Transport Policy Institute. He has independently come up with a figure almost equally as mind-blowing: $3.4 trillion (Litman 2011). If we were to fold those costs into, for example, the price of gasoline, that works out to a tax of between $25.40 per gallon (for the $3.4 trillion figure) and $38.10 per gallon (for the $5.1 trillion figure). To drive or not to drive? What at first blush looks like an individual choice starts looking more and more like a decision that was largely made for us long ago (see ECOnnection 7.4).

We also know, following the "fundamental law of highway congestion" first articulated back in the early 1960s (Downs 1962), that something different *must* be done. More roads, in the long term, only make traffic congestion worse (see Case Study 7.3). The fundamental law of highway congestion is this: any increase in road capacity will be met with a proportional (or greater) increase in traffic volume. In one study, a 10 percent increase in the interstate network within the typical urban country was met with a 10.3 percent increase in vehicle distance traveled on those roads (Duranton and Turner 2009). In this case, congestion actually *grew* with an increase in road capacity, as the additional lanes led to more people driving more frequently.

## ECOnnection 7.4
## High-Occupancy Vehicle Lanes

High-occupancy vehicle (HOV) lanes are for automobiles, at least in the United States, carrying two or more passengers. (It says something about our transportation values when a car with two people is considered "high occupancy.") The goal of HOV lanes is to encourage ride sharing and thus reduce the total automobile volume on roads. There are a couple of inherent problems with ride sharing, however, that disincentivize its use. For one, the total commute time must be significant to overcome the time lost while waiting for the carpool to arrive and during travel when picking up and dropping off fellow carpoolers. In many cases, these additional costs more than offset the savings from traveling in the HOV lane. There are also what might be called inconveniences—different schedules, the need to run errands during the trip, and so on—that further make ride sharing unattractive to commuters.

So, do they work? Between 50 to 80 percent of HOV lanes are used by members of the same households. Other significant users are friends on an outing or a date. In other words, HOV lanes are overwhelmingly used by people who would have carpooled anyway.

*Source: Schiller, Bruun, and Kenworthy (2010).*

### From Street Hierarchy to Interconnectivity

Urban planners have also been incentivizing the car—and disincentivizing alternatives—in how they have gone about laying out streets. Prior to the automobile, street systems maximized connectivity, as evidenced by the relatively high number of street intersections per square mile in older communities. Think about pre-automobile city centers—as found in any European city—and note the narrowness of streets and the diverse ways they interconnect. Connectivity in these spaces exists because these street systems provide multiple paths to reach surrounding major streets.

In the twentieth century, a concept known as **street hierarchy** came to dominate urban planning. Street hierarchy seeks to eliminate connections, funneling traffic up the hierarchy. Cul-de-sac streets are at the lowest level of the hierarchy, followed by primary or secondary collector streets. At this point, traffic is fed onto arterial streets (also occasionally called a boulevard), eventually ending up on intercity highways, which rest atop the hierarchy. This system has become a ubiquitous feature of the landscape in most modern cities (see Case Study 7.4).

A more interconnected street model is often criticized for the fact that it actually seeks to slow traffic down (a tough selling point in countries like the United States). Yet we must keep in mind that by resisting congestion, these systems also *save* us a tremendous amount of time that is otherwise lost in bumper-to-bumper traffic. Moreover, we are learning that as speeds slow down in a transportation system, the *scale* of the urban landscape is reduced too, thus making speed less important. In other words,

# "Daylighting" the Cheonggyecheon Stream in South Korea

**IMAGE 7.2**

Source: Ken Smith Landscape Architect, © 2010.

For more than fifty years, concrete (in the form of a major freeway) entombed a three-mile stretch of the Cheonggyecheon Stream that ran through the heart of Seoul, South Korea. It was finally liberated in 2001, when the former chief executive officer of Hyundai Engineering and Construction, Lee Myung-bak, was elected mayor of Seoul. One campaign promise was to remove the freeway and restore the Cheonggyecheon Stream. This practice of uncovering previously concealed natural amenities like streams is known as **daylighting** within the urban planning community. Four years and $384 million later, the Cheonggyecheon was flowing freely through the heart of downtown Seoul (see Image 7.2).

The project has enhanced the quality of life, public health, and social interaction of those living downtown, though it has increased the property values near the stream, pushing some poorer families out. Roughly ninety thousand pedestrians visit the stream banks on an average day. Biodiversity along the Cheonggyecheon has increased, with the number of fish, bird, and insect species expanding from 4 to 25, 6 to 36, and 15 to 192, respectively. Air pollution along the corridor has decreased, now that the tens of thousands of cars are gone. Small-particle air pollution along the corridor dropped to forty-eight micrograms per cubic meter from seventy-four. Moreover, summer temperatures are now routinely five degrees cooler near the stream than in nearby areas because of a reduced-heat island effect. Finally, even with the loss of a major freeway, traffic speeds in the areas have actually *increased* thanks to transportation changes such as expanded bus services, restrictions on cars, and higher parking fees.

*Source: Lonsdorf (2011); Revkin (2009).*

communities that have slowed down no longer need the range and speed provided by the automobile—a truly remarkable discovery.

An excellent example of this comes to us from Home Depot. Store location and size formula for this company depend heavily on two factors: the income range of families living in the service area and the number of trips per day through the nearest intersection to the proposed site. *Service area* is an estimation of a reasonable distance people would drive to get to the store. Thus, the more taxpayers spend on hierarchical car-oriented infrastructure, the larger the service area—and thus the store and parking lot—will be. Yet, given the aforementioned fundamental law of congestion, forces are exerting themselves on today's auto-oriented system in such a way that is making congestion inevitable. In response, Home Depot has recently altered the formula used to calculate store location and size, leading the company to build smaller stores more frequently spaced across the urban landscape (Condon 2010). The company realizes that traffic congestion is essentially *shrinking* the distance consumers are willing to cover in their cars. This is an interesting development. A major concern has been finding alternatives to the automobile that mimic its speed and range. Yet the Home Depot example contradicts this assumption, indicating that cities may actually scale down as we slow down. Quite a counterintuitive finding: that one strategy for decreasing the time we spend going from point A to point B is *to slow down.*

Another benefit of slowing down: pedestrian safety. Research examining Longmont, Colorado, cataloged and entered into a database some twenty thousand police accident reports (Swift, Painter, and Goldstein 2006). Each accident location was mapped and described by several physical characteristics. To compare injury accidents per mile per year against other factors, several correlations were explored. The most significant relationship to injury accidents was street width. The authors of the study explain that "as street widths widen, accidents per mile per year increase exponentially, and the safest residential street widths are the narrowest" (1).

## CASE STUDY 7.4
# Breaking Through the Street Hierarchy

In Salem, Oregon, new development plans must include street assignments according to the street hierarchy before they can be approved. In 2003 the designers of a new sustainable community submitted plans without assigning streets according to this hierarchy. They argued that their plans sought to distribute traffic throughout the network rather than concentrate it in a few arterial streets. City planners, noting their hands were tied, demanded the inclusion of a street hierarchy as stipulated by the city code. The designers reluctantly identified the new community's street with shops and community facilities like libraries and schools as the arterial. This, in turn, caught the eye of school district officials, noting that their policy expressly prohibited elementary schools from being located on arterial streets. So the school was relocated to a less accessible cul-de-sac, with ample space for parents to drop off and pick up their children . . . in their cars.

*Source: Condon (2010).*

Then there is the issue of public safety, such as in regards to fire equipment access. Even here, the data do not support the need for either wide roads or the street-hierarchy model. No difference was detected in fire-related fatalities or response times between communities with narrow streets and those with wider ones (Swift, Painter, and Goldstein 2006). Any costs that come with narrower streets are more than offset by increased housing density, which reduces overall travel distance, and the benefit of having multiple routes to choose from (Condon 2010).

## Disincentivizing the Car

How might we go about making the car a less attractive form of transportation? I have already discussed the importance of making the alternatives more attractive; after all, we can't expect people to choose to leave their cars at home if the alternatives take appreciably more time, cost more money, and might even be dangerous. What has not been discussed, however, are ways to make the car more costly to drive, a move that would effectively make alternatives immediately more attractive. Before criticizing such a scheme, remember all the money we already spend to incentivize the car (which makes any such criticism seem more than a bit insincere and hollow). In light of all these incentivizing structures, I am not a bit surprised that the vast majority of individuals in affluent nations "choose" to drive (though this might be changing; see ECOnnection 7.5). Who wouldn't choose an activity when they're paying for only a fraction of its real costs?

One widely discussed policy mechanism is a gas tax (or a further increase in existing gas taxes). The economic models are pretty clear as to their efficacy: such a tax would encourage consumers to drive less, switch from two vehicles to one, or buy more fuel-efficient vehicles (Eric, Sarica, and Tyner 2015). In addition to encouraging motorists to drive less, such taxes would signal to manufacturers to incorporate fuel-saving technologies in new vehicles, in response to consumers' choosing smaller, fuel-efficient vehicles. If implemented, however, we would need to make sure this tax wasn't regressive and therefore not unduly burdensome to those already socially and economically vulnerable (see Movement Matters 7.1). The other population such a tax would immediately affect is commuters. Of course, the goal of such a tax would be to discourage precisely this type of behavior. We must remember, however, that while people commute for a variety of reasons, one is because they cannot afford to live near where they work. I see this variable at play in Fort Collins, Colorado, where my employer (Colorado State University) is located. I know that a number of the janitorial and office staff, who make appreciably less than tenure-track professors, reside in surrounding communities because of the lower housing prices. The fact that I do not commute—I can actually walk to work—is a luxury not everyone can afford.

An even more promising policy is **pay-as-you-drive auto insurance**, where one's insurance rate (but not coverage) is contingent on, among other things, the amount of miles driven. Nobel Prize–winning economist William Vickrey once quipped, "The manner in which [auto insurance] premiums are computed and paid fails miserably to bring home to the automobile user the costs he [or she] imposes in a manner that will appropriately influence his [or her] decisions" (1968, 464). Little has changed in the fifty or so years since Vickrey made these comments. The current lump-sum pricing of auto insurance remains inefficient and inequitable (Nichols and Kockelman 2014). It is

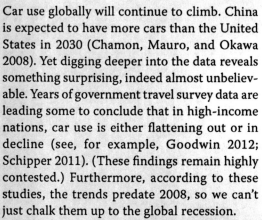

**ECOnnection 7.5**

## Have Cars Reached Their Peak?

Car use globally will continue to climb. China is expected to have more cars than the United States in 2030 (Chamon, Mauro, and Okawa 2008). Yet digging deeper into the data reveals something surprising, indeed almost unbelievable. Years of government travel survey data are leading some to conclude that in high-income nations, car use is either flattening out or in decline (see, for example, Goodwin 2012; Schipper 2011). (These findings remain highly contested.) Furthermore, according to these studies, the trends predate 2008, so we can't just chalk them up to the global recession.

Why this might be happening is unclear. Rising fuel costs and road congestion would be the most obvious reasons. Yet other variables are no doubt also at work, some of which possibly include stagnating wages among the middle class, growing income inequality, and increasing vehicle operating costs (Cohen 2012). We also know that younger people today are less enamored with driving and car ownership than generations past. One survey found that 46 percent of American drivers ages eighteen to twenty-four said they would choose having access to the Internet over owning a car (Chozick 2012). In response, car manufacturers are taking major steps to reach out to new drivers. General Motors, for example, recently announced collaborating with MTV Scratch, a unit of Viacom that specializes in connecting with younger consumers, in an attempt to better understand the millennials market as a market (Chozick 2012).

widely recognized that, just as an all-you-can-eat restaurant encourages more eating, all-you-can-drive insurance pricing encourages more driving, which also means more accidents, congestion, and greenhouse gas emissions. It is also terribly inequitable, in that miles driven is positively correlated with income. Low-mileage (and low-income) drivers therefore subsidize insurance costs for high-mileage (high-income) drivers (Bordoff and Noel 2008).

The results of a recent study indicate that the average American will drive 2.7 percent less (237 fewer miles per year) if auto insurance is pay-as-you-drive (Nichols and Kockelman 2014). Another study, by the Brookings Institution, goes even further, calculating that if all motorists in the United States paid for auto insurance on a per-mile basis rather than in a lump sum, driving would decline by 8 percent nationwide, saving society the equivalent of about $50 billion to $60 billion a year through reduced driving-related harms (Bordoff and Noel 2008). The study further estimates that this driving reduction would translate into a reduction in $CO_2$ emissions by 2 percent and oil consumption by about 4 percent. The authors note that it would take a $1-per-gallon increase in the gas tax to achieve the same reduction in driving. Yet unlike the gas tax, which would increase the cost of driving for everyone, roughly two-thirds of all US households would end up actually paying *less* for auto insurance; the average savings is estimated at $270 per car.

Other strategies to make driving less attractive could include doing away with ubiquitous free parking, which, as already mentioned, is a significant taxpayer-funded subsidy

### MOVEMENT MATTERS 7.1
## The Rise of Public Transit Movements

The public transit movement is an example of grassroots activism rooted in the belief that affordable and convenient public transit ought to be available to all. By organizing this previously invisible constituency—namely, lower-income riders that depend on public transit for their livelihoods—transit riders unions have emerged as an unlikely source of political power. The transit movement rose to prominence in Los Angeles in the 1990s, when bus riders, most of them black and Latino, came together to protest what was believed to be an unjust transit system that penalized riders from low-income neighborhoods. A recent success story occurred on March 1, 2015, in King County, Washington, when it introduced a reduced fare for low-income people—a major win for Seattle's Transit Riders Union. On the same day, San Francisco's transit riders convinced the city's Municipal Transportation Association (MUNI) to make transit free for disabled people and low-income seniors. One primary aim of these movements is to reduce the "affordability gap"—what workers are paid and what it costs to get to work. In the mid-1970s, a minimum-wage employee had to work for roughly ten minutes to pay for bus fare to and from work. Today, that same employee must work more than a half hour (Roe 2015). As the US economy emerges out of the Great Recession, it is adding jobs. However, job proximity—the number of jobs near where a person lives—is declining, a trend especially pronounced for low-income households and people of color, making affordable public transportation all the more important for these groups (Kneebone and Holmes 2015).

### CASE STUDY 7.5
## The London Congestion Charge

By the late 1990s, more than one million people were entering into central London on any given workday. A study from 1998 concluded that the average driver spent almost 30 percent of his or her time stationary during peak traffic periods. In response, a "congestion charge" was proposed in 2000. In 2003 the City of London, which is a small area within Greater London, referring to its historic core, began charging motorists for driving or parking within Central London between seven a.m. and six-thirty p.m. on weekdays. The standard charge is £10 (approximately $16) per day.

The number of private vehicles coming into the zone has declined 27 percent, which translated into some sixty-five to seventy thousand fewer daily trips made into the area. Bus, taxi, and bicycle use into Central London, conversely, is up 21, 22, and 28 percent, respectively. The average traffic speed within the zone has increased by almost 17 percent. Traffic has also decreased just outside the zone. Finally, surveys of retailers within the zone indicate that the congestion charge has had no significant effect on total sales (Skousen 2011).

to motorists. We might also think about eliminating minimum parking requirements that are embedded in city planning codes around the world. Another option would be to increase the cost of registering vehicles, which could be placed on a sliding scale so as to not unfairly affect low-income households. There is also the strategy of charging people to access a given area with their car (see Case Study 7.5). Or we could base urban design more around interconnectivity, to reference a point made earlier, and thus allow narrower streets, more intersections, and slower average car speeds to take precedence over the street-hierarchy logic.

There are numerous empirical reasons for criticizing the automobile, from, for example, its negative impacts on the environment, public health, and community cohesion to its links to climate change and air and noise pollution more generally. The good news is that there is nothing about the automobile that makes it an inherently superior form of transportation. Millions around the world choose this form of mobility over others not because of some quality inherent to the automobile but because societies have done such a good job of organizing around the car. Organize societies around the alternatives, and consumer choice will happily follow, with no sacrifice required.

## IMPORTANT CONCEPTS

- costs of transportation to public and environmental health and community cohesion
- effective speed
- free parking
- fundamental law of highway congestion
- habitat fragmentation
- peak car
- street hierarchy versus interconnectivity

## DISCUSSION QUESTIONS

- How has the automobile altered how we plan and organize communities?
- In what ways does society incentivize trips with the automobile and disincentivize alternative forms of transportation?
- Some argue people want to continue this love affair with the automobile, as evidenced by the fact of just how many people *choose* to drive: "Shame on environmentalists for wanting to go against what people clearly want!" How would you rebut this argument?
- What barriers keep you from choosing to leave your car at home and opting for alternative modes of transportation?
- Why might younger people today be less enamored with driving and car ownership than generations past?

## SUGGESTED ADDITIONAL READINGS

Fishman, E. 2015. "Bikeshare: A Review of Recent Literature." *Transport Reviews* 36(1): 92–113.
Moss, S. 2015. "End of the Car Age: How Cities Are Outgrowing the Automobile." *Guardian*, Apr. 28.

Renn, A. 2015. "Have We Really Reached 'Peak Car'?" *Guardian*, Apr. 30.

Tranter, P. 2014. "Active Travel: A Cure for the Hurry Virus." *Journal of Occupational Science* 21(1): 65–76.

## RELEVANT INTERNET LINKS

- www.foodmiles.com. Calculate the distance the food from your last meal has traveled (aka its food miles).
- www.nativeenergy.com/travel.html. Calculate your transportation footprint.
- www.nature.org/greenliving/carboncalculator/index.htm. Calculate your carbon footprint.
- www.youtube.com/watch?v=NJkZYCiXRA. Short video of the recently "daylighted" Cheonggyecheon River in Seoul, South Korea, mentioned in Case Study 7.3.

## SUGGESTED VIDEOS

- *Into the Future: Transport* (2015). Outlines the tremendous challenges associated with producing low-emission electric-powered vehicles, and convincing the public of their appeal as a viable, preferable option to traditional gas guzzlers.
- *Revenge of the Electric Car* (2011). Four different automobile visionaries race to capture the electric car market.
- *Taken for a Ride* (1996). www.youtube.com/watch?v=rAc4w11Yzys. An older but superb documentary about how American public mass transit was undermined and systematically destroyed during the first half of the twentieth century by General Motors and other corporations.
- *Urbanized* (2011). Architects, city planners, politicians, and others try to bring a fresh approach to dealing with the advantages and disadvantages of urban living.
- *Who Killed the Electric Car?* (2006). Details General Motors' efforts to hinder their own electric-car research and development.

# 8

# Food: From Farm to Fork

Few things are as obviously social *and* ecological as food and agriculture. Clearly, we need food to survive. As for *what* constitutes "food"—that too is a social act. Take bugs: an example of how one culture's pest is another's delicacy. As for agriculture, its links to the environment are obvious even to the uninitiated. *How* we produce food is also sociologically relevant, affecting society at all scales, from rural communities to entire nations. And how we've gone about feeding ourselves has changed drastically over the years.

One of the more consequential innovations in agriculture over the past two hundred years has been the substitution of capital for labor—known widely as the **mechanical revolution.** Examples vary widely: from the cotton gin in 1793, which separated the cotton lint from the seed (and initially increased the demand for slave labor in Southern slave states), to the threshing machine in 1816, which separated grain from the stalk; to Cyrus McCormick's reaper in 1834, which cut grain; and to the John Deere steel plow in 1837, which turned the soil cleanly, thereby minimizing the drag that bogged down earlier plows. Later in the nineteenth century came the tractor, which, unlike the horses it replaced, did not require food, water, or sleep and allowed the land used previously to raise hay and oats to feed one's horses to instead be put toward the production of commodities for sale.

This capital intensification (and energy intensification) had clear impacts on the **structure of agriculture,** at least in countries where this transition is well under way. (The term *structure of agriculture* is shorthand to describe how farms, rural populations, and agribusiness corporations are arranged to produce and distribute food and fiber.) Take, for example, the United States, where the requisite human hours to farm an acre of corn dropped rapidly throughout the first half of the twentieth century in no small part as a result of mechanization: from thirty-eight hours per acre in 1900 to thirty-three in 1920–1924, twenty-eight in 1930–1934, and twenty-five in 1940–1944. By 1955–1959, the figure had dropped to only ten hours of labor per acre. A study conducted by Iowa State College (now Iowa State University) in the 1930s concluded that a hired husker left between three and five bushels of corn per acre when the harvest occurred by hand. By comparison, a mechanical corn picker left two to three bushels. In addition, hired huskers charged on average $2.00 per acre, whereas custom mechanical pickers charged roughly $1.25 to $1.50 per acre. It is not surprising, then, that by 1938, between 33 and 50 percent of the laborers previously hired to handpick corn were replaced by mechanical pickers (Colbert 2000). The mechanical revolution was favored early on in the rapidly expanding agricultural sector in the United States, especially in the Midwest and Great Plains, where land was plentiful but labor scarce (Pfeffer 1983).

Mechanization, in turn, also encourages specialization and scale increases at the farm level. Though not the only force driving the specialization trends illustrated in Table 8.1, the mechanization of agriculture undoubtedly contributed to the state's shrinking commodity basket. Iowa, depicted in the table, is representative of the commodity erosion occurring throughout much of the world where grains and livestock are raised for export and agroindustrial purposes (e.g., feed for livestock, biofuels, high fructose corn syrup, Chicken McNuggets, and so on). Why is mechanization at least partially responsible for this? It makes economic sense to spread the cost of these expensive capital investments over as much land as possible, which, from a labor standpoint, is relatively easy to do, as mechanization allows one or two individuals to work large tracts of land in a short amount of time.

This represents the barest of introductions into the incredibly nuanced and increasingly complex subject of food production; for more detail, see, for example, Carolan 2011b, 2016. Food systems are not static; they're continually changing, as are their impacts. Although the impacts about to be discussed are significant, it is heartening to know it doesn't have to be this way. These systems did not just appear. As products of our (society's) own creation, we hold the collective capacity to recreate them.

## Fast Facts

- Industrial livestock farms—also known as CAFOs (Concentrated Animal Feeding Operations)—can produce more waste than many US cities. For example, a feeding operation with 800,000 pigs can produce over 1.6 million tons of waste a year, an amount that is one and a half times more than the annual sanitary waste produced by the city of Philadelphia. It is estimated that livestock in the United States produce annually between three and twenty times more manure than the country's human population: 1.2 to 1.37 billion tons of waste. And while sewage treatment plants are required for human waste, no such treatment facility requirements exist for livestock waste (Hribar 2010).
- The global food system, from fertilizer manufacture to food storage and packaging, is responsible for up to one-third of all human-caused greenhouse gas emissions (Gilbert 2012). Recent analysis by the Food and Agriculture Organization of greenhouse gas data shows that global emissions from agriculture, forestry, and fisheries have nearly doubled over the past fifty years and are poised to increase an additional 30 percent by 2050 if steps are not immediately taken to reduce them (FAO 2014). Digging further down into the data, we see that global emissions from energy use in the agricultural sector have increased a whopping 75 percent since 1990.
- Between 1995 and 2012, the US government paid out $293 billion in farm payments. Of this, 75 percent—or $178.5 billion—went to 10 percent of all farms (see Figure 8.1). The top recipient? From 1995 to 2012, Riceland Foods Inc. (Stuttgart, Arkansas) received over $554 million. That's more than what was paid to all the farmers in Alaska,

TABLE 8.1 Number of Commodities Produced for Sale in at Least 1 Percent of All Iowa Farms for Various Years from 1920 to 2012

| 1920 | (%) | 1935 | (%) | 1945 | (%) | 1954 | (%) | 1964 | (%) | 1978 | (%) | 1987 | (%) | 1997 | (%) | 2002 | (%) | 2012 | (%) |
|---|---|---|---|---|---|---|---|---|---|---|---|---|---|---|---|---|---|---|---|
| Horses | (95) | Cattle | (94) | Cattle | (92) | Corn | (91) | Corn | (87) | Corn | (90) | Corn | (79) | Corn | (68) | Corn | (58) | Corn | (54) |
| Cattle | (95) | Horse | (93) | Chicken | (91) | Cattle | (89) | Cattle | (81) | Soybns | (68) | Soybns | (65) | Soybns | (62) | Soybns | (54) | Soybns | (47) |
| Chicken | (95) | Chicken | (93) | Corn | (91) | Oats | (83) | Hogs | (69) | Cattle | (60) | Cattle | (47) | Hay | (42) | Hay | (37) | Hay | (30) |
| Corn | (94) | Corn | (90) | Horses | (84) | Chicken | (82) | Hay | (62) | Hay | (56) | Hay | (46) | Cattle | (42) | Cattle | (35) | Cattle | (30) |
| Hogs | (89) | Hogs | (83) | Hogs | (81) | Hogs | (79) | Soybns | (57) | Hogs | (50) | Hogs | (35) | Hogs | (19) | Horses | (13) | Horses | (11) |
| Apples | (84) | Hay | (82) | Hay | (80) | Hay | (72) | Oats | (57) | Oats | (34) | Oats | (25) | Oats | (12) | Hogs | (11) | Hogs | (07) |
| Hay | (82) | Potatoes | (64) | Oats | (74) | Horses | (42) | Chicken | (48) | Horses | (13) | Horses | (10) | Horses | (11) | Oats | (08) | Chicken | (04) |
| Oats | (81) | Apples | (56) | Apples | (41) | Soybns | (37) | Horses | (26) | Chicken | (09) | Sheep | (08) | Sheep | (04) | Sheep | (04) | Sheep | (03) |
| Potatoes | (62) | Oats | (52) | Soybns | (40) | Potatoes | (18) | Sheep | (17) | Sheep | (08) | Chicken | (05) | Chicken | (02) | Chicken | (02) | Oats | (03) |
| Cherries | (57) | Cherries | (34) | Grapes | (23) | Sheep | (16) | Potatoes | (06) | Wheat | (01) | Ducks | (01) | Goats | (01) | Goats | (01) | Goats | (02) |
| Wheat | (36) | Grapes | (28) | Potatoes | (23) | Ducks | (05) | Wheat | (03) | Goats | (01) | Goats | (01) | | | | | | |
| Plums | (29) | Plums | (28) | Cherries | (20) | Apples | (05) | Sorghum | (02) | Ducks | (01) | Wheat | (01) | | | | | | |
| Grapes | (28) | Sheep | (21) | Peaches | (16) | Cherries | (04) | Rdclover | (02) | | | | | | | | | | |
| Ducks | (18) | Peaches | (16) | Sheep | (16) | Peaches | (04) | Apples | (02) | | | | | | | | | | |
| Geese | (18) | Pears | (16) | Plums | (15) | Goats | (04) | Ducks | (02) | | | | | | | | | | |
| Stwberry | (17) | Mules | (13) | Pears | (13) | Grapes | (03) | Goats | (02) | | | | | | | | | | |
| Pears | (17) | Ducks | (12) | Rdclover | (10) | Pears | (03) | Geese | (01) | | | | | | | | | | |
| Mules | (14) | Wheat | (12) | Mules | (06) | Plums | (03) | | | | | | | | | | | | |
| Sheep | (14) | Geese | (11) | Stwberry | (06) | Wheat | (03) | | | | | | | | | | | | |
| Timothy | (10) | Sorghum | (10) | Ducks | (06) | Rdclover | (03) | | | | | | | | | | | | |
| Peaches | (09) | Barley | (09) | Wheat | (04) | Geese | (03) | | | | | | | | | | | | |
| Bees | (09) | Rdclover | (09) | Timothy | (04) | Popcorn | (02) | | | | | | | | | | | | |
| Barley | (09) | Timothy | (09) | Geese | (03) | Timothy | (02) | | | | | | | | | | | | |
| Raspbry | (07) | Stwberry | (08) | Rye | (02) | Swtpatoe | (02) | | | | | | | | | | | | |
| Turkeys | (07) | Soybns | (08) | Popcorn | (02) | Swtcorn | (01) | | | | | | | | | | | | |
| Wtmelon | (06) | Raspbry | (07) | Swtcorn | (02) | Turkeys | (01) | | | | | | | | | | | | |
| Sorghum | (06) | Turkeys | (06) | Rasbry | (02) | | | | | | | | | | | | | | |
| Goosebry | (03) | Popcorn | (06) | Bees | (02) | | | | | | | | | | | | | | |
| Swt corn | (02) | Swtcorn | (05) | Sorghum | (01) | | | | | | | | | | | | | | |
| Rye | (02) | Bees | (05) | | | | | | | | | | | | | | | | |
| Apricots | (02) | Goosebry | (04) | | | | | | | | | | | | | | | | |
| Tomatoes | (02) | Rye | (02) | | | | | | | | | | | | | | | | |
| Cabbage | (01) | Goats | (02) | | | | | | | | | | | | | | | | |
| Popcorn | (01) | | | | | | | | | | | | | | | | | | |
| Currents | (01) | | | | | | | | | | | | | | | | | | |
| n = 34 | | n = 33 | | n = 29 | | n = 26 | | n = 17 | | n = 12 | | n = 12 | | n = 10 | | n = 10 | | n = 10 | |

Source: Based on data from the US Census of Agriculture, 1920–2012.

**FIGURE 8.1** Asymmetries in USDA Farm Payments, 1995–2012

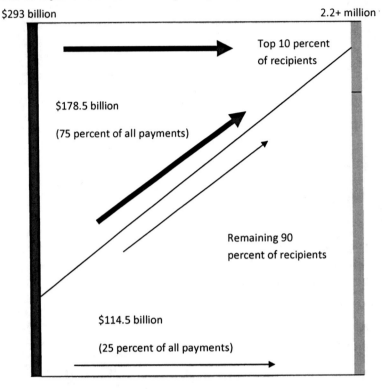

Source: Compiled using the databank maintained by Environmental Working Group (farm.ewg.org/progdetail.php?fips=00000&progcode=total&page=conc).

Connecticut, Hawaii, Maine, Massachusetts, Nevada, New Hampshire, New Jersey, and Rhode Island combined (Carolan 2016).

- Modern agricultural subsidy policy emerged in the early decades of the twentieth century. Initially, the policies were put into place to act as income redistribution measures. At this time farm incomes, on average, were considerably lower and less stable than those obtained in other sectors of the economy. The present realities surrounding farm incomes are very different. Today, farm incomes in affluent countries are, on average, above those of the average (nonfarm) household. And so, unlike three-quarters of a century ago, when subsidies served more as a safety net to protect those most in need, the overwhelming majority of farm subsidies today are going to the most wealthy.

- Farmers are likely to act proactively toward climate change if they perceive it as representing a real risk. Extensive survey research tells us, however, that the majority of US farmers do not perceive climate change as a threat (see, e.g., Stuart, Schewe, and McDermott 2014; White and Selfa 2013). Studies also indicate that farmers are more willing to participate in efforts focused on adaptation rather than mitigation. Arbuckle et al. (2013), for example, found that most of the farmers interviewed support adaptive actions, despite their beliefs about the causes of climate change, while few farmers support mitigation measures to reduce greenhouse gas emissions. Mitigation is dependent on the rationale that human emissions of greenhouse gases are the major driver of climate change. In contrast, adaptation to climate variability is something farmers believe they have always done whether or not they think climate change is the fault of human actions (see, e.g., Arbuckle, Morgan, and Hobbs 2015).

## Implications

At the risk of overgeneralizing, the impacts discussed in this section refer to those associated with what we might call the global **food system**, which can be defined as the entire array of activities—from input production and distribution to on-farm activities, marketing, processing, wholesale, and retail—that connect seed (and gene) to the mouths of consumers. To speak of a "system" is to make reference not just to certain agricultural practices but also (and equally) to regulatory, economic, social, and legal structures that reinforce the use of those practices (and even the ecological base that makes it all possible). Food production affects more than our stomachs, touching our lives in a variety of ways.

### Environmental Impacts

Where to begin? Let's start with water. As I have already discussed agriculture's link to water in Chapter 5, this discussion will be brief.

Let's begin with the concept of **irrigation efficiency**. Irrigation efficiency refers to the ratio of water that evaporates to what saturates the soil. The efficiency of traditional gravity irrigation, a method still widely used throughout the developing world, is about 40 percent—meaning that 60 percent of the water applied is lost to evaporation. Sprinkler systems, conversely, have an efficiency range of between 60 and 70 percent, whereas drip irrigation systems are between 80 and 90 percent efficient (Seckler 1996). Conventional understandings of irrigation efficiency refer to the minimal amount of water that can be applied to achieve maximum yield. Yet there are other ways to understand this concept. It could be defined as the maximization of crop production per unit of applied water. This admittedly means we stop striving for maximum yields, as the relationship between yields and applied water is linear only up to roughly 50 percent of **full irrigation** (which refers to the amount of water needed to achieve maximum yield). After this point, the yield curve takes on a curvilinear shape from increased surface evaporation, runoff, and deep percolation, until turning downward from anaerobic root-zone conditions, disease, and the leaching of nutrients (English, Solomon, and Hoffman 2002; see Figure 8.2). Conventional wisdom has farmers irrigating for maximum yield—the moment on the figure just prior to the curve turning downward. Yet if freshwater were to become additionally scarce, it might make more sense to strive for, say, 80 percent yields, especially if that could be achieved with half the water that would otherwise be needed to obtain the remaining 20 percent (and thus maximum) yield.

Another highly visible subject is agriculture-related **hypoxia**. Hypoxia refers to a state where oxygen concentrations in a body of water fall below the level necessary to sustain most animal life. The Gulf of Mexico is home to one of the Western Hemisphere's largest **dead zones**—the name given to bodies of water with low levels of dissolved oxygen. There are more than four hundred dead zones in the world today, 94 percent of which are in regions that will experience at least a 2° Celsius temperature

**FIGURE 8.2** General Relationships Between Yields and Total Amount of Water Applied

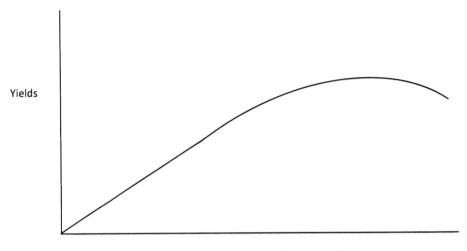

increase by the end of the century thanks to climate change; in other words, those areas are only going to get more "dead" (Altieri and Gedan 2015). The one found in the Gulf of Mexico is the product of excess nitrogen coming down through the Mississippi River. The majority of this excess nitrogen (roughly two-thirds) comes from agriculture and, to a lesser extent, lawns. Nitrogen levels in the Raccoon River, for example, which is part of the watershed of the Mississippi River, forced Des Moines Water Works in Iowa to build the world's largest nitrate-removal plant-treatment facility in 1991. Nitrate concentrations in this river have increased more than threefold since the 1950s (Eller 2015). After making its way into the Gulf, the nitrogen fuels the rapid growth of algae and plankton. When those organisms die and sink to the bottom, they decay and in doing so rob the water of oxygen (see Case Study 8.1). In 2014, the Gulf's dead zone measured 13,080 square kilometers (5,052 square miles), or more than twice the size of the state of Delaware (EPA 2015a).

According to the FAO (2013), the livestock sector generates an estimated 7.1 giga-tonnes of $CO_2$ equivalents a year, representing 14.5 percent of all human-generated greenhouse gas emissions. Beef and cattle milk production account for the majority of emissions, contributing 41 and 20 percent of the sector's emissions, respectively (see ECOnnection 8.1). Pig meat and poultry meat/eggs contribute 9 percent and 8 percent, respectively, to the sector's emissions. Emissions from this sector could also be broken down the following way. Feed production/processing and enteric fermentation (fermentation that takes place in the digestive systems of ruminant animals) are the two major sources of emissions, representing 45 and 39 percent of sector emissions, respectively. Manure storage and processing represent 10 percent, with the remainder attributable to the processing and transportation of animal products. The robust projected growth in the production and consumption of animal-based foods means higher emission shares and volumes in the years ahead.

## CASE STUDY 8.1
# Mobile Bay Jubilee

Jubilee is the name given to an event on the shores of Mobile Bay on Alabama's Gulf Coast when hordes of crab, shrimp, flounder, and eels leave deeper waters for shallower areas in the bay. The event often occurs more than once a year. The jubilee attracts many people, most of whom come looking to load up on free, abundant, and easy-to-catch seafood. It was not until the 1960s that a cause for the event was determined: hypoxia. During jubilees sea life becomes trapped between the shore and an advancing water mass low in dissolved oxygen (May 1973). Low levels of dissolved oxygen in the water can also cause marine life to become lethargic and slow, which further simplifies the task of catching these animals.

## ECOnnection 8.1
# Fish In Fish Out (FIFO) Ratio

Aquaculture has undergone many of the same structural changes as agriculture (Bunting 2013). These producers also find themselves trying to stay on the aquacultural treadmill, which is to say they are under tremendous pressure to raise as many fish as they can with as little feed as possible. This becomes especially challenging with larger predators such as salmon, which require comparatively large amounts of feed to produce body mass. The FIFO (Fish In Fish Out) ratio is the measurement of the amount they need. It indicates how much wild fish must be used as animal feed in order to produce an equivalent weight unit of farmed fish. So: if 1 kilogram of wild fish is used to produce the feed of 1 kilogram of farmed fish, the FIFO ratio is 1. Any value more than 1 means that more than 1 kilogram of wild fish is required to produce 1 kilogram of farmed fish. In the mid-1990s the FIFO ratio for salmon was 7.5 (that's right, it took 7.5 kilograms of wild fish to produce a kilo of farmed fish), while today the figure is between 3 and 0.5 (that's right, on some farms the ratio is *still* above one). Food for thought: If the current global consumption rate of fish of 17 kilograms per capita per year is to be maintained by 2050 (in light of a growing global population), aquaculture would have to reduce its average FIFO ratio from approximately 0.6 in 2008 to 0.3 units of marine fish to produce a unit of farmed fish. One way to do this would be to eat more of those fish with lower FIFO ratios, like catfish (at 0.5:1), tilapia (0.4:1), and milkfish (0.2:1), an already-popular fish in Asia.

Last, it is important that I say a few words about agriculture's links to soil erosion. A report released by the Environmental Working Group (EWG) indicates that the topsoil in America's top corn-producing state—namely, Iowa—is disappearing at an alarming rate (Cox, Hug, and Bruzelius 2011). This finding is all the more disturbing after considering the many millions of dollars spent on conserving this precious resource, involving programs that pay farmers to construct buffer strips and in some cases to have them remove their most highly erodible land from production entirely (to pay them, in other words, to *not* farm the land). Soil scientists at Iowa State University analyzed eighteen thousand samples gathered between 2002 and 2010 on Iowa farmland. With these data it was learned that far more soil was ending up in the Mississippi River watershed than what the US Department of Agriculture (USDA) considers sustainable. According to the USDA, five tons of soil per acre per year can be lost without reducing soil productivity. According to the EWG, soil erosion rates in Iowa are as great as twelve times that amount. This translates into roughly sixty-four tons of topsoil per acre per year. One reason for the high rates of erosion cited in the report is a highly inequitable incentive structure that delivers maximum rewards to farmers who ramp up production (think corn and ethanol subsidies) while providing a pittance, in comparison, to encourage them to conserve topsoil.

## Community Impacts

There is a large, rich body of literature looking at the impact of industrial agriculture on communities. The most famous of these studies, and one of the first, was conducted almost three-quarters of a century ago. Overseen by Walter Goldschmidt, a USDA anthropologist, and funded by the USDA, the study looks at two California communities in the early 1940s: Arvin, where large, absentee-owned, non-family-operated farms were more numerous, and Dinuba, where locally owned, family-operated farms were the norm (the names of both towns are pseudonyms). The researchers concluded that industrial agriculture had, overall, a negative impact on a variety of community quality-of-life indicators (Goldschmidt 1978). For example, relative to Dinuba, Arvin's population had a smaller middle class, a higher proportion of hired workers, lower mean family incomes, higher rates of poverty, poorer-quality schools, and fewer churches, civic organizations, and retail establishments. Residents of Arvin also had less local control over public decisions because of disproportional political influence by outside agribusiness interests. Goldschmidt's research was rediscovered in the 1970s, perhaps in response to rapid changes to agriculture during this time. Research since the 1970s has overwhelmingly supported the Goldschmidt thesis (Lobao and Stofferahn 2008; see ECOnnection 8.2).

It is important to clarify that *industrial agriculture* in this tradition often goes beyond the size of an operation by also incorporating indicators of farm organization. According to this literature, features like absenteeism (when land is leased and the owners live outside the community), contract farming, dependency on hired labor, and operation by farm managers (as opposed to owner-operator situations) place a greater burden on communities than when surrounding farms—even large ones—lack these characteristics. Large-scale, family-owned farms, for example, tend to still purchase their inputs, farm equipment, and services locally; volunteer their time at local organizations, such as church groups, school fund-raisers, and the like; and regularly interact with their neighbors.

Research has also looked at the impact of large-scale livestock-feeding operations— aka confined animal-feeding operations (CAFOs)—on community well-being and public health. Neighbors of CAFOs have been found to have higher levels of respiratory and digestive disturbances (Radon et al. 2007). They also have abnormally high rates

ECOnnection 8.2

# Negative Impacts of
# Industrialized Farms

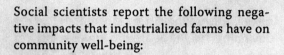

Social scientists report the following negative impacts that industrialized farms have on community well-being:

## SOCIOECONOMIC WELL-BEING

- greater income inequality, higher rates of poverty, or both
- higher rates of unemployment
- reduced employment opportunities

## SOCIAL FABRIC

- decline in local population
- social class structure becomes poorer (as a result of, for instance, increases in hired labor)

## SOCIAL DISRUPTION

- increases in crime rates and civil suits
- general increase in social conflict
- greater childbearing among teenagers
- increased stress and social-psychological problems
- swine CAFOs located in census blocks with high poverty and minority populations
- deterioration of relationships between farming neighbors
- more stressful neighborly relations

- deterioration in community organizations; less involvement in social life
- decrease in local-level political decision making (as outside interests gain influence)
- reduction in the quality of public services
- decreased retail trade and fewer, less diverse retail companies
- reduced enjoyment of outdoor experience (especially when living near CAFO)
- neighbors of hog CAFOs report upper-respiratory and digestive-tract disorders and eye problems
- residences closest to hog CAFOs experience declining values relative to those more distant

Social scientists report the following negative impacts that industrialized farms have on the health of the environment:

- depletion of water and other energy resources
- increase in Safe Drinking Water Act violations
- air-quality problems
- increased risks of nutrient overload in soils

*Source: Based on a review of literature by Lobao and Stofferahn (2008) and Stofferahn (2006).*

of psychological disorders, such as anxiety, depression, and sleep disturbances (Bokowa 2010). Children living on or near hog farms have abnormally high rates of asthma (Guidry et al. 2015). These rates are known to increase proportionally with the size of the operation (Donham et al. 2007). North Carolina school administrators report rates of asthma among the student population at levels well above the state average in schools within three miles of one or more large hog-feeding facilities (Mirabelli et al. 2006). Post-traumatic stress disorder has also been reported among residents living near CAFOs (Donham et al. 2007). This can result from such things as a reduction in one's quality of life or property values. For example, one study looking at a community in rural Kentucky found price reductions of 23 to 32 percent for residential properties sold within 1.25 miles of the facility, and much larger losses northeast (downwind) of the facility (Simons, Seo, and Robinson 2014). Researchers have also documented that a significant level of social tension—specifically between producers and their neighbors—can emerge when CAFOs are sighted within a community (Doane 2014).

## Malnutrition and the Green Revolution

The **green revolution** refers to a series of strategies developed during the mid- to late twentieth century to combat starvation by expanding the global production of staple food crops through crop breeding. Was the green revolution a success? It depends. For example, we unequivocally grow more calories today globally than we did a half century ago. So as a food calorie revolution, the green revolution *was* an unqualified success. But calories do not a nutritious diet make, as evidenced by the green revolution's links to **micronutrient malnutrition**—a condition that results from a diet lacking in sufficient quantities of micronutrients (Carolan 2013).

Micronutrient malnutrition plagues more than a billion around the world because of widespread deficiencies in key vitamins and minerals, particularly vitamin A, iodine, iron, and zinc. Most of these individuals live in low-income countries and are more often than not deficient in more than one micronutrient (CDC 2015). Children are a particularly sensitive population to micronutrient malnutrition because they have higher nutritional requirements per kilogram of body weight. Micronutrient deficiencies cause an estimated 1.1 million of the 3.1 million child deaths globally—in other words, more than one-third—that occur each year as a result of undernutrition (IFPRI 2014). A consensus is emerging that the growth lost in early years from malnutrition is, at best, only partially regained during childhood and adolescence with dietary improvements. One study, examining children who were between twelve and twenty-four months in age at the peak of the drought in rural Zimbabwe in 1994–1995 had average heights well below those of comparable children not affected by this event when measured at ages sixty to seventy-two months (Hoddinott and Kinsey 2001). Another study notes that among children in rural Zimbabwe who were exposed to the 1982–1984 droughts, average heights at late adolescence were reduced by 2.3 centimeters compared to children not exposed to this nutritional shock (Alderman, Hoddinott, and Kinsey 2006). Some studies have attempted to calculate the costs of malnutrition. An analysis estimates the burden of malnutrition to the national economy of Cambodia at more than $400 million annually—2.5 percent of the country's GDP (Bagriansky et al. 2014).

There is no disputing that the green revolution has occurred at the expense of dietary diversity. For evidence of this I point to a recent study published in the *Proceedings of the National Academy of Sciences* that reveals an emerging standard global food supply consisting increasingly of such energy-dense foods as soybeans, sunflower oil, and palm oil, along with more historically familiar staples like rice and wheat (Khoury et al. 2014). Wheat was found to be a major staple in 97.4 percent of all countries and rice in 90.8 percent, whereas soybean has become significant in 74.3 percent of countries. Meanwhile, many crops with long-held regional and cultural importance—cereals like sorghum, millet, and rye as well as root crops such as sweet potato, cassava, and yam—are disappearing from fields and diets. For example, a nutritious tuber crop known as

# Shifting Dietary Trends Among Low-Income Countries, 1969–2009

**FIGURE 8.3A** Since the inception of the CGIAR, diets in developing countries have shifted dramatically, including greater amounts of major oil crops and lesser quantities of regionally important staples.

**FIGURE 8.3B** Diets in developing countries are increasingly comprised of major globalized crops.

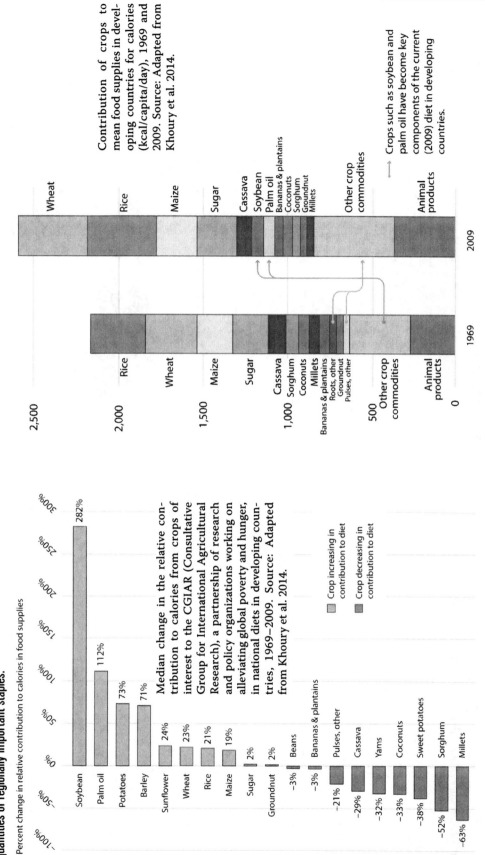

Percent change in relative contribution to calories in food supplies

Soybean 282%
Palm oil 112%
Potatoes 73%
Barley 71%
Sunflower 24%
Wheat 23%
Rice 21%
Maize 19%
Sugar 2%
Groundnut 2%
Beans –3%
Bananas & plantains –3%
Pulses, other –21%
Cassava –29%
Yams –32%
Coconuts –33%
Sweet potatoes –38%
Sorghum –52%
Millets –63%

Median change in the relative contribution to calories from crops of interest to the CGIAR (Consultative Group for International Agricultural Research), a partnership of research and policy organizations working on alleviating global poverty and hunger, in national diets in developing countries, 1969–2009. Source: Adapted from Khoury et al. 2014.

Crop increasing in contribution to diet

Crop decreasing in contribution to diet

Contribution of crops to mean food supplies in developing countries for calories (kcal/capita/day), 1969 and 2009. Source: Adapted from Khoury et al. 2014.

Crops such as soybean and palm oil have become key components of the current (2009) diet in developing countries.

# Shifting Global Dietary Trends, 1961–2009

**FIGURE 8.4A** A study of the world's countries finds that over the last fifty years, diets have become more similar.

**FIGURE 8.4B** Diets worldwide are increasingly comprised of major globalized crops.

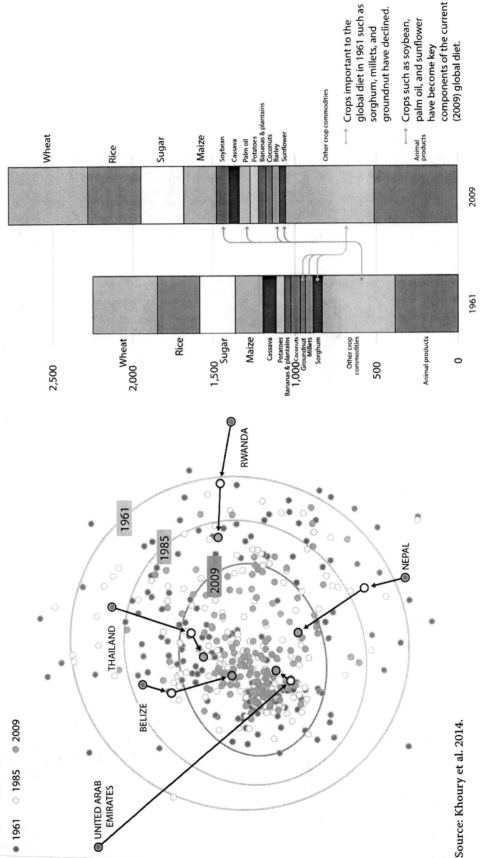

Relative contribution of major crops to the average food supply composition for calories (kcal/capita/day) worldwide, 1961 and 2009. Source: Khoury et al. 2014.

Source: Khoury et al. 2014.

oca, once grown throughout the Andean highlands, has declined significantly in this region both in cultivation and consumption.

Figure 8.3 illustrates these trends. As the figure details, soybean consumption has increase 282 percent in developing countries between 1969 and 2009, while the consumption of millet and sorghum has decreased by more than half during that same time period. There is a stark nutritional disparity between the foods at the top and bottom of the figure. Those being eaten at greater rates tend to be richer in macronutrients, while those disappearing are micronutrient rich. Not only that, many of the crops near the bottom of the figure are stress tolerant, which makes them particularly valuable when we talk about sustainably feeding future populations in the context of climate change.

Another way to visualize this move toward global diet homogeneity is through the following image constructed, and graciously provided to me, by the above study's lead author, Colin Khoury: Figure 8.4. Notice the dietary "spread"—a dispersed set of light-colored dots—that existed a half century ago around the world. The global diet today is represented by a clear clumping of darker dots closer to the middle of the figure.

Fortunately, micronutrient malnutrition has received greater attention in recent years. As evidence of this, note the rise of what is known as **biofortification**—the breeding and, increasingly, genetic engineering of plants with the aim of bolstering their micronutrient content. Biofortification strategies also do nothing to increase dietary diversity. They may, in fact, have just the opposite effect. Simply packing more nutrients in a handful of staple crops risks further shrinking the diets of those in the developing world, which have already seen their diets become dangerously narrow by the green revolution with its **monocultures** (an agricultural practice of producing a single plant species over a wide area for a number of consecutive years). There is also the concern that fortification programs will draw attention away from the more important issue of food access. As Tripp notes, biofortification schemes embrace, whether implicitly or explicitly, a "technical fix" attitude that "can tempt governments to believe they don't have to worry about nutrition because the plant breeders are handling this" (2001, 258).

## The "Treadmills" of Agriculture

In the 1950s, agricultural economist Willard Cochrane (1958) introduced the concept of the "agricultural treadmill." According to Cochrane, farmers are under tremendous economic pressure to adopt new technologies and increase the size of their operations. The logic behind the argument is straightforward. Those first to adopt a technology (especially one that increases yields or a farm's efficiency) initially experience windfall profits from increased output—like in the case of hybrid corn, which immediately upon adoption doubled a farmer's yield. Soon other farmers, seeing the relative advantage of the technology and wanting to capture additional profits, choose also to adopt. Yet the cumulative effect of the heightened output eventually exerts downward pressure on prices, as the market becomes flooded. It's important to realize that new agricultural technologies rarely do anything to directly increase consumer demand. At this point, those who have yet to adopt the technology now *must* adopt it if they wish to remain competitive in the market.

A consequence of being caught on the agricultural treadmill is the continual pressure to adopt the latest technologies and inputs while at the same time increasing the size of one's farming operation. This, however, increases one's operating costs, which in

## ECOnnection 8.3
## Yes! We Have
## No Bananas

The banana that Americans first came to know was called the Gros Michel banana—also known as "Big Mike." If you went to the store between 1906 and 1960, Big Mike was the banana for sale. It was ubiquitous in grocery stores around the world. Big Mike met with a tragic end, however. Panama disease—a fungus resistant to fungicide—wiped it from the face of the global marketplace. A hurried search for a viable replacement led to the discovery of the Cavendish cultivar, which was resistant to the disease. (A *cultivar* refers to a race or variety of a plant created or selected intentionally and maintained through cultivation.) Now it seems that a new strain of Panama disease is attacking the Cavendish in Asia, and if it were to spread to other continents, it could cause the Cavendish to go the way of the Big Mike (Koeppel 2007).

Banana corporations have developed their industry entirely around not only a single product but a single cultivar—talk about specialization! The industry has been likened to a pipe from many countries to local supermarkets. But this pipe fits only one variety of the world's one thousand banana varieties, which makes changing to a new variety very difficult and expensive.

The looming Panama disease threat has led to calls for the banana industry to move away from the monoculture (or, more accurately, monovarietal) model it has been using for more than a hundred years (Prisco 2015). Growing multiple varieties will ensure that no single disease will be able to wipe out the entire industry, bringing resiliency to the industry. There are, however, hurdles to overcome. Many varieties, for example, cannot withstand the transportation and handling requirements of long-distance shipping. Other hurdles are more cultural. Take "baby bananas." These taste best when eaten in a far browner state than a traditional Cavendish. Yet most people are accustomed to the signature yellow color that the Cavendish (and Big Mike before it) has, which indicates ripeness before it goes brown. It will take some work to get people used to eating a banana that looks, through a Cavendish lens, noticeably overripe.

turn requires farmers to continually seek out ways to increase their output. Yet there are other input-specific treadmills also at work here. The pesticide treadmill is perhaps the best known of these additional treadmills and was first discussed back in the 1970s (van den Bosch 1978). This is the phenomenon in which insects evolve to become resistant to pesticides, which leads to more applications, higher concentrations, and new chemicals, which leads to still further resistance, and so on. Studies going back as early as the 1970s note that despite large increases in pesticide use during the 1960s and 1970s, crop losses from insect pests were actually on the rise (Pimentel et al. 1978), a trend that continues to this day (Riggi et al. 2015). Whether we're discussing pesticides or fungicides (see ECOnnection 8.3), evolution has proven a formidable foe to agrichemical companies.

Another input-specific treadmill involves the use of synthetic fertilizers—also known as the fertilizer treadmill. Synthetic fertilizer can easily lead to a need for more fertilizer over time. This treadmill is particularly acute when tilth, which are levels of organic matter, and microorganism activity are diminished as a result of poor soil-management practices and a general mining of one's land—problems that are all too common on farmland where synthetic fertilizers are used. Under such a scenario, the only option becomes increasing the applications of fertilizer in order to maintain one's yield.

Last, there is the seed treadmill. A number of protections, as discussed in Chapter 4, are used by the seed industry that either discourage or outright prevent farmers from saving their seeds and replanting them the following season. Moreover, as also discussed in Chapter 4, the knowledge of how to save and replant seeds is another resource that farmers lose when they cease practicing seed saving. This creates a dependency on seed companies. In the United States, for example, the rate of saving corn seed fell from approximately 100 percent at the turn of the twentieth century to less than 5 percent by 1960, while rates for soybean saving dropped from 63 percent in 1960 to 10 percent in 2001 (Howard 2009).

## Solutions

In 2002 then UN secretary-general Kofi Annan asked an appointed panel of experts how a green revolution could be achieved in Africa. After more than a year of study, the group had their answer. Foremost, they questioned the one-size-fits-all approach to food security taken by the green revolution: "The diverse African situation implies that no single magic 'technological bullet' is available for radically improving African agriculture." The panel's strategic recommendations explain that "African agriculture is more likely to experience numerous 'rainbow evolutions' that differ in nature and extent among the many systems, rather than one Green Revolution as in Asia" (InterAcademy Council 2003, xviii).

I've found the term *rainbow evolutions* useful when talking to students and the public about issues pertaining to food security. The term alters the scope of the discussion by, first, directing attention away from single magic-bullet thinking—hence the term *rainbow*. Second, it emphasizes how agricultural development cannot be divorced from the social, economic, and agroecological conditions of place—which is why the word *evolutions* is so apt. And as every place is different and unique, the term reminds us that solutions cannot be overgeneralized. The following are some potential colors of this ever-changing rainbow.

### *Agroecology*

Small, diverse farms—also known as **polycultures**—that raise grains, fruits, vegetables, and livestock have been shown to outproduce, in terms of harvestable products per unit area, large, specialized (monoculture) operations. Yield advantages of small, diverse farms can range from 20 to 60 percent (Altieri and Nicholls 2008). A recent meta-analysis involving 26 studies and 301 observations examined whether polycultures can produce the following win-win relationship: increased yield *and* the internal control of crop pests. (Agroecology relies on internal versus external [pesticides] controls to keep problematic bugs—aka pests—in check. It's basic ecology: polycultures attract both "good" and "bad" bugs, and the former keep the latter under control. Agroecology therefore also refers to an **organic system**.) The findings of this research: "We

ECOnnection 8.4

# Agroecology: Growing More Than Food and Fiber

When we think about agriculture, we tend to view it as being solely about food and fiber production. This is a terribly narrow—and perhaps even dangerous—view of all that is provided by this sector. Agriculture is important to us in such additional ways as

### DIET
- enhancement of nutritional quality and the cycling of trace elements
- food security

### PUBLIC HEALTH
- protection of the health of farmworkers and consumers
- suppression of vectors of human disease (e.g., mosquitoes, snails, ticks)

### ENVIRONMENTAL SUSTAINABILITY
- preservation of biodiversity
- protection of wildlife
- preservation of our productive capacity against erosion, salinization, acidification, and compaction

- maintenance of an ecological community of natural enemies of pests and diseases of crops
- protection of the general environment against runoff, eutrophication, volatilization of nitrites, and dust in the atmosphere
- protection of water resources and quality

### RURAL DEVELOPMENT
- supporting employment, farm income, and rural life
- support for the economic independence of women

### NATIONAL DEVELOPMENT AND SOVEREIGNTY
- contributing to the international balance of payments
- defense of national sovereignty against possible dumping or political blackmail backed up by economic blockade
- food sovereignty

*Source: Based on Gliessman (2015).*

found win-win relationships between per-plant yield of the primary crop and biocontrol in polyculture systems" (Iverson et al. 2014, 1593; see ECOnnection 8.4).

The inverse relationship between farm size and productivity is the result of a more efficient use of land, water, biodiversity, and other agricultural resources by small farmers. Polycultures minimize losses from weeds, insects, and diseases by keeping ecological internal controls intact, and they more efficiently use water, light, and nutrients (Gliessman 2015). Small farms are also overwhelmingly owner operated, which, as discussed earlier, benefits rural communities and their economies.

Small, diverse operations are also more likely to be resilient to environmental events, pests, and disease. One reason is because polycultures tend to display more consistent yields than monocultures during extreme weather events (Gliessman 2015). In India, for example, the number of varieties a rice farmer grows increases with the variability of conditions (e.g., atmospheric, agronomic, pest ecology, and more). Thus, low terraces,

**IMAGE 8.1**

Representatives of La Via Campesina march in the streets of Dakar, Senegal. Source: "Representantes de la Via Campesina" by El Fondo Andaluz de Municipios para la Solidaridad Internacional (flickr.com/famsi_andaluciasolidaria) is licensed copyright © 2011 under CC BY-SA 2.0.

which are wetter and prone to flooding, are planted with indigenous long-growing rice varieties. Upper terraces, in contrast, dry out more rapidly after the rains, so they are planted with drought-resistant, fast-growing varieties. In total, a small Indian rice farmer can plant up to ten different rice varieties (Holdrege and Talbott 2008).

Small-farm efficiency can also be attained with surprisingly little investment, especially when compared to the massive capital expenditures required of industrial farms. In Peru, for example, several NGOs and government agencies have created initiatives to restore abandoned terraces and build new ones by offering peasant communities low-interest loans or seeds and other inputs. Terraces reduce the losses associated with frost and drought, minimize soil erosion, improve water efficiency, and increase crop yields between 45 and 65 percent compared to crops raised on sloping land (Altieri and Nicholls 2008, 476).

## La Via Campesina and Other Peasant-Based Movements

La Via Campesina is viewed by many as the world's most important transnational social movement (Claeys 2015; Desmarais 2008; Martínez-Torres and Rosset 2010), a fact that surprises a great many in countries like the United States, where most have never heard of the organization. As its website (www.viacampesina.org/en) explains: "La Via Campesina is the international movement which brings together millions of peasants, small and medium-size farmers, landless people, women farmers, indigenous people, migrants and agricultural workers from around the world. It defends small-scale sustainable agriculture as a way to promote social justice and dignity. It strongly opposes corporate driven agriculture and transnational companies that are destroying people and nature." (See Image 8.1.)

## CASE STUDY 8.2

# Landless Workers' Movement (MST)

The Landless Workers' Movement in Brazil (also known as the MST, after its Portuguese title, Movimento dos Trabalhadores Rurais Sem Terra), which includes members throughout Latin America, is an estimated 1.5 million strong (MST 2015). The energy of the movement is due to the perceived unjust distribution of land throughout the region and especially in Brazil, where 3 percent of the population own and control two-thirds of the country's arable land.

Under Brazilian law, a landowner risks losing title to his or her land by letting it lie idle, especially after someone else settles it and begins using it productively. Under such a scenario, the latter party could challenge the landholder's title to the land in court. The MST has sought to utilize this law to the advantage of landless peasants. To give their movement further legitimacy, MST leaders also point to a passage in Brazil's constitution that states that land should serve a "larger *social* function," which they interpret to mean that it should not be viewed through solely an economic lens. Members of the MST thus seek to identify and occupy idle land and make it agriculturally productive, arguing that such actions meet the constitutional requirement of a "social function." While doing this, the MST is also pushing for broader land reform throughout the region (Carolan 2011b).

La Via Campesina is made up of 164 local and national organizations in seventy-three countries from Africa, Asia, Europe, and the Americas and collectively represents about two hundred million peasant families. The movement is founded on the belief that for too long, rural and food policies have been developed in the absence of those most affected: namely, rural peoples, including women. The class profile of La Via Campesina is remarkably diverse: landless peasants, tenant farmers, sharecroppers, and rural workers largely in Latin America and Asia; small and part-time farmers in Europe, North America, Japan, and South Korea; peasant farmers and pastoralists in Africa; small family farms in Mexico and Brazil; middle-class (and some affluent) farmers in India; and poor urban (and urban-fringe) dwellers in countries like Brazil and South Africa.

A quick word about the term *peasant*, as it has historically signified a less than flattering identity. La Via Campesina, along with other peasant movements (see Case Study 8.2), seeks to recast the term *peasant* as an identity to be embraced. Delegates from the United Kingdom, when seeking to first name the movement, initially resisted the term La Via Campesina—which literally translates into "Peasant Way"—out of concern for the derogatory connotations attached to the term *peasant*. The delegates instead preferred the term *farmer*. Many outside the UK delegation, however, favored the term *peasant*, noting that *farmer* also had connotations that failed to capture the character of the movement and most of its participants (Desmarais 2008). A compromise was reached: keep the name La Via Campesina, but do not translate it into English. It has also been noted that the name La Via Campesina pays homage to Latin America's founding role in the movement.

## MOVEMENT MATTERS 8.1
## Food Sovereignty Movement Scores Victory in Ecuador

In 2008 the Ecuadorian Constitution declared food sovereignty a strategic goal and a government obligation, embracing many of the proposals put forth by Ecuadorian federations linked to La Via Campesina. (For a detailed analysis of this process see Giunta 2014.) For example, Article 13 of the Ecuadoran Constitution states: "Individuals and communities have the right to safe and permanent access to healthy, sufficient and nutritious food, preferably produced locally and in accordance with their different identities and cultural traditions." Regarding food sovereignty, Article 281 explains: "Food sovereignty is a strategic objective and an obligation of the State to guarantee that individuals, communities, towns and nationalities achieve permanent self-sufficiency with foods that are healthy and culturally appropriate."

La Via Campesina is responsible for elevating the term *food sovereignty* in the public consciousness (see Movement Matters 8.1). The term was first used publicly by the movement during the World Food Summit in 1996. As detailed in Table 8.2, food sovereignty speaks to a way of life that is in many ways diametrically opposed to the dominant view that presently dictates conventional food and agricultural policy.

The World Forum on Food Sovereignty was held in the village Nyéléni in Mali, Africa, in February 2007. The meeting brought together six hundred delegates from five continents to reaffirm the right to food sovereignty and to begin an international drive to reverse the worldwide decline in local community food production. The forum was organized through an alliance of diverse social movements: Friends of the Earth International, La Via Campesina, the World March of Women, the Network of Farmers' and Producers' Organizations of West Africa, the World Forum of Fish Harvesters and Fish Workers, and the World Forum of Fisher Peoples. The group wrote the Declaration of Nyéléni, in which you'll find the following lengthy definition of food sovereignty. I quote the definition in full to give the reader an idea of just how expansive the concept is:

> Food sovereignty is the right of peoples to healthy and culturally appropriate food produced through ecologically sound and sustainable methods, and their right to define their own food and agriculture systems. It puts the aspirations and needs of those who produce, distribute and consume food at the heart of food systems and policies rather than the demands of markets and corporations. It defends the interests and inclusion of the next generation. It offers a strategy to resist and dismantle the current corporate trade and food regime, and directions for food, farming, pastoral and fisheries systems determined by local producers and users. Food sovereignty prioritizes local and national economies and markets and empowers peasant and family farmer–driven agriculture, artisanal-fishing, pastoralist-led grazing, and food production, distribution and consumption based on environmental, social and economic sustainability. Food sovereignty promotes transparent trade that guarantees just incomes to all peoples as well as the rights

**TABLE 8.2** View of Dominant and Food Sovereignty Models

| ISSUE | DOMINANT MODEL VIEW | FOOD SOVEREIGNTY MODEL VIEW |
|---|---|---|
| Free Trade | Everything ought to be governed by the market | Food should be exempt from trade agreements, as it is fundamentally different from, say, cars |
| Production Priorities | Agro-exports | National and local markets |
| Subsidies | Claims to favor market logics yet relies heavily on government subsidies for the largest farms | Subsidies okay if they level the playing field and do not unduly harm small-scale farms in developing economies |
| Food | A commodity to be traded (fundamentally no different from any other commodity) | A unique commodity that everyone has a right to |
| Agriculture | Increasingly an occupation for those with access to significant amounts of credit, capital, land, and labor | A livelihood that should be available to all |
| Hunger | A technological/production problem | A problem of access (of food and of land to produce food) |
| Food Security | Achieve through trade and by adopting green revolution principles | Improved by enabling the hungriest to produce food and by embracing rainbow evolution policies |
| Seeds | Can be privatized (like land); a commodity with no cultural significance | A common heritage of humankind that everyone has a right to; an artifact that allows for the reproduction of culture |
| Overproduction | Is good (leads to cheap food) | Is bad (erodes food security around the world) |
| Peasantry | A holdover from feudalism (which no one wishes to return to); a pejorative term | "People of the land"; a proud identity for hundreds of millions around the world |

Source: Adapted from Desmarais (2008) and Martínez-Torres and Rosset (2010).

**IMAGE 8.2** Photo of Community Garden in Downtown Denver, Colorado

Source: Author and James Hale.

of consumers to control their food and nutrition. It ensures that the rights to use and manage lands, territories, waters, seeds, livestock and biodiversity are in the hands of those of us who produce food. Food sovereignty implies new social relations free of oppression and inequality between men and women, peoples, racial groups, social and economic classes and generations. (IPC 2016)

## Urban Gardens

As discussed in Chapter 6, more than half the world's population live in urban areas—a figure that is only going to increase in the decades ahead. The majority of those moving to cities in these rapidly urbanizing (low-income) nations are poor: those escaping hunger, conflict, and/or persecution from wherever they started out (Lundquist, Anderton, and Yaukey 2015). Most urban poor in low-income nations spend the majority of their incomes on food. An estimated 60 percent of all household income generated by the poor in Asia goes toward purchasing food, compared to Canada and the United States, where the figure is closer to 10 percent (Carolan 2013). Food insecurity among the urban poor is further exacerbated by diets composed heavily of tradable commodities (versus traditional foods) and a lack of space to grow their own food (Redwood 2010).

Although it is easy to brush urban agriculture aside as a nonviable strategy for developing food security, the role that urban agriculture currently plays in keeping millions from falling over the edge into abject hunger and poverty is quite surprising (see Image 8.2). One study examined urban centers in fifteen developing countries in Africa, Asia,

Eastern Europe, and Latin America, looking specifically at the role played by urban agriculture in promoting food and economic security and diet diversity among the urban poor (Zezza and Tasciotti 2010). Participation in urban agriculture among poor households in the countries studied was as high as 81 percent. Urban agriculture was also shown to be of major economic significance, making up more than 50 percent of the income for poor households in certain countries. Two-thirds of the countries analyzed were shown to have a correlation between active participation in agricultural activities and greater household dietary diversity, even after controlling for economic welfare and other household characteristics. There was also a link—albeit not as robust as the others—between urban agriculture participation and the consumption of fruits and vegetables.

Before ending this chapter, I need to stress one important point (which I've given evidence for in previous chapters): do not think for a moment that our food problems lie only in production. This is *good* news, as the thought of having to further industrialize food production is not an attractive one, given the associated costs to the environment (e.g., climate change and soil erosion), community well-being (recall the Goldschmidt thesis), and public health (e.g., pesticide exposure). For one thing, hunger is ultimately a problem of access and distribution. The United Nations, for example, calculates that the world's average daily calorie availability is projected to rise from 2,789 kilocalories per person per day in 2000 to 3,130 kilocalories per person per day in 2050 (United Nations 2013). That's how many calories would be available if the food raised went to feeding people and not, say, cars (as biofuels) or landfills (as food waste). As detailed in Chapter 6, in the discussion of Amartya Sen's work on famines, producing more food does not do the world's hungry any good if they cannot afford or more generally do not have access to it. We also waste, as described in Chapter 3, an outrageous amount of food. Why continue pushing for higher yields and greater agricultural output if we are going to continue to throw a significant chunk of those productivity gains away? Some food for thought . . .

---

## IMPORTANT CONCEPTS

- agroecology
- food sovereignty
- Goldschmidt thesis
- green revolution
- peasant-based movements
- rainbow evolutions
- the "treadmills" of agriculture

## DISCUSSION QUESTIONS

1. It seems as though labor abuses and injustices take a backseat to issues of environmental sustainability when thinking and talking about food. Why do you think that is? How can we make all those involved in the growing, manufacturing and processing, transportation, preparing, and selling of food more visible?

2. What are some of the links between the green revolution and micronutrient malnutrition?

3. In many respects, people from lower-income countries are at the forefront of challenging the dominant global food system (like La Via Campesina and the Landless Workers Movement). Why is that? What threats does this system pose to them?

4. Summarize the Goldschmidt thesis. Based on that literature, what policies would you recommend with the aim of enhancing rural community vitality and well-being?

## SUGGESTED ADDITIONAL READINGS

Carolan, M. 2013. *Reclaiming Food Security*. New York: Earthscan/Routledge.

Clausen, R., B. Clark, and S. Longo. 2015. "Metabolic Rifts and Restoration: Agricultural Crises and the Potential of Cuba's Organic, Socialist Approach to Food Production." *World Review of Political Economy* 6(1): 4–32.

Howard, P. 2016. *Concentration and Power in the Food System: Who Controls What We Eat?* London: Bloomsbury Academic.

Obach, B., and K. Tobin. 2014. "Civic Agriculture and Community Engagement." *Agriculture and Human Values* 31(2): 307–322.

## RELEVANT INTERNET LINKS

- www.fao.org/home/en. Food and Agriculture Organization of the United Nations.
- www.fcrn.org.uk. Food Climate Research Network. An excellent resource for those looking for cutting-edge research dealing with the food system's impact on the environment, in addition to many other agrifood-related issues.
- www.foodmiles.co. Calculate the distance the food from your last meal has traveled (aka its food miles).
- www.ruaf.org. Resource Centers on Urban Agriculture and Food Security.
- www.viacampesina.org/en. The website address for La Via Campesina.
- vimeo.com/27473286. Excellent short video about the movement La Via Campesina.

## SUGGESTED VIDEOS

- *Big River* (2010). A sequel of sorts to *King Corn* (see below) that investigates the socio-ecological impacts of the main characters' acre of corn.
- *Edible City: Grow the Revolution* (2012). A journey through the Local Good Food movement that's taking root in the San Francisco Bay Area, across the nation, and around the world.
- *The Harvest* (2011). A documentary about three of the close to half million migrant child farm laborers in the United States.
- *King Corn* (2008). Two friends learn about the food system by moving to Iowa and growing an acre of corn.
- *Lucent* (2014). An investigation of the practices of Australia's pig farms and slaughterhouses. Featuring a wealth of never-before-seen surveillance and handheld footage captured by a devoted team of animal rights activists.
- *Planeat* (2011). A look at the impacts of meat and dairy on the planet and our health.

- *Save the Farm* (2011). A popular organic farm in the middle of South Central Los Angeles is threatened by land developers, and community members take action.
- *Turlock* (2013). In February 2012, the owners of A&L Poultry (a fifty-thousand-hen egg farm) stopped feeding their hens, leaving the birds without food for more than two weeks. This documentary details what happened next.

# 9

# Energy Production:
# Our Sun-ny Prospects

In 2009, China became the world's number one consumer of energy, overtaking the United States, which had previously been on top for close to a century. China consumed 2.252 billion tons of oil equivalent in 2009, which was about 4 percent more than the United States' 2.17 billion tons (the oil-equivalent metric represents all forms of energy consumed, including crude oil, nuclear power, coal, natural gas, and renewable sources like hydropower and biofuel) (Swartz and Oster 2010). And 2009 proved not to be a fluke, as China has managed to hold onto that top spot, increasing its energy consumption to 2.6 billion tons (or 23 percent of the world's total) in 2012 (Li 2014). By 2035, China's energy consumption is expected to reach 3.83 billion tons of oil equivalent, more than India, the United States, and the European Union combined (Lin 2015).

Many in the United States expressed a collective sigh of relief in 2009, not so much because they were happy that China is, quite literally, killing hundreds of thousands of its people annually with its pollution (Li et al. 2015), but because they could finally point an indignant finger at someone other than themselves on the subject of energy consumption—how dare *they* do this? (I remember watching a couple of political pundits on television act precisely this way.) I still hear these expressions, even though they are dangerously misplaced. Although China might consume more energy in absolute terms, it comes nowhere close to outconsuming the United States on a per capita basis. So, in fairness, China's title as "top energy-consuming nation" is just a consequence of demographics. It has more than four times the population of the United States, a fact that also helps put into some perspective why China is investing heavily in its energy sector (see Case Study 9.1). If the United States had China's population, it would easily hold the title, outconsuming China by a factor of four.

The cloud of energy, however, has a silver lining. (It's there; we just can't see it at the moment, thanks to the layer of coal dust and other fine particulates that presently cover it.) While our thirst for energy is growing, as long as the sun exists we'll have plenty available to quench it, as electricity can be readily generated from solar, wind,

CASE STUDY 9.1

# Three Gorges Dam

Three Gorges is the world's most notorious dam. The dam's body was completed in 2006 and is located in China along the Yangtze River. Three Gorges Dam generates significant quantities of electricity, roughly eight times that of the US Hoover Dam. But at what cost, beyond the roughly $24 billion spent to build it?

The massive project, with its 1,045 square kilometers (403 square miles) wide reservoir, broke the record books for number of people displaced (more than 1.2 million) and number of cities (13), towns (140), and villages (1,350) flooded. The reservoir also submerged roughly one hundred archaeological sites, some dating back more than twelve thousand years. People who were displaced were allocated plots of land and small stipends as compensation. The dam itself also creates an impassable barrier to one endangered mammal (the Yangtze finless porpoise) and two that are threatened (the Chinese river dolphin and the Chinese paddlefish). The Chinese government went so far as to admit that two foreseen consequences were actually worse than anticipated: deteriorating water quality and erosion. Toxic algal blooms regularly blight the river's many tributaries as a result of reduced water flow and nutrients from land-use changes. Landslides are also a frequent occurrence, some of which are due to tremors and small earthquakes caused by the tremendous weight of the reservoir itself (which lies on two major fault lines). To mitigate these problems, China has embarked on a ten-year effort that will cost $26.45 billion—more than the cost of the entire dam!

*Source: Adapted from Hvistendahl (2008) and "The Legacy of Three Gorges Dam" (2011).*

geothermal, tidal, wave, and biomass. The sun, thanks to its energy and gravitational pull, is the source of all these renewables. At the moment, however, it's a case of where the "possible" and "probable" do not yet line up, though they could eventually, as I address in the Solutions section.

## Fast Facts

- More than 7,822 million tons (Mt) of coal was produced globally in 2013, up from 6,185 Mt in 2010. The top coal-producing nation was China, with 3,561 Mt (compared to 3,162 Mt in 2010); followed by the United States, with 904 Mt (*down* from 932 Mt in 2010); India, with 613 Mt (up from 538 Mt in 2010); Indonesia, with 489 Mt (*way up* from 173 Mt in 2010); Australia, with 459 Mt (up from 353 Mt in 2010); Russia, with 347 Mt (up from 248 Mt in 2010); and South Africa, with 256 Mt (up from 244 Mt in 2010). (See Image 9.1.) According to the World Coal Association (2014), proven global coal reserves are 892 billion tons, an amount, at current rates of production, that would last about 113 years.

- Nuclear power plants supplied 11.5 percent of the world's electricity in 2014, down from 13.5 percent generation in 2010. Countries generating the largest percentage of their electricity in 2014 from nuclear energy included France (76.9 percent compared to 74.1 percent in 2010), Slovakia (56.8 percent compared to 51.8 percent in 2010), Hungary (53.6 percent compared to 42 percent in 2010), Ukraine (49.4 percent compared to 48.1

**IMAGE 9.1**

Coal remains a popular source of energy in China, even for some households, which use it for heating and cooking. This truck is making a coal delivery in Beijing. Source: "Coal Consuming China" by Han Jun Zeng (flickr.com/67661012@N04) is licensed copyright © 2014 under CC BY-SA 2.0.

percent in 2010), and Belgium (47.5 percent compared to 51.1 percent in 2010). It is the United States, however, that leads the world in electricity generated from nuclear power (NEI 2012). As of August 2015, the United States had 99 reactors (down from 104 in 2010)—compared to France's 58 (the same number as in 2010)—that collectively produced 98.8 billion kilowatt hours (kWh) (compared to France's 63.1 billion kWh). In the future nuclear power will play a major role in China's energy portfolio. That country as of August 2015 has 26 reactors operating, 25 reactors under construction, 43 in the preconstruction phase, and another 136 proposed. These figures collectively are greater than all other countries combined. For example, France has one reactor under construction, zero in the preconstruction phase, and one proposed (WNA 2015).

- The countries with the greatest share of world crude oil reserves, as of 2014, are as follows: Venezuela, with 299.95 billion barrels representing 24.9 percent of OPEC's share; Saudi Arabia, with 266.58 billion barrels representing 22.1 percent of OPEC's share; Iran, with 157.53 billion barrels representing 13.1 percent of OPEC's share; Iraq, with 143.07 billion barrels representing 11.9 percent of OPEC's share; Kuwait, with 101.5 billion barrels representing 8.4 percent of OPEC's share; and United Arab Emirates, with 97.8 billion barrels representing 8.1 percent of OPEC's share (OPEC 2014).
- In 2014, the United States generated about 4,093 billion kWh of electricity. Approximately 67 percent of the electricity generated was from fossil fuels (coal, natural gas, and petroleum). Major energy sources and percent share of total US electricity generation in 2014 break down as follows: coal, 39 percent; natural gas, 27 percent; nuclear, 19 percent; hydropower, 6 percent; wind, 4.4 percent; biomass, 1.7 percent; petroleum, 1 percent; geothermal, 0.4 percent; and solar, 0.4 percent (EIA 2015b).

## Implications

Earlier chapters have covered many of the most significant socioecological implications of past and current energy use, with climate change chief among them. A substantial amount of time has also been spent describing the consequences of our collective addiction to oil and the car in particular. Yet the subject of energy *production* has yet to be given its due, particularly in regard to sources other than oil.

### "Clean" Coal

The aforementioned vastness of global reserves makes coal deserving of closer scrutiny. It is the most carbon intensive of all fossil fuels, which is why it has been called "the real global warming culprit" (Perrow 2010, 66). Coal is about as far from green as you can get when all available energy sources are lined up. Yet I doubt we'll abandon it anytime soon, primarily because of its great abundance in countries like China and the United States—numbers one and two, respectively, in terms of coal production *and* energy consumption. Thank goodness for **clean coal**, right?

What *clean coal* means depends on whom you ask. When I was writing the first edition of *Society and the Environment* the industry-sponsored American Coalition for Clean Coal Electricity had this definition posted on its website: "Clean coal technology refers to technologies that improve the environmental performance of coal-based electricity plants. These technologies include equipment that increases the operational efficiency of power plants, as well as technologies that reduce emissions." Broadly speaking, then, clean coal, according to the coal industry and its wide net of proponents, refers to any coal-burning technology that is an improvement over what we used to have. That definition of *clean* might work for my four-year-old son, who after washing his dinner plate (which remains covered in food) tells me how dirty it used to be prior to dipping it in the sink. The first time he did that, I remember going to the sink and showing him "what clean really means." Perhaps someone ought to do that for the coal industry. If you search the American Coalition for Clean Coal Electricity's website today, you will no longer find a definition of clean coal. The assumption is that all coal is clean, thus making the term *clean coal* redundant. Instead you'll find a description of technologies that make coal clean (www.americaspower.org/clean-coal-technologies-1663), but no definition of clean coal itself.

Outside the coal-lobbying industry, however, *clean coal* typically means something more befitting the name. That something typically involves capturing and storing the $CO_2$ produced by coal-fired power plants, thereby preventing this greenhouse gas from being emitted into the atmosphere and contributing to climate change. Unfortunately, while carbon-capture technology has been shown to work on a small scale, it has yet to be successfully scaled up (see Case Study 9.2).

Besides the large expense, carbon capture of clean coal still comes with a significant ecological footprint. Lest we forget, that coal has to come from somewhere. Millions of acres of habitat across the United States have been radically altered over the past 150 years by **strip-mining** (a practice involving the removal of soil and rock overlaying the mineral deposit). There were approximately 1,229 operational mines in the United States in 2012, 60 percent of which were strip mines (also known as surface mines) that

## CASE STUDY 9.2
## Experimenting with Carbon Capture in West Virginia

American Electric Power's coal plant on the Ohio River in New Haven, West Virginia, burns through a million pounds of Appalachian coal every hour. Back in 2009, plant operators began experimenting with carbon capture, which involved diverting and chilling roughly 1.5 percent of the smoke and sending it through a solution of ammonium carbonate, which absorbed the $CO_2$. The $CO_2$ was then compressed and injected into the porous sandstone formation that lies more than a mile below the banks of the Ohio River. For two years the plant captured and stored more than 37,000 metric tons of $CO_2$. While only a small fraction of what the plant produced, it was supposed to be just the beginning. The plan was to scale up the project to capture a quarter of the plant's emissions (1.5 million tons of $CO_2$ a year) by investing $334 million of American Electric Power's money coupled with matching funds from the US Department of Energy. To spend that amount, however, the company needed to know it would be able to recoup its investment. But since then-proposed climate change legislation failed to pass in Congress, state utility regulators told the company that it could not charge its customers for a technology not yet required by law. So in the spring of 2011 the project was abandoned. The plant had been the world's first to capture and store $CO_2$ from a coal-fired electric plant and had attracted engineers and politicians from around the world (Nijhuis 2014).

were responsible for 66 percent of domestic coal production (C2ES 2015; see ECOnnection 9.1).

A single five-hundred-megawatt coal-fired power plant emits three million tons of $CO_2$ and costs more than $500 billion a year when all the economic, health, and environmental impacts associated with each stage in the life cycle—extraction, transportation, processing, and combustion—are totaled (Epstein et al. 2011). Breaking this figure down a bit: $74.6 billion is "paid" by Appalachian communities—where much of the coal is extracted—in terms of increased health care costs, injury, and death; costs linked to emissions total more than $187 billion; and the mercury set loose into the environment, with its negative effects on human health, comes with a price tag of almost $30 billion. And let us not forget about climate change. Each five-hundred-megawatt coal-fired plant, in terms of climate change costs, passes onto the public, both present and future, an annual bill that can total more than $200 billion. Again, this is just *one* coal-fired power plant (see ECOnnection 9.2).

### *Hydraulic Fracturing (aka Fracking)*

Natural gas production is expected to increase rapidly in the decades ahead in countries with rich natural gas reserves. President Obama called the United States the "Saudi Arabia of natural gas," in his 2012 State of the Union address, thanks in no small part to shale gas. (This is where **fracking** comes into play—see below for a definition.) Recent

ECOnnection 9.1

# Mountaintop Removal Mining

**Mountaintop removal mining** involves clearing upper-elevation forests (typically at the summit of mountains), stripping the ground of topsoil, and using explosives to break up rocks to expose underlying yet relatively shallow coal seams. The practice is widespread throughout the central Appalachian region of the United States, particularly in eastern Kentucky, West Virginia, and southwestern Virginia. Studies have outlined the extensive environmental and public health consequences associated with this practice of coal extraction (e.g., Palmer et al. 2010; Crosby, Tatu, and Charles 2016). Those consequences include the following:

- ecological losses and downstream impacts: for example, burial of headwater streams leading to the permanent loss of ecosystems, declines in stream biodiversity, and elevated water concentrations of sulfate, calcium, and magnesium
- human health impacts: for example, contaminated groundwater and elevated levels of airborne and hazardous dust resulting in increased risk of lung and bronchus cancer
- mitigation problems: land reclaimed after a mine is closed has lower organic con-

tent, low water-infiltration rates (which increases the risk of flash flooding), and low nutrient content

Mountaintop mining is considerably more economical than traditional coal mining, as it is less labor intensive. Approximately 250 percent more coal can be extracted per worker using this technique than in traditional underground mines (NMA 2012). It is no coincidence that the recent expansion of mountaintop mining has coincided with the loss of thousands of jobs over the past twenty years in the US coal industry. The industry claims the lost jobs are due to increasing government regulations when the data indicate *it* is the one to blame. Proponents of the practice often cast critics as looking to damage the economic livelihood of mining communities, perpetuating the false "jobs versus the environment" argument. This criticism ignores the fact that mountaintop mining is doing the damage by replacing labor with dynamite and heavy equipment, and in the end (as all mines eventually close) leaving communities with a devastated natural resource base and no alternative opportunities for employment (Bell and York 2010).

estimates suggest the shale gas reserves in the United States are sufficient to cover current production rates for nearly a hundred years (GIBC 2015; see Image 9.2).

It is generally accepted that combustion of natural gas in power plants produces substantially less $CO_2$—35 to 66 percent lower, depending on the context—than that emitted by coal-fired power plants when equal amounts of energy are generated (US Department of Energy 2014). And yet, despite the fact that natural gas has lower greenhouse gas emissions than coal on a delivered power basis, we cannot ignore that the extraction and delivery of natural gas contributes meaningfully to climate change (see ECOnnection 9.3). The natural gas sector, from extraction to processing, transport to consumption, is responsible for 25 percent of US methane emissions and 2.2 percent of the country's greenhouse gas emissions (US Department of Energy 2014).

ECOnnection 9.2

# Floating on a Cloud . . . of Fossil Fuel Emissions

"The cloud" is an apt term, but not for the reasons you think. The name *cloud* in the context of the IT (information technology) sector does not have any single definition. The term is frequently applied to refer to a wide range of Internet-based platforms and services—from Facebook to Flickr, LinkedIn, and Google Maps—that store and deliver data from an online source to the gadget in front of you. The metaphor of a cloud certainly builds on the futurists' utopia of having finally overthrown matter. Cloud computing consumes nothing more than 1s and 0s. Right?

I do find the term apt, if the right metaphor were evoked. Cloud computing *clouds* our ability to see beyond the liquid crystal display in front of us. If "the cloud" were a country, it would have the fifth largest electricity demand in the world, at more than seven hundred billion kilowatt hours. Yet this demand is practically invisible. To give just one example: the antivirus software company McAfee calculates that the electricity required to transmit the trillions of spam emails sent annually is equivalent to the amount required to power more than two million homes in the United States and produces the same greenhouse gas emissions as over three million cars. Or another: Facebook's first two data centers in Oregon and North Carolina, while using a highly energy-efficient design and technology, were both located in areas where more than 60 percent of the electricity came from coal. So while the US Environmental Protection Agency continues to work with the IT sector to expand its EnergyStar rating system to apply to data centers, the fact that these server farms continue to obtain a significant amount of their energy from coal largely cancels out any efficiency gains made in server technology. And my last example: the consulting business McKinsey & Company analyzed energy consumption by data centers used by pharmaceutical companies, military contractors, banks, and government agencies and found them to be using, on average, only 6 percent to 12 percent of the electricity powering their servers to perform computations. The remaining energy—roughly 90 percent of it—went to idling servers.

*Source: Carolan (2014).*

Fracking works like this: a well is sunk several thousand feet into the shale formation, after which laterals are then drilled that fan out from the main vertical well. Fracking takes place when large amounts of water, sand, and a secret chemical mixture (it's considered proprietary knowledge) are injected into the well. The pressure from this mixture fractures the shale, which in turn releases the natural gas. Once the fracking process is done, the well goes into production, though some wells may require multiple frackings.

Fracking has come under increasing scrutiny, as many homeowners in areas where the practice is common say it has tainted their drinking water, either with methane or with the wastewater produced by the process. And the research is beginning to back up those claims. A highly cited study published in the *Proceedings of the National*

**IMAGE 9.2** Three Hydro-Fracking Derricks Drilling Natural Gas on the US Plains

Source: Jens_Lambert_Photography/iStock.

*Academy of Sciences* looked at sixty drinking-water wells in northeastern Pennsylvania and nearby areas in New York State (Osborn et al. 2011). Dissolved methane concentrations in water from the thirty-four wells located more than one kilometer from fracking operations were tested to have, on average, about 1.1 milligrams of dissolved methane per liter. In water taken from twenty-six wells within one kilometer of at least one fracking site, methane concentrations averaged 19.2 milligrams. Isotopic analyses of the carbon in the methane showed it to have the same signature as that being recovered from nearby shale operations, thus implicating the fracking process. Other gases were also detected, which too were unique to the active gas-drilling areas. Ethane, another component of natural gas, and additional hydrocarbons were detected in 81 percent of water wells near fracking operations but in only 9 percent of water wells farther away. Propane and butane were also more likely to be detected in wells closest to drilling areas.

According to a recent review of the literature (Werner et al. 2015), from January 1995 through March 2014 more than one thousand studies have been published on the impact of "unconventional natural gas development"—fracking—on public and environmental health. The authors conclude that while the "methodological rigor" of the literature is mixed, the following is clear: "there is also no evidence to rule out such [negative] health impacts" (Werner et al. 2015, 1127). Social scientists are also starting to examine the location of these fracking wells in relation to the sociodemographics of a region. The findings are disconcerting (see Movement Matters 9.1). As one recent study concludes:

## ECOnnection 9.3
## More Cheap Fracking Plastic

The vast majority of plastic manufactured in the United States is made from natural gas. Analysts have described shale gas as a "game changer," since it has allowed the United States to regain its position as a low-cost producer of all things plastic. These cheap disposable commodities are in turn being exported around the world, as evidenced by the fact that US exports of polyvinyl chloride—also known as PVC plastic—tripled between 2006 and 2011 (Carolan 2014). The price of ethane, a natural gas component that is converted to ethylene when exposed to heat and pressure—a process called *cracking*—has fallen dramatically in recent years in the United States. Ethylene is a key ingredient for the manufacture of polymers. In 2012 alone the cost of ethane dropped by 67 percent among Gulf Coast processors, driven in part by massive investments by chemical manufacturers in Texas (Kaskey

2012). Before the fracking boom, the most recent cracker (machinery used to convert ethane to ethylene) built in the United States was constructed in 2001. Now more than ten new crackers are in various stages of planning or construction. The plastic industry's interest in developing greener, biobased plastics has been tempered thanks to fracking. Back when oil and gas prices were high, major petrochemical companies were busy exploring ways to make plastics from things like corn, sugar cane, sugar beets, and algae. It was recently calculated that the proposed cracker projects have the potential to boost polyethylene production by as much as 50 percent, raising domestic production to more than 42 billion pounds a year—six pounds of this type of plastic for every living person on Earth (Freinkel 2015).

This study applies Geographic Information Systems (GIS) and spatial analysis to determine whether certain vulnerable human populations are unequally exposed to pollution from unconventional gas wells in Pennsylvania, West Virginia, and Ohio. . . . Sociodemographic indicators include age (children and the elderly), poverty level, education level, and race at the census tract level. . . . The results demonstrate that the environmental injustice occurs in areas with unconventional wells in Pennsylvania with respect to the poor population. There are also localized clusters of vulnerable populations in exposed areas in all three states: Pennsylvania (for poverty and elderly population), West Virginia (for poverty, elderly population, and education level) and Ohio (for children). (Ogneva-Himmelberger and Huang 2015, 165)

### Nuclear Power

The Nuclear Energy Agency (2010) has proclaimed that nuclear power "could provide around 25 percent of global electricity with almost no $CO_2$ emissions." But it's not just industry types who are singing the praises of nuclear power; many environmentalists are too. Patrick Moore, the cofounder of Greenpeace who has famously become a

MOVEMENT MATTERS 9.1

## The Fight Over Local Control

There has been a wave of local resolutions and proposals to ban or limit fracking and the disposal of fracking waste. For the oil and gas industry, however, giving local residents and governments control over energy reserves is bad for US energy policy, and of course bad for its business. But it is not as easy as merely voting fracking out. There is the issue, for example, of preemption. Namely, do towns have the right to limit oil and gas drilling through their local zoning laws, or do states' various oil, gas, and mining laws *preempt* any home-

rule authority to regulate land use? In 2014, the New York health commissioner ruled in favor of two communities that voted to keep fracking out, claiming the health risks of drilling outweighed the benefits of tapping the rich shale reserves. It was a major victory for the grassroots groups within those communities. In the words of a city council member of one of the towns, "This is simply a victory for local control. It is a victory for liberals and conservatives of all sorts. It is what democracy is all about."

*Source: Adapted from Mufson (2014).*

nuclear power advocate, noted in a bulletin for the International Atomic Energy Agency that "nuclear energy is the only non-greenhouse-gas-emitting power source that can effectively replace fossil fuels while satisfying the world's increasing demand for energy" (Moore 2006). These claims, while factually accurate, mask deeper, less green truths, which life-cycle analyses help make visible.

Some life-cycle analyses show nuclear power emitting up to twenty-five times more $CO_2$ emissions than wind energy once uranium refining and transportation, reactor construction, and waste disposal are considered. A typical nuclear plant uses roughly 900 miles of electrical cables, 170,000 tons of concrete, 32,000 tons of steel, 1,363 tons of copper, and 205,464 tons of other materials, many of which, like aluminum, are carbon intensive (Sovacool 2008). As for the other end of the life cycle, some estimates place the total energy required for decommissioning a nuclear plant to be as much as 50 percent more than the energy needed for its construction (Seier and Zimmermann 2014).

Figure 9.1 illustrates top-end and mean (signified by the $X$ and the corresponding number) emissions from a review of life-cycle analyses on nuclear power (Sovacool 2008). Proponents are correct when they say the operation phase has a relatively small $CO_2$ footprint. Yet nuclear plants and nuclear fuel do not just appear. Nor do they disappear at the end of their life cycle. After factoring in for the entire life cycle of nuclear power, a very different ecological footprint image emerges. Of the life-cycle studies reviewed, the mean total $CO_2$ estimate was 66.08 grams (g) of $CO_2$ equivalents ($CO_2$e) per kilowatt hour (kWh) (the highest was 288 g $CO_2$e/kWh), which is consistent with more recent research on the subject (e.g., Sheldon, Hadian, and Zik 2015; Zafrilla et al. 2014). This is still far better than, say, coal's $CO_2$ life cycle, which has been estimated to range from 1,000 g $CO_2$e/kWh (Gagnon, Belanger, and Uchiyama 2002) to as high as

**FIGURE 9.1** Range and Mean of $CO_2$ During the Life Cycle of Nuclear Power

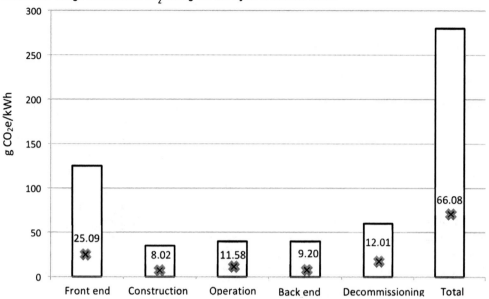

The mean is signified by the $X$ and the corresponding number in g $CO_2$e/kWh (grams of $CO_2$ equivalents per kilowatt hour). Source: Adapted from Sovacool (2008).

1,426 g $CO_2$e/kWh (Kiss and Rajovic 2015). Yet when compared to the $CO_2$ life-cycle footprint of wind and solar power, which according to a recent review of 153 life-cycle analyses places the means at 34.11 g $CO_2$e/kWh and 49.91 g $CO_2$e/kWh, respectively (Nugent and Sovacool 2014), nuclear comes up short.

Nuclear power is also expensive. Even with massive government subsidies, nuclear power remains uneconomical. One study calculates US subsidies to nuclear power to be 140 percent of the average wholesale price of power from this source (Koplow 2011). A recent study examines the cost of nuclear power relative to electricity generated from coal, natural gas, and wind. Nuclear power was found to be roughly 33 percent more expensive than that from coal, 20 percent more expensive than that from natural gas, and approximately the same price as electricity generated from wind (Boccard 2014). The technology also carries with it inherent—and to some degree incalculable—risk, not just of the meltdown variety but others related to weapons proliferation and the threat of terrorists targeting nuclear facilities. These realities further increase its costs, as expensive steps have to be taken to secure not only nuclear facilities but also the transportation of nuclear waste (see Case Study 9.3).

## Solutions

Ten years ago I couldn't have been as optimistic as I am today about energy generation. We have known for a long time that, theoretically, there's more potential renewable energy on this planet than we know what to do with. A popular statistic along these lines is that every hour, the energy equivalent to what all of humankind uses in an entire year

## CASE STUDY 9.3

# Fukushima Nuclear Disaster as "Normal Accident"

A magnitude 9 earthquake struck Japan on March 11, 2011, which was quickly followed by a devastating tsunami that rose to a peak of forty meters. Together, these events left twenty thousand people dead or missing and 125,000 buildings destroyed (Watts 2011). They also triggered a third disaster: the multiple meltdowns of three reactors at the Fukushima Daiichi nuclear plant, which ultimately released more radiation than any accident since the meltdown at Chernobyl in 1986, though a growing number of scientists say that the total release at Fukushima is worse than even this event (McNeill 2011).

Charles Perrow's *Normal Accidents* (1984) helps us think through events like the Fukushima nuclear disaster. Rather than ascribe the event to isolated equipment malfunction, operator error, or random acts of nature, Perrow makes the case that technological failures like what happened in Japan are the product of complex interacting systems. In this par-

ticular case, the root cause of failure lies in the tremendous complexity of nuclear plants. These "high-risk systems," as Perrow calls them, are inherently prone to failure regardless of how well they are managed or regulated. We therefore have two choices. One option is to radically redesign the systems to marginally reduce their complexity, by, say, moving the spent storage pools away from the site of power generation (Pidgeon 2011). The other option, which is also the surest way of avoiding these **normal accidents**, would be to abandon the technology entirely in favor of something less prone to catastrophic malfunction. A normal accident speaks of a failure that is inevitable, given the manner in which particular human and technological systems are organized. Extending this concept, might we call some of today's most pressing environmental problems—most notably global climate change—normal accidents?

strikes the earth's surface in the form of solar energy (Gilding 2011). Of course, we're a long way from capturing even a sizable fraction of this renewable energy. The point is that we can do it. It's now a matter of turning the technologically *possible* into the socially, economically, and politically *probable*.

## Efficiency and Curtailment

For decades, the principal solution to the energy problem was conservation and sacrifice. President Jimmy Carter in the late 1970s famously appeared on national television calling for energy conservation while wearing a sweater and sitting in front of a fireplace, a visual image that then presidential candidate Ronald Reagan later exploited when he argued that "energy conservation is being too cold in the winter and too warm in the summer" (as quoted in Kempton et al. 1985, 131). And to a significant degree, the mantra of sacrifice continues to be widely evoked among environmentalists. For example, of the seventy-seven "essential" skills touted to stop climate change in *The Life Earth Global Warming Survival Handbook* (Rothschild 2007), just three deal with efficiency-increasing actions. What's curious about these solutions is that comparisons of energy saved by curtailment versus those saved by increased efficiency show that the latter generally win out (Kastner and Stern 2015). While "turning out lights when leaving the room" continues to be parroted to our children, the evidence indicates that our focus might be better spent elsewhere.

I will be the first to admit that our energy problem will not be solved through efficiency gains alone; see Chapter 10, where the rebound effect and Jevons paradox are discussed. Yet as a pragmatic environmentalist, I think it is a mistake to ignore the low-hanging fruits that are sociotechnological solutions, so long as they do not get in the way of deeper socioecological change. If you had a very high temperature from an infection, you would treat the fever as well as the infection, wouldn't you? For the moment, let's talk about ways we can tinker with our consumption of energy at the margins and save the discussion of systemic change for later chapters.

Take the compact fluorescent (CFL) lightbulb. The average life of a CFL is between eight and fifteen times that of the traditional incandescent bulb but uses only 20 to 33 percent of the power of an equivalent incandescent—a truly remarkable gain in efficiency over the old lighting technology. Let's compare CFL and incandescent bulbs over a twelve-year period. During that time, you can either purchase fifteen incandescent bulbs and 1,500 kilowatt hours of electricity and spend roughly $225, or buy one CFL and 300 kilowatt hours of electricity at a cost of about $45. Yet the savings of CFLs pale when compared to the savings that could be had elsewhere through efficiency enhancements. The share of total world energy use (in 2015) by sector breaks down as follows: industrial, 51 percent; transportation, 20 percent; residential, 18 percent; and commercial, 12 percent (EIA 2015a). I'm not saying we should leave lights on in empty rooms, just that we need to turn off those lights and still do more—so much more.

One problem is that the average person does not fully understand how their actions use or save energy. In a national survey, 505 people were asked to report their perceptions of energy consumption and savings for various household, transportation, and recycling activities (Attari et al. 2010). The vast majority of respondents ranked curtailment, like turning off lights and driving less, above efficiency improvements, such as installing more efficient appliances and windows. When asked to indicate the most effective thing they could do to conserve energy, only 11.7 percent of participants mentioned efficiency improvements, whereas 55.2 percent mentioned curtailment (this does not add up to 100 because some gave very general answers like "recycle" and "conserve energy"). Moreover, when asked about certain activities, participants repeatedly underestimated energy use and savings, especially when it came to energy-intensive activities. The results of this exercise are illustrated in Figure 9.2. Although respondents' answers were close to accurate for less energy-intensive technologies and behavior, they *grossly underestimated* the energy consumption of appliances such as clothes washers, central air-conditioning systems, clothes dryers, and dishwashers. Take the case of lowering the hot water temperature in one's washing machine. Participants on average reported a savings of less than a hundred watt hours. The actual savings is closer to seven thousand watt hours.

Individuals also gave inaccurate answers when asked to compare consumption and savings related to transportation. For example, they significantly overestimated the

**FIGURE 9.2** Mean Perceptions of Energy Used or Saved Versus Actual Energy Used or Saved

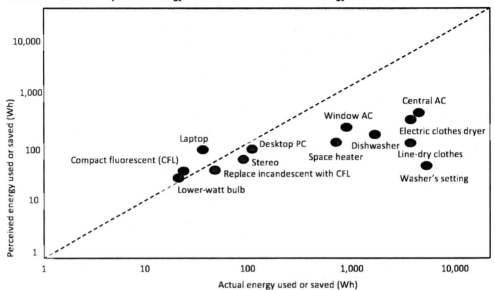

Wh: watt hours. The diagonal dashed line represents perfect accuracy. Source: Adapted from Attari et al. (2010).

savings attributable to reducing one's driving speed from seventy to sixty miles per hour for sixty miles. Conversely, they drastically underestimated—by almost a factor of ten—the energy savings derived from having their car tuned up twice a year. Pointing to these deficiencies in individuals' knowledge about energy consumption and savings, the study concludes that "the serious deficiencies highlighted by these results suggest that well-designed efforts to improve the public's understanding of energy use and savings could pay large dividends" (Attari et al. 2010, 16054).

Studies indicate that public understanding of energy use could be enhanced by merely changing how we talk about certain phenomena. Take, for example, how we in the United States talk about energy use as it pertains to automobiles: as a ratio of volume of consumption to a unit of distance—or specifically miles per gallon (mpg). Whereas people think that the amount of gas consumed by an automobile decreases as a linear function of a car's mpg, the actual relationship is curvilinear (see Figure 9.3). In one study, 171 participants from a national pool were given the following scenario: "A town maintains a fleet of vehicles for town employee use. It has two types of vehicles. Type A gets 15 miles per gallon. Type B gets 34 miles per gallon. The town has 100 Type A vehicles and 100 Type B vehicles. Each car in the fleet is driven 10,000 miles per year" (Larrick and Soll 2008, 1594). They were then asked to select a plan for replacing vehicles with the end goal of reducing overall gas consumption. Seventy-eight participants were given the following two options (framed in mpg terms): replace the 100 vehicles that get 15 mpg with vehicles that get 19 mpg, or replace the 100 vehicles that get 34 mpg with vehicles that get 44 mpg. Seventy-five percent chose the second option, which offers the largest gain in mpg *but not the greatest fuel savings.*

**FIGURE 9.3** Gallons of Gas Used per Ten Thousand Miles Driven

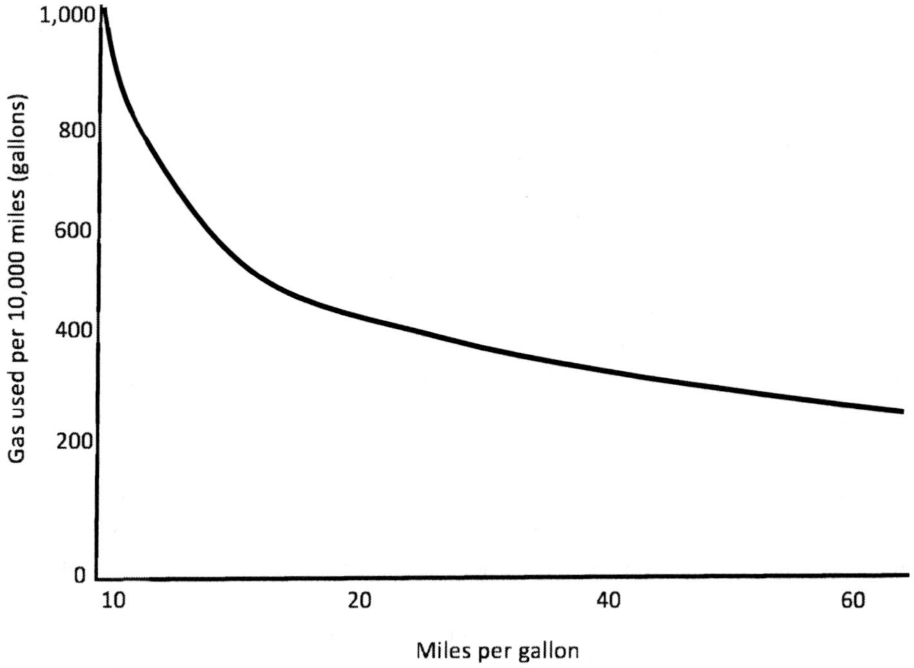

Source: Adapted from Larrick and Soll (2008).

The remaining participants were given a policy choice framed in terms of gallons per 100 miles (gpm). This group was told that the town "translates miles per gallon into how many gallons are used per 100 miles. Type A vehicles use 6.67 gallons per 100 miles. Type B vehicles use 2.94 gallons per 100 miles." Then they were given the same choices as the other group, though these options were expressed in gpm, versus mpg, terms. The percentage choosing the more fuel-efficient option increased from 25 percent in the mpg frame to 64 percent in the gpm frame. Based on this, the authors of the study conclude that whereas "mpg is useful for estimating the range of a car's gas tank, gpm allows consumers to understand exactly how much gas they are using on a given car trip or in a given year" (Larrick and Soll 2008, 1594).

## *Renewables*

The current global power demand is about eighteen terawatts (TW) (Marvel, Kravitz, and Caldeira 2013). If, however, the planet were powered by wind, solar, geothermal, tidal, and hydroelectric power, with no fossil-fuel or biomass combustion (that's right, *none*), something rather interesting occurs. Global power consumption would be considerably less, likely below fourteen TW (Jacobson and Delucchi 2009). How can the power-generating *method* impact consumption levels? The decline is due to the fact that, in most cases, electrification is a more efficient way to use energy. To take just one example: whereas roughly 18 percent of the energy in gasoline is used to move a vehicle (the vast majority is lost as heat), somewhere between 75 to 86 percent of the electricity delivered to an electric car is used to create motion.

## ECOnnection 9.4
# Windmills and Bird Fatalities

Windmills are often criticized for killing large numbers of birds. Do they? It depends on what they are being compared to. For instance, it is estimated that thirty thousand birds per year are killed by wind turbines in Denmark—a sizable number, especially considering windmills generate only 9 percent of the nation's electricity. But wait. Traffic kills one million birds annually in Denmark. If we abandon wind power because of avian fatalities, surely we should ban cars. After all, they are responsible for thirty times more bird deaths. And in Britain, fifty-five million birds are estimated to be killed every year by cats (MacKay 2009). Does this mean we should ban cats too?

Earlier I mentioned how every hour the energy equivalent of what humankind uses in an entire year strikes the earth's surface as solar energy. Clearly, some of that solar radiation—such as that falling on open seas and atop remote mountains—cannot be captured in a cost-effective manner. Yet even with subtracting for these and wind-deficient areas, humanity is still left with plenty. For example, a team of scientists from the Lawrence Livermore National Laboratory calculated that wind turbines placed on the Earth's surface could extract at least 400 TW annually, whereas high-altitude wind power (suspending airborne kite-like turbines hundreds or even thousands of feet off the ground) could extract more than 1,800 TW (Marvel, Kravitz, and Caldeira 2013). Presently wind adds only about 0.8 TW to our global energy portfolio every year (IEA 2015).

What about the often-expressed concern that a wind-powered future means a landscape blanketed with turbines? The footprint of the 3.8 million turbines needed to supply more than half of the total future global energy demand would be less than fifty square kilometers, or roughly half the size of Denver, Colorado. Granted, we will need to make sure there is proper spacing between each turbine so as not to unduly affect bird and bat migratory routes, among other reasons (see ECOnnection 9.4). Let's also not forget that sticking with fossil fuels means energy demand by 2030 will increase further than if we were to rely only or substantially on renewables. This future fossil-fuel demand will need to be supplied with some thirteen thousand new coal plants, each of which comes with its own land footprint, especially after factoring in for mining and mountaintop removal (Jacobson and Delucchi 2009).

Another dishonest critique of wind power is the "wind doesn't blow all the time" argument. First, a smart mix of renewable energy sources will ensure that something is always blowing, shining, turning, and so forth, so electricity is constantly being generated. Second, while wind does not blow all the time, coal plants are not online all the time, either. The average US coal plant is off-line 12.5 percent of the year for scheduled and unscheduled maintenance. Compare this to the average downtime for the newest generation of wind turbines: 2 percent on land and 4 percent at sea. Photovoltaic (solar) systems also fare well in this regard, with downtimes that factor out to about 2 percent of the year (Eccleston and March 2011).

## Incentivizing Renewables and Household Efficiency

We can do so much more than what we currently are doing to shift from a society based on fossil fuels to one based on renewable energy. Governments of affluent nations are spending tens of millions of dollars annually in renewable research and development (R&D). But relative to other expenditures, this is a remarkably small sum. According to the American Association for the Advancement of Science, the United States spent $4.36 billion on nondefense energy research in 2012. The good news is that's more than twice the amount from a decade ago, adjusted for inflation—still considerably less, however, than what the government was spending in the late 1970s at the height of the energy crisis. The bad news: that's a fraction of the federal budget for health and space research and a really small fraction of what the Pentagon spent on defense and international security assistance (more than $700 billion). And the ugly news: funding for energy-related research has *dropped* since 2012, thanks to congressional budget caps and the sequester (Plumer 2013).

A **carbon tax** is one widely discussed strategy to disincentivize the use of fossil fuels—especially coal—for electricity generation. The rationale behind such a tax is fairly simple. A carbon tax would make the market price of this fossil fuel more accurately reflect its true cost, for, as discussed earlier, electricity generated from this nonrenewable is currently incorrectly priced (to use standard economic parlance), as many of its real costs—such as to the environment and public health—are presently not accounted for. In other words, these costs are currently treated as an **externality** (a cost or benefit not transmitted through prices and incurred by a party who did not agree to the action causing the cost or benefit). It is also clear that coal-plant owners will only invest in technology like carbon capture and storage if they are convinced the price of carbon is going to remain high long enough to justify the additional expense associated with these facilities. A carbon tax would signal to investors that "cheap" (incorrectly priced) coal is a thing of the past and that investments in carbon capture make sense—and cents.

It is less clear, however, if a carbon tax would change consumer behavior (ECOnnection 9.5). Households historically have not responded to rising energy prices by making sufficient energy-efficiency investments. Part of the reason for this is because, as stated earlier, people on average poorly estimate how their actions consume or save electricity. (I mentioned previously how individuals tend to overemphasize curtailment over efficiency improvements.) This is in part because efficiency improvements—such as installing new windows or buying new energy-efficient appliances—almost always require out-of-pocket costs, whereas curtailment (like turning lights off) costs nothing. A carbon tax could conceivably, by making energy more expensive in the short term (before renewables catch up), cause individuals to place even more emphasis on curtailment. As rising energy costs would no doubt be at the forefront of consumers' minds—the media love to remind people when these are increasing—this would likely cause people to become even more vigilant to turn things off. Conversely, efficiency improvements might be seen as an expense that cannot be afforded at the moment. I see it all the time. As more of their paychecks are redirected toward paying for rising energy costs, the last thing many consumers want to do is to spend even more money on, say, heating and cooling their homes by investing in a high-efficiency furnace or so-called

## ECOnnection 9.5
## Social Norms and Behavior

The power of **social norms** tends to get properly emphasized in introductory sociology classes, but then, for some reason, it gets forgotten about in upper-level social science courses. The truth is social norms matter—a lot. Street musicians know this. So do baristas at coffee shops. That's why they put money into their guitar cases and tip jars: we know that when other people are doing something, the rest of us are more likely to follow. To be really effective, however, they should take it a step further and have a friend come by every few minutes and drop a dollar in. Why? The one predictor of giving money to a street musician is being near a person who gave money. How many times have you been in a hotel and read the following message: "Please reuse your towel and help us save the environment"? If you're like me, you've come across it too many times to count. And yet we know from experimental evidence that this is a terribly ineffective message (see, e.g., Goldstein, Cialdini, and Griskevicius 2008). So what works? Telling people that the average person actually does reuse their towels. For example, "More than 75 percent of the people in this hotel room reused their towels." We typically like to think of ourselves as normal, especially in relationship to our personally perceived reference groups. If we think our reference group is doing $X$, then we are more likely to start doing $X$ too. One of the problems is that we're so caught up in changing people's attitudes—making them "think more ecologically"—that we're missing what really motivates us most of the time. Yes, we do some things because we feel deeply connected to $X$. But more often, the reasons for our behaviors are more mundane.

*Source: Adapted from Cross (2014).*

high-performance windows, even though those short-term costs will eventually pay for themselves (many times over) in the long run.

Subsidies could play a useful role in changing behaviors. Financial incentives—from subsidized loans to deferred-payment loans, rebates, and tax credits—to reduce initial out-of-pocket costs would help consumers overcome certain barriers to improving household efficiency. We also need to be aware of nonmonetary barriers, which could be overcome by utilities or governments providing free energy audits, lists of approved contractors, and help in securing low-cost financing and inspection of completed work (Kastner and Stern 2015). Community-based efforts that rely on informal social networks to help spread information and knowledge on strategies for improving the energy efficiency of homes could also facilitate people making efficiency improvements to their homes (McKenzie-Mohr 2011).

There is an old saying that has been evoked in different forms over the centuries—from such diverse sources as Christianity, Eastern philosophy, and even Shakespeare—about how the depths of darkness also house the most brilliant light. There are clearly many ways that this can be interpreted. The one that interests me here is the environmental sociological interpretation. Namely, there is value in delving into the problems that plague us, for only through an understanding of their roots are lasting and real solutions proposed. Thus far, we've covered a lot of terrain that has encompassed both problems and solutions. But I dare say we have yet to roll up our sleeves and discuss what it is about how we organize society that makes environmental problems so prevalent. That changes in the proceeding chapters. The following section goes to depths yet to be explored in the hope of uncovering that light of understanding that we'll need to organize a truly sustainable society.

## IMPORTANT CONCEPTS

- clean coal
- energy curtailment versus efficiency
- hydraulic fracturing (aka fracking)
- normal accident
- nuclear power life cycle

## DISCUSSION QUESTIONS

1. The process of shifting away from certain energy sources and toward others will create winners and losers as, for instance, jobs move out of one region and into another. What becomes of the "losers" (like rural coal-mining communities) in a so-called green economy?
2. I have had people tell me that even if fracking does negatively affect those living near wells, we shouldn't place their interests above those of society. Some contaminated wells are a small price to pay for cheap, domestically produced energy, they tell me. What's your response to such a position?
3. Why are governments not investing more in renewable R&D? Or should research into renewable energy be entirely left up to the private sector?
4. Have you replaced all your old-fashioned incandescent lightbulbs with newer, more efficient illuminants (like CFLs)? If not, why? What other easy steps to reduce your energy footprint have you yet to do? And why haven't you?

## SUGGESTED ADDITIONAL READINGS

McAdam, D., and H. Boudet. 2012. *Putting Social Movements in Their Place: Explaining Opposition to Energy Projects in the United States, 2000–2005*. Cambridge: Cambridge University Press.

Selfa, T., C. Bain, and R. Moreno. 2014. "Depoliticizing Land and Water 'Grabs' in Colombia: The Limits of Bonsucro Certification for Enhancing Sustainable Biofuel Practices." *Agriculture and Human Values* 31(3): 455–468.

Steinhilber, S., P. Wells, and S. Thankappan. 2013. "Socio-Technical Inertia: Understanding the Barriers to Electric Vehicles." *Energy Policy* 60:531–539.

Williams, L., P. Macnaghten, R. Davies, and S. Curtis. 2015. "Framing 'Fracking': Exploring Public Perceptions of Hydraulic Fracturing in the United Kingdom." *Public Understanding of Science*, July 13.

## RELEVANT INTERNET LINKS

- www.eia.gov/countries. US Energy Information Administration. This site offers a wealth of energy-related data for more than two hundred countries.
- www.iaea.org. International Atomic Energy Agency. Information relating to nuclear power.
- www.thewindpower.net. An extensive global wind-turbine and wind-farm database.
- www.ucsusa.org. Union of Concerned Scientists' site on clean energy. Publications available for download and blogs.

## SUGGESTED VIDEOS

- *Aftermath: World Without Oil* (2010, series). Looks into the future and reveals what would happen if the world fundamentally changed.
- *The Cleantech Future* (2012). Explores what it takes to live in a clean world, a world where energy is 100 percent renewable, where water is no longer polluted, and where transportation is green.
- *The Ethics of Fracking* (2014). This documentary assesses all the costs that come with this form of energy extraction.
- *Fracking in America* (2012). A critical look at the politics behind fracking in the United States.
- *Fractured Earth* (2015). A short but impassioned documentary about the impact of fracking in rural Pennsylvania.
- *Fuel* (2010). More than eleven years in the making, the film documents the United States' addiction to fossil fuels and explores viable alternatives.
- *The Future of Energy* (2015). Set in Greensburg, Kansas, with a population of just under a thousand. In 2007, a tornado struck the town. The community decided to rebuild by harnessing the same power that was once the cause of its destruction: wind. Today, Greensburg is entirely operated on renewable wind energy.
- *GasHole* (2011). Film about the history of oil and existing viable alternatives to fossil fuels.
- *Gasland* (2010). An exposé of the widespread water pollution resulting from hydraulic fracturing.
- *Inside Chernobyl* (2012). A film based on current conditions in Chernobyl and Pripyat, where the Soviet government tried to cover up a catastrophic nuclear accident.
- *The Last Drop* (2011). A story about the tar sands in the Canadian wilderness.
- *The Last Mountain* (2010). A remarkable exposé on the threats of coal mining and corporate greed toward human, community, and environmental health.
- *Momenta* (2013). An environmental conservation film looking at communities in the Pacific Northwest and their fight against the coal export industry.
- *The Next Wave* (2013). A look at some of the aftermath of the disaster in Fukushima, Japan. Testing authorized by the government has detected a frightening spike in the occurrence of thyroid cancer in Fukushima children, and while doctors are unwilling to draw an authoritative link between the cancer and the nuclear radiation that spewed from the hazardous power plant, they're genuinely worried.

- *The Spill* (2010). www.pbs.org/wgbh/papges/frontline/the-spill. An investigation into the trail of problems—accidents, deaths, spills, and safety violations—that have long plagued the oil and energy company BP. Could the 2010 disaster in the Gulf of Mexico have been prevented?
- *Uranium: Is It a Country?* (2011). Highlights the opportunities and risks posed by nuclear energy, while paying particular attention to the costs of uranium mining.
- *Windfall* (2010). Highlights the benefits as well as the potential costs that come with large-scale wind-power generation.

Part III

# ORGANIZING A SUSTAINABLE SOCIETY

# 10

# Political Economy: Making Markets
# Fair and Sustainable

In his 1865 book, *The Coal Question*, in the chapter titled "Of the Economy of Fuel," William Stanley Jevons highlights the paradox of how the rising efficiency of coal used in production was associated with rising coal consumption. The Jevons paradox is based on a not-so-paradoxical principle: any time the cost of consuming a resource is reduced, people will respond by consuming more of it. Its implications, however, are profound. It suggests that in our rush to save the environment and natural resources through efficiency gains, we may be unintentionally hastening their demise. A related term is *the rebound effect,* which occurs when gains in efficiency fail to lead to proportional reductions in consumption—for example, when a 20 percent gain in efficiency leads to a reduction in consumption or waste of only 10 percent. When a rebound effect is more than 100 percent of the efficiency gain, it is called a Jevons paradox (see Case Study 10.1).

The line between where a rebounded effect ends and a Jevons paradox begins, however, is quite murky. Take the efficiency gains of hybrid cars. By going farther on each unit of gasoline, they are making travel by car cheaper, even with rising gas prices. And whenever something becomes cheaper, we respond by doing more of it. Let's say the efficiency gains accrued by your purchasing a new hybrid car still outweigh the losses incurred by your increases in driving—perhaps you now take more road trips on weekends after buying this vehicle. What precisely do you do with those savings? If you're like most people, you take those savings and spend them on something else—a vacation to Hawaii, a new iPhone, or perhaps on another vehicle. The problem is that we tend to reinvest efficiency gains in additional consumption, which arguably nullifies the ecological gain of *any* gain in efficiency (Owen 2011).

The amount of energy, for example, required to produce each unit of the world's economic output—what is known as **energy intensity**—has fallen more or less steadily over the past half century. Energy intensity in the United States is more than half what it was in 1975 (Lovins 2014). Since 1980, world real GDP, based on USDA Economic

## CASE STUDY 10.1

# Compact Fluorescent Bulbs: Jevons Paradox or Rebound Effect?

I have a confession to make: I sometimes leave lights on in my house for extended periods of time. It all started when my wife and I switched out all our incandescents for compact fluorescent bulbs. The average life of a CFL is between eight and fifteen times that of incandescents, and they use 20 to 33 percent of the power of equivalent incandescents—a truly remarkable gain in efficiency over the old lighting technology. Or it would seem. The problem is that our lighting behaviors changed with the adoption of the technology. Before the changeover, my wife and I hated leaving lights on for long periods of time. This meant no night-light for our daughter. We were also very hesitant to leave lights on in

the house when we went on extended trips. Not anymore. We now leave at least one light on all night for our two kids. And when we go on vacation, we always make sure at least one room is partially illuminated. We have the CFL bulbs to thank for this change in behavior. I cannot say whether this is a Jevons paradox or a rebound effect. I'd like to think the overall efficacy gained by switching over to CFLs outweighs our increased household bulb use, and as I think more about it, I am quite sure it does. Nevertheless, this remains a personal reminder of why efficiency gains alone should not be expected to solve all of our ecological ills.

Research Institute data, has also been growing faster than global energy use (based on BP Statistical Data). That is to say, global energy intensity has been decreasing, on average, about 0.8 percent annually. Meanwhile, global **carbon intensity**—the amount of $CO_2$ emitted for each unit of economic output produced—fell by an average of roughly 1 percent a year from 2000 to 2014.

This is great—right? It would be, if subsequent increases in productivity were not occurring faster than the aforementioned efficiency gains. To put it simply, while we are producing each unit more efficiently, we are also producing so many more units that we've more than offset any gains in efficiency (see Figure 10.1). Thus, even with those aforementioned reductions in carbon and energy intensities, global $CO_2$ emissions are projected to increase, according to BP estimates—yes, *that* BP (not known for its climate change doom and gloom messaging)—by 25 percent between 2013 and 2035 (BP 2015). It seems we need to develop a language whereby we clearly differentiate between two distinct types of efficiencies. There is, on the one hand, *relative efficiency*, which refers to the well-documented decreasing (per unit) intensities. But there is also, and this is where real sustainability resides, *absolute efficiency*, which refers to a reduction in total throughput and emissions. From a long-term sustainability perspective, what good is the former if we continue to increase our overall impact on the environment?

Don't get me wrong: it is not that we should entirely discount relative efficiency gains. We must not confuse them, however, for absolute efficiency gains, either. Otherwise,

**FIGURE 10.1** Carbon Intensity and Meeting Climate Change Goals

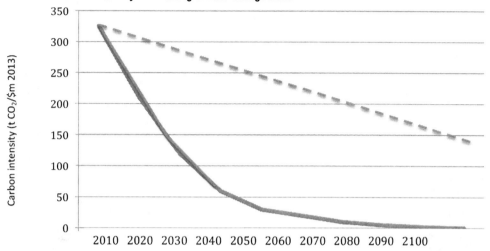

t $CO_2$/$m: tons of $CO_2$ emitted per each million dollars (in 2013 dollars) generated by the global economy. At current rates of reducing carbon intensity—roughly 0.8 percent annually (signified by the dashed line)—we would be heading toward the worst projected scenario of the IPCC, leading to a significant change of exceeding 4° Celsius of warming. To meet the global carbon emission goals to limit warming to 2° Celsius, the global economy needs to reduce carbon intensity by 6.2 percent a year for every year between now and 2100 (signified by the solid line). Doing that will mean the global energy system will be essentially zero carbon by the end of this century. Source: Adapted from PWC (2014).

we risk what I like to call **efficiency shifting**: namely, when money and resources saved through energy efficiency, such as from placing solar panels on the roof of a manufacturing plant, merely get shifted to and consumed by other goods and services, like increases in the use of air travel for shipping or business-related travel. Another example: industry-level efficiencies gains in the United States or United Kingdom that occur merely because those countries, through regulations, pushed polluting companies and industrial practices into other countries. We see this happen all the time. The money saved by homeowners through energy savings is used, for example, to buy more energy-using gadgets. Or note how the efficiency gains in the internal combustion engine made during the latter half of the twentieth century led to larger vehicles ultimately giving birth to the SUV boom in the late 1990s. Sociologist Richard York (2010) examined trends in $CO_2$ emissions and the carbon intensity of the global economy as well as for its top-five $CO_2$-emitting nations: China, the United States, Russia, India, and Japan. These countries, in 2006, accounted for 55 percent of total world emissions, 52 percent of world GDP, and 46 percent of world population. York found that although each economy (and the global economy as a whole) is trending toward improved relative efficiency gains in terms of $CO_2$ emissions (per inflation adjustment unit of GDP), their overall $CO_2$ footprints are growing at alarming rates. Figure 10.2 illustrates these trends for the United States.

This chapter, like those that follow, goes deeper than the ones preceding it. It does not take a professional sociologist, ecologist, or economist to realize there is something profoundly amiss with the current system, that the path we are presently on is

**FIGURE 10.2** $CO_2$ Emissions, United States, 1980–2006

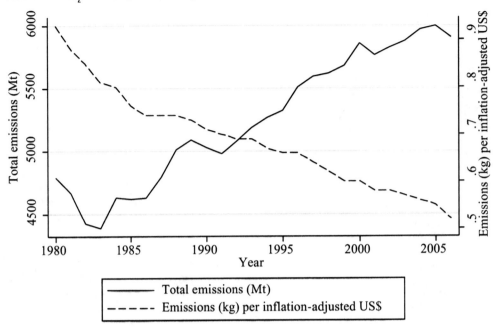

Source: Courtesy of Richard York.

fundamentally unsustainable, and that real social change is needed. What that current system is and how it might be changed are the subjects of this chapter and the remaining ones. I begin by outlining the structures of the current system while also taking time in the Solutions section to reorient us toward more sustainable directions.

## Fast Facts

- Market economies are narrowly conceived: corporations utilize people and capital—like buildings and machinery—to make goods and services that households in turn buy. The remainder of household income is then either saved or invested. These components collectively constitute what is known as the circular flow of the economy (Mankiw 2014).

- Narrow understandings of market economies are gravely short-sighted as they neglect a group of important variables: the laws of physics. As an article coauthored by a team of world-renowned ecologists, social scientists, and economists states: "We use a macro-ecological approach to integrate perspectives of physics, ecology, and economics with an analysis of extensive global data to show how energy imposes fundamental constraints on economic growth and development" (Brown et al. 2011, 19).

- **Natural capital** is not like typical capital assets such as bridges, roads, buildings, and machinery. Like capital assets, ecosystems depreciate when misused or overused. But they also differ from reproducible capital assets in three important ways (Dasgupta 2006). First, depreciated natural capital is often either slow to recover, like a polluted lake, or irreparable, such as a species extinction. Second, it is often difficult to substitute one depleted or exhausted ecosystem or ecosystem service for another. It would be impossible, for example, to replace the pollination services provided by bees. And third, ecosystems can collapse abruptly, with little prior warning, a point famously detailed in Jared Diamond's best-selling book *Collapse* (2006).

## Implications

Although environmental sociologists do not speak with one voice, they do share in the belief that business as usual is not an option. Economic growth is not only portrayed as the ideal contraceptive, as discussed earlier when talking about population, but cast as *the* cure-all elixir to whatever social or environmental ill might be ailing us. Are progress, prosperity, and well-being positively correlated with—and thus essentially reducible to—economic growth? And can economic growth go on indefinitely? These are empirical questions. In the chapters that remain, I look to see what the data have to say about economic growth, as to whether it's the cure, disease, or something in between.

In this chapter, I address a significant body of environmental sociology's theoretical core, particularly that which offers an explicit critique of the present system's unsustainable growth imperative. In doing this, I avoid subscribing to any totalizing narratives. Many of my colleagues, for example, feel strongly about chalking up most of the environment's (and humanity's) ills to capitalism. Although I agree with many of their central points, I don't find it particularly helpful to place blame without also offering pragmatic alternatives. Without well-thought-out alternatives, I am not convinced any of our problems would be solved by merely doing away with capitalism, an admittedly problematic mode of production. Moreover, echoing a point I made in Chapter 1, I am not convinced that any one thing is responsible for the mess we're in—an argument I intend to bolster in the remaining chapters. But I don't wish to minimize these scholars' valuable contributions: they are correct in highlighting the inherent problems associated with how we presently organize society and allocate its resources.

### The Growth Imperative

Capitalism, as currently practiced, makes growth an imperative rather than an option. Any business seeking to maintain rather than grow will be hastily eliminated from the market by its competitors. Going without economic growth for any length of time causes the entire global macroeconomic edifice to shake. Under this scenario, debts go unpaid, credit subsequently dries up, unemployment skyrockets, and the previously mentioned circular engine of growth begins to stall. And (infinite) growth *needs* (infinite) resources. By every aggregate measure, even with the aforementioned relative efficiencies, our impact upon the environment (our net throughput) is increasing. Global cement extraction just prior to the financial crisis was more than 125 percent greater than its 1990 level, iron ore roughly 100 percent higher, while bauxite, copper, and nickel extraction had increased more than 70 percent since 1990 (Jackson 2011). (Speaking of concrete, did you know China used more concrete in three years than the United States used in the entire twentieth century? Between 2011 and 2013 China consumed 6.6 gigatons of concrete, whereas the United States used 4.5 gigatons between 1901 and 2000 [McCarthy 2014].) This cannot go on indefinitely.

The hope—the *only* hope—for the status quo lies in something called **decoupling**, which refers to the ability of an economy to grow without corresponding increases in environmental pressure. Through decoupling, production processes are radically reconfigured and goods and services radically redesigned until economic output becomes entirely independent of material throughput. Right now, the two—economic output and material throughput—are tightly coupled: an increase in the former results in a more or less proportional increase in the latter. Only with decoupling can an economy grow indefinitely without risk of breaching ecological limits.

There is a small catch. Decoupling is looking more and more like a pipe dream. We cannot even achieve efficiency gains fast enough to offset global $CO_2$ increases in production and consumption. $CO_2$ is widely considered one of the easiest decoupling challenges for the simple reason that energy can be produced with no $CO_2$, as explained in Chapter 9. Compare this to, say, making a laptop with only renewable resources, which is at present an insurmountable challenge. The fact remains, energy production is tightly coupled to material resources and subsequently $CO_2$ emissions. So when I come across a statistic like the fact that the average American today buys a new piece of clothing every 5.4 days, up from 10.7 days just twenty years ago (Schor 2010), I get discouraged, as I know this growth in consumption comes with a growing ecological footprint. In 2015, the United States generated an average of twenty-five billion pounds of textile (clothing, footwear, towels, bedding, and so forth) waste per year—about eighty-two pounds per US resident (Council for Textile Recycling 2015). What does the environmental sociology literature have to say about this?

## The Treadmill of Production

The treadmill of production is one of the core theoretical frameworks in environmental sociology. Its roots extend back to Allan Schnaiberg's classic *The Environment: From Surplus to Scarcity* (1980), where the concept is given its first thorough treatment. It is a macrolevel framework, in that it places particular attention on institutions and social structures. It is also a quasi-Marxist framework. As John Bellamy Foster, a leading ecological Marxist, puts it, without directly naming "the system" at the heart of today's ecological crisis, this literature has developed the treadmill concept to the point that it has become the functional equivalent of capitalism (2005, 7–8).

According to treadmill-of-production scholars, modern capitalistic societies are driven by a never-ending commitment to growth, despite—and equally because of—its social and ecological costs. In pursuit of profit maximization, corporations are continually seeking ways to expand production. With the support of government and a complicit public, industrial production is allowed to expand, which in turn places still more demands on nature while creating growing amounts of waste. In other words, production begets more production, as all sectors of society depend on economic growth to solve the world's problems—e.g., unemployment, environmental degradation, and poverty and inequality—even though those very problems were caused, to various degrees, by growth itself. The following is a nonsequential breakdown of the treadmill logic from Schnaiberg and Gould (1994):

- Increasing accumulation and concentration of wealth as fewer businesses remain on the treadmill.
- Increasing movement of workers toward the private sector (as the public sector shrinks), thereby making it necessary to continually expand production in order to gain jobs and wages.

- Increasing allocations of wealth to businesses that replace labor with capital, which generates more profits for wealth holders and creates pressures for all wealth holders to adopt similar practices if they wish to remain competitive. This places smaller businesses, which do not have the capital to adopt these technologies, at a continual disadvantage. As smaller businesses then fall off the treadmill, wealth (point 1) and market share become further concentrated.
- The net result of ever-increasing production is an ever-increasing need for greater ecological withdrawals (resource extraction and utilization) and additions (pollution).
- Societies become increasingly vulnerable to socioeconomic disorganization as their ecological resource base is undermined.

## Internal Contradictions

Alongside capitalism's insatiable thirst for growth lie certain internal contradictions that threaten its very existence. Through the writings of Karl Marx, scholars have been able to identify some of these threats. Thus far, however, these contradictions have had just the opposite effect, speeding the treadmill up rather than slowing it down (or causing it to fall apart entirely). As highlighted in the previous section, capitalism has proven to be wily, using problems of its making to hasten the circular engine of growth and expand its reach, an invisible hand—to evoke Adam Smith's famous metaphor—that now extends not only around the globe but up into the heavens with the privatization of space (Dickens and Ormrod 2007) and all the way down to the genetic level (Carolan 2010a). The question remains: How long until these problems become so great, with climate change coming immediately to mind, that we can no longer turn to the market for our solutions?

## Metabolic Rift

One such argument draws on some of Marx's more obscure comments on matters of economic growth and natural resource exploitation and the rift these processes create. These writings were rediscovered largely thanks to Foster, who brought them to the attention of the environmental sociology community (1999). And so was born (or reborn) the metabolic rift thesis, as it has come to be known.

Mid-nineteenth-century environmental crises—from declining agricultural soil fertility to rising levels of sewage in cities—and the equally deplorable living conditions of urban workers were linked, according to Marx, to a disruption, or rift, in a previously sustainable socioecological metabolism. This rift, for Marx, is tied to the expansion of capitalist modes of production and urbanization—the latter made possible because of the rise of the former and in particular the displacement of small-scale agriculture. This process created a rift in ecological systems, leading to environmental degradation at points of production and consumption as people and their waste became concentrated in cities.

Inspired by the work of German chemist Justus von Liebig and his (later in life) ecological critique of modern agricultural methods, Marx derided the problem of "soil exhaustion"—what we today would call soil depletion. At one point in volume 1 of *Capital*, Marx writes that "all progress in capitalist agriculture is a progress in the art, not only of robbing the worker, but of robbing the soil" ([1863] 1976, 638). Concerns over soil exhaustion became rather acute in Britain in the early 1800s, arising as an important issue slightly later in North America and continental Europe in parallel with their emerging capitalist economies. Early on, the problem of diminished soil fertility was resolved by mixing into the soil guano (dung) imported from Peru, which eventually was replaced with artificial fertilizers.

Soil exhaustion during this period has been linked to the expansion of capitalism, which drew people into the cities to work in factories. As such, land had to be farmed utilizing more inputs to support a growing population and soon thereafter with machinery so a shrinking rural population could continue to farm all available arable land. Disconnecting people from the land caused major disruptions in the soil nutrient cycle in the form of too few nutrients in the countryside and far too many concentrated in cities, often in the form of sewage. The summer of 1858 in London was famously known as the summer of the Big Stink, as the Thames's smell was so foul that lawmakers were forced to flee Parliament for the countryside. These disruptions reeked both ecological and social havoc, a point Marx witnessed firsthand in London, where "they can do nothing better with the excrement produced by 4½ million people than pollute the Thames with it, at monstrous expense" ([1863–1865] 1981, 195). And what was the solution to this problem? Was it to repair the rift by bringing agricultural practices in line with ecological limits? No. Instead, the solution was to exacerbate the rift through artificial fertilizers—a solution that also sped up the treadmill, as those inputs had to be manufactured and purchased. This move might have resolved the problem of soil exhaustion in the short term, but it did nothing to deal with the root of the rift, as evidenced by the fact that our food continues to be produced in a fundamentally unsustainable manner.

The consequences of this rift are all around us (see ECOnnection 10.1). The first European Nitrogen Assessment (ENA) was released in 2011. It documents that nitrogen pollution is costing each person in Europe around $170 to $830 annually. The ENA represents the first time that the multiple threats of nitrogen pollution, including its impact on climate change and biodiversity, have been valued in economic terms on a continental scale. The study, carried out by two hundred experts from twenty-one countries and eighty-nine organizations, calculates that the annual cost of damage caused by nitrogen throughout Europe is $78 billion to $360 billion, a figure that is more than double the income gained from using nitrogen fertilizers in European agriculture (Sutton et al. 2011).

The overarching critique of the metabolic-rift thesis is the notion that capitalism, by its nature, is slowly yet undeniably destroying the very thing it needs to survive: its material productive base. Clark and York put it as follows: "'Metabolic rift' refers to an ecological rupture in the metabolism of a system. The natural processes and cycles (such as the soil nutrient cycle) are interrupted. The division between town and country is a particular geographical manifestation of the metabolic rift, in regards to the soil nutrient cycle. But the essence of a metabolic rift is *the rupture or interruption of a natural system*" (2005, 399; emphasis in the original).

## Another Contradiction of Capitalism

Capitalism, as I've already described, has proven most resourceful. Population growth has no doubt aided in its growth. There is also a geographical dimension to its success,

## ECOnnection 10.1
## Treadmill/Metabolic Rift: Declining Global Fish Stocks

Expansion of the capitalist enterprise into oceans has created another rift, signified by the depletion of fish stock (Clausen 2005; Longo, Clausen, and Clark 2015). As natural limits are approached, new technology is required to improve productivity and (temporarily) resolve tensions. Initially, making boats faster (so they can cover more territory) and larger (so they can stay out longer) and equipping them with technology to fish deeper (so greater depths can be exploited) seemed to do the trick. For a while, these gains in efficiency helped to keep supply up and the retail price of fish down, even as global fish stocks shrunk. These technological advances, however, did nothing to resolve the ecological tensions between capitalism and the aquatic ecosystems that are home to the world's ocean fish stock. In fact, they had precisely the opposite effect, as they sped up the treadmill. And so still more technological fixes were required. Enter capitalist aquaculture: a practice whereby fish are essentially treated like livestock. Yet the ecological limits still remain. As the most profitable farmed fish are carnivorous (e.g.,

Atlantic salmon), aquaculture continues to depend on wild fish, as they constitute the primary ingredient of fishmeal and fish oil. A farmed Atlantic salmon, for example, consumes four pounds of fishmeal for each one pound of live weight gain.

The treadmill of capital-intensive aquaculture is now running so fast that only a privileged few can compete in the market. A prawn farm in Queensland, Australia, for example, with all appropriate equipment, ponds, buildings, and processing facilities (*not* including land costs), is estimated to cost between AU$100,000 and $150,000 per hectare of pond. And the cost of an intensive pond-culture system that grows fifty tons of barramundi (also known as Asian sea bass) is AU$780,000. As the market becomes dominated by economically efficient (and ecologically inefficient) models of aquaculture, the small-scale fisher will find it increasingly difficult to remain economically viable. This is unfortunate, as the livelihoods of roughly fifty-five million people in less affluent nations are dependent on being able to sell the fish they catch (FAO 2012).

most notably globalization. Yet, as Marx and Engels ([1848] 1978) noted so long ago, these tendencies produce contradictions, which must be resolved in some form so as not to derail the circulation of capital. And therein lies capitalism's transformational engine: these contradictions and tensions that it then "resolves." This has allowed capitalism to continue on the tracks without (yet?) a major derailing of its logics.

Marx and Engels predicted that eventually such tensions would become too much for capitalism: "The development of Modern Industry, therefore, cuts from under its feet the very foundation on which the bourgeoisie produces and appropriates productions. What the bourgeoisie, therefore, produces, above all, is its own grave-diggers" (Marx and Engels [1848] 1978, 483). The first contradiction of capitalism, as described by Marx and Engels, is overproduction—that eventually there will simply be too much stuff and not enough people able to buy it all. Continually substituting labor for capital logic would suggest that capitalism will eventually reach a point where low salaries and unemployment (and underemployment) will make it impossible for consumption rates to increase indefinitely. Before we ever reach this point, however, capitalism may hit a wall that stops it in its tracks. That's James O'Connor's thesis at least, which he calls the second contradiction of capital. Whereas the contradiction discussed by Marx and Engels centers on a crisis of demand, for O'Connor capitalism will, over time, witness a crisis of supply. This underproduction will occur as industry and the state—both of which are directed by the logics of capital—fail to protect the conditions of production, namely, the environment. "Put simply," in the words of O'Connor, "the second contradiction states that when individual capitals attempt to defend or restore profits by cutting or externalizing costs, the unintended effect is to reduce the 'productivity' of the conditions of production" (1998, 245) (see ECOnnection 10.2). Or more simply still: no more resources, no more capitalism.

## Globalization of Environmental Goods and Bads

One myth that continues to be perpetuated is that economic growth is good for the environment. An example of a narrative supporting this myth comes from the Property and Environmental Research Center, the oldest pro–free market and private property institute in the United States. As one of the center's analysts writes, "Market forces also cause economic growth, which in turn leads to environmental improvements. Put simply, poor people are willing to sacrifice clean water and air, healthy forests, and wildlife habitat for economic growth" (Anderson 2004). What this quote misses is that well-off people do this too. And when you factor in for scale of impact, the environmental footprint of the impoverished turns out to be minuscule compared to the ecological damage inflicted daily to maintain the standard of living the affluent have come to expect. This should already be perfectly clear, based on what has been discussed thus far in the book. But in case you still need a little more convincing, allow me to take on a cherished concept among growth enthusiasts: the Environmental Kuznets Curve (EKC).

## Critiquing the Environmental Kuznets Curve

Simon Kuznets, who won a Nobel Prize in economics in 1971, famously postulated that a country's transition from preindustrial to industrial to postindustrial initially leads to increasing income inequality, followed by greater income equality, and overall increases in per capita incomes (1955). In the past two decades, the model was extended to environmental pollutants, as early analyses seemed to indicate that although air and water pollution levels frequently increased with initial economic growth, they eventually declined as countries reached a certain level of affluence (Dasgupta et al. 2002). This apparent pattern has come to be known as the Environmental Kuznets Curve. The EKC simply states that growth is (eventually) good for the environment. Although initially positively correlated with pollution, at some point economic growth becomes negatively associated with pollution and positively correlated with environmental quality (see Figure 10.3).

There was some early empirical support for the EKC. Grossman and Krueger (1994), for example, examined urban air pollution levels as well as water pollution for a number of countries. They found pollution indexes increased and then declined with economic affluence. In more recent years, however, the EKC has come under fire for

ECOnnection 10.2

# Capital Shaping Humans in Its Image: A Third Contradiction?

Some sociologists (e.g., Bates 2015; Dickens 2001, 2004; Meloni 2014) have applied Marx's writings in a unique way to speak about potential linkages between the biological and the social. According to one sociologist of this persuasion, Peter Dickens (2001, 106), "Capitalism, in conjunction with the various forms of biological predispositions . . . may over the long term have been shaping human biology in its own image." For evidence of this phenomenon, Dickens points to, among other things, epidemiological work suggesting that the effects of the mother's environment are transmitted to her unborn child. The implication is that inadequate prenatal care—which can alter normal (in developmental terms) rates of metabolism, hormonal excretion, blood flow, and the like within the uterus—can potentially lead to individuals born physiologically disadvantaged compared to those with adequate resources and capital. Or take a recent study published in the *Journal of Health and Social Behavior*, which found that the urban poor in the United States are experiencing accelerated aging at the cellular level and chronic stress, which is associated with a whole host of negative health outcomes (Geronimus et al. 2015). In short, the study demonstrates that these forms of physiological deterioration are linked to socioeconomic variables, namely income level and racial and ethnic identity. This research points to interesting questions concerning the interrelationship between society and biology. Can being socially underprivileged and disadvantaged produce physiological changes that amplify those aforementioned social conditions? Perhaps. It is a question worth exploring in greater detail.

mischaracterizing the extent of the environmental "efficiencies" that are said to be correlated with economic growth.

One criticism centers on what has come to be known as the Pollution Haven Hypothesis (PHH). Following the logic of comparative advantage, it is reasonable to assume that developing economies with weaker environmental regulations (and lax government enforcement of whatever regulations do exist) would attract polluting industries. Thus, the PHH posits that what we are seeing with the EKC is actually the result of polluting industry moving from developed to developing countries in search of governments more likely to ignore their activities. Though a reasonable hypothesis, it does not stand up well to empirical scrutiny. Studies have found "little" (Kearsley and Riddel 2010, 905) to at best "some" (Eskelanda and Harrison 2003, 1) evidence in support of the PHH. One major reason is that environmental costs are, for most industries, a relatively small share of overall operating costs. In other words, the benefit of being able to pollute does not typically outweigh other costs that would be incurred as a result of relocating to a haven, such as a poor infrastructure or undertrained labor force.

It is important to point out that the PHH speaks only to *emissions* associated with production, ignoring, for example, the mountains of toxic e-waste that end up being shipped annually to less developed countries to be recycled. As mentioned in Chapter

**FIGURE 10.3** Environmental Kuznets Curve

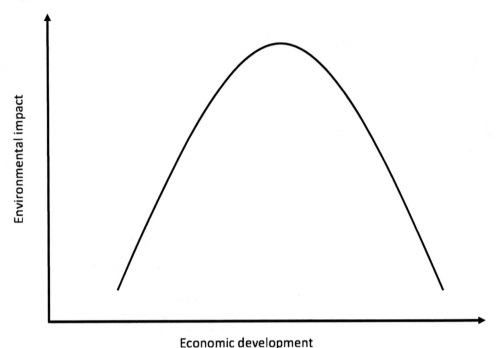

3, the evidence is mixed as to what actually gets recycled and what is landfilled or incinerated. My point is that the ecological footprint of a nation is more—*much* more—than its emissions. There is ample anecdotal evidence indicating that affluent nations are exporting their "environmental impact" (to reference the *y* axis in Figure 10.3) to other nations. We just have to look beyond industrial air emissions to find it. E-waste is only one well-publicized example. We also must realize that residents of affluent nations might also pollute *differently* from their contemporaries in lower-income nations. An example of this is air travel. Some 2 million people daily—or 730 million annually—fly in the United States (Burns 2010). In Indonesia, by comparison, which has roughly 75 percent of the population found in the United States, approximately 50 million flights are taken annually (Baskoro 2011). The EKC's most fatal flaw, however, resides in its mistaking *relative* efficiency for *absolute* efficiency. Technically speaking, as I tell my students, the EKC and its inverted-U curve are both right and wrong. It all depends on how you define ecoefficiency (see ECOnnection 10.3). The data on this are clear: while the most affluent nations tend to be the most ecoefficient, as measured by ecological footprint per unit of GDP, they are also guilty of having, in absolute terms, the largest ecological footprints (see, e.g., Brizga, Mishchuk, and Golubovska-Onisimova 2014; Toth and Szigeti 2016).

## World-Systems Framework

Another body of literature highly critical of the EKC is the world-systems approach. This tradition in environmental sociology has produced a diverse array of sophisticated analyses to assess the relationship between world-system factors and environmental

ECOnnection 10.3

# Forest Transition Theory

In the early 1990s, Alexander Mather (1990, 1992) began writing about what became known as the Forest Transition Theory (FTT). Much like the EKC, the FTT speaks to a recurring pattern that countries seem to go through as they industrialize and urbanize. First, the theory posits, they go through a process of rapid deforestation while initially industrializing. At some point, however, after ascertaining a certain level of economic development, deforestation stops and reforestation begins.

Early formulations focused almost exclusively on Europe and North America. In the past ten years, greater focus has been placed on less affluent countries. The results have been mixed. A number of studies, for instance, illustrate how agricultural retreat and forest recovery in one area typically occur only at the expense of agricultural expansion and deforestation elsewhere (see, for example, Pfaff and Walker 2010). Evidence is also beginning to emerge suggesting that reforestation, in countries fortunate enough to undergo it, may be only a temporary phase, eventually giving way to still further drivers of deforestation. This appears to be happening in the eastern portion of the United States (Drummond and Loveland 2010). After a period of reforestation, recent prospects for additional forested land have diminished, as accelerated rates of forest cutting, low-density development in the countryside, and pressures placed on land from biofuels are, once again, causing a net loss of forests in this region (see Figure 10.4).

FIGURE 10.4 Forest Cover Changes in the Eastern United States

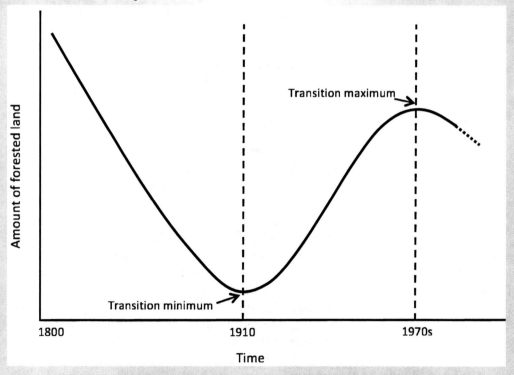

Source: Adapted from Drummond and Loveland (2010).

impacts. The relationship between affluent (aka "core") and less affluent (aka "periphery") nations, according to this literature, is an overwhelmingly exploitative one, as the former are able to extract far greater benefits from the present system than actors residing in the latter. Studies have shown, for example, that an EKC for $CO_2$ emissions may be fundamentally unattainable for many periphery nations, as their position in the global economy has effectively fixed them into a particular emissions trajectory. As a result, they are locked out of being able to adopt many of the greener technologies used in affluent nations, for reasons like a lack of credit, capital, expertise, and the like (see, e.g., Rosa et al. 2015). Other research in this tradition has extensively documented the gross asymmetry between core nations, which consume the vast majority of the world's resources and produce a sizable chunk of its pollution, and those that are more peripheral, which experience the vast majority of the environmental *impacts* (Jorgenson and Clark 2012). One study, for example, tracked how consumption in the United States, a core country, triggers pollution throughout global commodity chains (Prell et al. 2014). As the authors of this study argue, "our findings show how the production of commodities for US consumption tends to reify inequalities in the world-system: larger shares of value added (in comparison to shares of pollution) are generally prompted within the core, whereas the opposite effect tends to be experienced in the non-core" (405).

## Solutions

In light of the deeply embedded nature of the problems discussed throughout this book, I ask the reader for patience as solutions are rolled out over this chapter and the remaining ones that take aim at their roots. The problems we face are complex, which is why I am certain that no single proposed solution is sufficient. The problems are products of patterns of social organization, which though deeply flawed are not irreversible. I am not offering these solutions in an either/or spirit. Put them to work *collectively*—that's the source of my pragmatic optimism.

### Total Cost Accounting

Many of the goods supplied by the environment are public in nature. A good is said to be public if it is nonrival and nonexcludable. Many ecological phenomena that we value, like biodiversity and clean air, exhibit these characteristics. Their nonrival character is evidenced by the fact that my use and enjoyment of these phenomena do not affect your use and enjoyment of them. For instance, my breathing as much clean air as I want does not affect your ability to stand next to me and enjoy the clean air too. They are also nonexcludable in the sense that it is usually rather difficult to prevent others from benefiting from their existence. Short of erecting domes around people or communities, how could you possibly make clean air excludable? Or take biodiversity, which is more problematic still from the standpoint of excludability. It benefits humanity in so many ways—from food security to the manufacturing of drugs, purifying of water, and enriching of spirit—that excludability means more than just keeping people out of a biologically diverse space.

As already discussed, the prevailing cost-price system is poorly equipped to account for damage to ecosystems and human communities. Climate change—the most

**IMAGE 10.1**

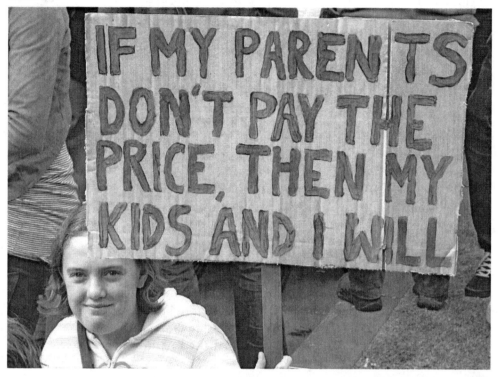

On World Environment Day, June 5, 2011, tens of thousands of people rallied around Australia to say yes to a carbon tax. This picture was taken on the lawn of the State Library in Melbourne, where thousands came to listen to speakers and music in a family-friendly rally. Source: "If my parents don't pay the price" by John Englart (flickr.com/takver) is licensed copyright © 2011 under CC BY-SA 2.0.

significant market failure in history—is proof that current market mechanisms cannot be entrusted to protect long-term public and environmental health. Public goods tend to be underprovided—and underprotected—if left to the market, as costs are externalized and paid disproportionately by third parties, future generations, or society at large. This practice of socializing costs not only makes for a terribly unsustainable economic system but is also incredibly unfair—a point I'll elaborate on in a moment. What, then, are our options if total cost accounting (or at least more honest cost accounting) is the goal? (See Image 10.1.)

One strategy that has been around for a while is known as **Pigovian taxes**—taxes levied on companies that pollute or create excess social costs (called negative externalities). English economist Arthur Cecil Pigou (1912) argued a century ago that the existence of externalities justifies government action. He advocated for pollution-avoidance charges and welfare-damage costs (aka taxes), which would be applied to any and all offending businesses and activities. Such taxes would not only serve to disincentivize certain behaviors but also generate revenue to pay whatever costs were socialized (e.g., to clean up a polluted river) as well as any expenses associated with the administration and monitoring of businesses.

The largest problem associated with Pigovian taxes involves getting the tax rate just right. If too low, the taxes will not sufficiently disincentivize the behavior or provide sufficient revenue to pay for cleanup and enforcement; if too high, businesses will be unduly burdened for costs that are not their own. Relatedly, information in these matters is always imperfect. For instance, when dealing with nonpoint-source pollution—like greenhouse gases—how can we be sure we're not overcharging some and undercharging others?

A notable challenge to the logic of Pigovian taxes came from economist Ronald Coase (1960), who argued that well-defined property rights to resources would nullify the need for government intervention and save society the inevitable efficiencies associated with antipollution taxes, noting the difficulty of getting tax rates just right. Coase's argument—or what is known today as the **Coase theorem**—alleges that when property rights are involved, parties naturally gravitate toward the most efficient and mutually beneficial outcome. Suppose a livestock producer holds the right to a stream (and thus the right—within limits—to pollute this stream) that a neighboring food processor draws its water from. Knowing precisely who owns what allows these individuals to negotiate an outcome that is suitable to both. The food processor has an incentive to pay the livestock producer to treat their wastewater, as long as that cost is less than the cost of treating their intake water. The livestock producer also has an incentive to accept payment, especially as they have an opportunity to profit from treating their waste. This is because the cost to the livestock producer of treating their concentrated manure will likely be less than the cost to the food processor for treating their more diluted intake water.

Unfortunately, real life is more complicated than idealized scenarios. What if there are thousands of competing businesses with interests in this outcome? What does the negotiating process look like, and how do we ensure all parties' interests are heard? Moreover, who decides what's sufficiently "clean" when talking about treating water? I promise you that a brewery's definition is astronomically stricter than a steel refinery's. There is also space to justify species extinction under such an arrangement. As long as the negotiating parties agree on a particular definition of *clean water*, what's to stop, say, an endangered bird that nests along the banks of the stream from going extinct if that definition does not suit the needs of wildlife? And what about future generations: Are they also to be left entirely out of this negotiating process?

Pricing tangible and visible costs is one thing, which is difficult enough. Yet there are no markets for many of the things we value that are associated with ecosystems and communities. The market price for a pickup load of logs, for example, says absolutely nothing about the value they played in a previous life for things like flood control, water purification, habitat, and carbon sinking. As William Rees, founding member and past president of the Canadian Society for Ecological Economics, correctly points out, "This is why the consumer purchasing a board foot of lumber—or just about anything else—doesn't come close to paying the full social cost of production" (2009, 470). So what are we to do? Again, Rees: "Such conclusions are not cause for despair but rather should liberate society from the dictates of oppressively wrong-headed economic models" (471). Merely coming to the realization that the market can't solve all our problems is half the battle. Once we realize this, a world of possibilities opens up.

## ECOnnection 10.4
## "Apolitical Ecologies" and Foucauldian Governance

The tendency to blame individuals for social and environmental problems is linked closely to the rise of neoliberalism and a shift toward neoliberal forms of what French philosopher Michel Foucault called "governance." Foucauldian governance, to admittedly oversimplify a highly nuanced concept, refers to the reduction of societal problems to an aggregate of individual ones. Doing this skillfully transfers responsibility for developing solutions from society as a whole onto individuals, making it up to individual consumers to do "the right thing." This move also supports the very system responsible for the problem in the first place. As good consumer-citizens, we are therefore taught to shop our way to safety, happiness, and sustainability by buying, in the case of environmental problems, ecofriendly products, high-efficiency gadgets, and carbon offsets.

Take the case of climate change. The most popular solutions are often individual ones, like buying hybrid cars, photovoltaic panels, and locally grown organic foods. Yet this disproportionately (and dangerously) places the focus on individual consumption choices rather than on creating policies that would enforce corporate accountability and lead to larger socioeconomic changes to the system responsible for the state we are in. In this sense, climate change can be seen as an **apolitical ecology**—a case in which explanations do not fully account for the asymmetries in power that first created it materially and then later define it as a problem to be solved by the same system that gave birth to it (Robbins 2012). This move effectively absolves that system of any blame.

### Fair Versus Free Trade

If markets are insufficient, what, then, are our options? Let's take a step back and look more closely at the precise type of capitalism that's driving today's global economy. It typically goes by the name of *neoliberalism*. As David Harvey explains in *A Brief History of Neoliberalism*, "Neoliberalism is in the first instance a theory of political economic practices that proposes that human well-being can best be advanced by liberating individual entrepreneurial freedoms and skills within an institutional framework characterized by strong private property rights, free markets, and free trade" (2005, 2). As opposed to individual liberties (the holy grail in classic liberalism), neoliberalism sees salvation only through free enterprise—and a really no-holds-barred, dog-eat-dog approach to free enterprise at that (see ECOnnection 10.4).

What, then, is free enterprise? Or, better yet, taking another step back, what does *freedom* mean? The term *free* comes up a lot when talking about markets: free markets, free enterprise, free trade, and so on. Like a small but growing cadre of economists (see, for instance, Sen 1984; Jackson 2009), I have found twentieth-century English philosopher Isaiah Berlin's dual understanding of freedom useful in this context (Carolan 2011b).

ECOnnection 10.5
# Fair Trade

Fair trade represents a producer-consumer relationship through a supply chain that attempts to distribute economic benefits more fairly between all stakeholders (Raynolds and Bennett 2015; see Image 10.2). This is in contrast to the conventional supply-chain model, which primarily seeks the maximization of return somewhere in the middle of the food system. Fair trade makes trade fairer through a number of practices. Some of these practices include the following (taken from Nicholls and Opal 2005, 6–7):

• *Agreed-upon minimum prices that are often higher than those set by the market.* This is in recognition that agricultural commodity market prices, thanks to things like subsidies and monopoly conditions, are rarely fair. Farmers are therefore given a living wage for their work.

• *An additional social premium paid on top of the fair trade price.* This allows producers and farm laborers to collectively implement larger development projects (like the building of new schools). How the

money is spent is usually decided democratically, through cooperatives.

• *Purchasing directly from producers.* This reduces the number of profit-taking "middle men" in the commodity chain and ensures that more of each dollar spent on the goods returns to producers.

• *Making credit available to producers.* As importers from affluent countries typically have greater access to credit than developing-country producers, importers must prefinance a significant portion of the year's harvest.

• *Democratically organized farmers and workers.* This helps minimize labor abuses (e.g., child and slave labor) and ensures socially responsible production practices.

A decade ago few had heard of *fair trade*. Today, the label is almost as widely recognized globally as *organic*. The extra income earned by fair trade producers from US sales alone has increased from almost zero in 1998 to roughly $40 million in 2012 (Dragusanu, Giovannucci, and Nunn 2014).

Conventional understandings of free markets remain dangerously fixated on only one side of this dual understanding, as evidenced by the fact that free markets are rarely ever fair (see ECOnnection 10.5). That is because most of this talk is heavily infused with, to draw from Berlin, "freedom *from*" rhetoric—freedom *from* other countries' production-oriented subsidies, freedom *from* government regulation, freedom *from* the state, and so forth. Freedom *from* talk is especially pervasive in neoliberal discourse. Isaiah Berlin describes this as "negative freedom," which refers to the "absence of interference" ([1958] 1969, 127). It seems as though when most people are asked about *freedom*, negative freedom is the type most have in mind—a freedom in which we are allowed to pursue actions unimpeded (see also Bell and Lowe 2000, 287–289).

In addition to its negative component, freedom also has a positive side. "Positive freedom"—or freedom *to*—refers to the ability "to lead one prescribed form of life . . . that derives from the wish on the part of the individual to be his [or her] own master"

**IMAGE 10.2**

Example of signage stores use to advertise their Fair Trade Certified products. Source: "fair trade certified" by kafka4prez (flickr.com/kafka4prez) is licensed copyright © 2006 under CC BY-SA 2.0.

(Berlin [1958] 1969, 127). Without the active pursuit of positive freedom, most people would not—indeed *could not*—feel free. To explain what I mean by this, I evoke an old English aphorism: "Freedom for the pike is death for the minnow." Without the pursuit of positive freedom for all—pikes and minnows alike—the pikes of the world would be clearly advantaged. And how do we actively pursue positive freedom for all? This is where the concept of *constraint*—which can only come from outside the market— comes into the picture. There must be some constraints if minnows are to prosper. Positive freedom, in other words, allows us to talk about constraint in the context of freedom without any sense of paradox (see Movement Matters 10.1).

Let's now apply this thinking to free markets, free enterprise, and the like. In order for me to be and feel free (and trade freely), I need some assurances that the pikes of the world will not freely have their way with me. This is why freedom—and, yes, free markets—*requires* some level of extramarket intervention. This intervention need not come solely in the form of government involvement. It can also exist as informal social norms, trust, and a shared sense of cooperation and responsibility. In a word, this constraint—where we seek to govern ourselves as well as our sustainable use of the ecological commons—can also emerge out of community (Ostrom 1999). (Community-based governance is discussed more fully in Chapter 11.)

There is nothing radical about this argument. We as citizens routinely support policies that tie our hands, whether through government-mandated retirement savings programs, restrictions on advertisements to children, or restrictions on commodities themselves (Kysar 2010). No one would support a society that allowed, say, unrestricted violence or the selling of poisoned food. Also remember that an argument *for*

## MOVEMENT MATTERS 10.1
# Italy's Gruppi di Aquisto Soledale (GAS): Solidarity Purchasing Groups

From just one group in 1994, the movement Gruppi di Aquisto Soledale (GAS) now has more than seven hundred registered groups in Italy, though the actual number is estimated to be closer to two thousand, involving some hundred thousand people (Soil Association 2011). When a purchasing group puts people and environment before—or at least on a level equal to—profit, the group becomes a *solidarity* purchasing group. Such a network chooses the products and enrolls producers on the basis of respect for the environment and the solidarity between members of the group. Groups are typically set up by friends or neighbors who decide to pool their buying power and purchase collectively from local, organic, small-scale producers. Members of these groups believed that these guidelines lead to the choice of local products (to minimize food miles); fair trade goods (to respect all producers by promoting their human rights, in particular those of women, children,

and indigenous groups); reusable or compostable goods (to promote sustainable lifestyles); seasonal foods (to, for example, reduce energy and water footprints that come with growing out-of-season foods in greenhouses); and organic goods produced without the use of such inputs as pesticides or herbicides.

Some additional facts and figures relating to GAS:

- Size varies from ten to three hundred families in a group, with an average group size of twenty-five families.
- There are more groups in the affluent and social-capital-rich northern regions of the country.
- In addition to food, some GAS groups in cities like Milan are working together to coordinate larger bulk purchases of things like PV cells, electricity, and "ethical finance."

restrictions is not an argument *against* a market economy (at least in some form). In the words of free-market advocate Tom Friedman (2008), writing in the wake of the 2008 financial collapse, "We need to re-establish the core balance between our markets, ethics and regulations. I don't want to kill the animal spirits that necessarily drive capitalism—but I don't want to be eaten by them either."

In the end, markets, even free ones, work only *because of* regulation. Business as we know it today could not exist without contracts, which are made possible by a web of government-enforced rules and regulations. Regulation even helps businesses function by laying out clear rules about what they can and cannot do. As Harvard business professor Michael Porter argues, *stricter* environmental regulations are actually in the best interests of many businesses and countries, as they provide these actors an important competitive advantage—what is known in the business community as the **Porter Hypothesis** (Frohwein and Hansjürgens 2005). The Porter Hypothesis notes that, among other things, regulation spurs innovation, as it creates incentives for businesses to adjust to social and environmental realities, like diminishing natural resources. Those nations and regions slow to commit to stricter environmental regulations are therefore doing themselves a grave disservice, a fact they will pay dearly for in the near future as their businesses struggle to compete against those better positioned to deal with the economic, social, and ecological realities of this century.

## IMPORTANT CONCEPTS

- Environmental Kuznets Curve (EKC)
- fair versus free trade
- first and second contradictions of capitalism
- Forest Transition Theory (FTT)
- Foucauldian governance
- Isaiah Berlin's dual understanding of freedom
- metabolic rift
- neoliberalism
- Pollution Haven Hypothesis (PHH)
- rebound effect and the Jevons paradox
- relative versus absolute efficiency
- total cost accounting
- treadmill of production
- world-systems theory

## DISCUSSION QUESTIONS

1. Have you ever invested in a more energy-efficient technology only to change your behavior and thus offset some (if not all) of those efficiency gains? Recall my example about switching all the incandescent bulbs in my house for CFLs.
2. In order for capitalism to be sustainable over the long term, what is going to need to happen?
3. Is the treadmill of production an optimistic or pessimistic theoretical framework? Why?
4. What are your thoughts on the position taken about how free markets actually presuppose a degree of restraint and government intervention in order to be free?

## SUGGESTED ADDITIONAL READINGS

Griffin, L., G. Pavela, and J. Arroyo. 2015. "Tourism and the Treadmill of Production: A Cross-National Analysis." *Environmental Sociology* 1(2): 127–138.

Holt, D. 2014. "Why the Sustainable Economy Movement Hasn't Scaled: Toward a Strategy That Empowers Main Street." In *Sustainable Lifestyles and the Quest for Plenitude: Case Studies of the New Economy*, edited by J. Schor and C. Thompson, 202–232. New Haven, CT: Yale University Press.

Owen, D. 2010. "Annals of Environmentalism: The Efficiency Dilemma." *New Yorker*, Dec. 20, 78.

Wold, M. 2012. "Beyond 'Free' or 'Fair' Trade: Mexican Farmers Go Local." *YES!*, Jan. 23. www.yesmagazine.org/peace-justice/beyond-free-or-fair-trade-mexican-farmers-go-local.

## RELEVANT INTERNET LINKS

- www.env-econ.net. An independently managed website on subjects related to environmental economics.
- www.fairtradeusa.org. Fair Trade USA.

## SUGGESTED VIDEOS

- *Canada's Toxic Chemical Valley* (2013). The burial ground of the First Nation of Aamjiwnaang is located in Sarnia, Ontario. About seventy years ago it got some new neighbors. The first thing you notice when you visit Sarnia is the smell. Imagine a mixture of gasoline, melting asphalt, and a trace of rotten egg smacking you in the face and crawling up your nose every time you breathe.
- *The Dark Side of Chocolate* (2010). A team of journalists investigates how human trafficking and child labor in the Ivory Coast fuel the worldwide chocolate industry.
- *Dukale's Dream* (2015). A documentary about the inspiration behind Hugh Jackman's—yes, *that* Hugh Jackman—fair trade coffee company.
- *Green Death of the Forests* (2012). An unconventional film. It portrays the causes and consequences of deforestation in Indonesia as well as the tranquility and calm of wild nature. It contains no narrative or dialogue and yet helps us understand complex commodity chains.
- *There's No Tomorrow* (2012). topdocumentaryfilms.com/theres-no-tomorrow. A half-hour animated documentary about resource depletion, energy, and the impossibility of infinite growth on a finite planet.

# Governance: Biases and
# Blind Spots

Informational and governance challenges make ecological sustainability a daunting enough goal at the national level. With globalization, the barriers to sustainability—*real* sustainability—increase exponentially. If individual countries will not properly regulate what happens within their borders, no one can do it for them. Whereas today's most pressing environmental problems are global in scope, the regulatory arms available to monitor and enforce environmental law and policy weaken considerably when extended beyond their respective geopolitical borders. Meanwhile, the arms of our pollution reach around the globe. What are we to do? There are various ways to combat those gangly arms of pollution, which go beyond creating equally long arms of government.

This chapter, among other things, is interested in detailing *why* current environmental regulations and policies look the way they do. Although there is an air of scientific objectivity to them, they ultimately rest on shifting sand, which is to say their logic is made possible only with the making of some questionable value judgments. In the Solutions section, alternative and arguably more just and sustainable methods of governance are suggested.

## Fast Facts

- In 2010 the US Fish and Wildlife Service, which administers one of the world's most potent environmental laws directed at species protection—namely, the Endangered Species Act—extended the law's protections to the polar bear by designating roughly 190,000 square miles of onshore barrier islands in Alaska as "critical habitat." And yet the agency is incapable of doing anything about the leading threat to this creature: climate change.
- Trans-Pacific transportation of pollution from Asia to North America is well documented (Lafontaine et al. 2015). For example, a recent study focusing on US air quality shows that Chinese air pollution related to production for exports contributes, at

a maximum on a daily basis, 12–24 percent of sulfate pollution over the western US states (Lin et al. 2014). The authors thus point out that while eastern states are seeing improvements in air quality partially as a result of importing goods from China—and thus not producing them and the associated emissions domestically—western states have not fared as well, because they're forced to breathe in this secondhand (for lack of a better word) pollution from Asia. US states are powerless to do anything about this transborder pollution. Consequently, they must include it in their planning, treating it essentially as if it were their own when seeking to meet federally mandated air-quality standards (Parrish et al. 2011).

- What about future generations? If current trends continue, we will leave for our children a world radically different from the one we inhabit today. Global sea levels will rise by 0.8 to 2.0 meters by 2100, which places low-lying countries like Bangladesh at severe risk of becoming submerged (US National Academy of Sciences 2011). Following current trends, the future will be less biologically and hence culturally diverse, drained of its resources and absorption capacities, and remarkably inequitable (United Nations 2015b).

## Implications

Policy makers have tried being objective. They have tried ripping themselves out of their political communities when assessing and developing environmental policy, to be nowhere and no one while simultaneously everywhere and everyone. They have tried to be fair by stripping policy decisions of all ethical consequence and significance. Guided by the so-called comprehensive rationality of cost-benefit analysis, they have attempted being and doing all these things. Yet for reasons that I will now detail, these goals have neither lived up to their promise nor made the world more sustainable. In fact, they may well have made many things worse.

### Welfare Economics and Cost-Benefit Analyses

At their core, cost-benefit analyses are guided by what is known as **welfare economics.** Welfare economics is a branch of microeconomics that seeks to evaluate well-being, with the assumption that human well-being is wholly reducible to *economic* well-being. Welfare economics thus subscribes to an extreme form of methodological reductionism, which involves reducing all choices and things to economic terms—usually a dollar amount. Whenever confronted with a choice, it is assumed humans, being the rational creatures we are, will always select the one that brings us the greatest benefit. Even proponents of this approach admit that this process inevitably involves making problematic value assignments. For instance, how does one assign value to biodiversity, a wetland, or a human life? Yet given the risk of regulatory agencies and politicians becoming captured by things like money and persuasive constituents, advocates of the cost-benefit analysis approach insist its objectivity preserves policy analyses' integrity by letting "the facts" decide things and not emotions, values, and subjective interests.

Insurmountable problems, however, remain with this approach. First, the framework is inherently incomplete. After all, it's naive to think all well-being can be reduced to economic well-being—a point I elaborate on in the next chapter. More problematic still, it is incapable of seeing its own flaws, as evidenced by the fact that the approach is based on an assumption of its own objectivity. Yet facts are incapable of speaking

# Unpacking "Science"

Funtowicz and Ravetz (1992) provide us with a well-known framework that allows us to move away from a singular view of science. When speaking of the highly ambiguous nature of today's environmental problems, they acknowledge that decisions can often only take place in a value-laden context. The practice of objective science, they contend, is ill-equipped to deal with any intermingling of facts and values and as such is grossly unprepared as a knowledge system for many of today's environmental problems. They develop their model around two variables, "systems uncertainty" and "decision stakes" (see Figure 11.1). When dealing with questions that involve low levels of each, they suggest the use of "applied science." When dealing with medium levels of both variables, "professional consultancy" is suggested. And when questions involve high levels of these two variables, "postnormal science" is called for. According to Funtowicz and Ravetz, the way we practice science must change as we move from that of "applied" to that of "postnormal," as scientific questions require the making of additional value judgments. American nuclear physicist Alvin Weinberg noted how there are questions "which can be asked of science and yet which cannot be answered by science" (1972, 209). So what should we do? According to Funtowicz and Ravetz, as scientific questions increase in their complexity and systems uncertainty, so too should there be an increase in who is involved in finding answers to them.

Funtowicz and Ravetz's framework, however, also makes subtle value judgments. For instance, who decides if something falls within the realm of applied science or professional consultancy? Where precisely do we lay down the boundaries between these three types of science? And who decides what constitutes high decision stakes? Questions like these are not unique to Funtowicz and Ravetz's model. We confront them every time we make an environmental policy decision.

FIGURE 11.1 Postnormal Science Diagram

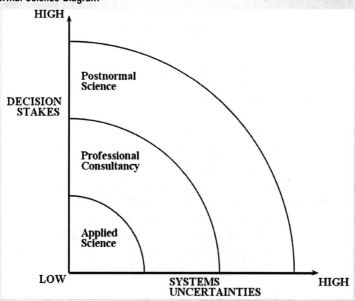

for themselves in matters of public health and environmental sustainability, given the tremendous level of uncertainties involved (see Ethical Question 11.1). *People* have to speak for those facts. And *who* those people are can matter tremendously.

The **Pareto optimality standard** is a core economic principle driving, and justifying, cost-benefit analyses and welfare economics more generally. The Pareto standard deems a policy acceptable only if at least one individual is better off and no individuals are made worse off. Without passing that minimal bar, a policy will not even be considered. Yet does it matter *who* is made better off? Let's say Policy A makes Bill Gates and Warren Buffett (and only Gates and Buffett) *minimally* better off and no one worse off, while Policy B makes many destitute persons *considerably* better off but costs Gates and Buffet twenty bucks each—pocket change for either of them. I know what policy I would root for: Policy B. According to the Pareto optimality standard, however, because it explicitly doesn't care about issues of equity, *who* is being helped is irrelevant. So anyone following the principle would have to choose Policy A, as it harms no one.

While claiming otherwise, this standard also makes normative assumptions by valuing only living human interests. But many other interests are worth valuing, like non-human life forms, future generations, and human communities, just to name a few. How are we ever going to make smart policy choices as long as we judge policies with a standard that is vastly prejudicial toward living human interests? Nobel Prize–winning economist Amartya Sen makes plain the aimlessness—or "pointlessness," as Guido Calabresi (1991) famously called it—of this standard: "An economy can be [Pareto] optimal . . . even when some people are rolling in luxury and others are near starvation as long as the starvers cannot be made better off without cutting into the pleasures of the rich. If preventing the burning of Rome would have made Emperor Nero feel worse off, then letting him burn Rome would have been Pareto-optimal. In short, a society or an economy can be Pareto-optimal and still be perfectly disgusting" (Sen 1970, 22).

The rush for welfare-economic policy analyses to make everything commensurate— that is to say, equal by way of reducing the world to monetary form—may make the approach appear objective, as technically all we are talking about are monetized costs and benefits. But this comes at great cost to society and the environment. One analysis of foreign aid policy calculates that the well-being of citizens in less affluent nations is one two-thousandth of the value of an American citizen (Kopczuk, Slemrod, and Yitzhaki 2005). With such a view of the citizens of poorer nations, is it any wonder why polluting industries and e-waste flow so readily to these parts of the world?

A widely circulated memo, dated December 12, 1991, leaked from the World Bank, articulated precisely such reasoning. Then chief economist for the World Bank Lawrence Summers (who was later appointed US Treasury secretary during the Clinton administration and subsequently served as president of Harvard University) penned the now-infamous memo. It argued that the lower marginal cost of waste disposal in a poor country compared with the higher marginal cost of waste disposal in a waste-producing affluent country justifies the latter polluting the former. The memo further argued that the poorest countries of Africa are vastly underpolluted, as they are underutilizing what affluent countries desperately need, namely, waste sinks.

In appearing to be nonethical, the welfare-economic approach ends up being terribly *un*ethical. In an essay titled "The Rights of Statistical People," Lisa Heinzerling puts the absurdity of this practice in plain sight:

We do not, for example, believe that so long as it is worth $10 million to one person to see another person dead, and so long as current estimates of the value of human life are lower than $10 million, it is acceptable for the first person to shoot and kill the second. . . . Yet when it comes to regulatory programs that prevent deaths—deaths also due to the actions of other people—it has become commonplace to argue that the people doing the harm should be allowed to act so long as it would cost more for them to stop doing the harm than the harm is worth in monetary terms. (2000, 189)

When we reduce human life to statistical terms, we deny those people the dignity to be thought of as humans. Similarly, by monetizing ecosystems and nonhuman life, we miss out on the opportunity to value things on their own terms. This can lead to, for example, the view that waste sinks in Africa ought to be filled with pollution from affluent nations just because sinks are substitutable.

It is entirely realistic to expect this approach to assign a lower value to those of lower socioeconomic status as well as to particular racial minorities, as certain ethnic groups are disproportionately overrepresented among lower-income strata. In having lower incomes and thus less buying power, welfare economics sees these people as having less value, literally, than those with higher incomes. Welfare economics therefore *justifies* certain types of environmental racism (Kysar 2010). Yet welfare economists are okay with this, as the outcome "would not be the result of a government decision to take racial characteristics into account; in fact it would not be a product of any group-level discrimination on the government's part" (Sunstein 2004, 391). So discrimination that can be justified with statistics is okay? And where's room for justice in all of this? How can we *ever* expect the economically disadvantaged to achieve upward mobility when our policy assessment tools view their lives as having less worth than the affluent's?

## Tyranny of the Present: Discounting

Welfare-economic policy analysis also has a distinct way of looking at the future. To its credit, it is consistent. It uses a technique to monetize future well-being, thus making it comparable with well-being today. Enter the practice of discounting.

Following this procedure, an increment of value today is worth more than that same increment in the future. Or, as noted by Cowen and Parfit, at a 5 percent discount rate, "one statistical death next year counts for more than a billion deaths in four hundred years" (1992, 147). Seen through this lens, the foot-dragging we've been witnessing in regards to climate change policy starts making sense. Thanks to discounting, it is entirely possible to settle on a policy option that may knowingly result in human extinction hundreds of years from now, but because it also lowers the well-being of some today, it is deemed unacceptable. Douglas Kysar has a wonderful term for this: "tyranny of the present" (2010, 148) (see ECOnnection 11.1).

Let's review some of the logic that underlies discounting. Proponents of the practice argue that the procedure is necessary to ensure that current generations maximize their investment of financial *and* natural capital opportunities. This benefits, or so the argument goes, not only the living but also future generations by maximizing the option set bequeathed to them—a type of "trickle forward" reasoning (Kysar 2010, 162). But *what* precisely are these benefits we are leaving the future? Answer: monetized well-being.

ECOnnection 11.1

# Discounting and Forest Management

With harvesting cycles that are often longer than twenty years—and for some tree species they can extend well beyond one hundred years—forestry management is premised on fairly long time horizons. The discount rate used therefore matters immensely. High discount rates greatly reduce the likelihood of sustainability, as it creates little or no incentive to replant after one rotation, especially as long as there remains a substantial amount of unlogged forest to be exploited (Kant and Alavalapati 2014). Lower discount rates, conversely, can make things like replanting incredibly attractive. All this matters enormously, as forestry provides us with so much more than just wood—from potential genetic materials to tourism, biodiversity, and carbon storage. Throughout much of the twentieth century, forestry discount rates were high and discouraged practices that would lead to truly sustainable yields.

The exact stuff left for later generations is irrelevant, according to the welfare-economic policy analysis. As articulated by two prominent welfare economists writing on the topic of sustainable development, "There is no abstract reason to believe that preserving a particular environmental amenity (a forest, a lake) is always better for posterity than other investments that do not involve the environment in particular (expenditures on basic research, reductions in national debt)" (Sunstein and Rowell 2007, 203). Remember, at the core of this approach is the assumption of ultimate substitutability among different types of capital. Money is just as good as anything else—in fact *better* because it can be converted into a variety of things (as long as they are not extinct, depleted, or soiled beyond repair).

Eric Neumayer, a prominent welfare economist, has argued that future generations might actually prefer to face higher skin-cancer rates if those risks come in exchange for some greater benefit. As Neumayer explains, "Whether future generations will accept an increase in the rate of skin cancer or not depends on what they get in exchange for it" (1999, 40). Even if he's right, how can we possibly know what future generations would accept in exchange for higher rates of skin cancer, and how can we be sure this Faustian bargain is agreeable to all and not just a privileged few? Welfare economists have even managed to justify the discounting of physical deformities, arguing that the cost to care for those deformities is likely to go down. In other words, we ought to value the avoidance of future deformities less than steps toward avoidance today (see, for example, Samida and Weisbach 2007). This argument, however, flatly misrepresents the ethical question at hand. "The nature of the ethical question on the table," remarks Kysar, "is not how to care for or cure a deformity that has already been suffered, but instead whether to inflict the pain in the first place." He continues: "By presuming that there is no ethically relevant distinction between living as a nondeformed individual and living as a deformed individual who has received compensation, the economist's response violated the most fundamental ethical precept, that individuals should not be used without their consent as a mean rather than as ends. Harm is inflicted—future individuals are used and indeed scarified without their consent—in order to promote well-being that they will not enjoy" (2010, 170; see Movement Matters 11.1).

## The Self-Interested Straw Person

When weighing policy options, the welfare economist also assumes the worst of people. I am talking about the selfish, self-interested depiction of individual behavior assumed by most policy analysts today. Curiously, economists seem to best fit this model, which makes me wonder if this "truth" speaks less about human nature and more about the power of perception, a bit of a case of what we call in the social sciences a self-fulfilling prophecy. It has been shown, for example, that economics majors are more likely than noneconomics students to free ride and are less likely to work cooperatively, just as their discipline would predict (Carter and Irons 1991; Marwell and Ames 1981). One of the dangers of this assumption comes across in international relations. Because national governments are believed to be an aggregate of self-interested people, international policy not surprisingly assumes states to be equally selfish. This stance is of tremendous policy consequence as far as the environment is concerned.

For example, through this lens international relations are viewed as occurring in a space of self-interested competition, leaving no room for anything like cooperation. Yet given that so many of our problems are global in character, trust and collaboration are precisely what we need more of. As long as nation-states assume the worst of other nation-states, it is hard to see how global sustainability will ever be practically attained.

We see this continually in international negotiations over climate change. Countries like the United States are unwilling to commit to any greenhouse gas reductions out of a fear that other developing economies will selfishly free ride and do nothing. President George W. Bush was making precisely this point when he said that without "an accord with China, China will produce greenhouse gas emissions that offset anything we do in a brief period of time" (Kysar 2010, 142). Indeed, this was the crux of the US government's argument in *Massachusetts v. EPA*.

*Massachusetts v. EPA* (549 US 497 (2007)) is a US Supreme Court case decided by a vote of five to four between twelve US states (and several US cities) and the Environmental Protection Agency (EPA). The former were seeking to force the latter to regulate $CO_2$ and other greenhouse gases as pollutants. The US government employed a couple of arguments in its defense. The first, building on this free-rider problem, went along the following lines: because it makes no difference at the global level whether the EPA does or does not regulate these emissions, as other countries (most notably China) will continue to pollute at ever-greater levels, why bother with such regulations? The other argument was based on a welfare-economic approach to international relations: namely, forcing the US government to act unilaterally in regard to greenhouse gas emissions "might hamper the President's ability to persuade key developing nations to reduce emissions." In other words, because states do not (and cannot) work together cooperatively, and respond only to various sticks and carrots, the US government would rather wait to regulate its greenhouse gas emissions. This would give it a bargaining chip to play at some future negotiation to show other countries its willingness to reduce emissions.

# Dams: Making Changes to How Things Are Counted

Perhaps you've heard the saying "Not everything that counts can be counted." But remember also, just because we can count something doesn't mean how we count it can't change. Dams are an excellent example of this. Generations ago cost-benefit analyses were elementary by today's standards. I can imagine how the planners of the Hoover Dam ran the numbers: comparing things like capital costs (e.g., pounds of concrete and steel rebar) and labor costs (they didn't even have to worry about lawsuits back then) to the revenue generated from hydroelectric power and water storage and allocation. Today, we do a lot better at internalizing costs, which means those cost-benefit analyses look different, as evidenced by the fact that we're actually starting to tear dams down—an unthinkable act a few decades ago.

The Elwha River, which slices through northwest Washington's Olympic Peninsula, once hosted rich runs of chinook and red salmon. That all came to an end in 1913 with the completion of the Elwha River dam (see Image 11.1). While supplying electricity to the region, it cut off salmon coming from the Strait of Juan de Fuca, which connects with the Pacific Ocean. "There's nothing more painful than to see red salmon banging up against the dam, which is what you saw when you went there," remarked Interior Secretary Sally Jewell at the annual meeting of the Society of Environmental Journalists in New Orleans on September 5, 2014 (Main 2014). When the removal of the dam began in September 2011, it was the outcome of a long process, involving many stakeholders and a lot of hard work. The Lower Elwha Klallam Tribe had for years advocated for the removal of the Elwha dam. The Federal Energy Regulatory Commission process requiring private hydropower dams to be licensed provided the tribe with an opportunity to intervene in an effort to restore the river and its salmon fisheries. In 1986, the tribe filed a motion to intervene. In 1992, thanks to growing support of several environmental groups, and after a lengthy administrative process, Congress passed the Elwha River Ecosystems and Fisheries Restoration Act. This act directed the US Department of the Interior to study the feasibility of the river and fisheries restoration. In the 1995 Elwha Report, the secretary of the interior recommended removal of the dam, along with the Glines Canyon dam. The primary source of funding for the Elwha River Restoration Act came from the National Park Service Construction Budget. In 2009, the American Recovery and Reinvestment Act provided the remaining funding necessary to accomplish removal of both dams (Guarino 2013).

**IMAGE 11.1**

Source: "Lower Elwha River Dam" by brewbooks (flickr.com/brewbooks) is licensed copyright © 2007 under CC BY-SA 2.0.

President George W. Bush, during a meeting with European leaders in 2007, explained that "each country needs to recognize that we must reduce our greenhouse gases and deal, obviously, with their own internal politics to come up with an effective strategy that hopefully, when added together, . . . leads to a real reduction" (Bush 2007). Given all that's at stake, I should think we need to rely on more than just hope when developing policies at both domestic and international levels. Yet that's what the welfare-economic approach asks us to do: to go it alone and hope that "when added together," our actions in the aggregate will amount to something that resembles global sustainability. That's a lot to ask for.

## Solutions

When I discuss with students the various social drivers that underlie today's environmental problems and equally create impediments to future solutions, many are initially frustrated. On the one hand, here is a case in which we literally just need to change how we think about things. On the other hand, the welfare-economic policy analysis is so entrenched in political, economic, and policy thought that it will require a lot of work to move away from it. The approach is also remarkably efficient at getting the job done, even though its outputs are highly problematic and ultimately unsustainable. I will now detail some alternatives, though it will require a collective rolling up of our sleeves if we want to see the welfare-economic policy approach overturned.

### From Tragedy to Drama

The assumption that a self-interested individual lies at the core of welfare-economic policy analysis is not without some empirical grounding. This caricature is famously detailed in Garret Hardin's classic essay from 1968, "The Tragedy of the Commons," which includes relevant passages like this one (1244):

> Picture a pasture open to all. It is to be expected that each herdsman will try to keep as many cattle as possible on the commons. Such an arrangement may work reasonably satisfactorily for centuries because tribal wars, poaching, and disease keep the numbers of both man and beast well below the carrying capacity of the land. Finally, however, comes the day of reckoning, that is, the day when the long-desired goal of social stability becomes a reality. At this point, the inherent logic of the commons remorselessly generates tragedy.

Assuming that each herder wishes to maximize their gain, they begin to ponder the consequences of adding one more animal to their herd. It quickly dawns on them that the costs and benefits of such an action are unevenly distributed. The herder receives all the proceeds from the sale of the additional animal. Yet the effects of overgrazing are shared by all. It is therefore perfectly rational for, and therefore expected that, herders in such a situation will continually add animals to their herd—*all* herders. And therein lies the tragedy: everyone acting in their own self-interests, when resources are shared and limited, will have catastrophic ends, leading Hardin to conclude, famously, "Freedom in a commons brings ruin to all" (1244).

CASE STUDY 11.1

# Central Government, Privatization, or Common-Property Regime?

David Sneath (1998) examined levels of grassland degradation in northern China, Mongolia, and Russia. Mongolia has allowed pastoralists to continue practicing their traditional group-property institutions, which involve large-scale movements between seasonal pastures, whereas Russia and China for much of the latter half of the twentieth century moved toward state-owned agricultural collectives with permanent settlements. (In the 1990s China began privatizing some of its pasturelands.) Interestingly, the grassland in Mongolia shows far fewer signs of degradation than comparable land in either China or Russia. About 75 percent of the pastureland in the Russian sector studied has been degraded, while more than one-third in the Chinese sector shows a significant level of degradation. Yet in the Mongolian sector examined, only one-tenth has suffered degradation. More recent research has corroborated these findings (see, e.g., Wang, Brown, and Agrawal 2013).

Yet as Dietz and colleagues (2002) highlight in their thorough review of the commons literature since Hardin's essay, prototypical scenarios—like Hardin's essay—always end up oversimplifying things. Some case studies tell a story similar to Hardin's. Many others have much happier endings.

One of the most relevant critiques leveled at Hardin is that he conflates common-property and open-access regimes. Common-property regimes are ones in which "the members of a clearly demarcated group have a legal right to exclude nonmembers of that group from using a resource. Open access regimes (*res nullius*)—including the classic cases of the open seas and the atmosphere—have long been considered in legal doctrine as involving no limits on who is authorized to use a resource" (Ostrom 2000, 335–336). This is an important distinction, as common property should not be mistaken to mean everyone's property (Ciriacy-Wantrup and Bishop 1975). Under common-property regimes, users already have use rights that are maintained through thick webs of social relationships. What from the "outside" may look ungoverned, as there may be no formal laws and rules and state-sanctioned monitoring, could actually be well governed through local customs, trust, and informal social norms (see, for example, Goldman 1998; Longo, Clausen, and Clark 2015).

It is concerning that resource privatization—one of Hardin's suggestions to avert the tragedy—may in fact be one of the reasons the tragedy is playing out in some parts of world (see Case Study 11.1). Late twentieth-century policy reforms are transforming common-property regimes into either state government–owned or private-property regimes. When this happens, however, especially in developing nations, rarely are sufficient moneys and resources devoted to the monitoring of these now noncommon-property resources. "Thus, what had been de facto common property with some limitation on access and use patterns became de jure government [or individual] property—but due to the lack of enforcement, it frequently became de facto open access" (Dietz et al. 2002, 13).

The late Elinor Ostrom and her various collaborators extensively documented that common-property resource governance need not end tragically. As it turns out, we are not as self-centered as the welfare-economic approach makes us out to be. There are many examples of long-enduring and sustainable common-property situations from around the world. Sustainable self-governance requires the development of rules and institutions that define such things as the physical boundaries of the property held in common, who has access to the resource, a sustainable rate of extraction and use, the methods for monitoring the resource, a system for resolving conflicts, and suitable sanctions and punishments for transgressions. Robert Netting (1981), in his classic study of a Swiss Alpine village, identifies five environmental variables that contribute to a resource being held as common rather than private property:

- the value of harvestable resource is low per unit of area
- what can be harvested varies considerably over time
- investment in improvements yields relatively small increases in the productivity of the resource
- overall costs can be reduced if activities (e.g., herding or processing dairy products) can be shared collectively
- infrastructure cost (e.g., fences and buildings) can be reduced if built on a larger scale

Perhaps the largest omission in Hardin's essay, and precisely why we are not as self-centered as the welfare-economic caricature assumes, is the fact that people *talk to one another*. The role of face-to-face interaction in building social capital and establishing those aforementioned thick social relationships that can rein in otherwise selfish behavior is well documented in the social science literature (Borg, Toikka, and Primmer 2015; Flora 2008; Flora et al. 2009; social capital was introduced in Chapter 7). Some interesting laboratory experiments have been conducted to better understand the role that communication plays in averting tragedy-like outcomes. The verdict: the ability to communicate and coordinate drastically alters outcomes.

Group communication fosters the formation of group identity and therefore reduces the likelihood of selfish behaviors. Individuals instead are more willing to think in terms of what's best for the collective versus what's exclusively best for them (Baumeister, Ainsworth, and Vohs 2015; Ostrom, Gardner, and Walker 1994).

When individuals are placed in a situation where they cannot communicate with others, they are more likely to act selfishly with regard to the use of shared resources (Ostrom, Gardner, and Walker 1994).

More recently, research has gone beyond studying resources at a particular scalar level, looking instead at common-property resources that cut across many levels. One obvious difference between global and local resources is the extent of the former and inherent difficulties associated with monitoring and enforcing sustainable use patterns (Dietz et al. 2002). Building and maintaining social capital between groups from different continents with different backgrounds also complicate matters. Some common-property resources—like freshwater in an international basin or marine ecosystems—are best viewed in an international context. Their effective management therefore depends on the cooperation of appropriate international institutions and national, regional, and local institutions (Ostrom et al. 1999).

Ultimately, the evidence indicates that while complicating matters, the global character of some of today's environmental problems should not be viewed as a guaranteed ticket to a world of despair (Agrawal 2014; Bulkeley et al. 2014; see Case Study 11.2). Elinor Ostrom, who was awarded the 2009 Nobel Prize in Economic Sciences for her work on this very subject, and her collaborators explained the future potential of global governance as follows:

> The lessons from successful examples of CPR [common-property resource] management provide starting points for addressing future challenges. Some of these will be institutional, such as multilevel institutions that build on and complement local and regional institutions to focus on truly global problems. Others will build from improved technology. For example, more accurate long-range weather forecasts could facilitate improvements in irrigation management, or advances in fish tracking could allow more accurate population estimates and harvest management. . . . In the end, building from the lessons of past successes will require forms of communication, information, and trust that are broad and deep beyond precedent, but not beyond possibility. . . . There is much to learn from successful efforts as well as from failures. (Ostrom et al. 1999, 282)

## Absolute Sustainability

Welfare-economic policy analyses have a very narrow understanding of "sustainability." According to proponents of this approach, it is necessary to ensure that current generations maximize their investment opportunities in the hope that benefits will trickle "forward" to later generations. Yet *what* are these benefits that we're leaving the future? The precise stuff, as I have mentioned, is irrelevant (see Sunstein and Rowell 2007, 203). Rather, what matters under this calculus is monetary value. This gives the approach the veneer of objectivity by removing from the decision-making process subjective values and emotions—after all, we're just talking about dollars and cents.

Clearly, however, *stuff* matters. To repeat a familiar adage: you can't eat GDP. Yet our welfare economist has a response to this: the perfect substitutability assumption. When resources become scarce, the higher market price will force innovation and lead, eventually, to suitable substitutes. Although the assumption might hold for some goods, like fuel (biofuels substituting for gasoline) and certain foods (high fructose corn syrup substituting for sugar), no one can seriously hold out similar hope for marine ecosystems, the ozone layer, clean air, and endangered species.

I return to my earlier call for absolute sustainability. Thomas Jefferson famously wrote in a letter to James Madison in 1789 that "the earth belongs in usufruct to the living" (Sloan 1993, 281). (*Usufruct* means to have a legal right to enjoy and profit from something that belongs to another.) Given that the survival of future billions rides on our actions today, it seems we do indeed have something akin to a duty to leave a sufficient amount of stuff intact and minimally adulterated for the future. Monetary wealth will indeed protect some people in the future from climate change and provide some people with fish if the marine ecosystem were to collapse. Yet I am far less worried about the well-being of the world's future affluent; they will likely have the resources to

# Reducing Emissions from Deforestation and Forest Degradation

Reducing Emissions from Deforestation and Forest Degradation (REDD) is a collaborative international initiative under negotiation within the UN climate talks and other international forums that will help to compensate governments, communities, companies, and individuals in low-income countries for actions that protect forests (see Image 11.2). By placing a monetary value on the role forest ecosystems play in carbon capture and storage, REDD allows intact forests to compete with historically more lucrative land uses that have resulted in their destruction.

Forests absorb $CO_2$ from the atmosphere, but when they are destroyed or degraded, they release large amounts of this greenhouse gas, contributing significantly to global warming. A study published in *Science* estimates that the total $CO_2$ sink (absorption or uptake) capacity of the world's regrowth forests is equivalent to half the world's fossil fuel $CO_2$ emissions (Pan et al. 2011). More than global carbon sinks, forests are also people's homes. There are roughly five hundred million forest-dependent people in the world, two hundred million of whom are indigenous peoples (FPP 2012). In short, forests directly support the livelihoods of millions who depend on these spaces for food, fuel, fodder for livestock, medicine, shelter, and religious/spiritual practices.

Initially, REDD was principally focused on reducing emissions from deforestation and forest degradation. By 2010, however, as set out in the Cancun Agreements, REDD became REDD+ to reflect the new components. REDD+ includes:

(a) reducing emissions from deforestation
(b) reducing emissions from forest degradation
(c) conservation of forest carbon stocks
(d) sustainable management of forests
(e) enhancement of forest carbon stocks

With this broader charge, REDD+ has the potential to simultaneously contribute to climate change mitigation and poverty alleviation while also conserving biodiversity and sustaining vital ecosystem services (REDD Desk 2015).

**IMAGE 11.2**

Source: "After the Rainforest, Uganda" by Rod Waddington (flickr.com/rod_waddington) is licensed copyright © 2014 under CC BY-SA 2.0.

protect and take care of themselves. It's the welfare of the other 99 percent of the world's population who will have considerably less that concerns me.

How, then, should we fold future generations into our thinking? Clearly, they cannot speak for themselves. Some economic theorists have begun to argue that the widely used constant discount rates are unjustified. When you set a fixed annual discount rate at, say, 5 percent, it is entirely possible to reject a policy option that may knowingly save the human race from extinction hundreds of years from now on the basis that it also lowers the well-being of some today. As opposed to the constant discount rate, some have suggested that the correct social discount rate should decrease with time, beginning, for example, for a short time at 3.5 percent and declining over the long run to 1 percent or less (Hepburn and Koundouri 2007).

More recently, Fleurbaey and Zuber (2013) suggest the following twist when thinking about discount rates: "Climate change policies [should] be evaluated with a negative discount rate . . . when the present donor is richer than the future beneficiary. Thus, if we consider long-run policies, the discount rate should be negative when the poorest contributors to the policy are richer than the poorest beneficiaries" (585–586). Do not most climate change policies satisfy this condition? Mitigation efforts, for instance, should put the financial burden on the high emitters, who are typically among the members of the present generation living in affluent countries. Such policies will benefit members of future generations, especially those most at risk from the threats of climate change, many of whom are (and will be) low-income households living in low-income countries. Can we really expect the poorest of future generations will be better off than the middle class of the present generation? If we cannot be absolutely sure of that, then perhaps the above suggestion has some ethical legs.

There are also some nondiscounting options. Schelling (1995), for example, argues we should make investments explicitly for future peoples just as we do with foreign aid today; we could call these investments *future aid*. One benefit of this approach is that it brings the subject of future well-being into the sphere of public consciousness, as opposed to the standard practice, which is generally to never talk about future generations unless it is politically expedient to do so. Of course, this practice does not guarantee anything for future generations, as evidenced by the recent sharp declines in foreign aid by most affluent nations. And it could conceivably make matters worse for the future, as it could provide justification for even more egregiously unsustainable behavior under the guise of "aiding the future in other ways."

Others have suggested abandoning discounting altogether for something more democratic in character. Kopp and Portney (1999), for instance, propose mock referenda, in which a random sample of the population is presented with a detailed description of the likely effects—current and future—of the various proposed policies. The participants would then vote for or against the policy (see also Page 2003). As opposed to the disinterested rationality of the welfare-economic approach, this style of "rationality depends on the virtues of collective problem solving; it considers the reasonableness of ends in relation to the values they embody and the sacrifices we must make to achieve them" (Sagoff 1988, 70). Importantly, this approach is not necessarily antithetical to the welfare-economic framework. Things could still be monetized but only after the policy has been chosen. Thus, rather than *determining* the policy selected, "the value will simply be an ancillary effect of a policy choice that was premised on social values" (Kysar

2010, 114). This technique could stop the policy foot-dragging that currently exists around climate change. I try something similar to this with my students. They are presented with reports that calculate projected costs associated with the taking of major steps to mitigate humans' greenhouse gas emissions and to adapt to changes already under way. They are then given other estimates as to the costs to society if nothing is done. This is followed by a conversation about the "value" of future generations and the impacts climate change could have on them. After these future costs are vaguely established (we never seem to settle on a fixed figure), I ask my students how they compare to the costs associated with implementing aggressive climate change policy today. Taking action today *always* proves the most cost-effective option.

## The Precautionary Principle

There was a time in the United States when we talked more about environmental rights than optimal trade-offs, of steward obligations more than discounted welfare maximization, and of international cooperation more than global competitiveness (Kysar 2010). The Endangered Species Act of 1973, for instance, placed the value of species at "incalculable," thereby, for a time, excluding from consideration *any* economic calculus. Similarly, the UN Environment Programme Participation Act of 1973 declared that it "is the policy of the United States to participate in coordinated international efforts to solve environmental problems of global international concern" (*United States Code, 2000* 2002, 159). As written in the National Environmental Policy Act of 1969, Congress recognized that it is the responsibility of the federal government to, among other things, "fulfill the responsibilities of each generation as trustee of the environment for succeeding generations." Finally, going back in time still further, we have the Delaney Clause. This 1958 amendment to the Food, Drugs, and Cosmetic Act of 1938 states that "the Secretary of the Food and Drug Administration shall not approve for use in food any chemical additive found to induce cancer in man, or, after tests, found to induce cancer in animals" (Merrill 1997, 313). Note the definitiveness of this language. There is no room for the comparing of an additive's health risks with its perceived economic benefits.

We currently assume the worst of people and the best of the technologies created by these self-centered, selfish people. When it comes to assessing the potential threats of novel technologies and setting up environmental, health, and safety regulations, the tendency, especially in the United States, is to take the position of "innocent until proven guilty." This represents, at its most basic level, the traditional risk assessment. Risk assessment, in effect, places the onus on regulatory agencies and the general public to prove that a given technology or industrial activity is not safe. Or, to put it another way, we have to falsify the statement "It's safe." This places us in a noticeably different regulatory environment from where we were when, say, the Delaney Clause was in full effect.

An alternative to the traditional risk assessment is the precautionary principle. The precautionary principle is generally recognized as having emerged in the 1970s, though its ethos dates back to the Hippocratic Oath, which states "First do no harm" (Steel 2014). Since then, the precautionary principle has flourished in a variety of settings. Arguably, its first international application came in 1984, at the First International Conference on Protection of the North Sea. From there, it has been integrated into numerous conventions and agreements, including, for example, the Maastricht Treaty on the European Union, the Barcelona Convention, the Global Climate Change Convention, and Principle 15 of the Rio Declaration. One popular definition of the precautionary principle comes from the 1998 Wingspread Statement on the Precautionary Principle: "When an activity raises threats of harm to human health or the environment, precautionary measures should be taken even if some cause and effect relationships are not established scientifically. In this context the proponent of the activity, rather than the public, should bear the burden of proof" (Raffensperger and Tickner 1999, 8).

Admittedly, this statement leaves the concept ill-defined, vague, and difficult to translate into practical action. For instance, what constitutes a "threat"? What about those cases in which human well-being is enhanced while the health of the environment is threatened? What does the term *precautionary measures* mean? And who are the "proponents" that this statement refers to: those producing the technology in question, those who benefit from it, or those who may profit from it?

Proponents would argue that the function of such an "open" definition is to ensure that the principle remains variable and contingent, which is admirable given the indeterminate nature of the systems (ecological, social, and so on) that it seeks to protect. Yet in the face of such ambiguity, it then becomes left to interested parties—regulators, industry representatives, environmental advocacy organizations, and the like—to work out the details. What guarantee is there, then, that powerful actors will not shape those policy specifics to benefit their interests, while excluding the interests of the less powerful?

There are two applications of the precautionary principle: one "strong" and one "weak" (Carolan 2007). The precautionary principle has frequently been interpreted as calling for the absolute proof of safety before new technologies are adopted; this is a popular reading among its critics. This "strong" formulation, for example, can be seen in a statement by environmental writer Jeremy Leggett (1990), when he argued that "the modus operandi we would like to see is: 'Do not emit a substance unless you have proof it will not do harm to the environment'" (459). Thus, whereas traditional risk assessments presume things to be safe until proven guilty (harmful), under this variant of the precautionary principle, the assumption is that technologies are guilty (harmful) until proven safe. In doing this, the responsibility of proof is placed on the shoulders of industry versus the general public and regulatory agencies.

In principle, this position is commendable. It holds a certain degree of moral currency by providing what many would consider a fair and just way of regulating technology: namely, those who stand to make millions from a given technology should likewise bear the burden of proof when demonstrating that such profits are not coming at the expense of humans, the environment, or both. Yet this approach has grave logical problems: namely, no product could ever meet the required threshold to be allowed onto the market. How does one prove that a given technology will do no harm to either humans or the environment? That is, how does one prove the statement "It's safe"? Karl Popper ([1934] 1961) famously argued that theories often take the following form: all Xs are Ys. For example: "All snow is white" or "All bodies attract one another with a force proportional to the product of their masses and inversely proportional to the square of their distance apart." To refute such a theoretical form requires that one find a single X that is not also a Y. To prove such a theory, however, would require that one observe every single X to make sure that it is indeed also a Y. Yet this would mean that one must engage in an exhaustive search of not only the entire universe but of the universe from the beginning to the end of time. Logically, therefore, while refutations of theories appear to be at least possible, confirmations (as a basis for proof) are not.

One way to salvage the precautionary principle is to weaken our interpretation of *proof*. Ultimately, nothing in this world is *totally* safe. Water can be lethal when too much is ingested. The same can be said for tea, coffee, apples, oxygen, sunlight. . . . Perhaps, then, a better way of putting it is seeking proof of being reasonably safe (Tickner 2003). With this move, we can now drink water and tea without the fear of regulatory agencies outlawing their use. Yet in doing this, the precautionary principle slips into something noticeably less novel. To speak of something being "reasonably safe" sounds an awful lot like risk assessment's claim of being about establishing "what's a reasonable risk."

Call it what you want: risk assessment, precautionary principle, or precautionary risk management—what we ultimately need are more open decision-making structures. And not just at the point of regulation. Regulation is something we do at the back end of the production process, *after* a product has been made. What about the decisions that are made at the front end of the production process, *before* a technology has been developed and mass-produced? As sociologist of science Brian Wynne (2002) points out, attempts to improve public participation in risk assessments, while admirable, have served to reinforce attention on only back-end science questions about consequences or risks instead of looking at why such widespread public dissatisfaction with modern technologies exists in the first place. In short, a democratic regulatory politics should not kick in only after a technology has been developed. It should inform the entire production process, from conceptual cradle to material grave. Doing this will encourage the production of technologies that are not only more just and less risky but also needed and that will enhance social welfare. This is radically different from the current model, which involves producing goods and leaving it up to marketing departments to convince the public they are things they need.

---

## IMPORTANT CONCEPTS

- discounting
- open-access versus common-property regimes
- postnormal science
- traditional risk assessment versus the precautionary principle
- tragedy of the commons
- welfare economics and cost-benefit analyses

## DISCUSSION QUESTIONS

1. How should future generations be factored into our thinking when assessing policy options?
2. As many of today's problems are global, do we need something akin to a global governing body to deal with these threats? What are some of the potential benefits and costs of this scenario?
3. Should we be more cautious in our approach to novel technologies?

4. How does Elinor Ostrom's research, and that of others, in the governing-the-commons tradition give us hope?

## SUGGESTED ADDITIONAL READINGS

Davies, P. 2014. "Green Crime and Victimization: Tensions Between Social and Environmental Justice." *Theoretical Criminology* 18(3): 300–316.

Dolsak, N., and E. Ostrom, eds. 2003. *The Commons in the New Millennium: Challenges and Adaptation.* Cambridge, MA: MIT Press.

Haarstad, H. 2014. "Climate Change, Environmental Governance and the Scale Problem." *Geography Compass* 8(2): 87–97.

Kark, S., A. Tulloch, A. Gordon, T. Mazor, N. Bunnefeld, and N. Levin. 2015. "Cross-Boundary Collaboration: Key to the Conservation Puzzle." *Current Opinion in Environmental Sustainability* 12:12–24.

## RELEVANT INTERNET LINKS

- www.iied.org/justice-forests-series-short-films. Two short films—*Tackling Forest Governance* and *Justice in the Forests*—about indigenous forest governance groups.
- www.youtube.com/watch?v=ByXM47Ri1Kc. Elinor Ostrom explains her pathbreaking research.
- www.youtube.com/watch?v=GgpEscvz168. An interview with a scholar who has studied REDD+ (see Case Study 11.2). Specifically, she explains the power and politics underlining this policy process, leading to its stalling out in some cases.

## SUGGESTED VIDEOS

- *Bikpela Bagarap (Big Damage)* (2011). www.bikpelabagarap.com. Filmed undercover, this documentary reveals the exploitation of forest communities in Papua New Guinea by Malaysian logging companies and corrupt politicians.
- *Canada's Toxic Chemical Valley* (2013). The burial ground of the First Nation of Aamjiwnaang is located in Sarnia, Ontario. About seventy years ago it got some new neighbors. The first thing you notice when you visit Sarnia is the smell. Imagine a mixture of gasoline, melting asphalt, and a trace of rotten egg smacking you in the face and crawling up your nose every time you breathe.
- *Green Gold* (2012). Documents large-scale ecosystem restoration projects in China, Africa, South America, and the Middle East, highlighting the enormous benefits to people and the planet of undertaking these efforts globally.
- *Rachel Carson's "Silent Spring"* (1993). Though twenty years old, this production from the PBS series *The American Experience* offers an excellent historical lesson for anyone not familiar with this landmark book and its pioneering author.
- *Seeing the Forest* (2015). A thirty-minute film documenting a case in Oregon where rather than just designating a forest as a wilderness preserve (and thus off-limits to everyone) the Forest Service instigated a remarkable experiment in collaborative governance.

# 12

# Inequality and Growth:
# Prosperity for All

Since Rachel Carson's *Silent Spring*—a book said to have helped spark the modern environmental movement (Lytle 2007)—a widespread understanding has emerged concerning the costs of growth to the environment. A variety of social theories were detailed in Chapter 10 that attempt to paint a fairly thick causal arrow from growth to environmental degradation. Growth nevertheless remains a sacred cow of sorts. Its costs may be great, but the costs of forgoing it, so the thinking goes, are even greater. Environmental degradation remains for many an unfortunate but necessary condition for future prosperity. We've also had some luck at pushing the "limits" further and further out. Some forty-five-plus years ago, a handful of widely circulated books were published on the subject of rapidly approaching limits, like *Limits to Growth* (Meadows et al. 1972) and *The Population Bomb* (Ehrlich 1968). These dire prophesies have yet to pan out. Their failure is relative rather than absolute. Their underlying premise about there being real limits is not wrong; we've just managed to delay hitting up against them. To which proponents of economic growth respond: What makes you so sure we will not delay hitting those limits indefinitely?

Critiquing economic growth on the grounds that it destroys the environment might resonate among the already converted. Yet experience has taught me that among the pro-growth diehards, another argumentative frame is required. What if I were to tell you that economic growth, beyond a certain point, contributes *nothing* to making us more prosperous, happy, or healthy? After a certain point, economic growth might even become regressive to society's overall well-being (Carolan 2013; Dietz, Rosa, and York 2012). Ecological economist Herman Daly (1999) calls this **uneconomic growth**: growth that costs us more than it benefits us. In other words, it is growth that makes us *less* well off.

For a time I too had thought economic growth was synonymous with prosperity, which made the subject in my mind ethically thorny. On the one hand, I wanted to do right to the environment; on the other, I wanted to do right to humanity. Turns out, it's not a zero-sum game. The environment's gain is ours too, and vice versa. Allow me to explain.

## Fast Facts

- Two hundred years ago, affluent, or what at the time were self-described as "civilized," countries had three times more wealth than so-called poor countries. By the end of colonialism, in the 1960s, the average inhabitant of the average affluent nation had become nine times wealthier relative to their contemporary in a low-income country. Today, they are roughly eighty times richer. The 250 richest people on earth, with a combined wealth of $2.7 trillion, have more than the poorest 3.5 billion, with a monetized combined worth of $2.2 trillion (Carolan 2014).

- According to the Millennium Ecosystem Assessment (2005), the total capital stock of the world—most notably natural capital—is degrading faster than wealth created in the formal economy. (Released in 2005, the *Millennium Ecosystem Assessment* involved more than thirteen hundred experts and provides one of the most thorough appraisals of the conditions and trends in the world's ecosystems and the services they provide.) To put it another way, more value is being destroyed than created—a classic case of uneconomic growth. Entities like the World Bank are thus starting to take greater notice of natural capital. In the bank's own words, "Gross Domestic Product (GDP) looks at only one part of economic performance—income—but says nothing about wealth and assets that underlie this income. For example, when a country exploits its minerals, it is actually depleting wealth. The same holds true for over-exploiting fisheries or degrading water resources" (World Bank 2015b).

- Although economic growth appears necessary in the world's poorest countries, its value diminishes tremendously after a country's average income hits roughly $15,000. Beyond this point, neither objective quality-of-life measures, such as average life expectancy, nor subjective ones, like happiness indicators, show any prominent improvement (Easterlin 2015; Jackson 2009; Wilkinson and Pickett 2009). Indeed, beyond a certain point, economic growth, especially when coupled with income inequality, may make us *less* happy—a fact that appears to hold as much for the affluent in those countries as for the poor (Delhey and Dragolov 2015; Wilkinson and Pickett 2009).

- Some countries are able to accomplish plenty, in terms of outcomes we can all get behind, without overly costing the environment. Costa Ricans, for example, live slightly longer than the average citizen of the United States and report having much higher levels of life satisfaction. And they do all this with an ecological footprint that is less than a quarter the size of the average person residing in the United States (Carolan 2013).

## Implications

It is only a couple of pages into this chapter, and I have already made a number of bold statements. I do not make them casually. They are based on a remarkable array of research conducted over the past ten years. The last seventy years, since the end of World War II, has been a tremendous social experiment. By practically every empirical indicator, this experiment has not gone as planned. I am not arguing that economic growth is in itself bad, just that after a certain point there ceases to be any empirical justification for it as an end in itself.

**FIGURE 12.1** Relationship Between Life Expectancy and Countries with a GDP Per Capita ($ Purchasing Power Parity) of $20,000 and Greater

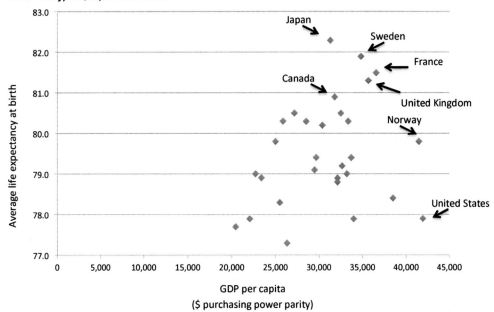

Source: Data obtained from the Food and Agriculture Organization.

## Rethinking Growth

First, let's look at the relationship between a country's average income and its life expectancy. Once a country surpasses a level where its average citizen makes approximately $15,000 annually, gains to life expectancy seem to become decoupled from subsequent economic growth. Although gains in life expectancy are still possible, as made clear by Figure 12.1, which looks only at higher-income countries, the gains appear to be more about how economic wealth is used and distributed than about growth per se. Indeed, some countries manage life expectancies that are higher than the United States with *half* the wealth.

The same holds for more subjective measures. After a certain point, economic growth does nothing to make people feel better off, as documented in Figure 12.2. Yet shouldn't the ultimate goal of development be about making us happier and more satisfied about life as a whole? Once we have our basic material needs satisfied, more stuff does little to make us happier. Again, any further happiness seems a product of how that additional wealth is used and distributed across society as a whole. As with life expectancies, there is remarkable variability across higher-income countries when it comes to how the average citizen feels about being satisfied with life as a whole. We finally have empirical evidence to back up what we've been saying for generations: money doesn't buy happiness (see ECOnnection 12.1).

This stands in stark contrast to conventional macroeconomic theory. Yet even economic theory has a term that recognizes the absurdity of this premise. The **diminishing marginal utility** of stuff, and ultimately of money itself, speaks to the fact that having

FIGURE 12.2 Relationship Between Average Per Capita Income and Percent of Population Reporting Happiness and Satisfaction with Life as a Whole, Select Countries

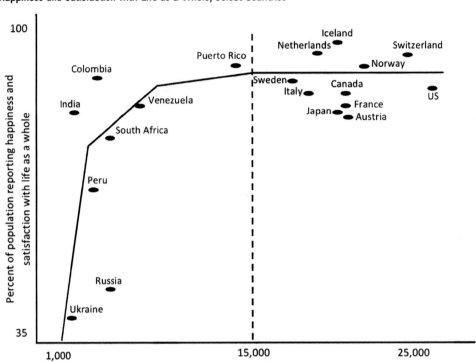

The solid line indicates the general relationship between *x* and *y* axes when all countries are tabulated. Source: Adapted from Carolan (2014) and Wilkinson and Pickett (2009).

more of something eventually provides less additional satisfaction. (The so-called law of diminishing marginal utility, plainly stated, is that the more units of something we consume, the less added enjoyment we get from each additional unit.) Although I am getting a bit ahead of myself, this helps us understand why economic growth after a certain point might indeed be *negatively* correlated with happiness.

Since 1990, inflation-adjusted per capita expenditures on furniture and household goods in the United States have increased a staggering 300 percent; for apparel, the rate of increase was 80 percent; for vehicles, housing, and food, the figure was 15–20 percent (Schor 2010). Clearly, all this stuff has done nothing to make the average American better off. This phenomenon of diminishing marginal utility also offers, as others have argued (Jackson 2009), justification for some level of redistribution. When you are starving, any food will bring an immediate bump in your feelings of satisfaction. At the opposite extreme, when a person in the United States is staring at a refrigerator and pantry overflowing with food, a little more will likely bring zero additional satisfaction. It might even be considered a burden, as they now have to find room for it. And for a growing number of people in high-income countries, the actual act of eating has become stressful, as they worry increasingly about obesity and obesity-related health risks. When talking about this in a class, I had a student thoughtfully ask, "Don't we

# Freedom Isn't Free, and Apparently Best in Moderation

The US-based think tank the Heritage Center and the *Wall Street Journal* compile data resulting in the Index of Economic Freedom. There's a good chance you've heard it mentioned on CNN, MSNBC, or Fox, often in the context of praise for those countries with high index scores. This index is a series of ten economic measurements that have been grouped into four broad categories: rule of law (property rights, freedom from corruption); limited government (fiscal freedom, government spending); regulatory efficiency (business freedom, labor freedom, monetary freedom); and open markets (trade freedom, investment freedom, financial freedom). Countries that score 80 to 100 are considered "free," 79.9 to 70 "mostly free," 69.9 to 60 "moderately free," 59.9 to 50 "mostly un-free," and 49.9 to 40 "repressed."

Setting that index to the side for a moment, I also want to introduce what are known as **Happy Life Years** (HLYs). While life expectancy and self-reported satisfaction surveys are indicative of how well people thrive in a country, neither captures this matter completely. One could imagine, for example, a society where people live long but not happily, such as in cases where medical technologies stretch life out well after quality life begins to diminish. Similarly, one could imagine that people live happily in a country but not for

long, perhaps as a result of overindulgence. Combining these measures resolves some of these limitations. It is common to measure the health of nations by the average number of years people live free from chronic illness: HLYs = life expectancy at birth x happiness score (on a scale of 0 to 1). For purposes of illustration, say life expectancy in Country X is 60 years. If everybody were perfectly happy (with a happiness score of 1), the average HLYs for this country would be 60. If, for example, the country's average happiness score was 0.5, the per capita HLYs lived would be 30.

Figure 12.3 examines the relationship between economic freedom (as captured in the Index of Economic Freedom) and HLYs. There are two rather striking features about this scatterplot. The first is that there is almost no correlation between the two variables. Economic freedom, in other words, appears to have little impact on a country's HLYs. More striking still is where the two variables do seem to have some relationship with each other. A relationship appears to materialize at the high end of the economic freedom score, and it is a negative one. Note how "mostly free" and "free" countries cannot seem to generate very high HLYs scores. Not a single country with an economic freedom score of 70 or greater averages 50 HLYs or more.

**FIGURE 12.3** Relationship Between Economic Freedom Score and Happy Life Years

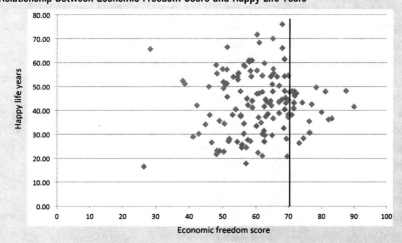

Source: Adapted from Carolan (2013).

at least need pro-growth policies to alleviate poverty? What will happen to them—the poor?" The evidence just does not support the argument that current pro-growth policies do much for the poor. For every $100 of economic growth between 1990 and 2001, a mere *60 cents* went toward poverty reduction for those earning less than $1 a day (Gilding 2011). The poverty-alleviating logic of growth looks something like this: the rich get richer so the poor can be a little less poor (but still poor in the end).

If you dig a little deeper, the data get even more interesting. The problem with growth as currently practiced is not that it degrades the quality of life for some of the world's inhabitants. It is true that levels of global inequality have never been worse; after all, 2016 marked the first time in human history where the richest 1 percent has a combined wealth greater than the remaining 99 percent of the world's population (Oxfam 2015). Yet the rich suffer under this system too—though obviously their suffering is qualitatively different from that of someone in abject poverty. According to the data, economic growth makes life less satisfying for *all* of humanity, rich and poor alike.

Whereas absolute wealth is a poor indicator of a country's level of prosperity, inequality proves to be a strong indicator, as it is negatively correlated with a whole host of prosperity and well-being indicators. This holds even for a nation's affluent. The economically advantaged are better off if the country they live in is more equal. The data on this subject are compelling. More equal societies have fewer health and social problems (see Figure 12.4), treat women and children better, have a greater sense of collective responsibility to those in other countries (see Figure 12.5), have lower rates of mental illnesses, are more willing to cooperate with international environmental agreements, and are more food secure (Carolan 2013; Wilkinson and Pickett 2009; Wilkinson, Pickett, and De Vogli 2010).

Perhaps it is no coincidence that welfare economics, as detailed in the previous chapter, has found such favor in the United States. More equal countries tend to be more cooperative (Wilkinson and Pickett 2009). The high levels of inequality in the United States offer the perfect environment for a perspective that assumes people are self-interested and selfish. This also helps us make some sense of why most of the industrialized world chose to continue with the Kyoto Protocol despite the noninvolvement of major greenhouse gas–emitting countries like the United States and China. (The Kyoto Protocol is an international agreement linked to the United Nations Framework Convention on Climate Change, which sets targets for thirty-seven industrialized countries and the European community for reducing greenhouse gas emissions. Recognizing that developed countries are principally responsible for the majority of greenhouse gas emissions in the atmosphere, the protocol places a heavier burden on developed nations under the principle of "common but differentiated responsibilities." The protocol was adopted in Kyoto, Japan, on December 11, 1997. It entered into force on February 16, 2005.) From a purely self-interested perspective, it makes no sense to comply with the protocol, given that any greenhouse gas reductions would easily be offset by nonsignatory countries. Perhaps these countries chose to do so out of a heightened sense of global responsibility (Kysar 2010), a sentiment, perhaps not coincidentally, more likely to be found among more equal societies (Delhey and Dragolov 2015).

Innovation also appears to be enhanced by equality, as more equal societies have higher levels of patents granted per capita. This may be due in part to their higher levels of social mobility and educational achievement: more equal societies are less likely to

**FIGURE 12.4** Relationship Between Health and Social Problems and Income Inequality, Select High-Income Countries

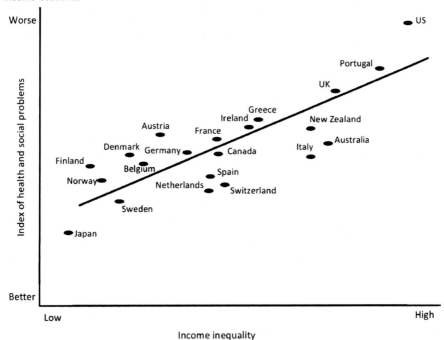

Source: Adapted from Wilkinson and Pickett (2009).

**FIGURE 12.5** Relationship Between Foreign Aid Spending and Income Inequality, Select High-Income Countries

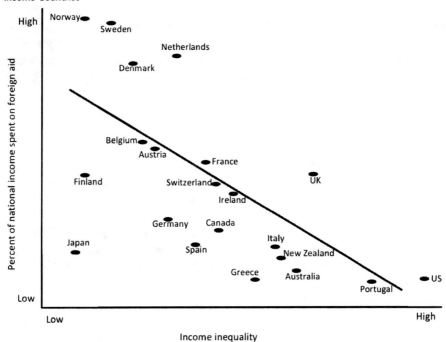

Source: Adapted from Wilkinson and Pickett (2009).

waste their potential human capital, since they provide greater opportunities for all of their members (Wilkinson, Pickett, and De Vogli 2010). Think about this in the context of renewable energy. Those countries first to transition to renewable energy sources will have done so because they are highly adaptable and innovative. Are countries like the United States hindering their ability to make this transition with their high levels of inequality? In sum, inequality is a tremendous source of inefficiency. The efficiency through which a society utilizes its resources to enhance its well-being increases at low to moderate levels of economic development but *declines* at high levels, particularly when combined with high levels of inequality (Dietz, Rosa, and York 2012; Knight and Rosa 2011). A high level of inequality in a society is therefore not only morally problematic but bad policy, as it reduces everyone's welfare.

## The Sociology of Consumption

Why do we consume so much stuff? The following five sociological mechanisms have been linked to escalating levels of consumption: social comparison, creation of self-identity, specialization, sociotechnical systems, and planned obsolescence. I briefly take each in turn, recognizing that this discussion represents the barest of overviews of a richly complex literature.

### SOCIAL COMPARISON

More than a century ago Thorstein Veblen ([1899] 1967), in his analysis of Western European countries, introduced us to the now commonplace term **conspicuous consumption**: the idea that we consume, at least in part, to display to others our social power and status. In centuries past, the displaying of power and status was relatively straightforward, involving things like commanding large armies, possessing huge castles, and ruling over entire societies. Individuals today, however, no longer possess great armies or rule over a peasant class. According to Veblen, we therefore make social statements in other ways, such as by surrounding ourselves with nice things to signal to others our placement in the socioeconomic hierarchy. The mechanism of social comparison also has a ratcheting-up effect on consumption. Individuals attempt to display a social status above what their household income levels allow, as they constantly strive to outdo those around them—a phenomenon commonly known as "keeping up with the Joneses."

### CREATION OF SELF-IDENTITY

Consumption is more than just the pursuit of status. It can also have a much deeper function. Our very sense of self is tied to it. The term *lifestyle* is important here, as attachment to groups, according to this argument, is an important source of personal identity. Thus, whether you have chosen, for example, a green lifestyle or one of someone who likes outdoor recreation (both popular among my students), consumption is tied to both. Association with the green lifestyle might require that you buy, say, organic food, a Toyota Prius, or solar panels for your house; at least these represent recent purchases by a friend of mine who embraces this lifestyle. If your identity is that of an outdoors person, you might, for example, walk around wearing clothes from Cabela's or Patagonia, depending on the type of outdoors persona you're trying to communicate to others.

## SPECIALIZATION

Henry Ford famously claimed that you could have the Model T automobile in any color as long as that color was black. That mentality reflects the logic of mass production. Today, more producers—perhaps to fit the aforementioned lifestyles and identities they support—are widening their range of what they produce to fit the specialized "needs" of consumers. An example of this is shoes. When my grandmother was growing up in rural Iowa in the 1920s, she had two pairs of shoes: one for work and one for dress. Fast-forward some ninety years to today. Now, two pairs of shoes would never do. We seem instead to "need" a specialized pair of shoes for almost every one of the day's activities: shoes for in the house, shoes for the garden, shoes for the gym (actually, there you'll need numerous different shoes depending on what you're doing), shoes for work, and so forth.

## SOCIOTECHNICAL SYSTEMS

This concept reminds us that there are broader sociological reasons that belie the concept of consumer choice. We should be careful not to look too exclusively at the individual, in other words, to understand why they choose to consume as they do. In some instances, that choice is made for them (as earlier discussed when talking about choosing to drive). Millions around the world, for example, did not choose to have their nondigital television sets become obsolete as analog television broadcasting was converted to and replaced by digital television. Similarly, if your grocery store does not carry organic food, you cannot choose to have an organic diet (nor can we say you're choosing a nonorganic diet). We can only choose what the sociotechnical system lets us choose.

## PLANNED OBSOLESCENCE

After World War II, US automobile manufacturers were facing an uncertain future as more Americans became car owners. Once every household (or at least those that could afford one) owned a car, who would be left to buy new automobiles? The answer was to get people to purchase a new car every couple of years. But how? A well-maintained car would theoretically last decades, perhaps even a person's entire life. How, then, could a car owner be cajoled into choosing to buy a new car even if the one currently owned was—from a functionality standpoint—perfectly fine? Enter planned obsolescence. The goal of planned obsolescence as it applies to automobiles is to make the one you currently have in your garage appear obsolete. This is accomplished with the occasional redesign of the car's interior and exterior so as to literally make your current model appear old (even if you just bought it last year). This process is also helped along by incrementally adding "upgrades"—like rearview cameras, eleven-speaker surround sound, and satellite navigation—and convincing the buyer that they need these extra bells and whistles.

Planned obsolescence can take other forms too, like designing devices that cannot be easily taken apart and repaired (see Image 12.1). When things break down—and we know they will because there's no incentive to make products that last a lifetime—we're effectively required to buy new. I remember when the "on" button broke off my blender and how I was forced to get a new blender because there was no way to get it fixed—just because of a defective "on" button!

**IMAGE 12.1**

Phones are being rendered obsolete even before you buy them! Source: "New phone coming soon" by Jason Tester Guerrilla Futures (flickr.com/streamishmc) is licensed copyright © 2012 under CC BY-ND 2.0.

## Environmental Justice

Closely related to the above discussion is the subject of environmental justice. As defined by the Environmental Protection Agency, environmental justice is about the "fair treatment and meaningful involvement of all people regardless of race, color, national origin, or income with respect to the development, implementation, and enforcement of environmental laws, regulations, and policies. Fair treatment means that no population, due to policy or economic disempowerment, is forced to bear a disproportionate share of the negative human health or environmental impacts of pollution or environmental consequences resulting from industrial, municipal, and commercial operations or the execution of federal, state, local and tribal programs and policies" (EPA 2012; see Image 12.2).

Our understanding of environmental justice has grown as scholarship accumulates, showing the unequal distribution of environmental threats. These threats disparately affect not only those of lower socioeconomic status but also certain ethnic minorities. Pollution-based racial discrimination goes by the name of **environmental racism** (though the concept can be defined much more broadly to include racial discrimination in environmental policy making and enforcement of regulations and laws, in addition to the targeting of communities of color for toxic waste disposal and siting of polluting industries).

**IMAGE 12.2**

Source: "PeoplesClimateMarch-2014" by Annette Bernhardt (flickr.com/mtumesoul) is licensed copyright © 2014 under CC BY-SA 2.0.

The birth of the term *environmental racism* has been traced back to 1982, when civil rights activists organized to stop the state of North Carolina from dumping 120 million pounds of soil laced with polychlorinated biphenyls in the predominantly African American county of Warren (Bullard 1990; Mohai, Pellow, and Roberts 2009). Out of this was born a new social movement whose aim has been to address concerns ignored by mainstream middle-class white environmentalists. The environmental justice movement has heavily (and rightly) criticized the conventional environmental movement for focusing too much on pristine ecological landscapes and not enough on people whose lives are threatened daily by ecological risk.

Some of the earliest research into this subject focused on the location of hazardous waste sites. The first was conducted by the US General Accounting Office in 1983 (GAO 1983). The study documented how African American communities in Southern US states hosted a disproportionate share of waste sites. This study was followed famously by the United Church of Christ (UCC) Commission for Racial Justice's national study in 1987 (Chavis and Lee 1987). This pathbreaking study showed that toxic-waste facilities across the United States were far more likely to end up in the backyards of people of color. According to the UCC study, race was the most important factor in predicting where these waste sites were located. In 1990 sociologist Robert Bullard (1990) published the now-classic book *Dumping in Dixie*. This work represents the first comprehensive examination of environmental racism by systematically linking hazard-ous facility siting with historical patterns of segregation in the Southern United States. Bullard documents in exquisite detail how communities of color have been deliberately targeted when locations were sought for society's waste (see ECOnnection12.2).

Some twenty-five years after the UCC study, similar findings continue to be made. Some of the recent research utilizes GIS (geographic information system) technology and new methodological techniques to better control for proximity. Employing these new tools, environmental justice scholars in fact "find that the magnitude of racial dis-parities around hazardous waste facilities is *much greater* than what previous national studies have reported" (Mohai and Saha 2007, 343; emphasis added). Those who be-lieve we live in a postracial society will be surprised to learn that the evidence suggests that environmental racism is more pronounced today than it was fifty years ago. One longitudinal study looking at Michigan from 1950 to 1990 concludes that "whereas significant racial, socioeconomic, and housing disparities at the time of siting were not in evidence for facilities sited prior to 1970, patterns of disparate siting were found for facilities sited after 1970" (Saha and Mohai 2005, 618).

Prior to the 1970s, we knew far less about the ecological risks associated with busi-ness as usual. The affluent therefore did not have as much reason to oppose living next to industrial facilities. Fortunately, we did not remain ignorant forever about ecological risk. The 1970s marked the beginning of unprecedented growth in public environmen-tal concern and opposition to facilities that bring with them environmental harms. With this came growing opposition to the siting of facilities that threatened environ-mental and human health. People no longer wanted these operations sited in their back-yards. Yet not everyone is in possession of sufficient resources to keep their backyards free of these facilities. Not surprisingly, then, the siting of hazardous waste facilities followed the path of least political resistance. And as inequalities continue to grow in countries like the United States, the haves have a lot more to apply to resist polluting industries being sited in their backyards than the have-nots. Hence the growing levels of environmental injustice.

Even when controlling for economic and sociopolitical variables, factors uniquely associated with race continue to correlate strongly with the location of the nation's haz-ardous waste facilities (Stretesky and McKie 2016). It's hard for me to believe that in each of those cases, there is overt racial discrimination going on. Perhaps some of this envi-ronmental racism is actually an artifact of environmental economism. **Economism**, for those unfamiliar with the term, refers to the act of reducing the world to economic di-mensions, a practice, as discussed in Chapter 11, lying at the heart of welfare economics and a specific example of methodological reductionism. When assessing the costs and benefits of policy options, this approach assigns a lower value to those of lower socioeco-nomic status. As certain ethnic minorities make on average less than other groups, they will be disproportionately penalized by this approach. The welfare-economics approach, in other words, legitimizes environmental racism in some cases.

Whereas early environmental racism studies originated in the United States, the scope of research in recent years has spanned the world (see Case Study 12.1). Two types of envi-ronmental injustice are being increasingly cited: international and global (Martinez-Alier et al. 2016). On the one hand, in reference to the former and as discussed in previous chapters, polluting industries are moving around the world. In doing this, they too often

ECOnnection 12.2

# The Plight of Native Americans

The term *ecocide* has been used to describe the US government's twentieth-century treatment of its Native peoples (Grinde and Johansen 1995), a fact that's not entirely denied by the US Department of Defense (DOD 2001): "In order to ensure that it meets its national security mission, DOD operates and trains on vast amounts of land, including American Indian and Alaska Native lands. Evidence of DOD's past use of these lands remains: hazardous materials, unexploded ordnance (UXO), abandoned equipment, unsafe buildings, and debris. This contamination degrades the natural environment and threatens tribal economic, social and cultural welfare."

Fifty years after the conclusion of the so-called Indian Wars, Native Americans were again uprooted from their land when the US government seized more than three hundred thousand acres of the Pine Ridge Reservation in South Dakota. (Families there were paid three cents an acre.) The government wanted this land as a practice bombing range for pilots before being sent off to fight for the Allies in World War II, an activity that laced the environment with contaminants (Bordewich et al. 2007).

The US government continues to unduly burden Native Americans with ecological risks up to this day. An analysis looking at closed military bases in the United States found that Native Americans are significantly more likely to be living next to these contaminated spaces than any other ethnic group (Hooks and Smith 2004). One particular risk highlighted by this study is unexploded ord-

nance, including mines and explosive shells, which have killed, maimed, and injured many. Native Americans continue to be threatened by their environment at levels that would be patently unacceptable to any less marginalized social group. Then there is the case of Native Hawaiians seeking restitution for damage to the island of Kaho'olawe, degraded by close to fifty years of abuse from the US military through use as a target range for warplanes (Blackford 2004). Or take the case of the Mescalero Apache tribe of New Mexico, which has experienced decades of exploitation after uranium deposits were discovered on its land in the 1950s. Initially, uranium extraction was an involuntary activity imposed on tribes for purposes of nuclear power and out of the US military's desire for weapons-grade uranium. However, in recent decades the resource has developed into an economic necessity for the Mescalero Apache. For instance, when the tribe was approached with a proposal to build a monitored retrievable storage facility for nuclear waste on its land in the 1990s, the chief and tribal council welcomed the opportunity. The "need" for this facility arose from the tribe's socioeconomic vulnerability: the unemployment rate within the tribe was greater than 33 percent, and more than half of the tribe lived below the federal poverty line. This case is a reminder that environmental injustice can involve not only direct exploitation but also indirect exploitation through forced consent under severe economic and social pressures (Vickery and Hunter 2016).

## CASE STUDY 12.1
# Environmental Racism in Cape Town, South Africa

On June 23, 2000, the bulk ore carrier *MV Treasure* sank off the coast of South Africa, spilling more than thirteen hundred tons of bunker oil in a marine ecosystem that supported the largest and third-largest colonies of African penguins worldwide. (Six years earlier, some ten thousand African penguins had been oiled after the sinking of the *Apollo Sea* bulk ore carrier.) The world was outraged, prompting environmental organizations from around the world to respond at breakneck speed. Newspapers as far away as North America carried advertisements requesting donations for the army of volunteers who worked tirelessly to clean, rehabilitate, and release the affected birds and scour their ravaged habitat. Within just a few weeks, almost twenty-five thousand birds had been treated.

At the same time, an equally (or arguably more) calamitous ecological event was occurring on the mainland in Cape Town. If the cameras and volunteers would have ventured just a few miles inland, they would have seen hundreds of thousands of poor, black Capetonians living in some of the most squalid conditions imaginable. Here pollution, sewage, uncollected waste, standing water, disease, and pestilence ravaged those living in these low-income communities. The environment was killing these people, just the way it had turned against the beloved African penguin. But there was one big difference between the two cases: the world didn't seem to care about the people living in the slums. Making this case even more sad is the fact that the postapartheid constitution, finalized in 1996, includes a bill of rights that grants all South Africans the right to an "environment that is not harmful to their health or well-being" and the right to "ecologically sustainable development" (section 24) (McDonald 2005). Apparently, this group was not even viewed by the South African government as worthy of its attention.

---

follow the path of least political resistance, which places them squarely in the backyards of some of society's most marginalized. Then there are risks that are truly global in character, like climate change (Shue 2014). These threats exacerbate existing inequalities, as those best positioned in terms of resources to keep themselves safe are also often those most responsible for the problems in the first place.

## Solutions

The solution to the above problems, we know, does not lie in doing away entirely with inequality. People *are* different—in terms of their contributions, skills, and interests—and need to be treated (and rewarded) as such. Differential rewards motivate people to make the world a better place, though clearly people are not motivated by *only* reward. Moreover, there are diminishing marginal returns in those rewards. The opportunity to make another $10,000 means a whole lot more to someone currently making $10,000 a year than it does to someone whose annual salary is a couple of million dollars. At

## ETHICAL QUESTION 12.1
# Is There a Right Level of Inequality?

Although most people believe extreme poverty to be morally wrong, the morality of inequality is far from settled terrain. Most can agree that some inequality is not only fair but best for society, as differential reward (especially when that reward is equally available to all) encourages people to make the world a better place. Empirical evidence (and common sense) also indicates that too much inequality stifles innovation and drive. Where's the incentive when the haves have everything and the rest of society has little chance of ever having anything? Getting the level of differential reward right is therefore not only an ethical question but also one with profound practical consequences.

To help us think through this question, Herman Daly (1999) offers the following instructive observation. He proposes a factor of ten as an inequality ceiling. The US military and universities have managed to keep their ratios close to or even below this level while maintaining tremendous drive among individuals within these organizations. In the military, for instance, the highest-paid generals

make roughly ten times the wages of a private. In a university, the prized rank of distinguished professor brings with it a salary that is roughly six to eight times that of a full time non–tenure track instructor. Compare this to the corporate world. Take Walmart: in 2007 its CEO, H. Lee Scott, made $29,682,000—that's 1,314 times more than the company's average full-time workers (Anderson et al. 2008). The CEO of Walmart also makes roughly 150 times more than a top-ranking US general and distinguished professor. Is that an efficient and effective distribution of resources? Is the CEO of Walmart 150 times more motivated than US generals and distinguished professors? Do we believe the head of Walmart is delivering 150 times more value to society than a top military commander or, say, a Nobel Prize–winning professor?

One way to frame this discussion is to talk about growing the middle class and expanding opportunities so people can have the freedom and liberty to pursue a life that is meaningful to them. Right now, far too many people lack these basic freedoms.

what point, then, is a society's innovative spirit maximized, and after which point does more inequality begin being responsible for more harm than good? This is a question we need to be discussing (see Ethical Question 12.1).

## A Postgrowth Society

It's curious why so many people continue to be enamored with growth even in the face of mounting evidence that we shouldn't be, particularly after a certain point of affluence is attained. John Stuart Mill, one of the founding parents of economics, wrote clearly about the limitations of economic growth: "It is scarcely necessary to remark that a stationary condition of capital and population implies no stationary state of human improvement. There would be as much scope as ever for all kinds of mental culture, and moral and social progress; as much room for improving the Art of Living and much more likelihood of its being improved, when minds cease to be engrossed by the art of getting on" (1848, 317).

Economists Robert Ayres and Benjamin Warr (2009) argue that "the historic link between output (GDP) growth and employment has been weakened, if not broken" (xvi). For the last two centuries, job losses in one sector were absorbed in another. This was particularly the case in higher-income countries, where, for example, workers displaced out of agriculture could often find employment in a thriving manufacturing sector. The problem, however, is that sectors expected to flourish this century employ very few people; think data server farms. (Two examples: a three-thousand-square-foot Facebook data center in Oregon that employs *thirty-five* full-time people; the $46 million in tax breaks North Carolina gave to Apple so they would build a server farm within the state that created fifty jobs [Carolan 2014].) Over the last fifteen years countries in North America, Europe, and Southeast Asia have witnessed a dramatic increase in labor productivity. Yet, unlike in the past, this productivity has yielded few if any additional jobs. The recent recession has only exacerbated this process. The US economy lost almost eight million jobs between 2008 and 2010 (Isidore 2010). During this process of shedding jobs businesses have learned to do more with less labor. Most of those jobs lost are therefore not coming back. The Dow has recovered all of its losses from the Great Recession, gaining more than 120 percent from its low in March 2009—the third strongest bull market for the Dow since World War II. And yet the US job market has recovered only 5.5 million of the 8.7 million jobs lost because of the financial crisis—the worst labor-market recovery since World War II. This helps explain why inflation-adjusted average income in 2014 is 8 percent lower than in 2007, when the Dow hit its previous high, and why almost all—93 percent to be exact—of pretax income gains of the current economic recovery have thus far gone to the top 1 percent. And the recovery has been even harder on households of color: the wealth of white households was thirteen times the median wealth of black households in 2013, compared with eight times the wealth in 2010 (Pew Research Center 2014).

The great twentieth-century economist John Maynard Keynes ([1930] 1963), writing some eighty years ago, believed that by the dawn of the twenty-first century, people would be working just a couple of days a week as a result of the remarkable productivity increases he (correctly) foresaw coming. He predicted (incorrectly) that rather than practicing overconsumption in order to keep everyone working *more* hours—to buy more stuff we would need to work more—we would instead choose to take advantage of those increases in productivity to work less and increase our leisure time. Employment for everyone is possible when the average worker works, depending on the society, twenty hours a week (see Case Study 12.2). In such a scenario, overconsumption is neither possible, as a twenty-hour workweek doesn't allow for it, nor necessarily desired; with everyone in the same boat, the social pressures to overconsume are dramatically weakened. How could Keynes have predicted that we would instead decide to continue working longer hours that make us terribly unhappy so we can buy products that do nothing to enhance our well-being while depleting our natural resources and destroying the health of ourselves and our planet? Does that make any sense? Keynes didn't think so either.

There is an enormous difference between an economy purposefully designed to be indifferent to growth, where prosperity and well-being increase in the absence of economic growth, and a failing growth economy, where growth, prosperity, and well-being

## CASE STUDY 12.2
## Kellogg's Six-Hour Day

Breakfast cereal giant W. K. Kellogg implemented a policy back in 1930 that we could learn from today. In response to the Great Depression, Kellogg made his workforce of fifteen hundred go from a traditional eight-hour to a six-hour workday instead of laying off some three hundred workers. The new arrangement meant everyone had to take a slight pay cut, but Kellogg also initiated production-based bonuses that could offset most of those losses. The policy was an unqualified success. The employees used their newly available time to pursue things of their choosing, which often involved activities that built family, community, and citizenship. In general, employees were happier under this new arrangement (Hunnicutt 1996). They also worked harder. The production of, for example, boxes of shredded whole-wheat biscuits per hour increased from eighty-three to ninety-six once the workday was shortened (Botsman and Rogers 2010).

World War II changed everything. Franklin Roosevelt signed an executive order demanding, among other things, longer workdays so the production needs of a war economy could be met. The labor unions initially opposed a policy to return to an eight-hour workday but eventually acquiesced, as they fully expected a return to a six-hour workday after the war's conclusion (Hunnicutt 1996). Workers polled as late as 1946 found that 77 percent of men and 87 percent of women actually preferred a thirty-hour workweek even if it meant lower wages (Fitz 2009). And the longer hours and larger paychecks did little to actually make the employees any better off. As one employee later reported, "Everybody thought they were going to get rich when they got that eight-hour deal and it really didn't make a big difference. . . . Some went out and bought automobiles right quick and they didn't gain much on that because the car took the extra money they had" (Botsman and Rogers 2010, 46).

all decline while inequality increases. In a failing growth economy, out-of-control unemployment and crushing state, household, and personal debt seriously threaten that society's social and political stability. A failing economy, for instance, helped precipitate the 2011 Egyptian revolution. Conversely, an economy indifferent to growth—even one designed to hold steady and not grow—can avoid all this if intentionally constructed with these ends in mind.

How do we do that? We can start by redirecting taxes away from things we generally want (like labor) to things we generally don't want (like pollution and waste). This encourages employment—a key difference from a failing growth economy—and discourages wasteful resource use and dependence, which can help buffer an economy from the shocks that come when access to those resources is disrupted (Gilding 2011). We can also institute policies that encourage a shorter workweek. The government already regulates how much children can work. Why can't it do the same with everyone? By working less, we will also spend less. And as growth is no longer an imperative, we can tighten access to credit, thereby reducing or eliminating entirely personal debt. What would you choose, if given the choice: being caught on what Juliet Schor (1992) has termed the **work-spend cycle** (where we work to spend, which in turn requires us to work more) or having an extra month (or more) of vacation time a year to spend with family and friends? If you are anything like the people I have asked this question, you very likely will prefer the latter.

As noted earlier, once we're well fed, clothed, adequately sheltered, educated, and feel generally secure, happiness comes from something other than just more stuff and additional wealth. By working less, we will have time to finally engage in those activities that truly make us happy. We will have time to engage in "mental culture" and "social progress" and improve overall the "Art of Living," to borrow terms used by John Stuart Mill. Decades of social capital research point to the benefits that accrue to individuals and society as a whole when people have the opportunity to engage with one another on a personal level (see Bartolini, Bilancini, and Luigi 2016). Moving away from our current obsession with growth will also address the aforementioned problems associated with rabid inequality. As the late Henry Wallich (former governor of the US Federal Reserve) famously put it, "Growth is a substitute for equality of income. So long as there is growth there is hope, and that makes large income differential tolerable" (1972).

We also shouldn't hold out hope for so-called service-based, postindustrial, or information-based economies. *Postindustrial* does not mean *postpollution*. These societies are built on an economy whereby manufacturing is reduced through trade, while consumption skyrockets, with the help of an expanding financial sector so we can buy all this stuff. When all ecological impacts are actually accounted for, most service- or information-based economies are at least as resource hungry as industrial economies. We will also have to rethink how we do leisure and recreation in this new economy. With current practices, these sectors are terribly energy and resource intensive, suggesting that we need to rethink not only what we consume but also how we recreate and relax (Huang and Wang 2015). Recreation is also becoming expensive. Today many worry about whether they can afford the next big trip (Rojek 2010). I guess that's why I increasingly hear people comment when on vacation that they need a vacation from their vacation. In a postgrowth economy, leisure will once again be leisurely.

It is also worth asking why leisure today must involve going someplace. Or perhaps it is more accurate to characterize it as getting away—after all, that's often how we characterize vacations. Maybe, if we enhanced the attractiveness of communities, we could reduce the "need" to travel to distant places. This would not only be a tremendous ecological gain, recognizing the significant environmental footprint associated with air travel and everything else one does when touring a distant land, but also help dampen the need we feel to (over) work, as we would no longer have this large expense looming on the horizon. And in the long term, this would have a virtuous effect. At present, contemporary communities are so lowly regarded that they offer few inducements to encourage people to stick around when they have free time. Making communities places we actually *want* to be will keep people within the community and thus further enhance the social and ecological dynamics of this space still further.

One modeling attempt by a Canadian economist illustrates how economic stabilization (growth of less than 0.1 percent annually) can successfully occur, though the entire transition will take a couple of decades (Victor 2008). Under the modeled Canadian scenario, unemployment and poverty were halved, the debt-to-GDP ratio was reduced by some 75 percent, and greenhouse gas emissions for the nation were cut 20 percent. The model revealed a couple of important insights. Changes to investment and the structure of the labor market have to be handled carefully to make a postgrowth society work. While net business investment was reduced in the modeled scenario, there was also a significant shift in investment to public goods through changes in taxation and public spending. The model supports the point made earlier that it is not wealth per se that improves societal well-being and resilience but how that money is spent and distributed. Unemployment was avoided both by reducing the average number of working hours (while assuming that labor productivity continues to increase) and by sharing the work more equally across the available workforce. As certain European labor policies have already shown, reducing the working week is a relatively simple solution to the challenge of maintaining full employment with nonincreasing output (Jackson 2009).

Although it is difficult for some to conceive of how companies can flourish without growth, consider that this is precisely how small businesses—like so-called mom-and-pop establishments—have operated for centuries. Businesses under this model have costs and revenues. When profits are earned, some are reinvested back into the business to replace or upgrade worn-out equipment. The goal is not to "grow" but rather to reduce costs in the hope of increasing profits. As Juliet Schor (2010) notes, businesses can be quite successful in the market when they offer better quality for a given price, a strategy that can be easily hindered when owners become obsessed with growth. Continual expansion is neither necessary nor sufficient for profitability.

The point that prosperity comes not from wealth but from the efficient use of resources lies at the heart of alternative measures to GDP. Throughout much of the twentieth century, GDP was the gold standard of progress and prosperity; it was long assumed that growth could deliver unlimited happiness. Now that we know it does not, alternative measures of process and prosperity are being developed. One of the most popular alternative measures is the Human Development Index. The HDI factors in a country's life expectancy as well as measures of literacy, education, and standards of living. The HDI was originally devised by the Pakistani economist Mahbub ul Haq and Indian economist Amartya Sen in 1990. Its goal, in the words of Mahbub ul Haq, is to give "human capital"—*humanity* (versus money)—"the attention it deserves" when talking about and implementing policies directed at this nebulous thing we call development (1995, 3). The HDI is now used widely in the international development community and by organizations like the United Nations. In line with all that has already been discussed, beyond a certain level of affluence, wealth has no correlation to a country's HDI ranking.

In recent years, attempts have also been made to combine HDI with ecological indicators, as presently HDI ignores environmental variables. Figure 12.6 provides an example, plotting countries according to their HDI ranking and ecological footprint. Note the wide disparity between countries with high HDI scores and ecological footprints behind those corresponding levels of well-being. One country has managed to produce a high HDI score within the parameters of what ecological-footprint scholars deem to be a truly sustainable economy (a footprint of 2.1 hectares per person or less): Cuba. It will be interesting to see if and how the new relationship between the United States and Cuba changes these scores in the future.

**FIGURE 12.6** Human Development Index Plotted Against Ecological Footprint

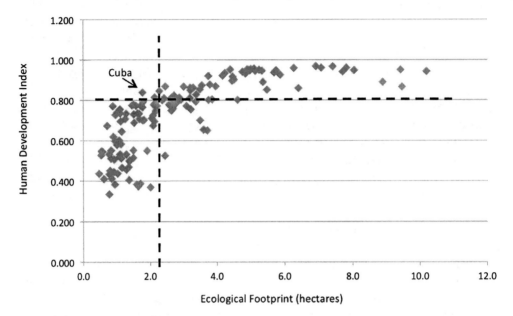

The Human Development Index (HDI) is calculated on a scale from 0 to 1, where 0 is the lowest and 1 is the highest. Source: Carolan (2013).

Another widely cited measure of progress, which takes into account a country's ecological condition, is the Happy Planet Index (HPI). The fundamental premise of the HPI is the acknowledgment that real prosperity can be said to have been reached only when the well-being of humankind does not come at the earth's expense (New Economics Foundation 2012). HPI scores range from 0 to 100. High scores reflect a society with high life expectancy, high life satisfaction, and a low ecological footprint. This measure turns convention on its head. For example, the United States ranks an unflattering 105th place, while Costa Rica comes out on top. Costa Ricans live slightly longer than Americans, report having much higher levels of life satisfaction, and do all this with an ecological footprint that is less than a quarter the size of the average US citizen. The HPI also supports the argument that it is not environmental throughput (aka growth) that makes a society great. For example, Vietnam and Nigeria have the same ecological footprints (1.4 hectares). Yet whereas the average resident of Nigeria lives to only 51 years and reports low life satisfaction, the average Vietnamese lives as long as most Europeans (75.2 years) and reports being roughly as happy as the average Japanese citizen (ibid.).

## Development as Freedom, Justice, and Empowerment

There is also good reason to believe readjustments to developmental policies and practices like those just mentioned would go a long way toward alleviating many of the environmental injustices described earlier. To work through this idea, I'll turn to Amartya Sen's thoughts on the subject and in particular his theory of justice when he speaks specifically on the pitfalls that come with making economic growth an end in itself.

# Community Capitals Framework

There are a variety of ways to translate Sen's thinking about capabilities into a pragmatic developmental program. The HDI represents one attempt to put Sen's thoughts into practice. Yet arguably, any developmental approach that works to empower—rather than just enrich—squares well with Sen's writings.

Take the community capitals framework. According to this approach, sustainable development is the product of a triple bottom line, involving economic, social, and environmental accountability (Flora 2008). These three sustainability pillars come together when a variety of capitals are present in sufficient degree, including natural, built, financial, political, social, human, and cultural capitals. Although equally important in the achievement of the aforementioned triple bottom line, investments in social and human capitals in particular, research shows, can produce a "spiraling up" effect that leads to the enhancement of all capitals over time (Emery and Flora 2006). We can see in Table 12.1 the role of the various capitals at play in rural development and how they build on each other. A community capitals approach expands our understanding of return on investment, noting that it should be measured in terms of an increase in *all* capitals, rather than just in terms of economic growth (financial capital). Furthermore, community capitals research believes in involving people so they can direct change from within a community, a point that also fits with Sen's point that only the communities—through debate and public reasoning—can determine what's best for them.

TABLE 12.1. Seven Capitals and Their Role in Sustainable and Just Agroecosystems and Communities*

| CAPITAL | DEFINITION | ROLE IN SUSTAINABLE AND JUST AGRO-ECOSYSTEMS AND COMMUNITIES |
|---|---|---|
| Natural | The natural biophysical assets of any given locale – can include natural resources (e.g., water, soil, air, minerals), amenities (e.g., trout streams and National Parks), and ecosystem services. | Represents the ecological productive base for the long-term growth and maintenance of other capitals |
| Cultural | Cultural understandings and practices that shape how we grasp the world, including what we take for granted and how we envision possible alternatives for social change. | Represents a measure to understand embodied knowledge and worldview diversity within a community. The richer the stock the greater the options for envisioning social change. Embodied knowledge is vital for "problem" definitions and the creation of just solutions. |
| Human | Representational knowledge and skills (as opposed to embodied knowledge) acquired through more formal educational channels. | Represents a measure of a community's formal knowledge base. Representational knowledge is vital for problem solving. |
| Social | The social glue of a community, which includes mutual trust, reciprocity, and respect and empathy for others. | Represents a measure of community cohesiveness. Social capital is a social lubricant that reduces the transaction costs of enhancing the other capitals. |
| Political | Access to structures of power and power brokers as well as the ability to influence the rules and regulations that shape access to resources. | Represents a measure of a community's power as well as a way to assess its distribution across stakeholders. The more evenly distributed the better the likelihood for just, equitable solutions. |
| Financial | The financial resources available to invest in things like community capacity building, knowledge exchange, the built environment, and entrepreneurship. | Represents a measure a community's economic wealth. The more evenly distributed across the community the better the likelihood for just, equitable solutions. |
| Built | The built environment, which includes constructed natural areas (e.g., parks, reconstituted wetlands, ski runs) and the physical "things" of communities (e.g., sidewalks, internet access, public transportation). | Represents a measure of a community's physical assets; assets that not only support other capitals but which could be repurposed for multiple ends and thus substituted for economic assets (e.g., versus constructing something new utilizing an existing physical structure). |

* Note: While the authors utilized these definitions it is understood that there is variability in the literature in how these concepts are understood and applied.

Source: Carolan and Hale 2016.

What makes Sen's approach to justice so interesting is his focus on capabilities, which are necessary for people to function fully in the lives they choose. It is Sen's contention that justice should not be about the distribution of goods and services but be about how individuals are able to use those goods and services so they can flourish. In Sen's words, the "focus has to be, in this analysis, on the freedoms generated by commodities, rather than on the commodities seen on their own" (1999, 74). Our current focus on economic growth, conversely, cares nothing about what commodities do for people; all that matters is that commodities are produced and sold. In sum, Sen's focus on capabilities forces us to ask what is needed to transform mere economic growth into a truly prosperous life while also considering what might interrupt the process.

This discussion links up with something discussed back in Chapter 10, when I wrote about Berlin's dual understanding of freedom. Sen (1993) draws inspiration from Berlin in his writings on the subject. Prosperity requires positive rights, like the right to utilize goods and services in ways that allow people to flourish. But it also, and equally, requires negative rights, such as the right to live in an environment where that process is not interrupted by, say, toxic waste, environmental racism, patriarchy, or runaway inequality. Instead of offering a universal set of capabilities, Sen believes the communities in question are best positioned to decide what it is they value and the life they wish to live: "[The] problem is not with listing important capabilities, but with insisting on one pre-determined canonical list of capabilities, chosen by theorists without any general social discussion or public reasoning. To have such a fixed list, emanating entirely from pure theory, is to deny the possibility of fruitful public participation on what should be included and why" (2005, 158; see ECOnnection 12.3).

Environmental justice movements have much in common with Sen's theory of justice and his emphasis on capabilities. This is especially true for movements originating in low-income countries, where the development priorities of outsiders have threatened the functioning of local communities (Schlosberg 2013). One key component of almost any type of environmental justice activism is building community capacity and facilitating community empowerment (Roark 2015; see Movement Matters 12.1).

Evidence of capability building in the environmental justice movement is ubiquitous, especially at the local level. And I'm not just talking about strengthening social ties *within* communities. The reason why, for instance, a study looking at the location of waste incinerators in France discovered that "each additional 1 percent of a town's population that is foreign-born increased the odds that the town received an incinerator by 29 percent" (Laurian and Funderburg 2014, 424) is not solely because individuals within communities with incinerators fail to interact with each other. The communities *themselves* are marginalized, which is to say they are not well integrated with, say, community activists in other communities and broader structures of power (e.g., politicians). We must also not forget that one community's environmental justice movement victory is another's hazardous waste facility, as these "successes" typically just displace an unwanted land use onto another community (see, for example, Malin 2015; Mohai, Pellow, and Roberts 2009).

The movement has also succeeded in making meaningful changes at the national level. Perhaps the most celebrated US example is President Clinton's Executive Order 12898, which mandates all federal agencies to ensure environmental justice in their operations. Another example is the EPA's National Environmental Justice Advisory

MOVEMENT MATTERS 12.1

## The Metales Plant in Tijuana, Mexico

Owned by San Diego–based New Frontier Trading Corporation, the Metales and Derivados battery-recycling plant in Tijuana began smelting in 1972 to recover lead and copper from automobile batteries and other sources. One 1990 study of a local water source found lead and cadmium levels three thousand times and one thousand times, respectively, higher than US standards (Carruthers 2008). The plant was eventually closed in 1994, after repeated noncompliance with environmental regulations. The owners of the plant promptly headed north, to San Diego, California, beyond the reach of Mexican authorities, leaving behind more than six thousand metric tons of lead slag and an additional twenty-four thousand tons of mixed hazardous waste, such as antimony, arsenic, cadmium, and copper (ibid.; Hendricks 2010). The Federal Ministry for Environmental Protection (PROFEPA) took control of the site, built a containment wall, and covered the slag with plastic tarps to prevent air exposure. Activists and some scientists, however, argued that such measures did little to protect the health of local residents, a point that later became obvious as the containment wall eroded and the plastic tarp degraded.

In 1998 local residents formed an alliance with the San Diego–based Environmental Health Coalition and began holding news conferences, vigils, and protests while also launching letter-writing and direct-action campaigns. After more than five years of hard work and network building—what Sen might call ground-up *capability* building—the activists were able to finally pressure the EPA and its Mexican counterpart, the PROFEPA, to find funding for a cleanup strategy. In June 2004, the activists and the Mexican government signed an agreement for the site's cleanup, a promise that has largely been fulfilled (Bachour 2015).

Council, which is meant to provide advice and oversight of its environmental justice activities, though the effectiveness of this council has long been questioned by environmental justice scholars and activists. Although a lot of work remains to be done, the movement as a whole *has* empowered communities throughout the United States, and increasingly throughout the world, making "it extremely difficult for firms to locate incinerators, landfills, and related LULUs [locally unwanted land uses] anywhere in the nation without a political struggle" (Brulle and Pellow 2006, 111).

## IMPORTANT CONCEPTS

- Amartya Sen's theory of justice
- community capitals framework
- conspicuous consumption
- environmental justice
- five sociological mechanisms of consumption

- Happy Life Years (HLYs)
- Happy Planet Index (HPI)
- Human Development Index (HDI)
- limits to growth and postgrowth

## DISCUSSION QUESTIONS

- What could you change about your own life that would both improve your well-being and reduce your ecological footprint? What's stopping you from making the change?
- As long as we create waste, we are going to have to put that waste somewhere. How do we keep that waste from finding its way into the backyards of *any* marginalized population?
- What do *progress* and *prosperity* mean to you?
- What conditions would have to be met for an economy to grow indefinitely? In such a scenario, would our happiness and well-being increase indefinitely too?

## SUGGESTED ADDITIONAL READINGS

Flavin, P., and B. Pacek. 2014. "Assessing the Impact of the Size and Scope of Government on Human Well-Being." *Social Forces* 92(4): 1241–1258.

New Economics Foundation. 2012. *The Happy Planet Index: 2012 Report*. London. b.3cdn.net/nefoundation/d8879619b64bae461f_opm6ixqee.pdf.

Vickery, J., and L. M. Hunter. 2016. "Native Americans: Where in Environmental Justice Research?" *Society & Natural Resources* 29(1): 36–52.

Warde, A. 2014. "After Taste: Culture, Consumption and Theories of Practice." *Journal of Consumer Culture* 14(3): 279–303.

## RELEVANT INTERNET LINKS

- hdr.undp.org/en/statistics. Get the latest Human Development Index data and rankings here.
- www.neweconomics.org. New Economics Foundation—home of the Happy Planet Index, among other interesting things.
- topincomes.g-mond.parisschoolofeconomics.eu. The World Top Incomes Database. An excellent resource that illustrates how inequality levels have changed for many countries.
- steadystate.org. Information about the steady-state economy.
- www.ted.com/talks/nic_marks_the_happy_planet_index.html. Nic Marks of the New Economics Foundation gives a TED talk titled "The Happy Planet Index."

## SUGGESTED VIDEOS

- *Growthbusters: Hooked on Growth* (2011). A documentary that questions society's most fundamental beliefs about prosperity.
- *Last Call* (2014). The story of one of the most controversial and inspiring environmental books of all times, *The Limits to Growth* (1972). And yet, its message today is more relevant than ever, or so the film argues.

- *Life After Growth* (2009). The story about the de-growth movement.
- *The Light Bulb Conspiracy* (2010). dotsub.com/view/aed3b8b2-1889-4df5-ae63-ad85f5572f27. Documents the strategic use of planned obsolescence over the past one hundred years to increase the purchase frequency of consumer goods.
- *Tipping Point: The Age of the Oil Sands* (2011). For years, residents in a small community in northern Alberta, Canada, have been plagued by rare forms of cancer. This film chronicles their struggle as they attempt to get answers from the oil industry that is operating upstream from them.

Part IV

# SHIFTING THE FOCUS TO RESULTS

# From Our Beliefs to Our Behaviors: Pragmatic Environmentalism in Action

We come now to the final social driver that I address: us. Sometimes in sociology we get so caught up talking about structures, capital, organizations, and the like that we forget that people "mutually constitute"—to evoke a popular term among agency and structure theorists—those things that otherwise seem to have such power over us. In this chapter, I take a closer look at understandings, perceptions, and attitudes relevant to the problems and solutions discussed throughout this book, noting that these seemingly mental artifacts are fundamentally sociological, as they affect and are an effect of one's socioecological environment. Any positive change has to ultimately start with us. This point is important, as it takes us back to where this book began: talking about pragmatic environmentalism. The chapter concludes by revisiting this concept.

## Fast Facts

- Democrats have consistently expressed more concern about climate change than Republicans in the United States, a divide that has grown particularly pronounced in recent years (McCright and Dunlap 2011b). Research has shown that US believers and skeptics have distinct social identities, beliefs, and emotional reactions that systematically predict their support for action to advance their respective positions (Bliuc et al. 2015). Therefore the divisions between these groups are unlikely to be overcome solely through communication and education strategies. We need to move beyond attempts to improve the public's understanding of science and include approaches that transform intergroup relations—in other words, strategies that reduce social distance and improve understandings about what the other side values (ECOnnection 13.1).
- An ambitious study examining data from 119 countries identified the factors that most influence climate change awareness and risk perception for 90 percent of the world's population (Lee et al. 2015). In North America, Europe, and Japan, more than 90 percent of the public is aware of climate change. But in many developing countries relatively

ECOnnection 13.1

# The Growing Scourge of Social Distance

So much work is being done around reducing geophysical distance—think local food! What about social distance? The two are not the same. Social distances have grown so large in countries like the United States that bringing people together for face-to-face encounters is becoming a challenge. Forget about getting people around the same table to eat. Even meeting in the same room is harder than ever. We know, for example, that even if we were to get socially distant people together, those with higher social status generally ignore those with less power. This phenomenon has been observed in studies. Within a minute or two of meeting, the person with greater status begins to disengage from the conversation— less nodding and laughing—when paired with someone far below them on the social hierarchy. They are also more likely to take over the conversation, interrupt, and look past the individual they are paired with, perhaps looking for someone more worthy of their time. Part of this empathy gap appears to be due to wealth. To put it plainly, the wealthy can hire help, while those lacking material capital have to reinvest more in their social assets—the neighbor who watches one's child occasionally, the friend who is good with cars, or the woman down the street who is handy with a plumber's wrench. Financial differences help produce behavioral differences, thus creating social distance at multiple levels. These differences go deep, shaping how these groups feel about those around them. This growing social distance, in all its various forms, can help us understand some of the dynamics being expressed in Congress, from its members' insistence on cutting financing for food stamps to their rejection of universal health care coverage. Redistricting and gerrymandering have created visceral echo chambers, where elected officials have less and less interaction with those different from themselves, which means they also empathize less with others.

This is yet another example of why unchecked inequality is not just an ethical issue. It is a deeply social one: it is producing gross divisions within societies, to the point where growing numbers of people—and politicians (lest we forget, they are people too)—live their lives inside bubbles and are clueless about others not like them, like the immigrant laborers who pick their strawberries, the single mother receiving government assistance, or the children in low-income countries who stitch their clothes.

*Source: Adapted from Carolan (in press).*

few are aware of it, although many do report having observed changes in local weather patterns. Overall, the authors found that about 40 percent of adults worldwide have never heard of climate change. This rises to more than 65 percent in some developing countries, like Egypt, Bangladesh, and India. The research also reveals some stark differences between countries in terms of predictors of climate change awareness. In the United States, the key predictors of awareness are civic engagement, communication access, and education. Meanwhile in China, climate change awareness is most closely associated with education, proximity to urban areas, and household income.

- A study with twenty-two authors, from five continents, looked at television food advertisements directed at children (Kelly et al. 2010). Ads for highly processed, nutritiously shallow foods accounted for between 53 and 87 percent of all food advertisements recorded. The rate of advertisements for these foods was higher during children's peak viewing times.
- Marketing textbooks estimate that the average North American is exposed to one thousand advertisements every day (Arens 2005), though other advertising insiders have given numbers as high as three thousand (Alexander, Crompton, and Shrubsole 2011).
- A study out of the United Kingdom found that 36 percent of the two thousand sixteen- to twenty-three-year-olds surveyed did not know bacon comes from pigs, 40 percent failed to link milk with dairy cows (7 percent attributed it to wheat), and 33 percent were unaware of the origins of eggs (11 percent attributed it to wheat or corn). The study also discovered that three in ten of those surveyed born in the 1990s haven't visited a farm in more than ten years (*Telegraph* Reporters 2012).

## Implications

As detailed in this section, what and how we think are of tremendous sociological consequence. Unfortunately, there is not enough space to offer an exhaustive account of how and why attitudes and understandings are sociologically relevant to matters relating to the environment and pro-environmental behaviors. Instead, I concentrate on three quite different subjects, looking at how we think about nature, the roots of climate denial, and the values and attitudes that help drive consumerism.

### Knowledge and Worldviews

A lot has been written about how Western philosophy itself, going all the way back to the ancient Greeks (Whitehead [1920] 1964), is responsible for bestowing on nature a type of secondary status (see, for example, Carolan 2008a; Ingold 2000; Zwart 1997). According to this **worldview** (which refers to a fundamental cognitive orientation shared by individuals within which is rooted the entirety of their knowledge), nature is inherently alien to us; while we perceive it, we dwell in a realm separate from it. This creates, in the words of the great twentieth-century philosopher Alfred North Whitehead, "the nature apprehended in awareness and the nature [a.k.a. Nature] which is the cause of awareness" ([1920] 1964, 30–31). Western philosophy thus leaves us with an understanding of the universe as being filled with nothing more than dead, static matter—as exemplified, for instance, in the writings of Newton. The living and dynamic in this philosophical outlook reside only in human consciousness. This separation between thought (mind) and matter (body) has perplexed philosophers for centuries—and more recently even some environmental sociologists. How is it that these two realms interact if indeed they are truly independent of each other (see Ethical Question 13.1)? Such a division inevitably creates the need for a third thing that connects the two. Yet the slope this creates is a slippery one, for what then connects this third thing to the other two?

By making nature something separate from us—and the human condition more generally—we've objectified it. **Ecofeminism** offers a rich literature detailing the historical link between the objectification of women and the objectification of nature. *The Death*

ETHICAL QUESTION 13.1

# Is Pollution Natural?

Ecologically minded scholars like to talk about breaking free of the dichotomies of Western thought (e.g., mind-body, society-nature, human-animal, and so on). Yet where does that leave something like pollution? If humans are really part of nature, rather than separate from it, doesn't the same then hold for the *effects* of human activity? Pushing the question further: What about human-induced climate change? If humans and all their activities are natural, wouldn't anthropomorphically driven climate change then hold the same status? Is that natural too?

The first (and obvious) response to these questions is that we make conceptual distinctions all the time and need to if we want to talk about anything, though we should be careful how we create those distinctions and be willing to revisit them if they prove problematic or oppressive. (I am doing something a bit unusual here and weighing in on these questions because they can be and have been used to undermine the case for taking action toward climate change, and I want to make sure readers have some reasoned responses at their disposal when confronted by such arguments.) A second, slightly more sophisticated, response would be to point out that the

questions asked above evoke what is known as the "is-ought problem." First articulated by seventeenth-century philosopher David Hume, the problem goes something like this: just because something *is* doesn't automatically mean it *ought* to be. Or to put it another way: statements of knowledge (e.g., "X is") are not statements of value (e.g., "X is how it ought to be"). For example, the *fact* that women have historically been subservient to men does not lead one to logically conclude that they *should* be treated this way. We can therefore say that the fact that life can and has changed the earth's atmosphere for billions of years does not mean humans have a right to do so. To conflate these statements of fact with statements of value is to commit a **naturalistic fallacy**. As a statement of value, the question "What impact *should* humans have on climate?" is entirely open for debate. This is why public participation is so crucial when developing environmental policy. Science alone is incapable of translating statements of "what is" (a scientific question) to statements of "what ought to be" (a policy question). Arguably, the best avenue for answering questions of value—questions of what ought to be—is through democratic means.

*of Nature* (Merchant 1980) argues that casting nature in the female gender (e.g., Mother Nature) strips it of activity and renders it passive, just as casting women as being closer to nature (as, for example, the "nurturing" sex) has had similar effects. As Merchant argues, "As women's womb had symbolically yielded to the forceps, so nature's womb harbored secrets that through technology could be wrested from her grasp for use in the improvement of the human condition" (169).

Metaphysics aside, I'm also convinced that our understandings of nature are in part a consequence of our relationship to this realm (Carolan 2008b, 2011a). Knowledge, after all, is relational. Take, for example, the Batek, one of the indigenous ethnic minorities of peninsular Malaysia. These hunting and gathering "people of the forest"—a self-imposed identity (Tuck-Po 2004, 50)—have lived in the forest for centuries. For them, concepts like "nature" and "forest" are multivariate categories, depending largely on who is living within this environment. And there is always a *who* in their understandings of nature, as evidenced by the fact that they do not even have a word for *wilderness* (Tuck-Po 2004). Or take research examining how understandings of nature differ between the Menominee—Wisconsin's oldest continuous residents—and their Anglo-European neighbors. Whereas children of European descent expressed problems recognizing that people are animals, the Menominee children grasped this idea fully (Longbottom and Slaughter 2016). As for the adults, Anglo-Europeans cited the importance of teaching their children that nature needs to be protected and if possible protected from humans (a viewpoint that places humans outside of nature), whereas Menominee adults stressed to their youth that people are part of nature (Bang, Medin, and Atran 2007). Perhaps not surprisingly, compared to their European neighbors, Menominee children and adults spend more of their time engaged in outdoor practices, where the natural world is foregrounded, and relatively less time engaged in practices where nature is backgrounded. Researchers point out how "the Menominee ecological orientation in reasoning strategies is paralleled in their framework orientation and practices" (Bang, Medin, and Atran 2007, 13871).

Tuck-Po (2004) explains how the Batek of peninsular Malaysia are able to identify native animals by their calls, a particularly important skill given the dense canopy of the forest, making visual identification nearly impossible. Yet such local knowledge is being lost as embodiments and practices around the world change (recall the earlier discussion of memory banks in Chapter 4). Among the Seri, an indigenous community in the Mexican state of Sonora, the younger generation is losing their ability to identify native animals in photographs as a result of their reduced interactions with these creatures (Nabhan 1997). Among the Salish people of Washington, young people are less successful than previous generations at identifying local plants according to their medicinal properties (Turner 2016). At one time, the language of the Rio Grande Pueblos allowed them to distinguish between many types of trees and plants. Today, children increasingly use their native term for *firewood* when speaking of trees and the word for *weed* when speaking of herbaceous plants because they've lost the local knowledge of their natural surroundings (Nabhan 1997). Yet it is more than just a problem of languages lost. We are losing the socioecological relationships that language is tethered to, for, as Abram explains, we "learn our native languages not mentally but bodily" (1996, 75).

## Denial, Ambivalence, and Apathy

In her study of a small community in Norway, Norgaard (2011) finds evidence that a lack of action against climate change is often not the result of poor or incomplete knowledge. Those she interviewed knew climate change was happening. The area had experienced very late snowfall and warmer winter temperatures while she was conducting her research. October, November, and December of that year were 4° Celsius, 5° Celsius, and 1.5° Celsius, respectively, warmer than the 30-year average, and the winter as a whole was the second warmest in the previous 130 years. Consequently, the local ski area opened late, which had a noticeable negative recreational and economic impact on the community. Moreover, a popular lake used heavily for ice fishing did not freeze.

*Literal denial* describes when people hold onto beliefs that are demonstrably false, as found among, say, climate change skeptics. *Implicatory denial* is when we fail to respond according to the moral and rational codes of the day; most citizens of Nazi

Germany could be placed in this category. Norgaard's work describes another type of denial: how thinking about climate change raises disturbing emotions of fear about the future, guilt, and a sense of helplessness, which are resisted collectively through participation in such cultural practices as emotion management, norms of conversation, and the use of narratives to justify past and current actions. This type of denial, the ability to *collectively* ignore disturbing information, points to, among other things, the role of emotion in social movements and political action and highlights how global warming raises new threats to the workings of democracy. Norgaard explains how denial allowed citizens of this small community to acknowledge climate change while also pushing it from their conscious mind. One tactic was blame shifting. Many of her respondents were quick to blame, for example, "Amerika" and the Bush administration (the US president at the time). When asked about Norway's role in climate change, as the world's second-largest exporter of oil, they were quick to dismiss this fact as insignificant, though the subject did make some uncomfortable.

Norgaard reminds us that "citizens of wealthy nations who fail to respond to the issue of climate change benefit from their denial in short-run economic terms." She continues, "They also benefit by avoiding the emotional and psychological entanglement and identity conflicts that may arise from knowing that one is doing 'the wrong thing'" (2006, 336). Many who live in affluent nations can also afford to deny climate change. Although the subjects of Norgaard's study will not escape the consequences of climate change, their social positioning was such that climate change will profoundly affect people in less affluent nations long before it drastically alters their own lives.

The roots of climate denial have also been shown to be fed by political ideology and can span (and in turn be further reinforced by) countermovements. A **countermovement** is a social movement that arises to explicitly oppose an existing social movement. Meyer and Staggenborg (1996, 1635) point to three conditions that lead to openings for countermovements: the original movement shows signs of success, the interests of some population are threatened by the original movement's goals, and political allies are available to aid oppositional mobilization. Jacques and colleagues (2008) look to these conditions to understand why the conservative movement in the United States launched a major countermovement against the environmental movement in the 1990s.

Environmentalism emerged as a global movement in the early 1990s with the aid of such events as the 1992 Earth Summit in Rio. This, combined with the fall of the Soviet Union, prompted the conservative movement to switch its talk of the "red scare" to a "green scare." The Republican takeover of Congress in 1994 also gave the countermovement access to political allies. Last, and perhaps most significantly, as environmentalists began calling for significant changes, the countermovement sought to brand environmentalism as a threat to not only economic progress but also the "American way of life." Jacques and colleagues point to the role that conservative think tanks (CTTs) have played in creating counterenvironmental knowledge and thereby espousing **environmental skepticism**—a position that attempts to undermine knowledge claims supporting the argument that environmental problems are real and that they are the result of human activity. Their search of English-language environmentally skeptical books published between 1972 (nothing prior to this could be found) and 2005 found 92.2 percent to have a clear link to one or more CTTs, either through author affiliation, or because the book was published by a CTT, or, the most common scenario, both (Jacques, Dunlap, and Freeman 2008).

McCright and Dunlap (2011a, 2011b) shed light on why political values matter when it comes to shaping views on climate change. They point to, among other things, research showing that political conservatives are more likely to justify and be apologetic for the status quo, even when it comes to climate change, whereas liberals are more open to critiques toward business-as-usual attitudes. Climate change also represents an existential threat to conservatives' faith in industrial capitalism and unfettered economic growth. This is especially the case when talk of global warming turns to the creation of internationally binding treaties to curb greenhouse gas emissions and the like. Such proposals are viewed as antithetical to many key ideas conservatives hold dear, such as beliefs about American exceptionalism, free markets, and minimal governmental regulation. It's not an understatement to say climate change threatens the entire worldview of conservatives, rocking their political philosophy to its core.

Climate deniers are not only conservative but also white and male, have higher than average incomes, and are overly confident in their views no matter how demonstrably false those views are (McCright and Dunlap 2011a). This privileged position helps explain their unshakable confidence that climate change will never happen. According to McCright and Dunlap, "Conservative white males have disproportionately occupied positions of power within our economic system. Given the expansive challenge that climate change poses to the industrial capitalist economic system, it should not be surprising that conservative white males' strong system-justifying attitudes would be triggered to deny climate change" (2011a, 1166). Having all these resources at their disposal also makes it far less likely that they will be severely threatened anytime soon by the harms caused by climate change, so they can afford to be skeptical (Klein 2011).

A recently published study also shows the influence those aforementioned worldviews have on understandings of climate change. A survey of 1,927 Australians involving members of four religious groupings—Buddhists, Christian literalists and nonliteralists, and secularists—looked at their attitudes toward and their beliefs about (1) whether climate change is human-induced, (2) the level of consensus they think exists among scientists, (3) their own efficacy to be able to doing anything about it, and (4) the need for policy responses (Morrison, Duncan, and Parton 2015). The study shows that religion explains these differences even after taking into account sociodemographic factors. The atheist/agnostic/no religion group (43.8 percent) and Buddhists (45.7 percent) have a much higher percentage of people located in the "alarmed" and "concerned" segments than the sample overall (33.3 percent). Further, atheist/agnostic/ no religion (16.3 percent) and Buddhists (2.9 percent) have a lower percentage of people located in the "doubtful" and "dismissive" segments than the sample overall (20.6 percent). The respondents who indicate affiliation with Christian denominations that have a literal interpretation of scripture have a smaller proportion of people located in the "alarmed" and "concerned" categories (19.6 percent). The Christian literalists also had a much higher percentage of people located in the "doubtful" and "dismissive" segments (30.2 percent) than the sample overall.

Our failure to act on climate change has also been attributed to ambivalence. Ambivalence is not the same as indifference, though the two terms are often used interchangeably. When someone is said to be ambivalent, they possess feelings, attitudes, and beliefs that are in tension with each other. **Sociological ambivalence** "focuses on the ways in which ambivalence comes to be built into the structure of social statuses and role" (Merton 1976, 5). A slightly more elaborate definition explains sociological ambivalence as referring "to incompatible or contradictory normative expectations or attitudes, beliefs, and behavior assigned to a status or to a set of statuses in a society or even incorporated into a single status" (Stebbins 1967, 247).

Tying this back to climate change, I offer a couple of quotes from some of my own research on the subject:

> "I care about the environment, biodiversity, conservation, all that. That's one hat I wear, as an environmentalist. But like everyone else I wear other hats: dad, democratic, entrepreneur, husband. . . . They [these different statuses] come with different expectations. For example, while I care about the environment I care about my kids more. So when faced with driving my daughter to school four miles each way in the winter and putting her on a bike, because we can't bus her, I'm going to pick the car. Yes, it has a bigger carbon footprint than a bike but my hat of dad outweighs that of environmentalist." . . .
>
> "I mean, we live in a society that makes it next to impossible to do the right thing as far as the environment is concerned. We have to drive. We're pinched for time so we need modern labor saving conveniences . . . I could live in a thatched hut in the forest but I have responsibilities to my family that keep me from rejecting the modern lifestyle, even though this lifestyle has considerable ecological implications." (Carolan 2010b, 317)

For both of these self-identified "environmentalists," ambivalence toward climate change does not mean indifference. Both professed caring for the environment and worrying about greenhouse gas emissions and climate change. The ambivalence emerged out of a perceived tension between what respondents *wanted* to do and what they believed they *could do* within the existing socio-organizational structures of society. The first person quoted also makes reference to what sociologists call **role strain**: tensions that emerge when expectations from holding multiple roles clash. The roles "environmentalist" and "dad" are often complementary—after all, environmentalists are deeply concerned about leaving a healthy planet for future generations. Yet sometimes those roles conflict, like when freezing temperatures (and concerns about exposure) momentarily elevate the "dad" role above that of "environmentalist" and result in the bike being left at home in exchange for fossil fuel–based mobility.

Sociological denial and ambivalence might also tell us something about the apathy being reported by surveys when it comes to today's environmental problems. One such study found levels of "informedness, confidence in scientists, and personal efficacy" regarding climate change interact such that the "more informed respondents both feel less personally responsible for global warming, and also show less concern for global warming" (Kellstedt, Zahran, and Vedlitz 2008, 113). As others have suggested, perhaps apathy isn't about caring too little but a paralysis that arises out of caring too much for too many different things (Lertzman 2010). Some of this apathy can also be attributed to the fact that people are more likely to tune out those problems they feel they have no control over (Snow et al. 2015).

## Consumerism, Advertising, and Status Attainment

The following stunning admission is taken from an article by Rory Sutherland, vice chair of the marketing firm Ogilvy UK and then president of the Institute of Practitioners in Advertising: "The truth is that marketing raises enormous ethical questions every day—at least it does if you're doing it right. If this were not the case, the only possible explanations are either that you believe marketers are too ineffectual to make any difference, or you believe that marketing activities only affect people at the level of conscious argument. Neither of these possibilities appeals to me. *I would rather be thought of as evil than useless*" (Sutherland 2010, 59; emphasis added).

Decades of studies note how advertising promotes rabid consumerism (see, for example, Galbraith 1958). After all, economic growth relies on the unending creation of insatiable needs. As Ezra Mishan, longtime professor of economics at the London School of Economics, famously noted a half century ago, "Therefore to continue to regard the market, in an affluent and growing economy, as primarily a 'want-satisfying' mechanism is to close one's eyes to the more important fact, that it has become a want-*creating* mechanism" (1967, 149; emphasis in the original). We also know that advertising further reinforces the values it reflects by normalizing them. On this point, talking specifically about smoking, Rory Sutherland further confessed, "While I can accept that the purpose of tobacco advertising was not to encourage people to smoke, I find it astounding that anyone could barefacedly suggest that cigarette posters seen everywhere did not serve to normalise the habit" (2010, 59).

A growing body of research examines links between intrinsic and extrinsic values and consumption. *Intrinsic values* refer to aspects of life that we find inherently rewarding, whereas the reward of *extrinsic values* lies in the validation given to us by others. When you place greater importance on extrinsic values, you are more likely to express prejudice toward others, be less concerned about the environment and human rights, and express lower levels of personal well-being and happiness (Alexander, Crompton, and Shrubsole 2011; Goldsmith 2015). Adolescents who strongly endorse extrinsic values report being less likely to turn off lights in unused rooms, recycle, and engage in other pro-environmental behaviors (Kasser 2005). Other studies report a strong positive correlation between the ecological footprints of adults and their possession of extrinsic values (Kasser 2016). So which values do you suppose advertisers target? The vast majority of advertising is directed at appealing to extrinsic values, the very values associated with lower motivation to address social and environmental problems (Alexander, Crompton, and Shrubsole 2011). Advertisers have also learned that it is possible to advertise so-called green products through an appeal to extrinsic values, like using a famous celebrity to advertise the latest hybrid car. Such a marketing campaign promotes extrinsic values by encouraging status competition and social comparison.

What are the cumulative effects of being endlessly seduced into becoming envious, status-seeking hyperconsumers who are looking for our next "happiness fix" with a swipe of the credit card or click of the mouse? Obviously, we do not rush to purchase everything we see advertised. But if almost every advertisement we see seeks to fuel our extrinsic values, it's reasonable to think this is going to have a measurable effect on people over the long term. Perhaps, to refer back to a point discussed in the previous chapter, this helps partially explain why so many in the United States report such low levels of well-being and happiness: Americans are overexposed to advertisements directed at appeals to extrinsic values. A study examined the impact of the use of Channel One—a daily ten-minute news bulletin with two minutes of advertisements—in US schools (Greenberg and Brand 1993). It compared the importance attached to extrinsic values in teenagers from two neighboring schools with very similar student and parent demographics: one had Channel One; the other did not. Teenagers enrolled at the school with Channel One had much higher levels of extrinsic values than the control group. This corroborates more recent research pointing to links between hours of watching television, a lack of concern about environmental problems, and an increased prevalence of extrinsic values (Macias and Williams 2015).

A lot of television is watched in the United States. This country is also, as discussed in the previous chapter, a society with excessive levels of inequality. This is a powerful double whammy, as we know that inequality is perhaps the greatest driver of overconsumption (Aggarwal 2016). For one thing, status competition drives hyperconsumerism. Second, inequality—by heightening the distance between the haves and the have-nots and thus increasing the status of being a have—intensifies status competition. Throw endless hours of television watching into this mix, and you have an environment ripe for materialism that we see in affluent countries today.

## Solutions

Changing how we think about things is no small feat. Fortunately, we have the benefit of decades of excellent social science research and illustrative examples from other countries to light our way. The task ahead may be daunting, but it's most definitely possible.

### *Advertisements, Freedom, and the Public Good*

Although the majority of parents feel they are primarily responsible for their children, they do not feel they alone own this responsibility, especially when it comes to competing with the deep pockets of multinational corporations and advertising companies that are trying to get into the minds and wallets of today's youth. The vast majority of the world's parents thus favor restrictions on advertising aimed at children (Oates and Tziortzi 2014). These sentiments have been found among parents in countries as diverse as, for example, the United States (Tripicchio et al. 2016), the Netherlands (van der Voort, Nikken, and van Lil 1992), and China (Chan and McNeal 2003).

Consumption is a thoroughly social activity. Once we accept this undeniable empirical truth, the argument against the regulation of advertisements falls apart. That argument goes something along the lines of the following: in the name of protecting individual freedom, one should be able to buy as much of whatever one likes; after all, the consumer knows best what they need. Establishing that those needs are products of social activity diminishes the argument that government intervention takes away from individual freedoms. For example, almost 60 percent of nine- to fourteen-year-olds in one US study explained how they feel pressure to buy stuff in order to fit in (Schor 2005). In fact, it could easily be argued that government intervention *increases* personal freedoms by helping to shield individuals from the dictates of these particular sociological forces.

We could begin by regulating advertisements directed at children, as this population in the classical liberal tradition is often seen as needing more protection than adults. We could also create advertising-free zones. Most places of religious worship are advertisement free. Why can't we do the same with schools and other public places where children are frequently present? Why not limit specific types of advertisement that are clearly meant for children? In Greece, for example, television advertisements for toys are banned from seven a.m. to nine p.m. In Norway and Sweden, it is illegal to target through advertisements children under the age of twelve. We also need to be aware of the dangers of putting all the responsibility on the shoulders of parents. As market-driven trends increasingly structure social interaction among children and teens, well-meaning parents who place restrictions on their kids' consumption patterns risk setting them up for social exclusion, which does not do their children any good. Finally, advertisements in countries like the United States are a tax-deductible expense. By spending money on advertisements, which increases brand loyalty and the purchase frequency of the product advertised, businesses are also able to reduce their tax liability: a clear win-win scenario for companies. Yet this win comes at the expense of individual and public health. The general public in the United States is subsidizing advertisements. Moreover, the hundreds of millions of dollars saved by businesses annually through these deductions could help pay for public services that are currently paid for by taxpayers.

## Collaborative Consumption

Aristotle is said to have written that "on the whole, you find wealth much more in use than in ownership" (Rifkin 2000, 76). Kevin Kelly, founder of the influential magazine *Wired*, has argued passionately that "access is better than ownership" (2012). We have become so wrapped up in fighting for our right to own that we seem to have forgotten why we wanted to own in the first place: for access and use. We are also guilty of overlooking the fact that markets are not ends in themselves. Markets were developed to solve problems of resource allocation; they were never meant to be the Holy Grail they have become. What's important is efficient and fair resource allocation. Markets have long been viewed as the best option to deliver those ends. But what if something better came along?

Michael Spence, a 2001 Nobel laureate in economics and a senior fellow at Stanford's Hoover Institution, wrote an article in *Forbes* titled "Markets Aren't Everything" (2009). In this piece, Spence celebrates the work of scholars like Elinor Ostrom who have highlighted how common-property resources can quite effectively be managed without the aid of formal markets. As Ostrom (1999) and others (e.g., Vishal and Vij 2016) have detailed, common-property resources (e.g., forests) have been effectively managed—in some cases for centuries—thanks to things like informal social norms, trust, and social capital. Yet what if, in this age of social media, Twitter, and the Internet more generally, something like a traditional commons is forming for consumers?

A generation ago, the thought of the nonmarket coordination of large groups of people from around the world for purposes of resource allocation seemed absurd. The transaction costs of such an endeavor were too great. If you had something and wanted to get rid of it, your options were limited. You could put an ad in the paper or place fliers on community bulletin boards around your neighborhood. And even if someone got back to you, the chance of a successful transaction was low (they might have wanted a different color, model, and so on). That has all changed, which explains why the godfather of *Wired* is proclaiming the virtues of access over ownership. For many consumer items, we no longer need the market. Enter what has become known as "collaborative consumption" (ECOnnection 13.2).

One example of collaborative consumption is **peer-to-peer renting**: the process of one private individual renting an underused item of theirs to another individual (aka P2P renting). There are a number of peer-to-peer sites that create a low transaction cost environment, allowing a type of commons to appear, like irent2you.com, rent mineonline.com, and iletyou.com. These sites enable individuals to make use of those underused goods we all are guilty of having by renting them to others, which in turn keeps those renters from purchasing the goods new. It has been estimated that if the United States shifted a mere fifth of its household spending from purchasing to renting, the country would cut $CO_2$ emissions by roughly 2 percent, or 13 million tons, annually (Botsman and Rogers 2010).

Another example of providing access rather than ownership is Zipcar, the world's largest **car sharing** company. Car sharing is a short-term (often by the hour) car rental model where the cars are scattered throughout a community to improve access rather than all being centrally housed at one location, as with traditional car rentals. Zipcar allows members to reserve a car for as little as one hour. Reservations can be made online or even through a mobile phone app. The cars are widely available in communities serviced by Zipcar, so access is often not a problem for members (I can even see two Zipcars from my university office window). As of June 2015, the company has close to one million members and offers nearly ten thousand vehicles throughout the United States, Canada, the United Kingdom, Spain, France, Austria, and Turkey.

Then there's Uber, which allows a person, at the push of a smartphone button, to hail a car within minutes, even during rush hour. (The service uses a surge-pricing model, which means the fares increase during high-demand periods.) Here's how it works: A customer requests a car using a smartphone app, and Uber sends its closest driver to their location using the phone's GPS. The fare, meanwhile, is charged directly to the customer's credit card. Uber provides five types of services. UberX is the least expensive option, which allows for the hiring of regular car drivers with a smartphone. These drivers use their personal auto insurance policy while driving for Uber and are not required to get commercial liability insurance. (According to the company website, all ride-sharing drivers are thoroughly screened, and the company conducts ongoing reviews of drivers' motor vehicle records throughout their time with Uber.) Other options include Uber Taxi (lets you e-hail a yellow cab), Uber Black (a private hire car), Uber SUV (the vehicle seats up to six people), and Uber Lux (for those wanting to ride around in a luxury car).

There is an old saying: when you walk around with a hammer, everything starts looking like a nail. Similarly, when you have a car in your garage, every trip starts looking as if it can only be accomplished with an automobile. Car sharing, conversely, makes you rethink whether a car is necessary for any particular trip. When people share cars, they begin to realize they don't actually need them as much as originally thought.

Let's also not forget about the *social* value added through collaborative consumption. When you consume collaboratively, you build social networks, nurture trust, and

ECOnnection 13.2

# Every Cloud Has a Silver Lining: From "Waste" to "Untapped Idling Capacity"

*So* much stuff—we're practically swimming in it! And apparently our homes and garages are not growing fast enough to contain it all. We increasingly feel the need to rent additional space for all that stuff we never or rarely use. (For those eighteen and older—as there is adult language—search "George Carlin talks about stuff" online for a witty sociological breakdown of our obsession over material things.) According to the Self-Storage Association (SSA), there are more than fifty-three thousand personal storage facilities in the United States alone. The total self-storage rentable space in the United States totals some 2.3 billion square feet (SSA 2012). That is more than 78 square miles of self-enclosed space (or more than three times the size of Manhattan Island in New York). Want to talk about some of the costs of overconsumption? Even when just focusing on those directly incurred by consumers—as consumers—the numbers are rather remarkable. On top of the roughly $150 billion a year Americans waste on goods they will never use, they are also spending, as all this unused stuff has to be put somewhere, an additional $22 billion in storage fees—the annual revenue generated by the self-storage industry in the United States (ibid.).

Rather than being wrenched by despair, I prefer taking a more optimistic slant on the above statistics, while also recognizing that we still need to change our ways. All that unused stuff has already extracted a significant toll on the environment. Why not, then, put it to use so more stuff does not meet a similar fate, of consuming still more resources only to be born and lie idle in some rented storage space for years? All those unused goods represent an enormous idling capacity. The fact is, while the owners might not use that stuff, others could. So let's get it into the hands of those who would.

Just about every semester I survey my class of one hundred undergraduate students and ask them about the things they own but never or rarely use. Recently I had a class that reported owning collectively eighty-eight power drills—eighty-eight! Granted, four students reported owning more than one. But still, for something that was on average said to be used once a year, that is a tremendous amount of hole-making idling capacity. Even the cars the students owned spent more time parked than in use—a lot more. They reported being in their cars, on average, about ten minutes a day. That leaves 1,430 minutes where the car was just sitting, yet still racking up costs in terms of depreciation, tax, title, license, insurance, and (in most cases) parking. How about you? Do you own things like a drill, car, snow blower, power saw, or camping equipment? How often do *you* use them, honestly?

generate social capital. As a sociologist, I cannot deny the social nature of shopping. Yet when we shop, we do not really establish any new social networks. We might build trust and a sense of camaraderie among the family and friends we are shopping with, though, equally, shopping has been shown to create animosity and jealousy among even loved ones who shop together (Kasser 2016; see ECOnnection 13.3). The tentative early evidence suggests that collaborative consumption not only strengthens already existing

## ECOnnection 13.3
# Collaboration Might Build Trust but It Also Needs It to Work

A big barrier to getting from the me-based status quo to a we-based sharing economy is trust. It is one thing to rent a power drill from a neighbor, quite another to let a total stranger sleep in your house. At the moment, most sharing platforms build trust into the exchange by building a self-policing community, in which users are required to have profiles and there is a community rating system. The next step looks to be developing a community rating system that travels with you from website to website—a second life reputation that may one day grow to be just as important, from an exchange standpoint, as your first life reputation (such as your credit score). An example of this is TrustCloud, which creates the equivalent of a sharing economy credit rating only for trust. Using proprietary algorithms, TrustCloud aims to measure individuals' trustworthiness by analyzing transactions on the web while also drawing on information from sites like Facebook, LinkedIn, Twitter, and Google+. This trail of online data exhaust, it is believed, can be a reliable predictor of our consistency, responsiveness, and overall trustworthiness. And while "there's always the argument that anyone can be an ax murderer," admits TrustCloud cofounder Xin Chung,

"you get a lot more indicators in data exhaust than you do in walking up to somebody in khakis and a crisp white shirt on the street. I'd pick the data exhaust any day" (Sacks 2011). Sites like Yelp, TripAdvisor, and eBay use pseudonyms that may reveal very little about the user's actual identity. Even so, they have created systems that are surprisingly effective and efficient at eliciting desired behaviors. Research indicates that sellers receive positive feedback on eBay 99 percent of the time and buyers 98 percent (Botsman and Rogers 2010). Users realize their behavior today is not one off and therefore strive—sometimes going to great lengths—to achieve that positive feedback, knowing, for example, that highly reputable sellers receive on average an 8 percent premium over identical items offered by sellers with lower or few ratings (Botsman and Rogers 2010). A bad review on eBay, however, stays on eBay and does not follow you around. Another way around this self-policing system is simply to create another "personality" on eBay by generating another nameless and faceless pseudonym. There is no reset button with things like TrustCloud—no chance, in other words, to declare trust bankruptcy and start anew.

(aka strong) ties but also builds new (aka weak) ones between people with different backgrounds (Ozanne and Ozanne 2016). Perhaps these ties could even be used to further push for social change by way of consumer activism, such as through traditional boycotts or more recently through "buycotts" (see Case Study 13.1).

## Globalization of Environmental Concern

Here's some good news: there appears to be a global diffusion of views and values concerning environmental protection (Dunlap and York 2008; Mohai, Simões, and Brechin 2010; Pampel 2014). Environmental concern has been defined by Dunlap and Jones as "the degree to which people are aware of problems regarding the environment and

## CASE STUDY 13.1

# The Carrotmob (aka Buycott)

Rather than punish stores and other businesses for their environmental atrocities, why not reward those for their pro-environmental actions with mass purchases? "Traditional activism revolves around conflict," explains Brent Schulkin (Caplan 2009). Schulkin is the founder of a movement of activist consumers employing a kind of reverse boycott that he calls a **carrotmob**. Simply defined, the carrotmob is a type of consumer activism based on the idea of using carrots (or incentives) to reward businesses for engaging in socially or environmentally responsible practices. Instead of creating enemies, a carrotmob focuses on positive cooperation. Schulkin solicited bids from twenty-three stores in his area to find which business would promise to spend the highest percentage of the carrotmob's profits on more energy-efficient lighting. In return, Schulkin promised to deliver, with the help of social media and social networks, a horde of consumers who pledged to buy stuff from the highest bidder, things that these consumers would have had to purchase anyway (namely, household and food items). The buycott occurred on March 29, 2008, when hundreds of green-minded patrons waited their turn in an hour-long line to spend their money at K&D Market. In all, the carrotmob spent more than $9,200, and K&D Market, in turn, promised to spend 22 percent of the day's revenue on energy-efficient lighting—enough to make all the improvements recommended by an energy auditor. Since 2000, activists have initiated hundreds of carrotmobs across North and South America, Europe, Asia, Australia, and New Zealand (Hoffmann and Hutter 2012).

support efforts to solve them and/or indicate a willingness to contribute personally to their solution" (2002, 485). As environmental attitudes are often taken to be synonymous with environmental concern (Dunlap and Jones 2002; Ester 1981), I will use the two concepts interchangeably (see ECOnnection 13.4).

Until recently, there was quite a debate between scholars about the globalization of environmental concern. Conventional wisdom had long assumed that widespread citizen concern for environmental quality was confined to wealthy nations. This presumption was grounded in the belief that residents of poor countries are too preoccupied with their material needs to support the postmaterialist value of environmental protection. The most famous champion of this view is Ronald Inglehart. Inglehart grounds his argument in two theories: Maslow's hierarchy of human needs and Mannheim's socialization hypothesis. Maslow argued that higher-order needs (e.g., concern for the environment) cannot be fully developed in people worried where their next meal is going to come from (a lower-order material need), whereas Mannheim's socialization hypothesis holds that "one's basic values reflect the conditions that prevailed during one's pre-adult years" (Inglehart 1990, 68). With these two theories in tow, Inglehart argues that individuals residing in affluent countries will hold more postmaterialist values and that these values will grow as a result of generational cohort replacement (Inglehart 1990, 1997). Inglehart's argument was and still is attractive in some political corners, as it justifies the status quo and the belief—no matter how disconnected it is

## ECOnnection 13.4
# The New Environmental Paradigm (NEP)

The New Environmental Paradigm (NEP) has been called "the most widely used measure of EA [environmental attitudes] since its publication in 1978" (Hawcroft and Milfont 2010, 144). The original scale was first published in 1978 by Dunlap and Van Liere and consisted of twelve items—eight pro-NEP and four anti-NEP—on a four-point Likert scale, anchored by "strongly agree" and "strongly disagree." The higher the NEP score, the greater an individual's level of environmental beliefs or ecological worldview (Dunlap 2008). In 2000 Dunlap and colleagues revised the NEP scale. The revised scale consists of fifteen items, eight pro-NEP and seven anti-NEP. Table 13.1 displays the twelve and fifteen items from the original and revised scales, respectively.

Economists have found the NEP scale to be an accurate predictor of willingness to pay in **contingent valuation** studies (see, for example, Cooper, Poe, and Bateman 2004; Kotchen and Reiling 2000). (Contingent valuation is a survey-based economic technique for placing a value on nonmarket resources.) The NEP scale has also been shown to predict both reported and observed behavior (see, for example, Casey and Scott 2006). A growing body of evidence also indicates that environmental educational programs can lead to an increase in NEP scores among children (Atav, Altunoğlu, and Sönmez 2015; Manoli, Johnson, and Dunlap 2007) and college students (Woodworth, Steen-Adams, and Mittal 2011).

from empirical reality—that continued economic development will eventually lead all nations toward socially and politically tolerant, environmentally sustainable, and postmaterial futures.

Yet not all research has been kind to Inglehart's postmaterialism thesis. Take, for example, the results of the twenty-four-nation "Health of the Planet" survey (Dunlap and York 2008). Of the fourteen different measures of environmental concern employed, seven were found to be *negatively* related with national affluence. In other words, they indicated higher levels of environmental concern among residents of poor countries. As Dunlap and York explain, "citizens of poorer nations were significantly more likely to (1) express personal concern about environmental problems, (2) rate the quality of their national environments as poor, (3) rate the quality of their community environments as poor, (4) perceive environmental problems as health threats at present (5) and in the future, (6) rate six community-level environmental problems as serious, and (7) express support for six governmental environmental protection programs" (2008, 534).

More recently, a twenty-five-country analysis found that willingness to sacrifice to protect the environment is not unique to wealthy nations (Mostafa 2013). Even more devastating to the postmaterialism thesis, the study found that a country's ranking on a postmaterialism index was *negatively* correlated to pro-environmental intentions. Put another way, postmaterialist values were associated with *less* environmentalism. More recently still, Pampel (2014) found a high willingness to pay for environmental quality among all groups studied in a sample consisting of respondents from ninety-six nations.

**TABLE 13.1** New Environmental Paradigm (NEP), Original and Revised

| ORIGINAL NEP (1978) | REVISED NEP (2000) |
|---|---|
| 1) We are approaching the limit of the number of people the earth can support. | 1) We are approaching the limit of the number of people the earth can support. |
| 2) The balance of nature is very delicate and easily upset. | 2) Humans have the right to modify the natural environment to suit their needs. |
| 3) Humans have the right to modify the natural environment to suit their needs. | 3) When humans interfere with nature it often produces disastrous consequences. |
| 4) Mankind was created to rule over the rest of nature. | 4) Human ingenuity will insure that we do NOT make the earth unlivable. |
| 5) When humans interfere with nature it often produces disastrous consequences. | 5) Humans are severely abusing the environment. |
| 6) Plants and animals exist primarily to be used by humans. | 6) The earth has plenty of natural resources if we just learn how to develop them. |
| 7) To maintain a healthy economy we will have to develop a "steady-state" economy where industrial growth is controlled. | 7) Plants and animals have as much right as humans to exist. |
| 8) Humans must live in harmony with nature in order to survive. | 8) The balance of nature is strong enough to cope with the impacts of modern industrial nations. |
| 9) The earth is like a spaceship with only limited room and resources. | 9) Despite our special abilities humans are still subject to the laws of nature. |
| 10) Humans need not adapt to the natural environment because they can remake it to suit their needs. | 10) The so-called "ecological crisis" facing humankind has been greatly exaggerated. |
| 11) There are limits to growth beyond which our industrialized society cannot expand. | 11) The earth is like a spaceship with very limited room and resources. |
| 12) Mankind is severely abusing the environment. | 12) Humans were meant to rule over the rest of nature. |
| | 13) The balance of nature is very delicate and easily upset. |
| | 14) Humans will eventually learn enough about how nature works to be able to control it. |
| | 15) If things continue on their present course, we will soon experience a major catastrophe. |

In the original NEP, agreement with points 3, 4, 6, and 10 reflects an anti-NEP sentiment, while agreement with points 1, 2, 5, 7, 8, 9, 11, and 12 reflects a pro-NEP sentiment. In the revised NEP, agreement with the even numbered points reflects anti-NEP opinions, while agreement with odd numbers reflects pro-NEP opinions. Source: Adapted from Dunlap and Van Liere (1978) and Dunlap et al. (2000).

"These findings," in the words of the author, "support the global environmentalism theory, which points to burgeoning environmentalism across the world" (57).

The big question is, What's driving this global diffusion of environmental concern? Some argue, like Inglehart, that whatever environmental concern resides in less affluent countries is the result of local, objective environmental degradation. If your local environment is poisoned, so the argument goes, then of course you're going to express some concern about the environment. If this were true, then residents of poor nations should rate local environmental problems as more serious than their counterparts in affluent nations, where local environmental conditions are presumably better, whereas developed nations should rate global problems as more serious. Steve Brechin (1999) set out to test this hypothesis and found only partial support for it. Although citizens of less affluent nations rated local problems as more serious than their more affluent counterparts, ratings of global problems do not differ significantly between rich and poor nations.

Another variable deserving mention is democracy. As democracy grows in a country, so grows not only environmental concern but also environmental associations, which increase opportunities for activism and group formation (Longhofer and Schofer 2010; Sjöstedt and Jagers 2014). Information spreads more easily in a democracy than in an autocracy. Democracies also tend to be more responsive to the environmental needs of the public than nondemocracies (Quan and Reuveny 2006). After examining more than one hundred countries, Quan and Reuveny (2006) conclude that, relative to less democratic countries, more democratic countries emit less $CO_2$ per capita, less $NO_2$ per capita, and less organic pollution in water; experience lower deforestation rates and less land degradation; and have higher percentages of forested land.

I also wonder what effect inequality has on levels of environmental concern within a country, to draw on a variable discussed extensively in the previous chapter. We know, for example, that more equal societies have a greater sense of collective responsibility for those in other countries and that business leaders in more equal countries are more likely to agree that their governments should cooperate with international environmental agreements (Wilkinson and Pickett 2009). I would therefore not be surprised if more equal societies also have higher levels of environmental concern. That would explain why some studies find that citizens of wealthier countries are no more or less concerned about environmental issues than those from poorer nations (Sulemana, James, and Valdivia 2016), while others find a negative correlation between national affluence and environmental concern (Gelissen 2007). Perhaps "level of societal inequality" ought to be looked at in future studies gauging levels of global environmental concern (Lo 2016).

## Pro-Environmental Behavior

We know from decades of research that there is no magic bullet that triggers environmentally significant behavior. A classic study by Gardner and Stern (1996), for instance, examined four types of intervention: religious and moral appeals, education to change attitudes, efforts to change the incentive structure of behavior by providing various types of rewards and penalties, and community management (e.g., the establishment of norms, shared rules, and expectations). Each type was found to have some success at changing behavior, with moral and educational approaches performing the least well. Without question, the most effective behavioral change strategy involved combinations of intervention types. In another study, incentives and education were found to be more effective when combined than the sum of the two interventions when carried out separately (Stern 1999).

An even more seminal study in environmental behavior from the 1980s found that even when electric utility companies subsidized 93 percent of the cost of home insulation, consumer response to the program varied wildly across the regions studied, from 1 to almost 20 percent (Stern et al. 1986). Something other than the subsidy had to be accounting for the different insulation-adoption rates. Researchers found that in addition to reducing financial barriers, utilities also needed to provide information about how insulation can improve household energy efficiency as well as help direct consumers to a reliable contractor.

Social norms are incredibly important in all of this too. What's especially remarkable about social norms is that they seem to have the capacity to elicit behavioral changes without any changes in values or attitudes. I would like to discuss briefly one example where behavioral change occurred *absent attitudinal change.* This case study involves high schools from the school district where I live, Fort Collins, Colorado (Shelley et al. 2011, 2012).

Over a period of eight years, Rocky Mountain High School, which first opened in 1973, was able to reduce its electrical energy consumption to levels below that of the LEED-certified Fossil Ridge High School, built in 2005. (LEED stands for Leadership in Energy and Environmental Design and involves a rating system for the design, construction, and operation of green buildings, homes, and neighborhoods.) Although the LEED school was built for energy efficiency, it consumed electricity at a higher rate (6.24 kilowatt hours per square foot) than the much older Rocky Mountain High School (4.79 kilowatt hours per square foot) in 2007 because of the latter's highly successful energy-conservation efforts. What did Rocky Mountain High School do to achieve these impressive results, where it was able to cut its electrical energy consumption in half over the span of a few years? As indicated by earlier research, no single thing led to the behavioral changes. The authors of this study cite a number of factors:

- Physical structures were added in the school that "communicated environmental values." Examples of this include the recycling center, the "Thanks a Watt" signs above electrical switches, and the clearly marked waste and recycling bins. Making these changes made it easy to be green, regardless of one's actual beliefs.
- Everyone was made a vested stakeholder. Giving staff and students a voice in the process enhanced their desire to see the project become a success and increased their willingness to work toward that end.
- Providing communication and feedback also proved important. Providing students and staff with regular reports on their energy consumption, as well as on how their consumption compared to other schools in the district, kept them vested in the project.

As mentioned, none of the respondents conveyed an actual change in their attitudes. Nevertheless, "even without a sense of environmental concern and without engaging in environmentally responsible behaviors at home, they participated in energy conservation and other efforts (such as recycling) within the organizational setting" (Shelley et al. 2011, 338).

## Social Movements

It is impossible to cover the social movement literature in a few paragraphs, but that is no excuse not to cover it, however thinly, here. Social movements are a powerful mechanism—perhaps *the* most powerful—for change (see Image 13.1).

Social movements can be analyzed in many different ways. One is through the lens of social networks, as a *movement* implies a level of coordination between actors that can

**IMAGE 13.1**

About twenty community members protest in front of the office of state representative Brian Ellis in Lyndora, Pennsylvania, to demand justice for families whose water has been contaminated by fracking operations. Source: "IMG_0340" by shadbushcollective (flickr.com/79055302@N03) is licensed copyright © 2012 under CC BY 2.0.

only be achieved through sustained interaction, or networks. When movement activity is dense—high levels of interaction among members—there is a greater likelihood of solidarity, mutual support, and self-sacrifice (Crossley and Ibrahim 2012). Moreover, dense networks facilitate the establishment and transference of nonmainstream values and movement-specific subcultures, which further fuel intergroup cohesion and collective action (Krinsky and Crossley 2014). These networks also engage in **framing** processes. Social movements construct collective action frames as their participants negotiate a shared understanding of the problem, how it should be handled, and the motivations behind their actions—the diagnostic, prognostic, and motivation frames, respectively (Snow and Benford 1988). Framing is also strategic, as it involves frame alignment processes. These processes include frame bridging (linking two or more frames), frame amplification (embellishment or clarification of existing values), frame extension (extending a frame beyond its initial scope), and frame transformation (changing old understandings or generating new ones) (Snow et al. 1986). Regarding frame transformation: Pellow and Brehm (2015; see also Pellow 2014) conducted an exhaustive study of "radical earth and animal liberation activists" (2015, 207) documenting how they build on deep ecology, ecofeminism, an environmental justice paradigm, and ecological movements, resulting in something entirely new, what activists call a "total liberation" frame. This frame reorganizes what it means to reduce harm to humans and the environment thanks to "a complete reordering of human/nonhuman relations" resulting in a desire for "equality for all beings" (207).

Why some movements succeed and others fail can also be thought about in terms of organizational resources. Discontent and a sense of injustice are common occurrences.

And yet collective *grievances* do not always stimulate collective *action*. According to McCarthy and Zald (1977), movement actors must have access to resources—financial, social capital, leadership, effective organizers, and so forth—that allow them to turn grievances into action.

In addition to having resources, movement organizations' ability to effect change often depends on circumstances of the broader sociopolitical environment. While a **resource mobilization framework** focuses heavily on internal organizational resources, a **political opportunity approach** considers external factors, such as the political context within which social movements are embedded (McAdam 1996). Take the marriage equality movement. The story of this movement is radically different today from the one told a decade ago. This is in part due to there being a different sociopolitical reality in place currently from what existed even just a few years ago. This is not to suggest all hope is lost when political opportunities appear "closed," when, say, lawmakers are not only resistant but also potentially hostile to movement demands—a reality experienced by many environmental activists in a post-9/11 world (Deflem 2015). Instead, such an environment may compel activists to approach the court system as a venue in which they perceive a better chance of generating social change (McCammon and McGrath 2015). The Endangered Species Act, specifically thanks to its citizen suit provision, has a rich history of activists taking successful legal action when federal agencies appear to be dragging their feet in enforcing the act (Baur and Irvin 2010).

## Pragmatic Environmentalism

Pragmatic social theorists—as well as environmentalists—take actors' agency and creativity seriously. As a theoretical tradition, pragmatism offers an alternative to overt social structuralism (an approach giving priority to structures) and methodological individualism (an approach giving priority to individuals). Instead, it emphasizes the dynamic emergent interplay between the process of constructing and reconstructing meaning through action and routine, on the one hand, and structures and the environment, on the other. John Dewey, the great American philosopher and an early developer of pragmatism, worried about the interests, beliefs, and ideologies of elites becoming fixed, or static, and assuming a taken-for-granted status within the political and the dominant social cultures. To combat this, he prescribed the technique of experimentalism, which essentially involves the recruiting of the broader public to constantly reflect on and question conventional habits and beliefs. Dewey believed this constituted an important first step in breaking up imposed rules of order and action, which is necessary if meaningful social change is to occur. The most likely time for established rules to be reformed, Dewey argued, is when existing institutions fail. During these moments, publics form that are commonly united through a shared threat or actual harm. (Think of the possible "publics" that could be organized as a response to climate change.) Thus, social and environmental problems are inherently *hopeful*, in the sense that they create openings for creativity, change, and an enlivened democracy.

And what of those who choose not to be initially enrolled in this collective activity? Fortunately, there are many ways to engage people in selecting pro-environmental behaviors without having to make them into so-called environmentalists. For example, let's say we are able to get people to choose to leave their car in the garage, or perhaps not even buy one. As long as they are doing this, does it really matter—at least initially—what their attitudes toward the environment or even automobiles are? Anna Peterson (2009) reminds us that attitudes and values have the potential to change in radical ways in response to behavioral changes. She gives the example of the 1954 US Supreme Court decision *Brown v. Board of Education of Topeka,* the landmark court ruling that struck down the infamous "separate but equal" rule made famous in the *Plessy v. Ferguson* US Supreme Court ruling from 1899. Peterson points out that "while school desegregation certainly did not end racism, it has had a significant effect on the lives and values of both white and black southerners," ultimately concluding that "Brown generated major shifts in values that probably would not have occurred had institutions and practices not changed first." She goes on to suggest that an "environmental *Brown v. Board of Education*" could, over time, help generate "environmental values as well as positive practical results" (2009, 132).

Something else we've learned over the past couple of decades is that getting people *talking and working together* is an immensely powerful force. The late Elinor Ostrom, as mentioned in an earlier chapter, won a Nobel Prize in economics in 2009 for her tireless research on precisely this point, though the idea that thick social networks can overwhelm desires to act selfishly has been articulated by social and political theorists for quite some time (see, for example, Eckersley 1992; Dryzek 1990; Habermas 1962). Sometimes the formation of these collectivities is abrupt and immediate: think of the speed at which a shared global public formed in the wake of September 11. More often, however, their formation is a slow grind, even for threats that are global and significant in scope, like climate change. In the end, *people* are going to have to do the work; structures are not going to change themselves. What are you going to do?

---

## IMPORTANT CONCEPTS

- climate change denial
- collaborative consumption
- consumerism
- framing
- globalization of environmental concern
- Inglehart's postmaterialism thesis
- intrinsic and extrinsic values
- New Environmental Paradigm (NEP)
- political opportunity approach
- postmaterialism thesis
- pragmatic environmentalism
- resource mobilization framework

## DISCUSSION QUESTIONS

1. We have long practiced a type of collaborative consumption with public libraries. Why do we not collaboratively consume more stuff, beyond books, movies, and music?
2. In what ways do some of your own pro-environmental attitudes not match up with certain behaviors? Why do you think this gap exists?

3. What are your thoughts on *Wired* founder Kevin Kelly's argument that "access is better than ownership"?
4. To revisit a question first posed at the end of Chapter 2: Why do some people continue to deny the existence of anthropogenic climate change? What are your thoughts on some of the explanations given above to this question?
5. Have you used Airbnb or Uber or some other example of collaborative consumption? What factors motivated you to try these services out? If you haven't used them yet, why not?

## SUGGESTED ADDITIONAL READINGS

Khondker, H. 2015. "From 'The Silent Spring' to the Globalization of the Environmental Movement." *Journal of International & Global Studies* 6(2): 25–37.
McCright, A., and R. Dunlap. 2015. "Comparing Two Measures of Social Movement Identity: The Environmental Movement as an Example." *Social Science Quarterly* 96(2): 400–416.
Rifkin, J. 2014. "The End of the Capitalist Era, and What Comes Next." *Huffington Post*, Apr. 1. www.huffingtonpost.com/jeremy-rifkin/collaborative-commons-zero-marginal-co st-society_b_5064767.html.
Schor, J., and C. Fitzmaurice. 2015. "Collaborating and Connecting: The Emergence of the Sharing Economy." In *Handbook on Research on Sustainable Consumption*, edited by L. Reisch and J. Thogersen, 410–425. Cheltenham, UK: Edward Elgar.

## RELEVANT INTERNET LINKS

- www.democracynow.org/2014/9/18/capitalism_vs_the_climate_naomi_klein. Video titled "Capitalism vs. the Climate: Naomi Klein on the Need for a New Economic Model to Address the Ecological Crisis."
- www.scorai.org. Sustainable Consumption Research and Action Initiative (SCORAI) is a network of academics and practitioners interested in better understanding the interface of material consumption, human fulfillment, lifestyle satisfaction, and macroeconomic and technological change.
- www.ted.com/talks/rachel_botsman_the_case_for_collaborative_consumption.html. TED talk by Rachel Botsman, one of the authors of *What's Mine Is Yours: The Rise of Collaborative Consumption* (Botsman and Rogers 2010).
- www.youtube.com/watch?v=5-iDUcETjvo. Video titled "Jeremy Rifkin: 'The Zero Marginal Cost Society' Talks at Google."

## SUGGESTED VIDEOS

- *END: CIV Resist or Die* (2011). If your homeland were invaded by aliens who cut down the forests, poisoned the water and air, and contaminated the food supply, would you resist?
- *The Evolution of Ecological Consciousness* (2013). It wasn't until the 1930s when we started to agree that there were such things as ice ages. It wasn't until the 1970s that plate tectonics was understood in geology. Our understanding of this planet is constantly developing and evolving.

- *Fierce Green Fire* (2014). www.democracynow.org/2014/4/22/earth_day_special_fierce _green_fire. Explores the environmental movement's global rise.
- *Meet the Climate Sceptics* (2011). A journey into the heart of climate skepticism to examine the key arguments against human-made global warming and try to understand the people who are making them.
- *Shareconomy (Sharing Economy)* (2014). Ten-minute video on the sharing economy. Available, among other places, on YouTube.
- *We the Tiny House People* (2012). This is a journey into the tiny homes of people searching for simplicity, self-sufficiency, minimalism, and happiness by creating shelter in caves, converted garages, trailers, tool sheds, river boats, and former pigeon coops.
- *Words from the Edge* (2013). For many years the environmental movement has assumed that if you want to get people to do something, what you have to do is to make a sufficiently depressing film or write a sufficiently horrific and miserable leaflet and get that into their hands and they will simply act: "Oh my God, that's terrible, I'll go and plant some carrots." Actually it doesn't work that way.

# Glossary

**Abject poverty:** Most severe state of poverty. Those living in this state cannot meet basic needs for food, water, shelter, sanitation, and health care.

**Adaptation** (climate change): Actions taken to adjust socioecological systems in response to existing or predicted climatic effects in order to reduce harmful effects.

**Agrobiodiversity:** All forms of life directly relevant to agriculture, including crops and livestock but also many other organisms, such as soil, fauna, weeds, pests, and predators.

**Anaerobic decomposition:** The breaking down of biodegradable material by microorganisms in an environment lacking oxygen.

**Apolitical ecology:** When conventional explanations do not fully account for the asymmetries in power that first created a problem materially and then later define it as a problem to be solved by the same system that gave birth to it.

**Arable land:** Land that can be cultivated to grow crops.

**Biochar:** Charcoal derived from a thermochemical decomposition of organic material at heightened temperatures in the absence of oxygen. Biochar is used to improve soil fertility and sequester carbon. Biochar oil and gas by-products can also be used as biofuels.

**Biocultural diversity:** Recognizes that cultural diversity does not merely parallel biological diversity but is profoundly interrelated with it.

**Biodiversity hotspots:** A biogeographic region with a significant reservoir of biodiversity that is under threat from humans.

**Biofortification:** The breeding and, increasingly, genetic engineering of plants with the aim of higher micronutrient content.

**Biohazards:** Environmental threats resulting from biological agents or conditions.

**Biopiracy:** The loss of biocultural diversity through legal and sometimes illegal means.

**Birthrate:** The ratio of live births to total population of a specified community, usually expressed per one thousand people per year.

**"Bonding" social capital:** Social ties that link people together who are primarily alike according to established characteristics.

**"Bridging" social capital:** Social ties that link people together across social cleavages.

**Buyer power:** An effect that results when a market has numerous sellers but only one buyer or a few.

**Cap and trade:** A scheme that involves the trading of a limited number of emission allowances. A regulatory authority establishes this limit, which is typically lower than the historical level of emissions.

**Carbon credits:** Units of carbon emissions that can be purchased or sold to meet compliance with carbon emission caps.

**Carbon intensity:** The amount of $CO_2$ emitted for each unit of economic output produced.

**Carbon offsets:** Reduction in emissions of carbon dioxide (or greenhouse gases more generally) in order to compensate for (offset) an emission released elsewhere.

**Carbon tax:** Tax on fossil fuels that seeks to reduce the emission of carbon dioxide.

**Carrotmob:** A type of consumer activism based on the idea of using carrots (or incentives) to reward businesses for engaging in socially or environmentally responsible practices.

**Car sharing**: A short-term (often by the hour) car rental model where the cars are scattered throughout a community to improve access rather than all being centrally housed at one location, as with traditional car rentals.

**Clean coal**: Defined by the coal industry as any technologies that improve the environmental performance of coal-based electricity plants, which include equipment that increases the operational efficiency of power plants as well as technologies that reduce emissions. Elsewhere, it refers to the $CO_2$ capture and (long-term) storage of emissions.

**Climate change**: A change in climate patterns that results from human activity like burning fossil fuels.

**Climate change refugees**: Populations that have been displaced as a result of climate change.

**Coase theorem**: When property rights are involved, parties naturally gravitate toward the most efficient and mutually beneficial outcome.

**Collective coverage**: Proportion of an area serviced by the municipal waste stream.

**Commodity chain**: The collective networks that encompass the beginning and end of a product's life cycle.

**Community severance**: The physical or social separation of an individual from the rest of the community.

**Conspicuous consumption**: The idea that we consume, at least in part, to display to others our social power and status.

**Contingent valuation**: A survey-based economic technique for placing a value on nonmarket resources.

**Convention on Biological Diversity**: An international, legally binding treaty that entered into force in 1993. The convention has three main goals: conservation of biological diversity, sustainable use of biological resources, and fair and equitable sharing of benefits arising from genetic resources.

**Cornucopian**: Someone who believes unending progress, economic growth, and material abundance can be had with advancements in technology.

**Countermovements**: A social movement that arises to explicitly oppose an existing social movement.

**Cultural hotspots**: A biogeographic region with a significant reservoir of cultural diversity that is under threat of extinction.

**Daylighting**: The practice of uncovering previously concealed natural amenities.

**Dead zones**: The name given to bodies of water with low levels of dissolved oxygen.

**Decoupling**: The ability for an economy to grow without corresponding increases in environmental pressure.

**Demographic inertia**: A well-documented demographic phenomenon relating to how a time lag is to be expected before the full effects of changes to a fertility rate are seen.

**Demographic transition model**: A model detailing the historical changes in birthrates and death rates for explaining rapid population growth. A country is said to have passed through the demographic transition when it moves from a condition of high birthrates and death rates (and a relatively small population) to low birthrates and death rates (and a relatively large population).

**Desalinization**: The removal of salt and other minerals from saline water.

**Diminishing marginal utility**: The more units of something we consume, the less added enjoyment we get from each additional unit.

**Disability-adjusted life-years (DALYs)**: The sum of years of potential life lost from premature mortality and the years of productive life lost from disability.

**Disease vectors**: An organism, such as a mosquito or tick, that carries disease-causing microorganisms from one host to another.

**Diversionary reframing**: Diverting attention away from real problems by trying to reframe the debate as being about something else.

**Down-cycling**: The process of converting waste into new materials or products of lesser quality and decreased functionality.

**Ecofeminism**: An area of study that examines the historical (and present) links between the objectification of women and the objectification of nature.

**Economism**: The act of reducing the world to economic dimensions.

**Ecosystem services**: The processes by which the environment produces resources that we often take for granted but need for our survival, such as clean air and water, timber, habitat for fisheries, and pollination of native and agricultural plants.

**Efficiency shifting**: When money and resources saved through energy efficiency merely get shifted to and consumed by other goods and services.

**Embodied energy**: The sum total of the energy utilized throughout an entire product life cycle.

**Energy intensity**: The amount of energy required to produce each unit of the world's economic output.

**Environmental racism**: Racial discrimination in environmental policy making and enforcement of regulations and laws, in addition to the targeting of communities of color for toxic waste disposal and siting of polluting industries.

**Environmental skepticism**: A position that attempts to undermine knowledge claims supporting the argument that environmental problems are real and that they are the result of human activity.

**Exponential growth**: Constant growth in a system where the amount added is proportional to the amount present.

**Ex situ**: Sampling, transferring, and storage of a species in a place other than the original location in which it was found, like a zoo or seed bank.

**Extended producer responsibility**: Holding the manufacturer responsible for a product beyond the time of sale, thereby relieving consumers, governments, future generations, and the environment from the costs associated with landfilling and recycling hazardous materials.

**Externality**: Cost or benefit not transmitted through prices and incurred by a party who did not agree to the action causing the cost or benefit.

**Family planning**: Educational, social, and medical services that empower individuals to make choices around reproduction.

**Food sovereignty**: A movement and way of life that is diametrically opposed to the dominant view that presently dictates conventional food and agricultural policy.

**Food system**: The entire array of activities—from input production and distribution to on-farm activities, marketing, processing, wholesale, and retail—that connect seed (and gene) to the mouths of consumers.

**Footprint shifting** (life cycle): Making efficiency gains at one point in a commodity's life cycle while creating a larger environmental load at another point.

**Fracking**: A method of extracting natural gas from deep wells; also known as hydraulic fracturing.

**Framing**: Involves the social construction of social phenomena—by mass media, political or social movements, political leaders, or other actors and organizations—whereby symbols, words, or phrases are given distinct meanings with the aim of organizing people into social groups, e.g., social movements.

**Full irrigation**: The amount of water needed to achieve maximum yield.

**Greenhouse effect**: When a portion of the sun's radiation that enters the atmosphere is absorbed by the planet's atmosphere thanks to greenhouse gases like $CO_2$ rather than being reradiated back into space.

**Greenhouse gases**: Any gases in the atmosphere that absorb and emit radiation within the thermal infrared range.

**Green revolution**: A series of strategies developed during the mid- to late twentieth century to combat starvation by expanding the global production of staple food crops through crop breeding.

**Habitat fragmentation**: The emergence of discontinuities (or fragmentation) in an organism's preferred environment (or habitat).

**Happy Life Years (HLYs)**: A measurement of the health of a nation found through multiplying life expectancy at birth by happiness score (on a scale of 0 to 1).

**Heat island effect**: Because concrete, tarmac, and other common construction materials absorb heat readily, built-up areas tend to be warmer than nearby rural areas.

**Hypoxia**: A state when oxygen concentrations in a body of water fall below the level necessary to sustain most animal life.

**Indigenous knowledge**: Knowledge unique to a given community, culture, or society.

**Informal settlements**: Unplanned housing constructed on land illegally or not in compliance with current building regulations, or both.

**In situ**: The management of a species at the location of discovery.

**Intergovernmental Panel on Climate Change**: Established by two UN organizations, the United Nations Environment Programme and the World Meteorological Organization, in 1988 to provide scientific assessments on issues relating to climate change. With the IPCC as the internationally accepted authority on the subject, the world's governments look to it as the official advisory body on climate change.

**Irrigation efficiency**: The ratio of water that evaporates to what saturates the soil.

**Islandization** (habitat): The breaking up of habitats without wildlife corridors to connect them.

**Kyoto Protocol**: An international treaty brokered by the UN, signed in 1997, that binds signatory nations to reduce their emissions of greenhouse gases. At Kyoto (where the agreement was first signed), nations agreed to cut their emissions of six greenhouse gases by an average of 5 percent overall, compared with 1990 levels, in what was termed the first commitment period, which was to end in 2012.

**Landfill**: A method of solid waste disposal where refuse is buried between layers of dirt.

**Low-elevation coastal zones**: Areas within ten meters of mean sea level.

**Market concentration**: The dominance of a particular market by a few large firms as a result of acquisition, mergers, and other processes.

**Market environmentalism**: A theory that emphasizes markets as a solution to environmental problems.

**Maternal mortality ratio**: The number of women who die from pregnancy-related causes while pregnant or within forty-two days of pregnancy termination per one hundred thousand live births.

**Mechanical revolution**: The gradual substitution of capital for labor in agriculture.

**Megacities**: Cities with more than ten million residents.

**Memory banks**: Spaces that preserve not only genetic material but the skills to grow and save seeds and prepare the fruits of those labors.

**Micronutrient malnutrition**: A condition that results from a diet lacking in sufficient quantities of micronutrients.

**Mitigation**: Making reductions in the concentration of greenhouse gases by reducing their sources, increasing sink capacity, or both.

**Monocultures**: An agricultural practice of producing a single plant species over a wide area for a number of consecutive years.

**Mountaintop removal mining**: Clearing upper-elevation forests (typically at the summit of mountains), stripping the ground of topsoil, and using explosives to break up rocks to expose underlying yet relatively shallow coal seams.

**Municipal solid waste**: All solid waste originating from homes, industries, businesses, demolition, land clearing, and construction.

**Natural capital**: Assets indispensable for human survival and economic activity provided by the ecosystem.

**Naturalistic fallacy**: When statements of fact are conflated with statements of value.

**Neoliberalism**: A set of economic practices grounded in the belief that human well-being is best advanced by limiting (if not eliminating) government and liberating individual entrepreneurial freedoms within legal and institutional frameworks that support strong private property rights, free markets, and free trade.

**Neo-Malthusians**: Those who advocate for the control of population growth.

**Nongovernmental organization (NGO)**: Any legally constituted organization that operates independently from any government.

**Nonpoint-source pollution**: Pollution that is more diffuse, making the source harder to pinpoint.

**Normal accidents**: A failure that is inevitable, given the manner in which particular human and technological systems are organized.

**One-child policy**: First introduced in 1978, this policy restricts married urban couples in China to one child, though exceptions are allowed, such as for rural couples and certain ethnic minorities.

**Open source seeds**: Seeds that cannot be patented, licensed, or commodified in any way, even in those instances where they have been bred or genetically modified into something new.

**Organic system** (agriculture): A farm management system that seeks to enhance biodiversity while minimizing the use of off-farm inputs.

**Pareto optimality standard**: Deems a policy acceptable only if at least one individual is better off and no individuals are made worse off.

**Pay-as-you-drive auto insurance**: Insurance whose rate (but not coverage) is contingent on, among other things, the amount of miles driven.

**Peasant-based movements**: Social movements that began in the Global South and that centrally involve peasants. In this context "peasant" is not a pejorative term but one of empowerment.

**Peer-to-peer renting**: The process of one private individual renting an underused item of theirs to another individual.

**Pigovian taxes**: Taxes levied on companies that pollute or create excess social costs (called negative externalities).

**Point-source pollution**: Pollution with an identifiable source.

**Political opportunity approach**: Argues that success or failure of social movements is primarily affected by political opportunities.

**Polycultures**: Small, diverse farms that raise grains, fruits, vegetables, and livestock.

**Popular epidemiology**: A type of citizen science in which laypeople are involved and which requires a lower level of statistical confidence when claiming the existence of causal links.

**Porter Hypothesis**: Regulation spurs innovation, as it creates incentives for businesses to adjust to social and environmental realities.

**Pronatal social norms**: Individual attitudes and societal expectations that promote high fertility rates.

**Resource mobilization framework**: Emphasizes the ability of a movement's members to acquire resources and to mobilize people toward accomplishing the movement's goals.

**Role strain**: Tensions that emerge when expectations from holding multiple roles clash.

**Salinization**: The buildup of salt in soil and groundwater.

**Sequestering CO2**: The act of removing $CO_2$ from the atmosphere and holding it in a sink.

**Sink** (greenhouse gas): A natural or artificial reservoir—like a forest—that holds and stores greenhouses gases for an indefinite period, thus preventing their accumulation in the atmosphere.

**Social constructivism**: An approach that focuses entirely on the sociologically dependent knowledge of a phenomenon rather than on any inherent qualities that the thing possesses itself.

**Social norms**: Standards of behavior shared by a social group.

**Sociological ambivalence**: Incompatible or contradictory normative expectations or attitudes, beliefs, and behavior that people have because of their holding multiple statuses or when a single status has contradictory expectations.

**Sociological drivers**: Real phenomena that can only be fully grasped with the help of social theory that underlie today's environmental problems.

**Sociological imagination**: A way of thinking that involves making connections between the particular and the general over time and across scales.

**Species problem**: The inherent ambiguity surrounding the use and definition of the species concept.

**Street hierarchy**: Eliminates connections between streets by funneling traffic up the hierarchy, from cul-de-sac streets to primary or secondary collector streets, arterial streets, and ultimately highways.

**Strip-mining**: The removal of soil and rock overlaying the mineral deposit.

**Structure of agriculture**: How farms, rural populations, and agribusiness firms are arranged to produce and distribute food and fiber.

**Terminator technology**: Genetically engineered seeds that produce sterile plants.

**Tragedy of the commodity**: Rather than being its savior, commodification of so-called natural capital contributes to the decline of biodiversity and ecosystem services.

**Type I error**: Concluding there is a causal link when there isn't one.

**Type II error**: Concluding there is not a causal link when there is one.

**Uneconomic growth**: Growth that costs us more than it benefits us.

**Urban sprawl**: The spreading of urban development into areas adjoining cities.

**Vertical farming**: The practice of farming "up," rather than "out."

**Virtual water**: Water used during the growing, making, or manufacturing of a given commodity.

**Volatile organic compounds**: Compounds that evaporate from housekeeping, maintenance, and building products made with organic chemicals.

**Vulnerable road users**: As defined by the WHO, this population includes pedestrians, cyclists, and users of motorized two-wheel vehicles.

**Waste regimes**: The realization that institutions, regulations, policy initiatives, and social conventions determine not only what is waste but also how waste is valued.

**Water footprint**: An indicator of freshwater use that looks at both direct and indirect water use by a consumer or producer.

**Water privatization**: The treatment of water like any other commodity and leaving questions of access and sanitation to market mechanisms.

**Welfare economics**: A branch of microeconomics that seeks to evaluate well-being, with the assumption that human well-being is wholly reducible to economic well-being.

**Wildlife corridors**: Areas of habitat connecting wildlife populations and larger islands of habitat.

**Work-spend cycle**: Where we work to spend, which in turn requires us to work more.

**Worldview**: A fundamental cognitive orientation shared by individuals within which is rooted the entirety of their knowledge.

# References

AAA (American Automobile Association). 2015. *Your Driving Costs*. Heathrow, FL. exchange.aaa.com/wp-content /uploads/2015/04/Your-Driving-Costs-2015.pdf.

Abram, D. 1996. *The Spell of the Sensuous*. New York: Pantheon Books.

Agapow, P., O. Bininda-Emonds, K. Crandall, J. Gittleman, G. Mace, J. Marshall, and A. Purvis. 2004. "The Impact of Species Concept on Biodiversity Studies." *Quarterly Review of Biology* 79:161–179.

Aggarwal, R. M. 2016. "International Development and Sustainability." In *Sustainability Science*, edited by H. Heindricks, 273–282. Springer Netherlands.

Agrawal, A. 2014. "Studying the Commons, Governing Common-Pool Resource Outcomes: Some Concluding Thoughts." *Environmental Science & Policy* 36:86–91.

Alderman, H., J. Hoddinott, and B. Kinsey. 2006. "Long-Term Consequences of Early Childhood Malnutrition." *Oxford Economic Papers* 58(3): 450–474.

Alexander, J., T. Crompton, and G. Shrubsole. 2011. "Think of Me as Evil: Opening the Ethical Debates in Advertising." Public Interest Research Centre (PIRC) and WWF-UK. assets.wwf.org.uk/downloads/think_of_me_as _evil.pdf.

Alexandratos, N., and J. Bruinsma. 2012. *World Agriculture Towards 2030–50*. ESA Working Paper No. 12-03. Food and Agriculture Organization, United Nations, Rome. large.stanford.edu/courses/2014/ph240/yuan2 /docs/ap106e.pdf.

Altieri, A., and K. Gedan. 2015. "Climate Change and Dead Zones." *Global Change Biology* 21(4): 1395–1406.

Altieri, M., and C. Nicholls. 2008. "Scaling Up Agroecological Approaches for Food Sovereignty in Latin America." *Development* 51(4): 472–480.

American Public Health Association. 2010. *The Hidden Health Costs of Transportation*. Washington, DC. www .apha.org/NR/rdonlyres/E71B4070-9B9D-4EE1-8F43-349D21414962/0/FINALHiddenHealthCostsShortNew BackCover.pdf.

Anderson, S., J. Cavanagh, C. Collins, S. Pizzigati, and M. Lapham. 2008. *Executive Excess, 2008: How Average Taxpayers Subsidize Runaway Pay*. United for a Fair Economy and Institute for Policy Studies. www.ips-dc.org /wp-content/uploads/2008/08/ExecutiveExcess2008.pdf.

Anderson, T. L. 2004. "Why Economic Growth Is Good for the Environment." *Hoover Digest* 3. www.perc.org /articles/why-economic-growth-good-environment.

Ansar, A., B. Flyvbjerg, A. Budzier, and D. Lunn. 2014. "Should We Build More Large Dams? The Actual Costs of Hydropower Megaproject Development." *Energy Policy* 69:43–56.

Arbuckle, J. G., L. S. Prokopy, T. Haigh, J. Hobbs, T. Knoot, C. Knutson, A. Loy, A. S. Mase, J. McGuire, L. W. Morton, J. Tyndall, and M. Widhalm. 2013. "Climate Change Beliefs, Concerns, and Attitudes Toward Adaptation and Mitigation Among Farmers in the Midwestern United States." *Climatic Change* 117:943–950.

Arbuckle, J., L. W. Morgan, and J. Hobbs. 2015. "Understanding Farmer Perspectives on Climate Change Adaptation and Mitigation: The Roles of Trust in Sources of Climate Information, Climate Change Beliefs, and Perceived Risk." *Environment and Behavior* 47(2): 205–234.

Arens, W. 2005. *Contemporary Advertising*. Columbus, OH: McGraw-Hill.

Ashworth, D., P. Elliott, and M. Toledano. 2014. "Waste Incineration and Adverse Birth and Neonatal Outcomes: A Systematic Review." *Environment International* 69:120–132.

Atav, E., B. Altunoğlu, and S. Sönmez. 2015. "The Determination of the Environmental Attitudes of Secondary Education Students." *Procedia-Social and Behavioral Sciences* 174:1391–1396.

Atkinson, C. 2014. "Report Reveals Average US Family Owns Four Mobile Devices." *New York Post*, Feb. 10.

Attari, S., M. DeKayb, C. Davidson, and W. Bruine de Bruin. 2010. "Public Perceptions of Energy Consumption and Savings." *Proceedings of the National Academy of Sciences* 107(37): 16054–16059.

Ayres, R., and B. Warr. 2009. *The Economic Growth Engine: How Energy and Work Drive Material Prosperity.* Northampton, MA: Edward Elgar.

Bachour, M. K. 2015, February. "Disrupting the Myth of Maquila Disposability: Sites of Reproduction and Resistance in Juárez." *Women's Studies International Forum* 48:174–184.

Bachram, H. 2004. "Climate Fraud and Carbon Colonialism: The New Trade in Greenhouse Gases." *Capitalism Nature Socialism* 15(4): 5–20.

Bagriansky, J., N. Champa, K. Pak, S. Whitney, and A. Laillou. 2014. "The Economic Consequences of Malnutrition in Cambodia: More Than 400 Million US Dollars Lost Annually." *Asia Pacific Journal of Clinical Nutrition* 23(4): 524.

Balmford, A., R. Green, and J. Scharlemann. 2005. "Sparing Land for Nature: Exploring the Potential Impact of Changes in Agricultural Yield on the Area Needed for Crop Production." *Global Change Biology* 11:1594–1605.

Banerjee, A., and E. Duflo. 2011. "More Than 1 Billion People Are Hungry in the World: But What if the Experts Are Wrong?" *Foreign Policy* (May–June).

Bang, M., D. Medin, and S. Atran. 2007. "Cultural Mosaics and Mental Models of Nature." *Proceedings of the National Academy of Sciences* 104(35): 13868–13874.

Barbier, E. B. 2015. "Climate Change Impacts on Rural Poverty in Low-Elevation Coastal Zones." *Estuarine, Coastal and Shelf Science* 165:ii–iii.

Barnard, N. 2010. "Trends in Food Availability, 1909–2007." *American Journal of Clinical Nutrition* 91:1530S–1536S.

Bartlett, S., D. Dodman, J. Hardoy, D. Satterthwaite, and C. Tacol. 2009. "Social Aspects of Climate Change in Rural Areas in Low and Middle Income Nations." Contribution to the World Bank. www.dbsa.org/Vulindlela/Papers%20Library/Session1 Satterthwaite.pdf.

Bartolini, S., E. Bilancini, L. Bruni, and P. Porta, eds. 2016. *Policies for Happiness.* Oxford: Oxford University Press.

Baskoro, F. M. 2011. "Air Travel to Grow by 13% by Next Year, Industry Says." *Jakarta Globe*, Dec. 8.

Bates, S. 2015. "The Emergent Body: Marxism, Critical Realism and the Corporeal in Contemporary Capitalist Society." *Global Society* 29(1): 128–147.

Battisti, D., and R. Naylor. 2009. "Historical Warning of Future Food Insecurity." *Science* 323:240–244.

Baumeister, R. F., S. E. Ainsworth, and K. D. Vohs. 2015. "Are Groups More or Less Than the Sum of Their Members? The Moderating Role of Individual Identification." *Behavioral and Brain Sciences*, May 4.

Baur, D., and W. Irvin. 2010. *Endangered Species Act: Law, Policy, and Perspectives.* New York: American Bar Association.

Bayani, O. 2010. "U.S. Can Save $41.1 Billion Annually Through Building Retrofits." Ecoseed, Oct. 12. www.ecoseed.org/business/14085-u-s-can-save-41-1-billion-annually-through-building-retrofits.

BBC. 2003. "Argentina Fights Flood Waters." BBC News, May 2. news.bbc.co.uk/2/hi/americas/2994301.stm.

Bell, M., and P. Lowe. 2000. "Regulated Freedoms: The Market and the State, Agriculture, and the Environment." *Journal of Rural Studies* 16:285–294.

Bell, S., and R. York. 2010. "Community Economic Identity: The Coal Industry and Ideology Construction in West Virginia." *Rural Sociology* 75(1): 111–143.

Berlin, I. (1958) 1969. *Four Essays on Liberty.* London: Oxford University Press.

Blackford, M. 2004. "Environmental Justice, Native Rights, Tourism, and Opposition to Military Control: The Case of Kaho'olawe." *Journal of American History* 91(2): 1–43.

Bliuc, A., C. McGarty, E. Thomas, G. Lala, M. Berndsen, and R. Misajon. 2015. "Public Division About Climate Change Rooted in Conflicting Socio-Political Identities." *Nature Climate Change* 5:226–229.

Boccard, N. 2014. "The Cost of Nuclear Electricity: France After Fukushima." *Energy Policy* 66:450–461.

Bohra-Mishra, P., and D. Massey. 2011. "Environmental Degradation and Out-Migration: New Evidence from Nepal." In *Climate Change and Migration,* edited by E. Piguet, P. de Guchteneire, and A. Pecoud, 74–101. Paris: Cambridge University Press, UNESCO.

Bokowa, A. 2010. "The Review of Odour Legislation." *Proceedings of the Water Environment Federation* 20:492–511.

Bolles, A. 1878. *Industrial History of the United States.* Norwich, CT: Henry Bill.

Booker, A., D. Johnston, and M. Heinrich. 2015. "Value Chains of Herbal Medicines—Ethnopharmacological and Analytical Challenges in a Globalizing World." In *Evidence-Based Validation of Herbal Medicine,* edited by P. Mukherjee, 29–44. Amsterdam: Elsevier.

Bordewich, F., R. Klein, P. Smith, M. Buckingham, and E. Winograde. 2007. *No Reservations: Native American History and Culture in Contemporary Art.* Ridgefield, CT: Aldrich Contemporary Art Museum.

Bordoff, J., and P. Noel. 2008. "Pay-as-You-Drive Auto Insurance: A Simple Way to Reduce Driving-Related Harms and Increase Equity." Discussion paper 2008–2009, July. Brookings Institution, Washington, DC. www .brookings.edu/~/media/Files/rc/papers/2008/07_payd_bordoffnoel/07_payd_bordoffnoel_pb.pdf.

Borg, R., A. Toikka, and E. Primmer. 2015. "Social Capital and Governance: A Social Network Analysis of Forest Biodiversity Collaboration in Central Finland." *Forest Policy and Economics* 50:90–97.

Boserup, E. 1965. *The Conditions of Agricultural Growth: The Economics of Agrarian Change Under Population Pressure.* Chicago: Aldine.

Botsman, R., and R. Rogers. 2010. *What's Mine Is Yours: The Rise of Collaborative Consumption.* New York: Harper.

Boxall, B., and M. Stevens. 2015. "California Faces Fight over Historic Water Rationing Plans." *Los Angeles Times,* Apr. 16.

BP. 2015. *BP Energy Outlook, 2035.* Feb. www.bp.com/content/dam/bp/pdf/Energy-economics/energy-outlook-2015 /Energy_Outlook_2035_booklet.pdf.

Brechin, S. 1999. "Objective Problems, Subjective Values, and Global Environmentalism: Evaluating the Postmaterialist Argument and Challenging a New Explanation." *Social Science Quarterly* 80:793–809.

Bremner, B., and N. Lakshman. 2006. "Behind the Coke-Pepsi Pesticide Scare." *Business Week,* Aug. 24. www .businessweek.com/globalbiz/content/aug2006/gb20060824_932216.htm.

Brizga, J., Z. Mishchuk, and A. Golubovska-Onisimova. 2014. "Sustainable Consumption and Production Governance in Countries in Transition." *Journal of Cleaner Production* 63:45–53.

Brogaard, L., A. Damgaard, M. Jensen, M. Barlaz, and T. Christensen. 2014. "Evaluation of Life Cycle Inventory Data for Recycling Systems." *Resources, Conservation and Recycling* 87:30–45.

Brown, J., W. Burnside, A. Davidson, J. DeLong, W. Dunn, M. Hamilton, N. Mercado-Silva, J. Nekola, J. Okie, W. Woodruff, and W. Zuo. 2011. "Energetic Limits to Economic Growth." *BioScience* 61(1): 19–26.

Brown, K., and T. Kasser. 2005. "Are Psychological and Ecological Well-Being Compatible? The Role of Values, Mindfulness, and Lifestyle." *Social Indicators Research* 74:349–368.

Brown, L. 2009. *Plan B 4.0: Mobilizing to Save Civilization.* New York: W. W. Norton.

Brulle, R., and D. Pellow. 2006. "Environmental Justice: Human Health and Environmental Inequalities." *Annual Reviews of Public Health* 27:103–124.

Bulkeley, H., L. Andonova, M. Betsill, D. Compagnon, T. Hale, M. Hoffmann, P. Newell, M. Paterson, S. VanDeveer, and C. Roger. 2014. *Transnational Climate Change Governance.* New York: Cambridge University Press.

Bullard, R. 1990. *Dumping in Dixie: Race, Class, and Environmental Quality.* Boulder: Westview.

———, ed. 2005. *The Quest for Environmental Justice: Human Rights and the Politics of Pollution.* San Francisco: Sierra Club Books.

Bullock, C. 2008. "The Economic and Social Aspects of Biodiversity." Government of Ireland. www.environ.ie/en /Heritage/PublicationsDocuments/FileDownLoad,17321,en.pdf.

Bunting, S. 2013. *Principles of Sustainable Aquaculture: Promoting Social, Economic and Environmental Resilience.* New York: Routledge.

Burns, B. 2010. "TSA Myth or Fact: Leaked Images, Handcuffed Hosts, Religious Garb, and More!" TSA Blog, Nov. 18. blog.tsa.gov/2010/11/tsa-myth-or-fact-leaked-images.html.

Bush, G. W. 2007. "President Bush Meets with EU Leaders, Chancellor Merkel of the Federal Republic of Germany and President Barroso of the European Council and President of the European Commission." US Department of State Archive, Apr. 30. 2001–2009. state.gov/p/eur/rls/rm/84003.htm.

Buzby, J., and J. Hyman. 2012. "Total and Per Capita Value of Food Loss in the United States." *Food Policy* 37(5): 561–570.

C2ES (Center for Climate and Energy Solutions). 2015. "Coal." Arlington, VA. Accessed Aug. 17. www.c2es.org /energy/source/coal.

Cairns, M., ed. 2015. *Shifting Cultivation and Environmental Change: Indigenous People, Agriculture and Forest Conservation.* New York: Routledge.

Calabresi, G. 1991. "The Pointlessness of Pareto: Carrying Coase Further." *Yale Law Journal* 100(5): 1211–1237.

Caplan, J. 2009. "Shoppers, Unite! Carrotmobs Are Cooler Than Boycotts." *Time,* May 15.

Carbon Mitigation Initiative. 2011. *Carbon Mitigation Initiative: Annual Report, 2010.* Princeton University, Princeton, NJ. cmi.princeton.edu/annual_reports/pdfs/2010.pdf.

Cardinale, B. 2011. "Biodiversity Improves Water Quality Through Niche Partitioning." *Nature* 472:86–89.

Carnicer, J., J. Sardans, C. Stefanescu, A. Ubach, M. Bartrons, D. Asensio, and J. Peñuelas. 2015. "Global biodiversity, stoichiometry and ecosystem function responses to human-induced C–N–P imbalances." *Journal of Plant Physiology* 172:82–91.

Carolan, M. 2005a. "Realism Without Reductionism: Toward an Ecologically Embedded Sociology." *Human Ecology Review* 12(1): 1–20.

———. 2005b. "Society, Biology, and Ecology: Bringing Nature Back into Sociology's Disciplinary Narrative." *Organization and Environment* 18:393–421.

———. 2007. "The Precautionary Principle and Traditional Risk Assessment: Rethinking How We Assess and Mitigate Environmental Threats." *Organization and Environment* 20(1): 5–24.

———. 2008a. "I Do Therefore There Is: Enlivening Socio-Environmental Theory." *Environmental Politics* 18(1): 1–17.

———. 2008b. "More-Than-Representational Knowledge/s of the Countryside: How We Think as Bodies." *Sociologia Ruralis* 48(4): 408–422.

———. 2008c. "When Good Smells Go Bad: A Socio-Historical Understanding of Agricultural Odor Pollution." *Environment and Planning A* 40(5): 1235–1249.

———. 2010a. *Decentering Biotechnology: Assemblages Built and Assemblages Masked.* Burlington, VT: Ashgate.

———. 2010b. "Sociological Ambivalence and Climate Change." *Local Environment* 15(4): 309–321.

———. 2011a. *Embodied Food Politics.* Burlington, VT: Ashgate.

———. 2011b. *The Real Cost of Cheap Food.* New York: Earthscan.

———. 2013. *Reclaiming Food Security.* New York: Earthscan/Routledge.

———. 2014. *Cheaponomics: The High Cost of Low Prices.* New York: Earthscan/Routledge.

———. 2016. *The Sociology of Food and Agriculture.* New York: Earthscan/Routledge.

———. In press. *Feeling Food: Toward a Reenvisioned Gastro-Consciousness.* Washington, DC: Island.

Carolan, M., and J. Hale. 2016. "'Growing' Communities with Urban Agriculture: Generating Value Above and Below Ground." *Community Development.* DOI: 10.1080/15575330.2016.1158198.

Carolan, M., and D. Stuart. 2016. "Get Real: Climate Change and All That 'It' Entails." *Sociologia Ruralis* 56(1): 74–95.

Carruthers, D. 2008. "The Globalization of Environmental Justice: Lessons from the US-Mexico Border." *Society and Natural Resources* 21:556–568.

Carter, J., and M. Irons. 1991. "Are Economists Different, and if So, Why?" *Journal of Economic Perspectives* 5(2): 171–177.

Casey, P., and K. Scott. 2006. "Environmental Concern and Behavior in an Australian Sample Within an Ecocentric-Anthropocentric Framework." *Australian Journal of Psychology* 58:57–67.

Catton, W., and R. Dunlap. 1978. "Environmental Sociology: A New Paradigm." *American Sociologist* 13:41–49.

CDC (Centers for Disease Control and Prevention). 2015. "Micronutrient Facts." Atlanta, GA. www.cdc.gov /immpact/micronutrients.

Chamon, M., P. Mauro, and Y. Okawa. 2008. "Mass Car Ownership in the Emerging Market Giants." *Economic Policy* 23(54): 243–296.

Chan, K., and J. McNeal. 2003. "Parental Concern About Television Viewing and Children's Advertising in China." *International Journal of Public Opinion Research* 15(2): 151–166.

Charles, D. 2014. "Plant Breeders Release First 'Open Source Seeds.'" NPR, Apr. 17. www.npr.org/sections/thesalt /2014/04/17/303772556/plant-breeders-release-first-open-source-seeds.

Chavis, B., and C. Lee. 1987. *Toxic Wastes and Race in the United States: A National Report on the Racial and Socio-Economic Characteristics of Communities with Hazardous Waste Sites.* New York: Commission for Racial Justice, United Church of Christ.

Chazan, G. 2011. "Biofuels Industry Battles Past Bumps in the Road." *Wall Street Journal*, Apr. 7.

Chen, C., J. Harries, H. Brindley, and M. Ringer. 2007. "Spectral Signatures of Climate Change in the Earth's Infrared Spectrum Between 1970 and 2006." Fifteenth American Meteorological Society Satellite Meteorology and Oceanography Conference, Amsterdam, Sept. www.eumetsat.eu/Home/Main/Publications/Conference_and _Workshop_Proceedings/groups/cps/documents/document/pdf_conf_p50_s9_01_harries_v.pdf.

Chensheng, L., K. Warchol, and R. Callahan. 2014. "Sub-Lethal Exposure to Neonicotinoids Impaired Honey Bees Winterization Before Proceeding to Colony Collapse Disorder." *Bulletin of Insectology* 67(1): 125–130.

Chester, M., J. Sperling, E. Stokes, B. Allenby, K. Kockelman, C. Kennedy, L. Baker, J. Keirstead, and C. Hendrickson. 2014. "Positioning Infrastructure and Technologies for Low-Carbon Urbanization." *Earth's Future* 2(1): 533–547.

Chiu, M., B. Shah, L. Maclagan, M. Rezai, P. Austin, and J. Tu. 2015. "Walk Score and the Prevalence of Utilitarian Walking and Obesity Among Ontario Adults: A Cross-Sectional Study." *Health Reports* 26(7): 3–10.

Chozick, A. 2012. "To Draw Reluctant Young Buyers, G.M. Turns to MTV." *New York Times*, Mar. 22.

Chrisafis, A. 2015. "France to Force Big Supermarkets to Give Unsold Food to Charities." *Guardian* (London), May 22.

CIA (Central Intelligence Agency). 2015. *CIA World Fact Book, 2014.* Washington, DC. www.cia.gov/library /publications/the-world-factbook/rankorder/2127rank.html.

Ciriacy-Wantrup, S., and R. Bishop. 1975. "Common Property as a Concept in Natural Resource Policy." *National Resources Journal* 15(4): 713–727.

Claeys, P. 2015. *Human Rights and the Food Sovereignty Movement: Reclaiming Control.* New York: Routledge.

Clark, B., and R. York. 2005. "Carbon Metabolism: Global Capitalism, Climate Change, and the Biospheric Rift." *Theory and Society* 34:391–428.

Clausen, R. 2005. "The Metabolic Rift and Marine Ecology: An Analysis of the Ocean Crisis Within Capitalist Production." *Organization and Environment* 19(2): 422–444.

Clausen, R., and S. Longo. 2012. "The Tragedy of the Commodity and the Face of AquAdvantage Salmon." *Development and Change* 43(1): 229–251.

Coase, R. 1960. "The Problem of Social Cost." *Journal of Law and Economics* 3:1–44.

Cochrane, W. 1958. *Farming Prices: Myth and Reality.* Minneapolis: University of Minnesota Press.

Cohen, M. 2012. "The Future of Automobile Society: A Socio-Technical Transitions Perspective." *Technology Analysis and Strategic Management* 24(4): 377–390.

Cohen, S. 2010. "Growing Public Support for Sustainability." *Huffington Post*, Apr. 19. www.huffingtonpost.com /steven-cohen/growing-public-support-fo_b_542600.html.

Colbert, T. 2000. "Iowa Farmers and Mechanical Corn Pickers, 1900–1952." *Agricultural History* 74(2): 530–544.

Condon, P. 2010. *Seven Rules for Sustainable Communities.* Washington, DC: Island.

Conover, D., and S. Munch. 2002. "Sustaining Fisheries Yields over Evolutionary Time Scales." *Science* 297:94–96.

Conrad, S. 2011. "A Restorative Environmental Justice for Prison E-Waste Recycling." *Peace Review* 23(3): 348–355.

Conservation Measures Partnership. 2012. "Threats Taxonomy." Accessed May 17. www.conservationmeasures .org/initiatives/threats-actions-taxonomies/threats-taxonomy.

Cook, J., D. Nuccitelli, S. A. Green, M. Richardson, B. Winkler, R. Painting, R. Way, P. Jacobs, and A. Skuce. 2013. "Quantifying the Consensus on Anthropogenic Global Warming in the Scientific Literature." *Environmental Research Letters* 8(2): 024024.

Cooper, P., G. Poe, and I. Bateman. 2004. "The Structure of Motivation for Contingent Values: A Case Study of Lake Water Quality Improvement." *Ecological Economics* 50:69–82.

Costanza, R., R. d'Arge, R. de Groot, S. Farber, M. Grasso, B. Hannon, S. Naeem, K. Limburg, J. Paruelo, R. O'Neill, R. Raskin, P. Sutton, and M. van den Belt. 1997. "The Value of the World's Ecosystem Services and Natural Capital." *Nature* 387:253–260.

Costanza, R., R. de Groot, P. Sutton, S. van der Ploeg, S. Anderson, I. Kubiszewski, S. Farber, and R. Turner. 2014. "Changes in the Global Value of Ecosystem Services." *Global Environmental Change* 26:152–158.

Council for Textile Recycling. 2015. "The Facts About Textile Waste." Abingdon, MD. www.weardonaterecycle .org/about/issue.html.

Cowen, T., and D. Parfit. 1992. "Against the Social Discount Rate." In *Philosophy, Politics, and Society*, edited by P. Laslett and J. Fishkin, 144–161. New Haven, CT: Yale University Press.

Cox, C., A. Hug, and N. Bruzelius. 2011. *Losing Ground.* Environmental Working Group, Washington, DC. static .ewg.org/reports/2010/losingground/pdf/losingground_report.pdf.

Cox, J. 2009. "What Is Vertical Farming?" On Earth, Nov. 6. www.onearth.org/community-blog/what-is-vertical -farming.

———. 2014. "How Will the End of 'Buy One Get One Free' Affect Shoppers? Asks Extreme Couponer Jordon Cox." *Mirror* (London), Apr. 11.

Crane, K. 2015. "Smog Solutions: A Fix to China's Pollution Problem Is Expensive but Worth It." *US News and World Report*, Jan. 17.

Crosby, L., C. Tatu, and Charles. 2016. "Lung and Bronchus Cancer Deaths in Boone County, WV Before and After Mountaintop Removal Mining." *Journal of Rare Disorders: Diagnosis and Therapy* 2(1): 1. raredisorders .imedpub.com/lung-and-bronchus-cancer-deaths-in-boone-county-wv-before-and-after-mountaintop -removal-mining.pdf.

Cross, J. 2014. "Three Myths of Behavioral Change." TEDx Colorado State University lecture, Fort Collins, CO, Feb. 19. www.youtube.com/watch?v=l5d8GW6GdR0.

Crossley, N., and J. Ibrahim. 2012. "Critical Mass, Social Networks and Collective Action: The Case of Student Political Worlds." *Sociology* 46:596–612.

Crutzen, P. 2006. "Albedo Enhancement by Stratospheric Sulfur Injections: A Contribution to Resolve a Policy Dilemma?" *Climate Change* 77(3–4): 211–220.

Cunha, L. 2009. "Water: A Human Right or an Economic Resource?" In *Water Ethics*, edited by M. Ramón Llamas, L. Martínez-Cortina, and A. Mukherji, 97–113. Boca Raton, FL: CRC.

*Daily Mail* Reporter. 2008. "EU Forces Market Trader to Pulp Thousands of Kiwi Fruit Because They're One Millimeter Too Small." *Daily Mail* (London), June 27.

Daly, H. 1999. *Ecological Economics and the Ecology of Economics.* Northhampton, MA: Edward Elgar.

Dankelman, I., K. Alam, W. B. Ahmed, Y. D. Gueye, N. Fatema, and R. Mensah-Kutin. 2008. *Gender, Climate Change, and Human Security: Lessons from Bangladesh, Ghana, and Senegal.* Women's Environment and Development Organization, New York. www.wedo.org/wp-content/uploads/hsn-study-final-may-20-2008.pdf.

Dasgupta, P. 2006. "Nature in Economics." *Environmental Resource Economics* 39:1–7.

Dasgupta, S., B. Laplante, H. Wang, and D. Wheeler. 2002. "Confronting the Environmental Kuznets Curve." *Journal of Economic Perspectives* 16(1): 147–168.

Davis, A. 2015. "American Recycling Is Stalling, and the Big Blue Bin Is One Reason Why." *Washington Post*, June 20.

Deflem, M., and S. McDonough. 2015. "The Fear of Counterterrorism: Surveillance and Civil Liberties since 9/11." *Society* 52(1): 70–79.

Defra (Department for Environment, Food, and Rural Affairs). 2011. "Waste Data Overview." London, June. www .defra.gov.uk/statistics/files/20110617-waste-data-overview.pdf.

Delhey, J., and G. Dragolov. 2015. "Happier Together: Social Cohesion and Subjective Well-Being in Europe." *International Journal of Psychology* (Feb.).

Dell'Amore, C. 2013. "20,000 Species Are Near Extinction: Is It Time to Rethink How We Decide Which to Save?" *National Geographic*, Dec. 16.

Delucchi, M. 2004. "Summary of Theory, Data, Methods, and Results: Report #1 in the Series: The Annualized Social Cost of Motor-Vehicle Use in the United States, Based on 1990–91 Data." Institute of Transportation Studies, University of California, Davis, Research Report UCD-ITS-RR-96–03(01)_rev1.

Demirbas, A., and M. Demirbas. 2010. *Algae Energy: Algae as a New Source of Biodiesel*. New York: Springer.

Demographia. 2015. *Demographia World Urban Areas*. 11th ed. www.demographia.com/db-worldua.pdf.

Desmarais, A. 2008. "The Power of Peasants: Reflections on the Meanings of La Vía Campesina." *Journal of Rural Studies* 24:138–149.

Despommier, D. 2010. *The Vertical Farm: Feeding the World in the 21st Century*. New York: Thomas Dunne Books.

Diamond, J. 2006. *Collapse: How Societies Choose to Fail or Succeed*. New York: Penguin.

Dickens, P. 2001. "Linking the Social and Natural Sciences: Is Capital Modifying Human Biology in Its Own Image?" *Sociology* 35:93–110.

———. 2004. *Society and Nature: Changing Our Environment, Changing Ourselves*. Malden, MA: Polity.

Dickens, P., and J. Ormrod. 2007. *Cosmic Society: Towards a Sociology of the Universe*. New York: Routledge.

Dietz, T., N. Dolsak, E. Ostrom, and P. Stern. 2002. *The Drama of the Commons*. Washington, DC: National Academies Press.

Dietz, T., G. Gardner, J. Gilligan, P. Stern, and M. Vandenbergh. 2009. "Household Actions Can Provide a Behavioral Wedge to Rapidly Reduce US Carbon Emissions." *Proceedings of the National Academy of Sciences* 106(44): 18452–18456.

Dietz, T., F. Kenneth, C. Whitley, J. Kelly, and R. Kelly. 2015. "Political Influences on Greenhouse Gas Emissions from US States." *Proceedings of the National Academy of Sciences* 112(27): 8254–8259.

Dietz, T., and E. Rosa. 1994. "Rethinking the Environmental Impacts of Population, Affluence, and Technology." *Human Ecology Review* 1:277–300.

Dietz, T., E. Rosa, and R. York. 2012. "Environmentally Efficient Well-Being: Is There a Kuznets Curve?" *Environmental Geography* 32:21–28.

Di Ruocco, A., P. Gasparini, and G. Weets. 2015. "Urbanisation and Climate Change in Africa: Setting the Scene." In *Urban Vulnerability and Climate Change in Africa: A Multidisciplinary Approach*, edited by S. Pauleit, A. Coly, S. Fohlmeister, P. Gasparini, G. Jørgensen, S. Kabisch, W. J. Kombe, S. Lindley, I. Simonis, and K. Yeshitela, 1–35. Future City 4. Cham, Switzerland: Springer International.

D. M. 2014. "Japan's Demography: The Incredible Shrinking Country." Banyan (blog), *Economist*, Mar. 25. www .economist.com/blogs/banyan/2014/03/japans-demography.

Doan, L., and D. Murtaugh. 2015. "Americans Drove More Than 3 Trillion Miles Last Year." *Bloomberg Business*, Mar. 23.

Doane, M. 2014. "Politics and the Family Farm: When the Neighbors Poison the Well." *Anthropology Now* 6(3): 45–52.

DOD (Department of Defense). 2001. "American Indian and Alaska Native Initiatives." In *Fiscal Year 2001 Defense Environmental Quality Program Annual Report to Congress*. www.denix.osd.mil/arc/EQFY2001.cfm.

Dodman, D. 2009. "Urban Form, Greenhouse Gas Emissions, and Climate Vulnerability." In *Population Dynamics and Climate Change*, edited by J. Guzmán, G. Martine, G. McGranahan, D. Schensul, and C. Tacoli, 64–79. New York: UNFPA and IIED.

Domingo, J., and M. Nadal. 2009. "Domestic Waste Composting Facilities: A Review of Human Health Risks." *Environment International* 35:382–389.

Domingo, J., J. Rovira, L. Vilavert, M. Nadal, M. Figueras, and M. Schuhmacher. 2015. "Health Risks for the Population Living in the Vicinity of an Integrated Waste Management Facility: Screening Environmental Pollutants." *Science of the Total Environment* 518:363–370.

Donham, K., S. Wing, D. Osterberg, J. Flora, C. Hodne, K. Thu, and P. Thorne. 2007. "Community Health and Socioeconomic Issues Surrounding Concentrated Animal Feeding Operations." *Environmental Health Perspectives* 115(2): 317–320.

Doublet, V., M. Labarussias, J. Miranda, R. Moritz, and R. Paxton. 2015. "Bees Under Stress: Sublethal Doses of a Neonicotinoid Pesticide and Pathogens Interact to Elevate Honey Bee Mortality Across the Life Cycle." *Environmental Microbiology* 17(4): 969–983.

Downs, A. 1962. "The Law of Peak-Hour Express-Way Congestion." *Traffic Quarterly* 16(3): 393–409.

Dragusanu, R., D. Giovannucci, and N. Nunn. 2014. "The Economics of Fair Trade." National Bureau of Economic Research No. 20357. www.nber.org/papers/w20357.pdf.

Drummond, M., and T. Loveland. 2010. "Land-Use Pressure and a Transition to Forest-Cover Loss in the Eastern United States." *BioScience* 60(4): 286–298.

Dryzek, J. 1990. *Discursive Democracy: Politics, Policy, and Political Science.* New York: Cambridge University Press.

Dunlap, R. 2008. "The New Environmental Paradigm Scale: From Marginality to Worldwide Use." *Journal of Environmental Education* 40(1): 3–18.

———. 2010. "The Maturation and Diversification of Environmental Sociology: From Constructivism and Realism to Agnosticism and Pragmatism." In *The International Handbook of Environmental Sociology,* edited by M. Redclift and G. Woodgate, 15–32. Northampton, MA: Edward Elgar.

Dunlap, R., and R. Jones. 2002. "Environmental Concern: Conceptual and Measurement Issues." In *Handbook of Environmental Sociology,* edited by R. Dunlap and W. Michelson, 482–524. Westport, CT: Greenwood.

Dunlap, R., and K. Van Liere. 1978. "The New Environmental Paradigm." *Journal of Environmental Education* 9:10–19.

Dunlap, R., K. Van Liere, A. Mertig, and R. Jones. 2000. "Measuring Endorsement of the New Ecological Paradigm: A Revised NEP Scale." *Journal of Social Issues* 56:425–442.

Dunlap, R., and R. York. 2008. "The Globalization of Environmental Concern and the Limits of the Postmaterialist Values Explanation." *Sociological Quarterly* 49:529–563.

Duranton, G., and M. Turner. 2009. "The Fundamental Law of Road Congestion: Evidence from US Cities." NBER Working Paper no. 15376. National Bureau of Economic Research, Cambridge, MA. www.nber.org/papers/w15376.pdf.

Earthman, G. 2014. "Research on Green Schools and Student Performance." In *Marketing the Green School: Form, Function, and the Future,* edited by T. Chan, 38–52. Hershey, PA: IGI Global.

Easterlin, R. 2015. "Happiness and Economic Growth: The Evidence." In *Global Handbook of Quality of Life: Exploration of Well-Being of Nations and Continents,* edited by W. Glatzer, L. Camfield, V. Møller, and M. Rojas, 283–300. Dordrecht, Netherlands: Springer.

E. B. 2015. "In the Bin: Recycling in America." Democracy in America (blog), *Economist,* Apr. 22. www.economist.com/blogs/democracyinamerica/2015/04/recycling-america.

Eccleston, C., and F. March. 2011. *Global Environment Policy: Concepts, Principles, and Practice.* Boca Raton, FL: CRC.

Eckersley, R. 1992. *Environmentalism and Political Theory: Towards an Ecocentric Approach.* London: University College London Press.

Edmonds Institute. 2006. "Out of Brazil: A Peanut Worth Billions (to the US)." Edmonds, WA, March. www.edmonds-institute.org/outofbrazil.pdf.

Edney, M. 1997. *Mapping an Empire: The Geographical Construction of British India, 1765–1843.* Chicago: University of Chicago Press.

EEA (European Environment Agency). 2013. "Managing Municipal Solid Waste: A Review of Achievements in 32 European Countries." EEA Report No. 2/2013. www.eea.europa.eu/publications/managing-municipal-solid-waste/at_download/file.

Ehrhardt-Martinez, K., E. Crenshaw, and J. Jenkins. 2002. "Deforestation and the Environmental Kuznets Curve: A Cross-National Investigation of Intervening Mechanisms." *Social Science Quarterly* 83(1): 226–243.

Ehrlich, P. 1968. *The Population Bomb.* San Francisco: Sierra Club.

Ehrlich, P., and J. Holden. 1971. "Impact of Population Growth." *Science* 171:1212–1217.

EIA (Energy Information Administration). 2015a. "How Much Energy Is Consumed in the World by Each Sector?" www.eia.gov/tools/faqs/faq.cfm?id=447&t=3.

———. 2015b. "What Is U.S. Electricity Generation by Energy Source?" www.eia.gov/tools/faqs/faq.cfm?id=427&t=3.

Eisler, M., M. Lee, J. Tarlton, G. Martin, J. Beddington, J. Dungait, H. Greathead, J. Liu, S. Mathew, H. Miller, T. Misselbrook, P. Murray, V. Vinod, R. Van Saun, and M. Winter. 2014. "Agriculture: Steps to Sustainable Livestock." *Nature* 507:32–34.

Ekelund, R., and R. Hébert. 1997. *A History of Economic Theory and Method.* 4th ed. New York: McGraw-Hill.

Eller, D. 2015. "The Real Story on Nitrate Levels in Iowa's Rivers." *Des Moines Register,* Apr. 13.

Elliott, S., and I. Yusuf. 2014. "'Yes, We Can; but Together': Social Capital and Refugee Resettlement." *Kotuitui: New Zealand Journal of Social Sciences Online* 9(2): 101–110.

Emery, M., and C. Flora. 2006. "Spiraling-Up: Mapping Community Transformation with Community Capitals Framework." *Community Development* 37(1): 19–35.

Emperaire, L., and L. Eloy. 2015. "Amerindian Agriculture in an Urbanising Amazonia (Rio Negro, Brazil)." *Bulletin of Latin American Research* 34(1): 70–84.

English, M., K. Solomon, and G. Hoffman. 2002. "A Paradigm Shift in Irrigation Management." *Journal of Irrigation and Drainage Engineering* (Sept.–Oct.): 267–277.

EPA (Environmental Protection Agency). 2011. "Inventory of US Greenhouse Gas Emission and Sinks, 1990–2009." EPA 430-R-11-005. Office of Atmospheric Programs, EPA, Washington, DC, Apr. epa.gov/climatechange /emissions/downloads11/US-GHG-Inventory-2011-Executive-Summary.pdf.

———. 2012. "Environmental Justice Key Terms." Washington, DC. Accessed July 3. www.epa.gov/region07/ej /definitions.htm.

———. 2013. "Land Use Overview." Washington, DC. www.epa.gov/oecaagct/ag101/landuse.html.

———. 2015a. "Northern Gulf of Mexico Hypoxic Zone." Washington, DC. www.water.epa.gov/type/watersheds /named/msbasin/zone.cfm.

———. 2015b. "Sources of Greenhouse Gas Emissions." Washington, DC. www.epa.gov/climatechange/ghg emissions/sources/transportation.html.

Epstein, P., J. Buonocore, K. Eckerle, M. Hendryx, B. Stout, R. Heinberg, R. Clapp, B. May, N. Reinhart, M. Ahern, S. Doshi, and L. Glustrom. 2011. "Full Cost Account for the List Cycle of Coal." *Annals of the New York Academy of Sciences* 1219:73–98.

Eric, G., K. Sarica, and W. Tyner. 2015. "Analysis of Impacts of Alternative Policies Aimed at Increasing US Energy Independence and Reducing GHG Emissions." *Transport Policy* 37:121–133.

Eskelanda, G., and A. Harrison. 2003. "Moving to Greener Pastures? Multinationals and the Pollution Haven Hypothesis." *Journal of Development Economics* 70:1–23.

Ester, P. 1981. "Environmental Concern in the Netherlands." In *Progress in Resource Management and Environment Planning,* edited by T. O'Riordan and R. Turner, 81–108. New York: Wiley.

Euromonitor International. 2013. "Downsizing Globally: The Impact of Changing Household Structure on Global Consumer Markets." www.euromonitor.com/downsizing-globally-the-impact-of-changing-household -structure-on-global-consumer-markets/report.

Ewing, R., R. Brownson, and D. Berringan. 2006. "Relationship Between Urban Sprawl and Weight of United States Youth." *American Journal of Preventative Medicine* 31(6): 464–474.

Ewing, R., G. Meakins, S. Hamidi, and A. C. Nelson. 2014. "Relationship Between Urban Sprawl and Physical Activity, Obesity, and Morbidity—Update and Refinement." *Health and Place* 26:118–126.

Ewing, R., T. Schmid, R. Killingsworth, A. Zlot, and S. Raudenbush. 2003. "Relationship Between Urban Sprawl and Physical Activity, Obesity, and Morbidity." *American Journal of Health Promotion* 18(1): 47–57.

FAO (Food and Agriculture Organization). 2002. "Reducing Poverty and Hunger: The Critical Role of Financing for Food, Agriculture, and Rural Development." International Fund for Agricultural Development, World Food Program, United Nations, Rome. www.fao.org/docrep/003/Y6265e/y6265e00.htm.

———. 2012. "Fisheries and Aquaculture—Enabling a Vital Sector to Contribute More." United Nations. www.fao .org/news/story/en/item/150839/icode.

———. 2013. "Tackling Climate Change Through Livestock." United Nations, Rome. www.fao.org/docrep/018 /i3437e/i3437e.pdf.

———. 2014. "Agriculture's Greenhouse Gas Emissions on the Rise." United Nations, Rome, Apr. 11. www.fao.org /news/story/en/item/216137/icode.

Feldt, T., T. Fobil, J. Wittsiepe, M. Wilhelm, H. Till, A. Zoufaly, G. Burchard, and T. Göen. 2014. "High Levels of PAH-Metabolites in Urine of E-Waste Recycling Workers from Agbogbloshie, Ghana." *Science of the Total Environment* 466–467:369–376.

Finetto, C., C. Lobascio, and A. Rapisarda. 2010. "Concept of LUNAR Farm: Food and Revitalization Module." *Acta Astronautica* 66(9–10): 1329–1340.

Fischetti, M. 2012. "How Much Water Do Nations Consume?" *Scientific American,* May 21. www.scientificamerican .com/article/graphic-science-how-much-water-nations-consume.

Fisher, W. 1943. "The Bengal Famine: 50,000 Indians Weekly Succumb to Disease and Starvation in Spreading Catastrophe." *Life* 15(21): 16–20.

Fishman, E. 2015. "Bikeshare: A Review of Recent Literature." *Transport Reviews* 36(1): 92–113.

Fitz, D. 2009. "What's Wrong with a 30-Hour Work Week?" *Z Magazine,* July. www.zcommunications.org/whats -wrong-with-a-30-hour-work-week-by-don-fitz.

Fleurbaey, M., and S. Zuber. 2013. "Climate Policies Deserve a Negative Discount Rate." *Chicago Journal of International Law* 13(2).

Flora, C. 2008. "Social Capital and Community Problem Solving Combining Local and Scientific Knowledge to Fight Invasive Species." *Learning Communities* 2:30–39.

Flora, C., M. Livingston, I. Honyestewa, and H. Koiyaquaptewa. 2009. "Understanding Access to and Use of Traditional Foods by Hopi Women." *Journal of Hunger and Environmental Nutrition* 4:158–171.

Forgie, V., P. Horsley, and J. Johnston. 2001. "Facilitating Community-Based Conservation Initiatives." Science for Conservation Report no. 169. Department of Conservation, Wellington, New Zealand. www.doc.govt.nz/upload /documents/science-and-technical/Sfc169.pdf.

Foster, J. B. 1999. "Marx's Theory of Metabolic Rift: Classical Foundations for Environmental Sociology." *American Journal of Sociology* 105(2): 366–405.

————. 2005. "The Treadmill of Accumulation: Schnaiberg's Environment and Marxian Political Economy." *Organization and Environment* 18(1): 7–18.

Fox, T. 2013. *Global Food: Waste Not Want Not.* Institution of Mechanical Engineers, United Kingdom. www.imeche.org/docs/default-source/reports/Global_Food_Report.pdf.

FPP (Forest Peoples Programme). 2012. "Forest Peoples: Numbers Across the World." Moreton-in-Marsh, UK. www.forestpeoples.org/sites/fpp/files/publication/2012/05/forest-peoples-numbers-across-world-final_0.pdf.

Frank, L., M. Andresen, and T. Schmid. 2004. "Obesity Relationships with Community Design, Physical Activity, and Time Spent in Cars." *American Journal of Preventative Medicine* 27:87–96.

Fraser, C. 2009. *Rewilding the World.* New York: Henry Holt.

Freeman, L. 2001. "The Effects of Sprawl on Neighborhood Social Ties: An Explanatory Analysis." *Journal of the American Planning Association* 67(1): 69–77.

Freinkel, S. 2015. "Why the U.S. Plastics Industry Loves the Fracking Boom." *Salon,* June 1. www.salon.com/2014/06/01/why_the_u_s_plastics_industry_loves_the_fracking_boom_partner.

Frérot, A. 2011. *Water: Towards a Culture of Responsibility.* Lebanon: University of New Hampshire Press.

Friedman, T. 2008. "The Great Unraveling." *New York Times,* Dec. 16.

Frohwein, T., and B. Hansjürgens. 2005. "Chemicals Regulation and the Porter Hypothesis: A Critical Review of the New European Chemicals Regulation." *Journal of Business Chemistry* 2(1): 19–36.

Fukuda-Parr, S. 2003. "The Human Development Paradigm." *Feminist Economics* 9(2–3): 301–317.

Funtowicz, S., and J. Ravetz. 1992. "Three Types of Risk Assessment and the Emergence of Post Normal Science." In *Social Theories of Risk,* edited by S. Krimsky and D. Golding, 230–251. New York: Praeger.

Gagnon, L., C. Belanger, and Y. Uchiyama. 2002. "Lifecycle Assessment of Electricity Generation Options: The Status of Research in Year 2001." *Energy Policy* 30:1267–1278.

Galbraith, K. 1958. *The Affluent Society.* New York: Penguin.

GAO (General Accounting Office). 1983. *Siting of Hazardous Waste Landfills and Their Correlation with Racial and Economic Status of Surrounding Communities.* Washington, DC: US Government Printing Office.

Garcia, S., J. Rice, and A. Charles, eds. 2014. *Governance of Marine Fisheries and Biodiversity Conservation.* Hoboken, NJ: Wiley.

Gardner, G., and P. Stern. 1996. *Environmental Problems and Human Behavior.* Boston: Allyn and Bacon.

————. 2008. "The Short List." *Environment Magazine* 50(5): 12–25.

Garming, H., and H. Waibel. 2009. "Pesticides and Farmer Health in Nicaragua: A Willingness-to-Pay Approach to Evaluation." *European Journal of Health Economics* 10(2): 125–133.

Gelissen, J. 2007. "Explaining Popular Support for Environmental Protection: A Multi-Level Analysis of 50 Nations." *Environment and Behavior* 39:392–415.

Gemenne, F., J. Barnett, N. Adger, and G. Dabelko. 2014. "Climate and Security: Evidence, Emerging Risks, and a New Agenda." *Climatic Change* 123(1): 1–9.

Geronimus, A., J. Pearson, E. Linnenbringer, A. Schulz, A. Reyes, E. Epel, J. Lin, and E. Blackburn. 2015. "Race-Ethnicity, Poverty, Urban Stressors, and Telomere Length in a Detroit Community-Based Sample." *Journal of Health and Social Behavior* 56(2): 199–224.

GIBC (Global Investment and Business Center). 2015. *Brunei Energy Policy, Laws and Regulations Handbook.* Washington, DC.

Gilbert, N. 2012. "One-Third of Our Greenhouse Gas Emissions Come from Agriculture." *Nature,* Oct. 2. www.nature.com/news/one-third-of-our-greenhouse-gas-emissions-come-from-agriculture-1.11708.

Gilding, P. 2011. *The Great Disruption.* New York: Bloomsbury.

Gille, Z. 2007. *From the Cult of Waste to the Trash Heap of History: The Politics of Waste in Socialist and Postsocialist Hungary.* Bloomington: University of Indiana Press.

Giunta, I. 2014. "Food Sovereignty in Ecuador: Peasant Struggles and the Challenge of Institutionalization." *Journal of Peasant Studies* 41(6): 1201–1224.

Gliessman, S. 2015. *Agroecology: The Ecology of Sustainable Food Systems.* 3rd ed. Boca Raton, FL: CRC.

Goldman, M., ed. 1998. *Privatizing Nature: Political Struggles for the Global Commons.* New Brunswick, NJ: Rutgers University Press.

————. 2007. "How 'Water for All' Policy Becomes Hegemonic: The Power of the World Bank and Its Transnational Policy Networks." *Geoforum* 38:786–800.

Goldschmidt, W. 1978. *As You Sow: Three Studies in the Social Consequences of Agribusiness.* Montclair, NJ: Allanheld, Osmun.

Goldsmith, E. 2015. *Social Influence and Sustainable Consumption.* London: Springer.

Goldstein, N., R. Cialdini, and V. Griskevicius. 2008. "A Room with a Viewpoint: Using Social Norms to Motivate Environmental Conservation in Hotels." *Journal of Consumer Research* 35(3): 472–482.

Gooch, M., A. Felfel, and N. Marenick. 2010. "Food Waste in Canada." George Morris Center, University of Guelph. www.vcmtools.ca/pdf/Food%20Waste%20in%20Canada%20120910.pdf.

Goodwin, P. 2012. "Three Views on Peak Car." *World Transportation Policy and Practice* 17(4): 8–17.

Grant, K., F. Goldizen, P. Sly, M. Brune, M. Neira, M. van den Berg, and R. Norman. 2013. "Health Consequences of Exposure to E-Waste: A Systematic Review." *Lancet Global Health* 1(6): e350–e361.

Green Advocacy Ghana. 2011. "Ghana E-Waste Country Assessment." SBC E-Waste Africa Project. ewasteguide .info/files/Amoyaw-Osei_2011_GreenAd-Empa.pdf.

Greenberg, B. S., and J. E. Brand. 1993. "Television News and Advertising in Schools: The 'Channel One' Controversy." *Journal of Communication* 43(1): 143–151.

Grinde, D., and B. Johansen. 1995. *Ecocide of Native America: Environmental Destruction of Indian Lands and Peoples.* Santa Fe: Clear Lights.

Grossman, G., and A. Krueger. 1994. *Economic Growth and the Environment.* NBER Working Paper no. W4364. Cambridge, MA: National Bureau of Economic Research.

Grunwald, M. 2008. "The Clean Energy Scam." *Time*, Mar. 27.

———. 2015. "Inside the War on Coal." *Politico.* www.politico.com/agenda/story/2015/05/inside-war-on-coal-000002.

Guarino, J. 2013. "Tribal Advocacy and the Art of Dam Removal: The Lower Elwha Klallam and the Elwha Dams." *American Indian Law Journal* 2(1): 114–145.

Guidry, V., C. Gray, A. Lowman, D. Hall, and S. Wing. 2015. "Data Quality from a Longitudinal Study of Adolescent Health at Schools Near Industrial Livestock Facilities." *Annals of Epidemiology* 25(7): 532–538.

Gustavsson, J., R. Otterdijk, and A. Meybeck. 2011. *Global Food Losses and Food Waste.* Food and Agriculture Organization of the United Nations. www.fao.org/docrep/014/mb060e/mb060e00.pdf.

Habermas, J. 1962. *The Structural Transformation of the Public Sphere.* Darmstadt, Germany: Hermann Luchterhand.

Hamilton, C. 2010. *Requiem for a Species.* London: Earthscan.

———. 2015. "The Risks of Climate Engineering." *New York Times*, Feb. 12.

Haq, M. ul. 1995. *Reflections on Human Development.* New York: Oxford University Press.

Hardin, G. 1968. "The Tragedy of the Commons." *Science* 162:1243–1248.

Harley, B. 1989. "Deconstructing the Map." *Cartographica* 26:1–20.

Harries, J., H. Brindley, P. Sagoo, and R. Bantges. 2001. "Increases in Greenhouse Forcing Inferred from the Outgoing Longwave Radiation Spectra of the Earth in 1970 and 1997." *Nature* 410:355–357.

Harris, L., and H. Hazen. 2006. "Power of Maps: (Counter) Mapping for Conservation." *ACME: An International E-Journal for Critical Geographies* 4:99–130.

Harvey, D. 2005. *A Brief History of Neoliberalism.* New York: Oxford University Press.

Hasan, A. 2014. "A Tale of Two Cities: Density Regulations vs Reality." International Institute for Environment and Development. www.iied.org/tale-two-cities-density-regulations-vs-reality.

Hauck, J., C. Görg, R. Varjopuro, O. Ratamäki, J. Maes, H. Wittmer, and K. Jax. 2013. "'Maps Have an Air of Authority': Potential Benefits and Challenges of Ecosystem Service Maps at Different Levels of Decision Making." *Ecosystem Services* 4:25–32.

Hawcroft, L., and T. Milfont. 2010. "The Use (and Abuse) of the New Environmental Paradigm Scale over the Last 30 Years: A Meta-Analysis." *Journal of Environmental Psychology* 30:143–158.

Hazen, H., and P. Anthamatten. 2004. "Representation of Ecoregions by Protected Areas at the Global Scale." *Physical Geography* 25:499–512.

Hegarty, S. 2010. "Why Family Planning Saves Lives." *Guardian* (London), Nov. 19.

Heinzerling, L. 2000. "The Rights of Statistical People." *Harvard Environmental Law Review* 24:189–207.

Hendricks, T. 2010. *The Wind Doesn't Need a Passport: Stories from the US-Mexico Borderlands.* Berkeley: University of California Press.

Hepburn, C., and P. Koundouri. 2007. "Recent Advances in Discounting: Implications for Forest Economics." *Journal of Forest Economics* 13(2–3): 169–189.

Hertsgaard, M. 2010. "The Grapes of Wrath: Climate Change and the Wine Industry." PBS, Apr. 30. www.pbs.org /wnet/need-to-know/economy/the-grapes-of-wrath-climate-change-and-the-wine-industry/263.

HLPE (High Level Panel of Experts). 2012. *Food Security and Climate Change.* A Report by the High Level Panel of Experts on Food Security and Nutrition of the Committee on World Food Security, Food and Agriculture Organization, United Nations, Rome. www.fao.org/fileadmin/user_upload/hlpe/hlpe_documents/HLPE_Reports /HLPE-Report-3-Food_security_and_climate_change-June_2012.pdf.

Hoddinott, J., and B. Kinsey. 2001. "Child Growth in the Time of Drought." *Oxford Bulletin of Economics and Statistics* 63(4): 409–436.

Hoekstra, A. 2015. "The Water Footprint: The Relation Between Human Consumption and Water Use." In *The Water We Eat: Combining Virtual Water and Water Footprints*, edited by M. Antonelli and F. Greco, 35–50. Cham, Switzerland: Springer.

Hoekstra, A., and M. Mekonnen. 2012. "The Water Footprint of Humanity." *Proceedings of the National Academy of Sciences* 109(9): 3232–3237.

Hoffmann, S., and K. Hutter. 2012. "Carrotmob as a New Form of Ethical Consumption: The Nature of the Concept and Avenues for Future Research." *Journal of Consumer Policy* 35(2): 215–236.

Holdrege, C., and S. Talbott. 2008. *Beyond Biotechnology: The Barren Promise of Genetic Engineering*. Lexington: University Press of Kentucky.

Holt, W., ed. 2012. *Urban Areas and Global Climate Change*. Bingley, UK: Emerald.

Hooks, G., and C. Smith. 2004. "The Treadmill of Destruction: National Sacrifice Areas and Native Americans." *American Sociological Review* 69(4): 558–575.

House of Commons. 2010. *The Regulation of Geoengineering: Fifth Report of Session 2009–10*. Science and Technology Committee, House of Commons, Parliament of Great Britain.

House of Lords. 2014. *Counting the Cost of Food Waste: EU Food Waste Prevention*, HL paper 154. House of Lords, Parliament of Great Britain. www.parliament.uk/documents/lords-committees/eu-sub-com-d/food-waste-prevention/154.pdf.

Howard, P. 2009. "Visualizing Consolidation in the Global Seed Industry, 1996–2008." *Sustainability* 1:1266–1287.

Hribar, C. 2010. *Understanding Concentrated Animal Feeding Operations and Their Impact on Communities*. National Association of Local Boards of Health, Bowling Green, OH. www.cdc.gov/nceh/ehs/docs/understanding_cafos_nalboh.pdf.

Huang, K., and J. Wang. 2015. "Greenhouse Gas Emissions of Tourism-Based Leisure Farms in Taiwan." *Sustainability* 7(8): 11032–11049.

Hughes, T. 1969. "Technological Momentum in History: Hydrogenation in Germany, 1898–1933." *Past and Present* 44(1): 106–132.

Hunnicutt, B. 1996. *Kellogg's Six-Hour Day*. Philadelphia: Temple University Press.

Hunter, L., and E. David. 2011. "Climate Change and Migration: Considering Gender Dimensions." In *Climate Change and Migration*, edited by E. Piguet, P. de Guchteneire, and A. Pecoud, 306–330. Paris: Cambridge University Press, UNESCO.

Hunter, M., and J. Gibbs. 2007. *Fundamentals of Conservation Biology*. 3rd ed. Malden, MA: Blackwell.

Hurst, D. 2010. "Growers Go Bananas over Waste." *Brisbane Times*, Jan. 7.

Hvistendahl, M. 2008. "China's Three Gorges Dam: An Environmental Catastrophe." *Scientific American*, Mar. 25.

ICTSD (International Center for Trade and Sustainable Development). 2010. "Food Giant Nestlé Accused of Biopiracy." *Bridges Trade BioRes* 10(10): 3. ictsd.org/downloads/biores/biores10-10.pdf.

IEA (International Energy Agency). 2015. "Wind Power Seen Generating up to 18% of Global Power by 2050." Paris. www.iea.org/newsroomandevents/news/2013/october/wind-power-seen-generating-up-to-18-of-global-power-by-2050.html.

IFPRI (International Food Policy Research Institute). 2014. *2014 Global Hunger Index: The Challenge of Hidden Hunger*. Bonn.

Inglehart, R. 1990. *Culture Shift in Advanced Industrial Society*. Princeton, NJ: Princeton University Press.

———. 1997. *Modernization and Postmodernization: Cultural, Economic, and Political Change in 43 Societies*. Princeton, NJ: Princeton University Press.

Ingold, T. 2000. *The Perception of the Environment: Essays on Livelihood, Dwelling, and Skill*. New York: Routledge.

INRIX. 2014. "Economic and Environmental Impact of Traffic Congestion in Europe and the US." inrix.com/economic-environment-cost-congestion.

Institute for Lifecycle Energy Analysis. 2002. "Reusable Versus Disposable Cups." sustainability.tufts.edu/downloads/Comparativelifecyclecosts.pdf.

InterAcademy Council. 2003. *Realising the Promise and Potential of African Agriculture: Science and Technology Strategies for Improving Agricultural Productivity and Food Security in Africa*. Amsterdam. www.cgiar.org/pdf/agm04/agm04_iacpanel_execsumm.pdf.

IPC (International Planning Committee for Food Sovereignty). 2016. "What Is IPC?" Accessed Mar. 3. www.foodsovereignty.org/about-us.

IPCC. 2014. *Climate Change 2014: Mitigation of Climate Change*. Cambridge: Cambridge University Press.

Ipsos. 2015. "Nine in Ten 8th Graders Agree That Climate Change Is Real and Human Activity Significantly Contributes to Climate Change." Mar. 13. www.ipsos-na.com/news-polls/pressrelease.aspx?id=6792.

Ipsos/Reuters. 2015. "Poll: Drought, May 28." www.ipsos-na.com/news-polls/pressrelease.aspx?id=6864.

Isidore, C. 2010. "7.9 Million Jobs Lost—Many Forever." CNN, July 2. money.cnn.com/2010/07/02/news/economy/jobs_gone_forever/index.htm.

Israel, E., and A. Frenkel. 2015. "The Distribution of Capital Forms Between Cities and Suburbs and Their Impact on Social Justice in Space." *Urban Geography* 36(4): 578–607.

IUCN (International Union for Conservation of Nature). 2010. *Addressing Climate Change: Issues and Solutions from Around the World*. Gland, Switzerland.

Iverson, A., L. Marín, K. Ennis, D. Gonthier, B. Connor-Barrie, J. Remfert, B. Cardinale, and I. Perfecto. 2014. "Do Polycultures Promote Win-Wins or Trade-Offs in Agricultural Ecosystem Services? A Meta-Analysis." *Journal of Applied Ecology* 51(6): 1593–1602.

Jackson, T. 2009. *Prosperity Without Growth.* London: Earthscan.

———. 2011. "'Peak Stuff' Message Is Cold Comfort." *Guardian* (London), Nov. 1.

Jacobson, M., and M. Delucchi. 2009. "A Plan to Power 100 Percent of the Planet with Renewables." *Scientific American*, Oct. 26.

Jacques, P., R. Dunlap, and M. Freeman. 2008. "The Organisation of Denial: Conservative Think Tanks and Environmental Skepticism." *Environmental Politics* 17(3): 349–385.

Jebaraj, P. 2011. "Development of Bt Brinjal: A Case of Bio-Piracy." *Hindu*, Aug. 10.

Jevons, W. 1865. *The Coal Question.* London: Macmillan.

Jones, C., and D. Kammen. 2014. "Spatial Distribution of US Household Carbon Footprints Reveals Suburbanization Undermines Greenhouse Gas Benefits of Urban Population Density." *Environmental Science & Technology* 48(2): 895–902.

Jorgenson, A. 2006. "Unequal Ecological Exchange and Environmental Degradation: A Theoretical Proposition and Cross-National Study of Deforestation, 1990–2000." *Rural Sociology* 71(4): 681–712.

Jorgenson, A., and B. Clark. 2012. "Are the Economy and the Environment Decoupling? A Comparative International Study, 1960–2005." *American Journal of Sociology* 118:1–44.

Kahl, V. F. S., D. Simon, M. Salvador, C. D. S. Branco, J. F. Dias, F. R. da Silva, C. T. de Souza, and J. da Silva. 2016. "Telomere Measurement in Individuals Occupationally Exposed to Pesticide Mixtures in Tobacco Fields." *Environmental and Molecular Mutagenesis* 57(1): 74–84.

Kant, S., and J. Alavalapati. 2014. *Handbook of Forest Resource Economics.* New York: Earthscan/Routledge.

Kashem, S., A. Irawan, and B. Wilson. 2014. "Evaluating the Dynamic Impacts of Urban Form on Transportation and Environmental Outcomes in US Cities." *International Journal of Environmental Science and Technology* 11(8): 2233–2244.

Kaskey, J. 2012. "Cheap Gas from Fracking Fuels Profits at LyondellBasell." *Bloomberg News*, Oct. 16. www.bloomberg.com/news/2012-10-15/cheap-gas-from-fracking-fuels-profits-at-lyondellbasell-energy.html.

Kassam, A., R. Scammell, K. Connolly, R. Orange, K. Willsher, and R. Ratcliffe. 2015. "Europe Needs Many More Babies to Avert a Population Disaster." *Guardian* (London), Aug. 22.

Kasser, T. 2005. "Frugality, Generosity, and Materialism in Children and Adolescents." In *What Do Children Need to Flourish? Conceptualizing and Measuring Indicators of Positive Development,* edited by K. Moore and L. Lippman, 357–373. New York: Springer Science.

———. 2016. "Materialistic Values and Goals." *Annual Review of Psychology* 67:489–514.

Kastner, I., and P. Stern. 2015. "Examining the Decision-Making Processes Behind Household Energy Investments: A Review." *Energy Research & Social Science* 10:72–89.

Katz, J. 2008. "Poor Haitians Resort to Eating Mud." *National Geographic*, Jan. 30. news.nationalgeographic.com/news/2008/01/080130-AP-haiti-eatin.html.

Kauman, L. 2010. "Toxic Metals' Ties to Work in Prisons." *New York Times*, Oct. 26.

Kaye, L. 2015. "Unilever, P&G Join Closed Loop Fund to Boost Municipal Recycling." *Triple Pundit: People, Planet, Profit*, Feb. 9. www.triplepundit.com/2015/02/unilever-pg-join-closed-loop-fund-boost-municipal-recycling.

Kearsley, A., and M. Riddel. 2010. "A Further Inquiry into the Pollution Haven Hypothesis and the Environmental Kuznets Curve." *Ecological Economics* 69:905–919.

Keegan, P. 2009. "Zipcar: The Best New Idea in Business." CNNMoney, Aug. 27. money.cnn.com/2009/08/26/news/companies/zipcar_car_rentals.fortune.

Keith, D. 2013. *A Case for Climate Engineering.* Cambridge: MIT Press.

Kellstedt, P., S. Zahran, and A. Vedlitz. 2008. "Personal Efficacy, the Information Environment, and Attitudes Toward Global Warming and Climate Change in the United States." *Risk Analysis* 28(1): 113–126.

Kelly, B., J. Halford, E. Boyland, K. Chapman, I. Bautista-Castaño, C. Berg, M. Caroli, B. Cook, J. Coutinho, T. Effertz, E. Grammatikaki, K. Keller, R. Leung, Y. Manios, R. Monteiro, C. Pedley, H. Prell, K. Raine, E. Recine, L. Serra-Majem, S. Singh, and C. Summerbell. 2010. "Television Food Advertising to Children: A Global Perspective." *American Journal of Public Health* 100(9): 1730–1736.

Kelly, K. 2012. "Access Is Better Than Ownership." *Exponential Times.* Accessed July 3. www.exponentialtimes.net/videos/access-better-ownership-0.

Kempton, W., C. Harris, J. Keith, and J. Weihl. 1985. "Do Consumers Know What Works in Energy Conservation?" In *Families and the Energy Transition,* edited by J. Byrne, D. Schulz, and M. Sussman, 115–132. New York: Haworth.

Kennedy, D. 2012. *Rooftop Revolution: How Solar Power Can Save Our Economy—and Our Planet—from Dirty Energy.* San Francisco: Berrett-Koehler.

Kernan, M., R. Battarbee, and B. Moss, eds. 2010. *Climate Change Impacts on Freshwater Ecosystems.* Hoboken, NJ: Blackwell.

Kerr, J. 2013. "Deal Allowing Nestlé to Draw Ontario Water During Droughts Under Review." *Globe and Mail* (Toronto), Aug. 19.

Keynes, J. M. (1930) 1963. "Economic Possibilities of Our Grandchildren." In *John Maynard Keynes: Essays in Persuasion,* 358–373. Reprint, New York: Norton.

Khoury, C., A. Bjorkman, H. Dempewolf, J. Ramirez-Villegas, L. Guarino, A. Jarvis, L. Rieseberg, and P. Stuik. 2014. "Increasing Homogeneity in Global Food Supplies and the Implications for Food Security." *Proceedings of the National Academy of Sciences* 111(11): 4001–4006.

Kirkham, M. 2011. *Elevated Carbon Dioxide: Impacts on Soil and Plant Water Relations.* Boca Raton, FL: CRC.

Kiss, F., and V. Rajovic. 2015. "Life Cycle Inventory Analysis of Lignite-Based Electricity Generation: Case Study of Serbia." *Journal of Production Engineering* 18(1): 61–64.

Klein, N. 2011. "Capitalism vs. the Climate." *Nation,* Nov. 9.

Kloppenburg, J. 2014. "The Unexpected Outcome of the Open Source Seed Initiative's Licensing Debate." Open-Source, June 3. opensource.com/law/14/5/legal-issues-open-source-seed-initiative.

Kneebone, E., and N. Holmes. 2015. *The Growing Distance Between People and Jobs in Metropolitan America.* Washington, DC: Brookings Institute. www.brookings.edu/~/media/research/files/reports/2015/03/24-job -proximity/srvy_jobsproximity.pdf.

Knight, K., and E. Rosa. 2011. "The Environmental Efficiency of Well-Being: A Cross-National Analysis." *Social Science Research* 40:931–949.

Koeppel, D. 2007. *Banana: The Fate of the Fruit That Changed the World.* New York: Hudson Street.

Kopczuk, W., J. Slemrod, and S. Yitzhaki. 2005. "The Limitations of Decentralized World Redistribution: An Optimal Taxation Approach." *European Economic Review* 49(4): 1051–1079.

Koplow, D. 2011. *Nuclear Power: Still Not Viable Without Subsidies.* Union of Concerned Scientists, Cambridge, MA. www.ucsusa.org/sites/default/files/legacy/assets/documents/nuclear_power/nuclear_subsidies_report.pdf.

Kopp, R., and P. Portney. 1999. "Mock Referenda for Intergenerational Decisionmaking." In *Discounting and Intergenerational Equity,* edited by P. Portney and J. Weyant, 87–98. Washington, DC: Resources for the Future.

Kotchen, M., and S. Reiling. 2000. "Environmental Attitudes, Motivations, and Contingent Valuation of Nonuse Values." *Ecological Economics* 32:93–107.

Kozloff, N. 2010. *No Rain in the Amazon: How South America's Climate Change Affects the Entire Planet.* New York: Palgrave.

Krinsky, J., and N. Crossley. 2014. "Social Movements and Social Networks: Introduction." *Social Movement Studies* 13(1): 1–21.

Kuznets, S. 1955. "Economic Growth and Income Inequality." *American Economic Review* 45(1): 1–28.

Kysar, D. 2010. *Regulating from Nowhere: Environmental Law and the Search for Objectivity.* New Haven, CT: Yale University Press.

LAB (League of American Bicyclists). 2012. "Ride for the Environment." Washington, DC. Accessed June 6. www .bikeleague.org/resources/why/environment.php.

Lafontaine, S., J. Schrlau, J. Butler, Y. Jia, B. Harper, S. Harris, L. Bramer, K. Waters, A. Harding, and S. Simonich. 2015. "Relative Influence of Trans-Pacific and Regional Atmospheric Transport of PAHs in the Pacific Northwest, US." *Environmental Science & Technology* 49(23): 13807–13816.

Lappé, A. 2014. "World Bank Wants Water Privatized, Despite Risks." American Aljazeera, Apr. 17. america .aljazeera.com/opinions/2014/4/water-managementprivatizationworldbankgroupifc.html.

Larrick, R., and J. Soll. 2008. "The MPG Illusion." *Science* 320:1593–1594.

Laurian, L., and R. Funderburg. 2014. "Environmental Justice in France? A Spatio-Temporal Analysis of Incinerator Location." *Journal of Environmental Planning and Management* 57(3): 424–446.

La Viña, A., and L. Ang. 2011. "Implementing the REDD-Plus Safeguards: The Role of Social Accountability." Affiliated Network on Social Accountability, East Asia and the Pacific, Working Paper, Philippines, Sept. www .theredddesk.org/sites/default/files/resources/pdf/2011/implementing_the_redd_safeguards_the_role_of _social_accountability.pdf.

Leach, M., and I. Scoones. 2015. *Carbon Conflicts and Forest Landscapes in Africa.* London; New York: Routledge.

Lee, T., E. Markowitz, P. Howe, C. Ko, and A. Leiserowitz. 2015. "Predictors of Public Climate Change Awareness and Risk Perception Around the World." *Nature Climate Change* 5:1014–1020.

"The Legacy of Three Gorges Dam." 2011. *Science* 333(6044): 817.

Leggett, J. 1990. "Global Warming: A Greenpeace View." In *Global Warming: A Greenpeace Report,* edited by J. Leggett, 457–480. Oxford: Oxford University Press.

Lehmann, J. 2007. "A Handful of Carbon." *Nature* 447:143–144.

Leiserowitz, A., E. Maibach, C. Roser-Renouf, G. Feinberg, and S. Rosenthal. 2015. *Climate Change in the American Mind.* Yale Project on Climate Change Communication, Yale University, and Center for Climate Change Communication, George Mason University. environment.yale.edu/climate-communication/files/Global-Warming -CCAM-March-2015.pdf.

Leiserowitz, A., N. Smith, and J. Marlon. 2010. *Americans' Knowledge of Climate Change.* Yale Project on Climate Change Communication, Yale University. environment.yale.edu/climate/files/ClimateChangeKnowledge2010 .pdf.

Lertzman, R. 2010. "The Myth of Apathy: Psychosocial Dimensions of Environmental Degradation." PhD thesis, Cardiff University.

Levasseur, M., M. Généreux, J. Bruneau, A. Vanasse, E. Chabot, C. Beaulac, and M. Bédard. 2015. "Importance of Proximity to Resources, Social Support, Transportation and Neighborhood Security for Mobility and Social Participation in Older Adults: Results from a Scoping Study." *BMC Public Health* 15(1):503.

Li, F., Y. Liu, J. Lü, L. Liang, and P. Harmer. 2015. "Ambient Air Pollution in China Poses a Multifaceted Health Threat to Outdoor Physical Activity." *Journal of Epidemiology and Community Health* 69(3): 201–204.

Li, M. 2014. *Peak Oil, Climate Change, and the Limits to China's Economic Growth*. New York: Routledge.

Lin, C. 2015. "The Dragon's Rise in the Great Sea: China's Strategic Interests in the Levant and Eastern Mediterranean." In *The Eastern Mediterranean in Transition: Multipolarity, Politics, and Power*, edited by A. Tziampris and S. Litsas, 63–78. Burlington, VT: Ashgate.

Lin, J., D. Pan, S. Davis, Q. Zhang, K. He, C. Wang, D. Streets, D. Wuebbles, and D. Guan. 2014. "China's International Trade and Air Pollution in the United States." *Proceedings of the National Academy of Sciences* 111(5): 1736–1741.

Lindhqvist, T., and K. Lidgren. 1990. "Modeller för Förlängt Producentansvar (Model for Extended Producer Responsibility)." In *Från vaggan till Graven: Sex Studier av Varors Miljöpåverkan (From the Cradle to the Grave: Six Studies of the Environmental Impacts of Products)*, 7–44. DS1991:9. Stockholm: Ministry of the Environment.

Litman, T. 2010. "Community Cohesion as a Transport Planning Objective." Victoria Transport Policy Institute, Victoria, BC, Apr. 15. www.vtpi.org/cohesion.pdf.

———. 2011. "Transportation Cost and Benefit Analysis Techniques, Estimates and Implications." Victoria Transport Policy Institute, Victoria, Canada. www.vtpi.org/tca/tca00.pdf.

Liu, J., G. Daily, P. Ehrlich, and G. Luck. 2003. "Effects of Household Dynamics on Resource Consumption and Biodiversity." *Nature* 421:530–533.

Liu, Y., and D. Apollon. 2011. *The Color of Food*. Applied Research Center, New York, Feb. foodchainworkers.org/wp-content/uploads/2011/05/Color-of-Food_021611_F.pdf.

Lo, A. Y. 2016. "National Income and Environmental Concern: Observations from 35 countries." *Public Understanding of Science*. DOI: 10.1177/0963662515581302.

Lobao, L., and C. Stofferahn. 2008. "The Community Effect of Industrial Farming: Social Science Research and Challenges to Corporate Farming Laws." *Agriculture and Human Values* 25:219–240.

Lomax, T., D. Schrank, S. Turner, L. Geng, Y. Li, and N. Koncz. 2011. "Real-Timing the 2010 Urban Mobility Report." University Transportation Center for Mobility, Texas Transportation Institute, Texas A&M University, College Station, TX. utcm.tamu.edu/publications/final_reports/Lomax_10-65-55.pdf.

Longbottom, S. E., and Slaughter, V. 2016. "Direct Experience With Nature and the Development of Biological Knowledge." *Early Education and Development*. DOI: 10.1080/10409289.2016.1169822.

Longhofer, W., and E. Schofer. 2010. "National and Global Origins of Environmental Association." *American Sociological Review* 75(4): 505–533.

Longo, S., R. Clausen, and B. Clark. 2015. *The Tragedy of the Commodity: Oceans, Fisheries, and Aquaculture*. New Brunswick, NJ: Rutgers University Press.

Lonsdorf, K. 2011. "From Freeways to Waterways: What Los Angeles Can Learn from Seoul." KCET, Aug. 9. www.kcet.org/socal/departures/landofsunshine/la-river/from-freeways-to-waterways-what-los-angeles-can-learn-from-seoul.html.

Lovejoy, T. 1980. "A Projection of Species Extinctions." In *The Global 2000 Report to the President*, edited by G. Barney, 2:328–373. Washington, DC: US Government Printing Office.

Lovins, E. 2014. "Energy Intensity: The Secret Revolution." *Forbes*, July 18. www.forbes.com/sites/amorylovins/2014/07/18/energy-intensity-the-secret-revolution.

Lovins, L. H., and B. Cohen. 2011. *Natural Capitalism: Capitalism in the Age of Climate Change*. New York: Hill and Wang.

Lundquist, J., D. Anderton, and D. Yaukey. 2015. *Demography: The Study of Human Population*. 4th ed. Long Grove, IL: Waveland.

Lupala, Z., L. Lusambo, Y. Ngaga, and A. Makatta. 2015. "The Land Use and Cover Change in Miombo Woodlands Under Community Based Forest Management and Its Implication to Climate Change Mitigation: A Case of Southern Highlands of Tanzania." *International Journal of Forestry Research* 459102. www.hindawi.com/journals/ijfr/2015/459102/abs.

Lytle, M. 2007. *The Gentle Subversive: Rachel Carlson and the Rise of the Environmental Movement*. New York: Oxford University Press.

Macias, T., and K. Williams. 2015. "Know Your Neighbors, Save the Planet: Social Capital and the Widening Wedge of Pro-Environmental Outcomes." *Environment and Behavior* 48(3): 391–420.

MacKay, D. 2009. *Sustainable Energy: Without the Hot Air*. Cambridge, UK: UIT Cambridge.

MacKenzie, D., and G. Spinardi. 1995. "Tacit Knowledge, Weapons Design, and the Uninvention of Nuclear Weapons." *American Journal of Sociology* 101(1): 44–99.

Maffi, L., and E. Woodley. 2010. *Biocultural Diversity Conservation: A Global Sourcebook*. London: Earthscan.

Main, D. 2014. "As World's Largest Dam Removal Is Completed, Fish Already Returning." *Newsweek*, Sept. 9.

Malin, S. 2015. *The Price of Nuclear Power: Uranium Communities and Environmental Justice.* New Brunswick, NJ: Rutgers University Press.

Mankiw, N. 2014. *Essentials of Economics.* Boston: Cengage Learning.

Manoli, C., B. Johnson, and R. Dunlap. 2007. "Assessing Children's Environmental Worldviews: Modifying and Validating the New Ecological Paradigm Scale for Use with Children." *Journal of Environmental Education* 38(4): 3–13.

Marcotullio, P., S. Hughes, A. Sarzynski, S. Pincetl, L. Sanchez Peña, P. Romero-Lankao, D. Runfola, and K. Seto. 2014. "Urbanization and the Carbon Cycle: Contributions from Social Science." *Earth's Future* 2(1): 496–514.

Marinelli, J. 2011. *Landscape for Life.* US Botanic Garden and the Lady Bird Johnson Wildflower Center, University of Texas at Austin. www.landscapeforlife.org/publications/LFL_Workbooks_Print_downloadable.pdf.

Markovich, J., and K. Lucas. 2011. "The Social and Distributional Impacts of Transport: A Literature Review." Working Paper no. 1055. Transport Studies Unit, School of Geography and the Environment, Oxford University, Aug. www.tsu.ox.ac.uk/pubs/1055-markovich-lucas.pdf.

Martin, D. 2014. *Edible: An Adventure into the World of Eating Insects and the Last Great Hope to Save the Planet.* New York: Houghton Mifflin.

Martin-Ortega, J., R. Ferrier, I. Gordon, and S. Khan. 2015. *Water Ecosystem Services: A Global Perspective.* New York: Oxford University Press.

Martinez-Alier, J., L. Temper, D. Del Bene, and A. Scheidel. 2016. "Is There a Global Environmental Justice Movement?" *The Journal of Peasant Studies* 43(3): 731–755.

Martínez-Torres, M., and P. Rosset. 2010. "La Vía Campesina: The Birth and Evolution of a Transnational Social Movement." *Journal of Peasant Studies* 37:149–175.

Marvel, K., B. Kravitz, and K. Caldeira. 2013. "Geophysical Limits to Global Wind Power." *Nature Climate Change* 3(2): 118–121.

Marwell, G., and R. Ames. 1981. "Economists Free Ride, Does Anyone Else?" *Journal of Public Economics* 15:295–310.

Marx, K. (1863) 1976. *Capital.* Vol. 1. New York: Vintage.

———. (1863–1865) 1981. *Capital.* Vol. 3. New York: Vintage.

Marx, K., and F. Engels. (1848) 1978. "Manifesto of the Communist Party." In *The Marx-Engels Reader*, 469–500. New York: Norton.

Mather, A. 1990. *Global Forest Resources.* London: Bellhaven.

———. 1992. "The Forest Transition." *Area* 24:367–379.

Mattisson, K., C. Håkansson, and K. Jakobsson. 2015. "Relationships Between Commuting and Social Capital Among Men and Women in Southern Sweden." *Environment and Behavior* 47(7): 734–753.

May, E. 1973. "Extensive Oxygen Depletion in Mobile Bay, Alabama." *Limnology and Oceanography* 18:353–366.

Mayden, R. 1997. "A Hierarchy of Species Concepts: The Denouement in the Saga of the Species Problem." In *Species: The Units of Biodiversity*, edited by M. Claridge, H. Dawah, and M. Wilson, 381–424. New York: Chapman and Hall.

Mbuvi, M., J. Musyoki, W. Ayiemba, and J. Gichuki. 2015. "Determining the Potential for Introducing and Sustaining Participatory Forest Management: A Case Study of South Nandi Forest of Western Kenya." *International Journal of Biodiversity and Conservation* 7(3): 190–201.

McAdam, D. 1996. "Conceptual Origins, Current Problems, Future Directions." In *Comparative Perspectives on Social Movements*, edited by D. McAdam, J. McCarthy and M. Zald, 23–40. New York: Cambridge University Press.

McCammon, H., and A. McGrath. 2015. "Litigating Change? Social Movements and the Court System." *Sociology Compass* 9(2): 128–139.

McCarthy, J., and M. Zald. 1977. "Resource Mobilization and Social Movements: A Partial Theory." *American Journal of Sociology* 82:1212–1241.

McCarthy, N. 2014. "China Used More Concrete in Three Years Than the US Used in the Entire 20th Century." *Forbes*, Dec. 5. www.forbes.com/sites/niallmccarthy/2014/12/05/china-used-more-concrete-in-3-years-than-the-u-s-used-in-the-entire-20th-century-infographic.

McCright, A., and R. Dunlap. 2011a. "Cool Dudes: The Denial of Climate Change Among Conservative White Males in the United States." *Global Environmental Change* 21(4): 1163–1172.

———. 2011b. "The Politicization of Climate Change and Polarization in the American Public's View of Global Warming, 2001–2010." *Sociological Quarterly* 52:155–194.

McDonald, D. 2005. "Environmental Racism and Neoliberal Disorder in South Africa." In *The Quest for Environmental Justice: Human Rights and the Politics of Pollution*, edited by R. Bullard, 255–278. San Francisco: Sierra Club Books.

McGranahan, G., D. Balk, and B. Anderson. 2007. "The Rising Tide: Assessing the Risks of Climate Change and Human Settlements in Low Elevation Coastal Zones." *Environment and Urbanization* 19(1): 17–37.

McKenzie-Mohr, D. 2011. *Fostering Sustainable Behavior: An Introduction to Community Based Social Marketing.* Gabriola Island, BC: New Society.

McMichael, P. 2009. "Banking on Agriculture: A Review of the World Development Report, 2008." *Journal of Agrarian Change* 9(2): 235–246.

McNeill, D. 2011. "Why the Fukushima Disaster Is Worse Than Chernobyl." *Independent* (London), Aug. 29.

Meadows, D., D. Meadows, J. Randers, and W. Behrens. 1972. *The Limits to Growth.* New York: Universe Books.

Meijaard, E., and V. Nijman. 2003. "Primate Hotspots on Borneo: Predictive Value for General Biodiversity and the Effects of Taxonomy." *Conservation Biology* 17:725–732.

Mekonnen, M., and Y. Hoekstra. 2011. "The Green, Blue and Grey Water Footprint of Crops and Derived Crop Products." *Hydrology and Earth System Sciences* 15(5): 1577–1600.

Mellino, C. 2015. "Three Young Entrepreneurs Find Revolutionary Way to Cut Out Food Waste." *EcoWatch*, Feb. 25. ecowatch.com/2015/02/25/entrepreneurs-reduce-food-waste.

Meloni, M. 2014. "How Biology Became Social, and What It Means for Social Theory." *Sociological Review* 62(3): 593–614.

Menon, G. 1991. "Ecological Transition and the Changing Context of Women's Work in Tribal India." *Purusartha* 14:291–314.

Merchant, C. 1980. *The Death of Nature: Women, Ecology, and the Scientific Revolution.* San Francisco: HarperCollins.

Merrill, R. 1997. "Food Safety Regulation: Reforming the Delaney Clause." *Annual Review of Public Health* 18:313–340.

Merton, R. 1976. *Sociological Ambivalence, and Other Essays.* New York: Free Press.

Meyer, D. S., and S. Staggenborg. 1996. "Movements, Countermovements, and the Structure of Political Opportunity." *American Journal of Sociology* 101:1628–1660.

Mill, J. S. 1848. *Principles of Political Economy.* Boston: Charles C. Little and James Brown.

Millennium Ecosystem Assessment. 2005. *Ecosystems and Human Well-Being: Synthesis.* Washington, DC: Island.

Ministry of Home Affairs. 2013. Sample Registration System Survey. Government of India. www.censusindia.gov.in/vital_statistics/SRS_Reports_2013.html.

Mirabelli M., S. Wing, S. Marshall, and T. Wilcosky. 2006. "Asthma Symptoms Among Adolescents Who Attend Public Schools That Are Located Near Confined Swine Feeding Operations." *Pediatrics* 118:e66–e75.

Mishan, E. 1967. *The Costs of Economic Growth.* Middlesex, MA: Penguin.

Mohai, P., D. Pellow, and J. T. Roberts. 2009. "Environmental Justice." *Annual Reviews Environmental Resources* 34:405–430.

Mohai, P., and R. Saha. 2007. "Racial Inequality in the Distribution of Hazardous Waste: A National-Level Reassessment." *Social Problems* 54(3): 343–370.

Mohai, P., S. Simões, and S. Brechin. 2010. "Environmental Concerns, Values, and Meanings in the Beijing and Detroit Metropolitan Areas." *International Sociology* 25(6): 778–817.

Møllegaard, S., and M. Jæger. 2015. "The Effect of Grandparents' Economic, Cultural, and Social Capital on Grandchildren's Educational Success." *Research in Social Stratification and Mobility* 42:11–19.

Moore, P. 2006. "Nuclear Re-Think." *International Atomic Energy Agency Bulletin* 48(1): 56–58.

Mora, C., D. Tittensor, S. Adl, A. Simpson, and B. Worm. 2011. "How Many Species Are There on Earth and in the Ocean?" *PLOS ONE* 9(8): e1001127.

Morris, J. 2005. "Comparative LCAs for Curbside Recycling Versus Either Landfilling or Incineration with Energy Recovery." *International Journal of Life Cycle Assessment* 10(4): 273–284.

Morrison, M., R. Duncan, and K. Parton. 2015. "Religion Does Matter for Climate Change Attitudes and Behavior." *PLOS One* 10(8): e0134868.

Mostafa, M. 2013. "Wealth, Post-Materialism and Consumers' Pro-Environmental Intentions: A Multilevel Analysis Across 25 Nations." *Sustainable Development* 21(6): 385–399.

Mozell, R., and L. Thach. 2014. "The Impact of Climate Change on the Global Wine Industry: Challenges and Solutions." *Wine Economics and Policy* 3(2): 81–89.

MST (Movimento dos Trabalhadores Rurais Sem Terra). 2015. "What Is the MST?" Friends of the MST. Accessed Aug. 7. www.mstbrazil.org.

Mufson, S. 2014. "Here's the Grassroots Political Story Behind the New York Fracking Ban." *Washington Post*, Dec. 18.

Myrskyla, M., H.-P. Kohler, and F. Billari. 2009. "Advances in Development Reverse Fertility Declines." *Nature* 460:471–743.

Nabhan, G. 1997. *Cultures of Habitat.* Washington, DC: Counterpoint.

Narain, V., and Vij, S. 2016. "Where Have All the Commons Gone?" *Geoforum* 68:21–24.

Nash, M. P., director. 2010. *Climate Refugees: The Human Face of Climate Change.* Video. Los Angeles: LA Think Tank; Preferred Content.

Nazarea, V. 2005. *Heirloom Seeds and Their Keepers: Marginality and Memory in the Conservation of Biological Diversity.* Tucson: University of Arizona Press.

NEI (Nuclear Energy Institute). 2012. "World Statistics." Washington, DC. Accessed June 7. www.nei.org /resourcesandstats/nuclear_statistics/worldstatistics.

Netting, R. 1981. *Balancing on an Alp: Ecological Change and Continuity in a Swiss Mountain Community.* New York: Cambridge University Press.

Neumayer, E. 1999. "Global Warming: Discounting Is Not the Issue, but Substitutability Is." *Energy Policy* 27:33–34.

New Economics Foundation. 2012. *The Happy Planet Index: 2012 Report.* London. b.3cdn.net/nefoundation /d8879619b64bae461f_opm6ixqee.pdf.

Newman, A. 2011. "N.J. to Leave Regional Cap-and-Trade Scheme." *New American*, May 31. www.thenewamerican .com/tech-mainmenu-30/environment/7689-nj-to-leave-regional-cap-and-trade-scheme.

NHDES (New Hampshire Department of Environmental Services). 2012. "Time It Takes for Garbage to Decompose in the Environment." Concord, NH. Accessed March 28. des.nh.gov/organization/divisions/water/wmb /coastal/trash/documents/marine_debris.pdf.

Nicholls, A., and C. Opal. 2005. *Fair Trade: Market Drive Ethical Consumption.* Thousand Oaks, CA: Sage.

Nichols, B., and K. Kockelman. 2014. "Pay-as-You-Drive Insurance: Its Impacts on Household Driving and Welfare." *Transportation Research Record: Journal of the Transportation Research Board* 2450:76–82.

Nijhuis, M. 2014. "Coal." *National Geographic*, Apr. ngm.nationalgeographic.com/2014/04/coal/nijhuis-text.

N. L. 2010. "What's Up Pussycat? Saving the Tiger." Babbage (blog), *Economist*, Nov. 24. www.economist.com/blogs /babbage/2010/11/saving_tiger.

NMA (National Mining Association). 2012. "Most Requested Statistics." Washington, DC. Accessed June 7. www .nma.org/pdf/c_most_requested.pdf.

Norgaard, K. 2006. "'We Don't Really Want to Know': Environmental Justice and Socially Organized Denial of Global Warming in Norway." *Organization and Environment* 19(3): 347–370.

———. 2011. *Living in Denial: Climate Change, Emotions, and Everyday Life.* Cambridge: MIT Press.

Norman, E., C. Cook, and A. Cohen, eds. 2015. *Negotiating Water Governance: Why the Politics of Scale Matter.* Burlington, VT: Ashgate.

NPR (National Public Radio). 2011. "Among the Costs of War: Billions a Year in A.C.?" June 25. www.npr.org/2011 /06/25/137414737/among-the-costs-of-war-20b-in-air-conditioning.

Nuclear Energy Agency. 2010. "Nuclear Energy and Addressing Climate Change." Nov. www.oecd-nea.org/press /in-perspective/2010-addressing-climate-change.pdf.

Nugent, D., and B. Sovacool. 2014. "Assessing the Lifecycle Greenhouse Gas Emissions from Solar PV and Wind Energy: A Critical Meta-Survey." *Energy Policy* 65:229–244.

Oates, C., and N. Tziortzi. 2014. "Parents' Beliefs About, and Attitudes Towards, Marketing to Children." In *Advertising to Children: New Directions, New Media*, edited by M. Blades, C. Oates, F. Blumberg, and B. Gunte, 115–136. New York: Palgrave.

O'Brian, E. 2006. "Habitat Fragmentation Due to Transport Infrastructure." In *The Ecology of Transport*, edited by J. Davenport and J. Davenport, 191–203. Dordrecht, Netherlands: Springer.

O'Connor, J. 1998. *Natural Causes: Essays in Ecological Marxism.* New York: Guildford.

OECD (Organization for Economic Cooperation and Development). 2015a. *Aligning Policies for a Low-Carbon Economy.* Paris: OECD.

———. 2015b. *OECD Studies on Water Stakeholder Engagement for Inclusive Water Governance.* Paris: OECD.

Ogneva-Himmelberger, Y., and L. Huang. 2015. "Spatial Distribution of Unconventional Gas Wells and Human Populations in the Marcellus Shale in the United States: Vulnerability Analysis." *Applied Geography* 60:165–174.

Ohring, G., P. Romanov, R. Ferraro, A. Heidinger, I. Laszlo, C.-Z. Zou, and M. Foster. 2014. "Satellite Observations of North American Climate Change." In *Climate Change in North America*, edited by G. Ohring, 95–165. Cham, Switzerland: Springer.

Olivier, J., G. Janssens-Maenhout, M. Muntean, and J. Peters. 2014. *Trends in Global CO2 Emissions: 2014 Report.* The Hague: PBL Netherlands Environmental Assessment Agency; Ispra, Italy: European Commission, Joint Research Centre. edgar.jrc.ec.europa.eu/news_docs/jrc-2014-trends-in-global-co2-emissions-2014-report -93171.pdf.

OPEC (Organization of the Petroleum Exporting Countries). 2014. "OPEC Share of World Crude Oil Reserves, 2014." www.opec.org/opec_web/en/data_graphs/330.htm.

Osborn, S. G., A. Vengosh, N. R. Warner, and R. B. Jackson. 2011. "Methane Contamination of Drinking Water Accompanying Gas-Well Drilling and Hydraulic Fracturing." *Proceedings of the National Academy of Sciences* 108(20): 8172–8176.

Ostrom, E. 1999. *Governing the Commons: The Evolution of Institutions for Collective Action.* New York: Cambridge University Press.

———. 2000. "Private and Common Property Rights." In *Encyclopedia of Law and Economics*, edited by B. Bouckaert and G. De Geest, 3:332–379. London: Edward Elgar.

Ostrom, E., J. Burger, C. Field, R. Norgaard, and D. Policansky. 1999. "Revisiting the Commons: Local Lessons, Global Challenges." *Science* 284(5412): 278–282.

Ostrom, E., R. Gardner, and J. Walker. 1994. *Rules, Games, and Common-Pool Resources.* Ann Arbor: University of Michigan Press.

Owen, D. 2011. *The Conundrum.* New York: Riverhead Books.

Oxfam. 2015. "Richest 1% Will Own More Than All the Rest by 2016." London. www.oxfam.org/en/pressroom /pressreleases/2015-01-19/richest-1-will-own-more-all-rest-2016.

Ozanne, L., and J. L. Ozanne. 2016. "How Alternative Consumer Markets Can Build Community Resiliency." *European Journal of Marketing* 50(3/4): 1–17.

Pacala, S., and R. Socolow. 2004. "Stabilization Wedges: Solving the Climate Problem for the Next 50 Years with Current Technologies." *Science* 305:968–972.

Page, T. 2003. "Balancing Efficiency and Equity in Long-Run Decision-Making." *International Journal of Sustainable Development* 6:70–86.

Palmer, M., E. Bernhardt, W. Schlesinger, K. Eshleman, E. Foufoula-Georgiou, M. Hendryx, A. Lemly, G. Likens, O. Loucks, M. Power, P. White, and P. Wilcock. 2010. "Mountaintop Mining Consequences." *Science* 327:148–149.

Pampel, F. 2014. "The Varied Influence of SES on Environmental Concern." *Social Science Quarterly* 95(1): 57–75.

Pan, Y., R. Birdsey, J. Fang, R. Houghton, P. Kauppi, W. Kurz, and O. Phillips. 2011. "A Large and Persistent Carbon Sink in the World's Forests." *Science* 333(6045): 988–993.

Pariatamby, A., and M. Tanaka, eds. 2014. *Municipal Solid Waste Management in Asia and the Pacific Islands.* Singapore: Springer.

Parker, L. 2015. "Ocean Trash: 5.25 Trillion Pieces and Counting, but Big Questions Remain." *National Geographic,* Jan. 11. news.nationalgeographic.com/news/2015/01/150109-oceans-plastic-sea-trash-science-marine-debris.

Parrish, D., H. Singh, L. Molina, and S. Madronich. 2011. "Air Quality Progress in North American Megacities: A Review." *Atmospheric Environment* 45:7015–7025.

Pellow, D. 2014. *Total Liberation: The Power and Promise of Animal Rights and the Radical Earth Movement.* Minneapolis: University of Minnesota Press.

Pellow, D., and H. Brehm. 2015. "From the New Ecological Paradigm to Total Liberation: The Emergence of a Social Movement Frame." *Sociological Quarterly* 56:185–212.

Perrow, C. 1984. *Normal Accidents: Living with High Risk Technologies.* Princeton, NJ: Princeton University Press.

———. 2010. "Organizations and Global Warming." In *Routledge Handbook of Climate Change and Society,* edited by C. Lever-Tracy, 59–77. New York: Routledge.

Peterson, A. 2009. *Everyday Ethics and Social Change: The Education of Desire.* New York: Columbia University Press.

Peterson, A., and A. Navarro-Siguenza. 1999. "Alternative Species Concepts as Bases for Determining Priority Conservation Areas." *Conservation Biology* 13:427–431.

Peterson, E. 2009. *A Billion Dollars a Day: The Economics and Politics of Agricultural Subsides.* Malden, MA: Wiley-Blackwell.

Pew Research Center. 2014. "Wealth Inequality Has Widened Along Racial, Ethnic Lines Since End of Great Recession." Washington, DC, Dec. 12. www.pewresearch.org/fact-tank/2014/12/12/racial-wealth-gaps-great -recession.

Pfaff, A., and R. Walker. 2010. "Regional Interdependence and Forest 'Transitions': Substitute Deforestation Limits the Relevance of Local Reversals." *Land Use Policy* 27:119–127.

Pfeffer, M. 1983. "Social Origins of Three Systems of Farm Production in the United States." *Rural Sociology* 48(4): 540–562.

Pickering, A. 1999. *Constructing Quarks: A Sociological History of Particle Physics.* Chicago: University of Chicago Press.

Pidgeon, N. 2011. "In Retrospect: Normal Accidents." *Nature* 477(7365): 404–405.

Pigou, A. C. 1912. *Wealth and Welfare.* London: Macmillan.

Pimentel, D. 2005. "Environmental and Economic Costs of the Application of Pesticides Primarily in the United States." *Environment, Development, and Sustainability* 7:229–252.

Pimentel, D., and M. Burgess. 2014. "Environmental and Economic Costs of the Application of Pesticides Primarily in the United States." In *Integrated Pest Management,* Volume 3, edited by D. Pimentel and R. Peshin, 47–72. New York: Springer.

Pimentel, D., J. Krummel, D. Gallahan, J. Hough, A. Merrill, I. Schreiner, P. Vittum, F. Koziol, E. Back, D. Yen, and S. Fiance. 1978. "Benefits and Costs of Pesticide Use in United States Food Production." *BioScience* 28(772): 778–784.

Pimm, S., C. Jenkins, R. Abell, T. Brooks, J. Gittleman, L. Joppa, P. Raven, C. Roberts, and J. Sexton. 2014. "The Biodiversity of Species and Their Rates of Extinction, Distribution, and Protection." *Science* 344(6187): 1246752.

Plumer, B. 2013. "Four Charts That Show the US Spends Too Little on Energy Research." *Washington Post,* Apr. 9.

Popper, K. (1934) 1961. *The Logic of Scientific Discovery.* New York: Science Editions.

Potter, D. 2015. "Why Isn't Desalination the Answer to All California's Water Problems?" KQED, Dec. 18. ww2.kqed.org/science/2015/12/18/why-isnt-desalination-the-answer-to-all-californias-water-problems.

Pouchard, A. 2014. "San Francisco Is Rapidly Becoming the Recycling Capital of the World." *Business Insider*, June 17. www.businessinsider.com/san-francisco-is-rapidly-becoming-the-recycling-capital-of-the-world-2014-6.

Pradhan, E., K. West, J. Katz, S. LeClerq, S. Khatry, and S. Shrestha. 2007. "Risk of Flood-Related Mortality in Nepal." *Disasters* 31(1): 57–70.

Prell, C., K. Feng, L. Sun, M. Geores, and K. Hubacek. 2014. "The Economic Gains and Environmental Losses of US Consumption: A World-Systems and Input-Output Approach." *Social Forces* 93(1): 405–428.

Prisco, J. 2015. "Why Bananas as We Know Them Might Go Extinct (and What to Do About It)." CNN, July 22. www.cnn.com/2015/07/22/africa/banana-panama-disease.

Putnam, R. 2001. *Bowling Alone: The Collapse and Revival of American Community*. New York: Simon and Schuster.

PWC (Price Waterhouse Coopers). 2014. *Two Degrees of Separation: Ambition and Reality—Low Carbon Economy Index 2014*. London. www.pwc.co.uk/assets/pdf/low-carbon-economy-index-2014.pdf.

Quan, L., and R. Reuveny. 2006. "Democracy and Environmental Deregulation." *International Studies Quarterly* 50:935–956.

Rabobank Group. 2010. *Sustainability and Security of the Global Food Supply Chain*. Utrecht, Netherlands. www.rabobank.nl/images/rabobanksustainability_29286998.pdf.

Radon, K., A. Schulze, V. Ehrenstein, R. van Strien, G. Praml, and D. Nowak. 2007. "Environmental Exposure to Confined Animal Feeding Operations and Respiratory Health of Neighboring Residents." *Epidemiology* 18:300–308.

Raffensperger, C., and J. Tickner, eds. 1999. *Protecting Public Health and the Environment: Implementing the Precautionary Principle*. Washington, DC: Island.

Ramon, K. 2011. "Debates on Protecting Traditional Knowledge in an Age of Globalization." In *Interdisciplinary Perspectives in Political Theory*, edited by M. Kulkarni, 189–215. Thousand Oaks, CA: Sage.

Ravallion, M., S. Chen, and P. Sangraula. 2007. "New Evidence on the Urbanization of Global Poverty." Policy Research Working Paper 4199, World Bank. siteresources.worldbank.org/INTWDR2008/Resources/2795087-1191427986785/RavallionMEtAl_UrbanizationOfGlobalPoverty.pdf.

Ray, D., N. Mueller, P. West, and J. Foley. 2013. "Yield Trends Are Insufficient to Double Global Crop Production by 2050." *PLOS* 8(6): e66428.

Raynolds, L., and E. Bennett, eds. 2015. *Handbook of Research on Fair Trade*. Cheltenham, UK: Elgar.

REDD Desk. 2015. "Forests: Why Are They Important?" July 10. theredddesk.org/what-redd#toc-1.

Redwood, M. 2010. "Commentary: Food Price and Volatility and the Urban Poor." In *Urban Agriculture: Diverse Activities and Benefits for City Society*, edited by C. Pearson, 5–6. London: Earthscan.

Rees, W. 2009. "True Cost Economics." In *Berkshire Encyclopedia of Sustainability*, edited by C. Laszlo, 468–471. Great Barrington, MA: Berkshire Publishing.

REN21 Secretariat. 2010. *Renewables 2010: Status Report, Renewable Action Policy Network for the 21st Century (REN21)*. Paris.

Revi, A. 2008. "Climate Change Risk: An Adaptation and Mitigation Agenda for India Cities." *Environment and Urbanization* 20(1): 207–229.

Revkin, A. 2009. "Peeling Back Pavement to Expose Watery Havens." *New York Times*, July 17.

Rideout, B. 2005. "The Effect of a Brief Environmental Problems Module on Endorsement of the New Ecological Paradigm in College Students." *Journal of Environmental Education* 37(1): 3–11.

Riffle, C. 2011. "Can Cities Lead the Way in Cutting Greenhouse Gas Emissions?" *Guardian* (London), June 7.

Rifkin, J. 2000. *The Age of Access: The New Culture of Hypercapitalism, Where All of Life Is a Paid-For Experience*. New York: Tarcher.

Riggi, L., V. Gagic, R. Bommarco, and B. Ekbom. 2015. "Insecticide Resistance in Pollen Beetles over 7 Years: A Landscape Approach." *Pest Management Science* 72(4): 780–786.

Roark, P. 2015. *Social Justice and Deep Participation: Theory and Practice for the 21st Century*. New York: Palgrave.

Robbins, P. 2012. *Political Ecology*. 2nd ed. Malden, MA: Wiley.

Roberto, K. 2003. *How to Do Hydroponics*. 4th ed. Lindenhurst, NY: Futuregarden.

Roe, A. 2015. "Free the Buses: Riders Say Transit Is a Human Right." Equal Voice for Families, Apr. 14. www.equalvoiceforfamilies.org/free-the-buses-riders-say-transit-is-a-human-right.

Rojek, C. 2010. *The Labour of Leisure: The Culture of Free Time*. Los Angeles, CA: Sage.

Rosa, E., and T. Dietz. 1998. "Climate Change and Society: Speculation, Construction, and Scientific Investigations." *International Sociology* 13:421–455.

Rosa, E., T. Rudel, R. York, A. Jorgenson, and T. Dietz. 2015. "The Human (Anthropogenic) Driving Forces of Global Climate Change." In *Climate Change and Society: Sociological Perspectives*, edited by R. Dunlap and R. Brulle, 32–60. New York: Oxford University Press.

Roser, M. 2015. "Child Mortality." Our World in Data. ourworldindata.org/data/population-growth-vital-statistics/child-mortality.

Rothschild, D. 2007. *The Life Earth Global Warming Survival Handbook*. New York: Rodale Books.

Ruitenberg, R. 2014. "World Biodiesel Output Seen by Oil World Reaching Record." *Bloomberg News*, June 10. www.bloomberg.com/news/articles/2014-06-10/world-biodiesel-output-seen-by-oil-world-reaching-record.

Sacks, D. 2011. "The Sharing Economy." Fast Company, Apr. 18. www.fastcompany.com/1747551/sharing-economy.

Sagoff, M. 1988. *The Economy of the Earth*. New York: Cambridge University Press.

Saha, R., and P. Mohai. 2005. "Historical Context and Hazardous Waste Facility Siting: Understanding Temporal Patterns in Michigan." *Social Problems* 52(4): 618–648.

Samida, D., and D. Weisbach. 2007. "Paretian Intergenerational Discounting." *University of Chicago Law Review* 74(1): 145–170.

Sarthi, P., A. Agrawal, and A. Rana. 2015. "Possible Future Changes in Cyclonic Storms in the Bay of Bengal, India, Under Warmer Climate." *International Journal of Climatology* 35(7): 1267–1277.

Schade, C., and D. Pimentel. 2010. "Population Crash: Prospects for Famine in the Twenty-First Century." *Environment, Development and Sustainability* 12(2): 245–262.

Schelling, T. 1995. "Intergenerational Discounting." *Energy Policy* 23:395–401.

Schiller, P., E. Bruun, and J. Kenworthy. 2010. *An Introduction to Sustainable Transportation: Policy, Planning, and Implementation*. London: Earthscan.

Schipper, L. 2011. "Automobile Use, Fuel Economy, and $CO_2$ Emissions in Industrialized Countries." *Transportation Policy* 18:358–372.

Schlesinger, J., E. Munishi, and A. Drescher. 2015. "Ethnicity as a Determinant of Agriculture in an Urban Setting: Evidence from Tanzania." *Geoforum* 64:138–145.

Schlosberg, D. 2013. "Political Challenges of the Climate-Changed Society." *PS: Political Science & Politics*, 46(01): 13–17.

Schnaiberg, A. 1980. *The Environment: From Surplus to Scarcity*. New York: Oxford University Press.

Schnaiberg, A., and K. Gould. 1994. *Environment and Society: The Enduring Conflict*. New York: St. Martin's.

Schor, J. 1992. *The Overworked American*. New York: Basic Books.

———. 2005. *Born to Buy*. New York: Scribner.

———. 2010. *Plenitude: The New Economics of True Wealth*. New York: Penguin.

Seckler, D. 1996. *The New Era of Water Resources Management: From "Dry" to "Wet" Water Savings*. International Irrigation Management Institute, Colombo, Sri Lanka. www.iwmi.cgiar.org/Publications/IWMI_Research _Reports/PDF/pub001/REPORT01.pdf.

Seier, M., and T. Zimmermann. 2014. "Environmental Impacts of Decommissioning Nuclear Power Plants: Methodical Challenges, Case Study, and Implications." *International Journal of Life Cycle Assessment* 19(12): 1919–1932.

Sen, A. 1970. *Collective Choice and Social Welfare*. San Francisco: Holden-Day.

———. 1981. *Poverty and Famines: An Essay on Entitlement and Deprivation*. New York: Oxford University Press.

———. 1984. "The Living Standard." *Oxford Economic Papers* 36:74–90.

———. 1993. "Markets and Freedom." *Oxford Economic Papers* 45:519–541.

———. 1994. "Population and Reasoning." Working Paper Series no. 94.06. Cambridge, MA: Harvard Center for Population and Development Studies, Harvard School of Public Health, Harvard University.

———. 1999. *Development as Freedom*. New York: Anchor.

———. 2005. "Human Rights and Capabilities." *Journal of Human Development* 6(2): 151–166.

Seo, B., and R. Chiu. 2014. "Social Cohesiveness of Disadvantaged Communities in Urban South Korea: The Impact of the Physical Environment." *Housing Studies* 29(3): 407–437.

Seshadri, S. 2001. "Prevalence of Micronutrient Deficiency Particularly of Iron, Zinc, and Folic Acid in Pregnant Women in South East Asia." *British Journal of Nutrition* 85:S87–S92.

Seto, K., B. Guneralp, and L. Hutyra. 2012. "Global Forecasts of Urban Expansion to 2030 and Direct Impacts on Biodiversity and Carbon Pools." *Proceedings of the National Academy of Sciences* 109(40): 16083–16088.

Sheldon, S., S. Hadian, and O. Zik. 2015. "Beyond Carbon: Quantifying Environmental Externalities as Energy for Hydroelectric and Nuclear Power." *Energy* 84(1): 36–44.

Shelley, C., J. Cross, W. Franzen, P. Hall, and S. Reeve. 2011. "Reducing Energy Consumption and Creating a Conservation Culture in Organizations: A Case Study of One Public School District." *Environment and Behavior* 4(3): 316–343.

———. 2012. "How to Go Green: Creating a Conservation Culture in a Public High School Through Education, Modeling, and Communication." *Journal of Environmental Education* 43(3): 143–161.

Shemkus, S. 2014. "Fighting the Seed Monopoly." *Guardian* (London), May 2.

Shove, E., F. Trentmann, and R. Wilk. 2009. *Time, Consumption, and Everyday Life: Practice, Materiality, and Culture*. New York: Berg.

Shue, H. 2014. *Climate Justice: Vulnerability and Protection*. New York: Oxford.

Simon, J. 1981. *The Ultimate Resource*. Princeton, NJ: Princeton University Press.

Simons, R., Y. Seo, and S. Robinson. 2014. "The Effect of a Large Hog Barn Operation on Residential Sales Prices in Marshall County, KY." *Journal of Sustainable Real Estate* 6(2): 93–111.

Sjöstedt, M., and S. Jagers. 2014. "Democracy and the Environment Revisited: The Case of African Fisheries." *Marine Policy* 43:143–148.

Skousen, M. 2011. *Econopower: How a New Generation of Economists Is Transforming the World.* New York: Wiley.

Sloan, H. 1993. "The Earth Belongs in Usufruct to the Living." In *Jeffersonian Legacies*, edited by P. Onuf, 281–315. Charlottesville: University Press of Virginia.

Smart, M., K. Ralph, B. Taylor, C. Turley, and A. Brown. 2014. "Honey, Can You Pick-Up Groceries on Your Way Home? Analyzing Activities and Travel Among Students and in Non-Traditional Households." University of California Transportation Center, UCLA, Las Angeles. www.uctc.net/research/papers/UCTC-FR-2014-07.pdf.

Smil, V. 2004. *China's Past, China's Future: Energy, Food, Environment.* New York: Routledge.

Smith, E. 2001. "On the Coevolution of Cultural, Linguistic, and Biological Diversity." In *Biocultural Diversity: Linking Language, Knowledge, and the Environment*, edited by L. Maffi, 95–117. Washington, DC: Smithsonian Institution Press.

Sneath, D. 1998. "State Policy and Pasture Degradation in Inner Asia." *Science* 281(5380): 1147–1148.

Snow, D., and R. Benford. 1988. "Ideology, Frame Resonance, and Participant Mobilization." *International Social Movement Research* 1:197–218.

Snow, D., E. Rochford, S. Worden, and R. Benford. 1986. "Frame Alignment Processes, Micro-Mobilization, and Movement Participation." *American Sociological Review* 51:464–481.

Snow, E., L. Allen, M. Jacovina, and D. McNamara. 2015. "Does Agency Matter? Exploring the Impact of Controlled Behaviors Within a Game-Based Environment." *Computers & Education* 82:378–392.

Society of the Plastics Industry. 1988. "Plastic Packaging Resins." American Chemistry Council. plastics .americanchemistry.com/Plastic-Resin-Codes-PDF.

Socolow, R. 2011. "Wedges Reaffirmed." *Bulletin of the Atomic Scientists*, Sept. 27. www.thebulletin.org/web -edition/features/wedges-reaffirmed.

Soil Association. 2011. "Organic Buying Groups: Case Study A." Bristol, UK. www.soilassociation.org/LinkClick .aspx?fileticket=1EQctvug1cE%3D&tabid=638.

Sovacool, B. 2008. "Valuing the Greenhouse Gas Emissions from Nuclear Power: A Critical Survey." *Energy Policy* 36:2950–2963.

Spence, M. 2009. "Markets Aren't Everything." *Forbes*, Oct. 12. www.forbes.com/2009/10/12/economics-nobel -elinor-ostrom-oliver-williamson-opinions-contributors-michael-spence.html.

Spilsbury, R. 2010. *Deforestation Crisis.* New York: Rosen.

"Spring Tide: Pollution Fears Are Driving the Chinese Towards Expensive Branded Waters." 2015. *Economist*, Feb. 26.

SSA (Self Storage Association). 2012. Fact Sheet, June 30. www.selfstorage.org/ssa/Content/NavigationMenu /AboutSSA/FactSheet/default.htm.

Statista. 2015. "Per Capita Consumption of Bottled Water Worldwide in 2009 and 2014, by Leading Countries (in Gallons)." www.statista.com/statistics/183388/per-capita-consumption-of-bottled-water-worldwide-in-2009.

Stebbins, R. 1967. "A Note on the Concept of Role Distance." *American Journal of Sociology* 73(2): 247–250.

Steel, D. 2014. *Philosophy and the Precautionary Principle.* New York: Cambridge University Press.

Stein, P. 2015. "Bike-Share Programs Are Expanding Worldwide; Are They Successful?" *Washington Post*, May 22.

Stephenson, J., F. Berkes, N. Turner, and J. Dick. 2014. "Biocultural Conservation of Marine Ecosystems: Examples from New Zealand and Canada." *Indian Journal of Traditional Knowledge* 13(2): 257–265.

Stepp J., S. Cervone, H. Castaneda, A. Lasseter, G. Stocks, and Y. Gichon. 2004. "Development of a GIS for Global Biocultural Diversity." *Policy Matters* 13:267–270.

Sterling, E., and E. Vintinner. 2012. "How Much Is Left? An Overview of the Crisis." In *A Pivotal Moment: Population, Justice, and the Environmental Challenge*, edited by L. Mazur, 193–204. Washington, DC: Island.

Stern, P. 1999. "Information, Incentives, and Pro-Environmental Consumer Behavior." *Journal of Consumer Policy* 22:461–478.

Stern, P., E. Aronson, J. Darley, D. Hill, E. Hirst, W. Kempton, and T. Wilbanks. 1986. "The Effectiveness of Incentives for Residential Energy Conservation." *Evaluation Review* 10(2): 147–176.

Stofferahn, C. 2006. "Industrialized Farming and Its Relationship to Community Well-Being: An Update of a 2000 Report by Linda Lobao." Office of the Attorney General, State of North Dakota, Sept.

Stone, B. 2008. "Urban Sprawl and Air Quality in Large US Cities." *Journal of Environmental Management* 86:688–698.

Stretesky, P. B., and R. McKie. 2016. "A Perspective on the Historical Analysis of Race and Treatment Storage and Disposal Facilities in the United States." *Environmental Research Letters* 11(3): 031001.

Stuart, D., R. L. Schewe, and M. McDermott. 2014. "Reducing Nitrogen Fertilizer Application as a Climate Change Mitigation Strategy: Understanding Farmer Decision-Making and Potential Barriers to Change in the US." *Land Use Policy* 36:210–218.

Stuart, T. 2009. *Waste: Uncovering the Global Food Scandal.* New York: Norton.

Subramaniam, M. 2014. "Neoliberalism and Water Rights: The Case of India." *Current Sociology* 62(3): 393–411.

Sulemana, I., H. S. James, and C. B. Valdivia. 2016. "Perceived Socioeconomic Status as a Predictor of Environmental Concern in African and Developed Countries." *Journal of Environmental Psychology*. DOI: 10.1016.

Sunstein, C. 2004. "Valuing Life: A Plea for Disaggregation." *Duke Law Journal* 54:384–445.

Sunstein, C., and A. Rowell. 2007. "On Discounting Regulatory Benefits: Risk, Money, and Intergenerational Equity." *University of Chicago Law Review* 74(1): 171–208.

Sutherland, R. 2010. "We Can't Run Away from the Ethical Debates in Marketing." *Market Leader*, Jan. www.marketing-society.org.uk/SiteCollectionDocuments/knowledge-zone/market-leader/january-2010.pdf.

Sutton, M., C. Howard, J. Erisman, G. Billen, A. Bleeker, P. Grennfelt, H. van Grinsven, and B. Grizzetti. 2011. *The European Nitrogen Assessment: Sources, Effects, and Policy Perspectives*. Cambridge: Cambridge University Press.

Swartz, S., and S. Oster. 2010. "China Tops US in Energy Use." *Wall Street Journal*, July 18.

Swift, P., D. Painter, and M. Goldstein. 2006. "Residential Street Typology and Injury Accident Frequency." VMT Congress of New Urbanism. massengale.typepad.com/venustas/files/SwiftSafetyStudy.pdf.

Szasz, A. 2007. *Shopping Our Way to Safety: How We Changed from Protecting the Environment to Protecting Ourselves*. Minneapolis: University of Minnesota Press.

Taylor, D., C. Taylor, and J. Taylor. 2012. *Empowerment on an Unsustainable Planet*. New York: Oxford University Press.

Taylor, J., and S. Lovell. 2015. "Urban Home Gardens in the Global North: A Mixed Methods Study of Ethnic and Migrant Home Gardens in Chicago, IL." *Renewable Agriculture and Food Systems* 30(1): 22–32.

*Telegraph* Reporters. 2012. "Where Do Milk, Eggs and Bacon Come From? One in Three Youths Don't Know." *Telegraph* (London), June 14.

Terry, G. 2009. "No Climate Justice Without Gender Justice: An Overview of the Issues." *Gender and Development* 17(1): 5–18.

Texas A&M Transportation Institute. 2013. "As Traffic Jams Worsen, Commuters Allowing Extra Time for Urgent Trips." College Station, TX, Feb. 5. tti.tamu.edu/2013/02/05/as-traffic-jams-worsen-commuters-allowing-extra-time-for-urgent-trips.

Thompson, M. 1979. *Rubbish Theory*. New York: Oxford University Press.

Thyberg, K. L., D. J. Tonjes, and J. Gurevitch. 2015. "Quantification of Food Waste Disposal in the United States: A Meta-Analysis." *Environmental Science & Technology* 49(24): 13946–13953.

Tickner, J. 2003. "The Role of Environmental Science in Precautionary Decision Making." In *Precaution: Environmental Science and Preventive Public Policy*, edited by J. Tickner, 3–20. Washington, DC: Island.

Torres, A., O. Sarmiento, C. Stauber, and R. Zarama. 2013. "The Ciclovia and Cicloruta Programs: Promising Interventions to Promote Physical Activity and Social Capital in Bogotá, Colombia." *American Journal of Public Health* 103(2): e23–e30.

Toth, G., and C. Szigeti. 2016. "The Historical Ecological Footprint: From Over-Population to Over-Consumption." *Ecological Indicators* 60:283–291.

Toulmin, C. 2009. *Climate Change in Africa*. New York: Zed Books.

Transparency Market Research. 2015. "Bottled Water Market (Still, Carbonated, Flavored and Functional): Global Industry Analysis, Size, Share, Growth, Trends and Forecast 2014–2020." www.transparencymarketresearch.com/bottled-water-market.html.

Tranter, P. 2012. "Effective Speed: Cycling Because It's 'Faster.'" In *City Cycling*, edited by J. Pucher and R. Buehler, 57–74. Cambridge, MA: MIT Press.

Tripicchio, G., M. Heo, L. Diewald, S. M. Noar, R. Dooley, A. Pietrobelli, K. S. Burger, and M. S. Faith. 2016. "Restricting Advertisements for High-Fat, High-Sugar Foods during Children's Television Programs: Attitudes in a US Population-Based Sample." *Childhood Obesity* 12(2): 113–118.

Tripicchio, G., M. Heo, L. Diewald, S. M. Noar, R. Dooley, A. Pietrobelli, K. S. Burger, and M. S. Faith. 2016. "Restricting Advertisements for High-Fat, High-Sugar Foods during Children's Television Programs: Attitudes in a US Population-Based Sample." *Childhood Obesity* 12(2): 113–118.

Tripp, R. 2001. "Can Biotechnology Reach the Poor? The Adequacy of Information and Seed Delivery." *Food Policy* 26:249–264.

Troped, P., H. Starnes, R. Puett, K. Tamura, E. Cromley, P. James, E. Ben-Joseph, S. Melly, and F. Laden. 2014. "Relationships Between the Built Environment and Walking and Weight Status Among Older Women in Three US States." *Journal of Aging and Physical Activity* 22(1): 114–125.

Trotman, R. 2008. *The Benefits of Community Conservation: A Literature Review*. Report prepared for the Auckland, New Zealand, Regional Council, Dec. www.arc.govt.nz/albany/fms/main/Documents/Auckland/Volunteers/Benefits%20of%20community%20conservation.pdf.

Trzupek, R. 2011. "Natural Gas Will Repower America." *Real Clear Energy*, Oct. 18. www.realclearenergy.org/articles/2011/10/18/natural_gas_will_repower_america_106319.html.

Tschakert, P. 2014. The Socioeconomic Capability to Adapt to Climate Change." In *Global Environmental Change*, edited by B. Freedman, 745–753. Handbook of Global Environmental Pollution. New York: Springer.

Tuck, S., C. Winqvist, F. Mota, J. Ahnström, L. Turnbull, and J. Bengtsson. 2014. "Land-Use Intensity and the Effects of Organic Farming on Biodiversity: A Hierarchical Meta-Analysis." *Journal of Applied Ecology* 51(3): 746–755.

Tuck-Po, L. 2004. *Changing Pathways.* Lanham, MD: Lexington Books.

Tudge, C. 2010. "How to Raise Livestock—and How Not To." In *The Meat Crisis,* edited by J. D'Silva and J. Webster, 9–21. London: Earthscan.

Turner, N. J. 2016. "We give them seaweed": Social economic exchange and resilience in Northwestern North America. *Indian Journal of Traditional Knowledge* 15(1): 5–15.

Twidell, J., and T. Weir. 2015. *Renewable Energy Resources.* New York: Routledge.

UNDP (United Nations Development Programme). 1990. *Human Development Report, 1990.* New York: Oxford University Press.

UNEP (United Nations Environmental Programme). 2007. *Declaration of the Rights of Indigenous People.* Sixty-First Session, UN General Assembly, New York.

———. 2008. *State and Trends of the Environment, 1987–2007.* New York. www.unep.org/geo/geo4/report/02 _Atmosphere.pdf.

———. 2009. "Recycling: From E-Waste to Resources." July. www.unep.org/PDF/PressReleases/E-Waste_publication _screen_FINALVERSION-sml.pdf.

United Nations. 2002. "General Comment Number 15." Economic and Social Council, United Nations, New York. www.citizen.org/documents/ACF2B4B.pdf.

———. 2004. "World Population to 2020." Economic and Social Affairs, United Nations, New York. www.un.org/esa /population/publications/longrange2/WorldPop2300final.pdf.

———. 2005. "Fact Sheet 7: Mega Cities." Working Paper no. ESA/P/WP/200. New York: UN Department of Economic and Social Affairs, Population Division. www.un.org/esa/population/publications/WUP2005/2005WUP _FS7.pdf.

———. 2009. "Water in a Changing World." Third UN World Water Development Report. www.unesco.org/water /wwap/wwdr/wwdr3/pdf/WWDR3_Water_in_a_Changing_World.pdf.

———. 2010. *Solid Waste Management in the World's Cities.* London: Earthscan.

———. 2013. *Global Food and Nutrition Scenarios: Final Report Millennium Institute Washington, DC.* United Nations, Washington, DC. www.un.org/en/development/desa/policy/wess/wess_bg_papers/bp_wess2013 _millennium_inst.pdf.

———. 2014. "Should International Refugee Law Accommodate Climate Change?" United Nations News Center, July 3. www.un.org/apps/news/story.asp?NewsID=48201#.VYqUa2CI1UQ.

———. 2015a. "Energy." United Nations Habitat. unhabitat.org/urban-themes/energy.

———. 2015b. *The Millennium Development Goals Report, 2015.* www.un.org/millenniumgoals/2015_MDG _Report/pdf/MDG%202015%20rev%20(July%201).pdf.

———. 2015c. "World Population Prospects." esa.un.org/unpd/wpp/Graphs.

*United States Code, 2000: Title 22, Foreign Relations and Intercourse.* 2002. Washington, DC: US Government Printing Office.

US Bureau of Reclamation. 2015. "Lower Colorado River Operations Schedule." www.usbr.gov/lc/region/g4000 /hourly/rivops.html.

US Department of Energy. 2014. "Life Cycle Analysis of Natural Gas Extraction and Power Generation." May 29. www.netl.doe.gov/File%20Library/Research/Energy%20Analysis/Life%20Cycle%20Analysis/NETL-NG-Power -LCA-29May2014.pdf.

US Department of Transportation. 2015. "Average Annual Miles per Driver by Age Group." Highway Commission, Washington, DC, Feb. www.fhwa.dot.gov/ohim/onh00/bar8.htm.

US National Academy of Sciences. 2011. *Climate Change, the Indoor Environment, and Health.* Washington, DC: National Academies Press.

Vallance, S., H. Perkins, and J. Dixon. 2011. "What Is Social Sustainability? A Clarification of Concepts." *Geoforum* 42(3): 342–348.

van den Bosch, R. 1978. *The Pesticide Conspiracy.* Garden City, NY: Doubleday.

Vandergeest, P. 1996. "Mapping Nature: Territorialization of Forest Rights in Thailand." *Society and Natural Resources* 9:159–175.

van der Hoek, W., F. Konradsen, K. Athukorala, and T. Wanigadewa. 1998. "Pesticide Poisoning: A Major Health Problem in Sri Lanka." *Social Science and Medicine* 46(4): 495–504.

van der Voort, T., P. Nikken, and J. van Lil. 1992. "Determinants of Parental Guidance of Children's Television Viewing: A Dutch Replication Study." *Journal of Broadcasting and Electronic Media* 36(1): 61–74.

Veblen, T. (1899) 1967. *The Theory of the Leisure Class: An Economic Study of Institutions.* New York: Funk and Wagnalls.

Verheijen, F., S. Jeffery, M. van der Velde, V. Peníček, M. Beland, A. Bastos, and J. Keizer. 2013. "Reductions in Soil Surface Albedo as a Function of Biochar Application Rate: Implications for Global Radiative Forcing." *Environmental Research Letters* 8(4): 044008.

Vernon, L. 2011. "Why All Plastic Containers Can't Be Recycled." *Eco Ramblings*, Feb. ecoramblings.com/why-all -plastic-containers-cant-be-recycled.

Vervoort, W. 2014. "Dams Are Not the Smart Way to Secure Water for Agriculture." *Conversation*, Oct. 21. theconversation.com/dams-are-not-the-smart-way-to-secure-water-for-agriculture-33193.

Vickery, J., and L. M. Hunter. 2016. "Native Americans: Where in Environmental Justice Theory and Research?" *Society & Natural Resources* 29(1): 36–52.

Vickrey, W. 1968. "Automobile Accidents, Tort Law, Externalities, and Insurance: An Economist's Critique." *Law and Contemporary Problems* 33:464–487.

Victor, P. 2008. *Managing Without Growth: Slower by Design, Not Disaster.* Northampton, MA: Edward Elgar.

Vijayan, V. 1987. *Keoladeo National Park Ecology Study.* Bombay: Bombay Natural History Society.

———. 1991. *Keoladeo National Park Ecology Study, 1980–1990.* Bombay: Bombay Natural History Society.

Voelcker, J. 2014. "1.2 Billion Vehicles On World's Roads Now, 2 Billion By 2035: Report." Green Car Reports, July 29. www.greencarreports.com/news/1093560_1-2-billion-vehicles-on-worlds-roads-now-2-billion-by-2035-report.

Wackernagel, M. 2013. "The Ecological Footprint and the Average American Family." Global Footprint Network. www.seeinnovation.org/Documents/Global%20Footprint%20Network%20article.pdf.

Wallich, H. 1972. "Zero Growth." *Newsweek*, Jan. 24, 62.

Wang, J., D. Brown, and A. Agrawal. 2013. "Climate Adaptation, Local Institutions, and Rural Livelihoods: A Comparative Study of Herder Communities in Mongolia and Inner Mongolia, China." *Global Environmental Change* 23(6): 1673–1683.

Watson, I. 2013. "China: The Electronic Wastebasket of the World." CNN, May 30. www.cnn.com/2013/05/30 /world/asia/china-electronic-waste-e-waste.

Watts, J. 2011. "Fukushima Disaster: It's Not Over Yet." *Guardian* (London), Sept. 9.

WEDO. 2008. "Gender, Climate Change, and Human Security: Lessons from Bangladesh, Ghana, and Senegal." Women's Environment and Development Organization, May. Retrieved March 15, 2012 (http://www.wedo.org/ wp-content/uploads/hsn-study-final-may-20-2008.pdf).

Weinberg, A. 1972. "Science and Trans-Science." *Minerva* 10:209–222.

Weinzettel, J., E. Hertwich, G. Peters, K. Steen-Olsen, and A. Galli. 2013. "Affluence Drives the Global Displace-ment of Land Use." *Global Environmental Change* 23(2): 433–438.

Werner, A., S. Vink, K. Watt, and P. Jagals. 2015. "Environmental Health Impacts of Unconventional Natural Gas Development: A Review of the Current Strength of Evidence." *Science of the Total Environment* 505:1127–1141.

Wesseling, C., L. Castillo, and C. Elinder. 1993. "Pesticide Poisonings in Costa Rica." *Scandinavian Journal of Work, Environment and Health* 19(4): 227–235.

White, L. 1967. "The Historical Roots of Our Ecologic Crisis." *Science* 155:1203–1207.

White, M., N. Diffenbaugh, G. Jones, J. Pal, and F. Giorg. 2006. "Extreme Heat Reduces and Shifts United States Premium Wine Production in the 21st Century." *Proceedings of the National Academy of Sciences* 103(30): 11217–11222.

White, S., and T. Selfa. 2013. "Shifting Lands: Exploring Kansas Farmer Decision-Making in an Era of Climate Change and Biofuels Production." *Environmental Management* 51:379–391.

Whitehead, A. N. (1920) 1964. *Concept of Nature.* Cambridge: Cambridge University Press.

Whitehead, L., A. Upward, P. Friedel, G. Cox, and M. Mossman. 2010. "Using Core Sunlight to Improve Illumina-tion Quality and Increase Energy Efficiency of Commercial Buildings." Proceedings of the ASME Fourth Inter-national Conference on Energy Sustainability, Phoenix, AZ, May 17–22. www.phas.ubc.ca/ssp/howdoesitwork /ASME_2010_paper.pdf.

White House. 2014. Fact Sheet: The Economic Challenge Posed by Declining Pollinator Populations. Office of the Press Secretary, Washington, DC, June 20. www.whitehouse.gov/the-press-office/2014/06/20/fact-sheet -economic-challenge-posed-declining-pollinator-populations.

WHO (World Health Organization). 2011. "Burden of Disease from Environmental Noise: Quantification of Healthy Life Years Lost in Europe." Geneva. www.euro.who.int/__data/assets/pdf_file/0008/136466/e94888 .pdf.

———. 2012a. "DALYs / YLDs Definition." Geneva. Accessed June 6. www.who.int/mental_health/management /depression/daly/en.

———. 2012b. "Media Center: Malaria." Geneva. www.who.int/mediacentre/factsheets/fs094/en.

———. 2012c. "WHO Definition of Health." Geneva. Accessed May 19. www.who.int/about/definition/en/print .html.

———. 2013. "Global Status Report on Road Safety." Geneva. www.who.int/iris/bitstream/10665/78256 /1/9789241564564_eng.pdf.

———. 2015. "Road Traffic Injuries." Geneva. www.who.int/mediacentre/factsheets/fs358/en.

Wichelns, D. 2010. "Agricultural Water Pricing: United States." Organisation for Economic Co-Operation and Development. www.oecd.org/unitedstates/45016437.pdf.

Wilkinson, R., and K. Pickett. 2009. *The Spirit Level: Why More Equal Societies Are Almost Always Better.* New York: Penguin Books.

Wilkinson, R., K. Pickett, and R. De Vogli. 2010. "Equality, Sustainability, and Quality of Life." *BMJ* 341(Nov. 27): 1138–1140.

Williamson, T. 2002. "Sprawl, Politics, and Participation: A Preliminary Analysis." *National Civic Review* 91(3): 235–244.

Wilson, E. O. (1992) 1999. *The Diversity of Life*. New York: Norton.

Wily, L. 1999. "Moving Forward in African Community Forestry: Trading Power, Not Use Rights." *Society and Natural Resources* 12(1): 49–61.

WNA (World Nuclear Association). 2015. "World Nuclear Power Reactors and Uranium Requirements." London. www.world-nuclear.org/info/Facts-and-Figures/World-Nuclear-Power-Reactors-and-Uranium-Requirements.

Wood, D. 1993. "The Power of Maps." *Scientific American* (May): 88–94.

Woodworth, B., M. Steen-Adams, and P. Mittal. 2011. "Role of an Environmental Studies Course on the Formation of Environmental Worldviews: A Case Study of a Core Curriculum Requirement Using the NEP Scale." *Journal of Environmental Studies and Sciences* 1(2): 126–137.

World Bank. 2012. *What a Waste: A Global Review of Solid Waste Management*. Washington, DC. siteresources .worldbank.org/INTURBANDEVELOPMENT/Resources/336387-1334852610766/What_a_Waste2012_Final .pdf.

———. 2015a. "Data: Indicators." data.worldbank.org/indicator.

———. 2015b. "Natural Capital Accounting." www.worldbank.org/en/topic/environment/brief/environmental -economics-natural-capital-accounting.

———. 2015c. "Renewable Internal Freshwater Resources per Capita." data.worldbank.org/indicator/ER.H2O .INTR.PC.

World Coal Association. 2014. "Coal Facts 2014." www.worldcoal.org/bin/pdf/ . . . pdf . . . /coal_facts_2014(12_09 _2014).pdf.

Wu, W., X. Yize, L. Guangchun, Z. Weilin, L. Hualiang, R. Shannon, and X. Yanjun. 2013. "Temperature-Mortality Relationship in Four Subtropical Chinese Cities: A Time-Series Study Using a Distributed Lag Non-Linear Model." *Science of the Total Environment* 449:355–362.

WWF. 2014. *Living Planet Report 2014: Species and Spaces, People and Places*. Morges, Switzerland. assets .worldwildlife.org/publications/723/files/original/WWF-LPR2014-low_res.pdf.

Wynne, B. 2002. "Risk and Environment as Legitimatory Discourses of Technology: Reflectivity Inside and Out?" *Current Sociology* 50:459–477.

Xichuan, H. 2014. "A Canal Too Far." *Economist*, Sept. 27.

Xing, Y., Z. Li, Y. Fan, and H. Hou. 2010. "Biohydrogen Production from Dairy Manures with Acidification Pretreatment by Anaerobic Fermentation." *Environmental Science and Pollution Research* 17(2): 392–399.

Xu, B. 2014. "China's Environmental Crisis." Council on Foreign Relations, Apr. 25. www.cfr.org/china/chinas -environmental-crisis/p12608.

York, R. 2006. "Review of *Cultures of Environmentalism*," by Steve Yearly. *Organization and Environment* 19:142–144.

———. 2010. "The Paradox at the Heart of Modernity: The Carbon Efficiency of the Global Economy." *International Journal of Sociology* 40(2): 6–22.

York, R., E. Rosa, and T. Dietz. 2003. "Footprints on the Earth: The Environmental Consequences of Modernity." *American Sociological Review* 68(2): 279–300.

Zafrilla, J., A. Cadarso, F. Monsalve, and C. de la Rúa. 2014. "How Carbon-Friendly Is Nuclear Energy? A Hybrid MRIO-LCA Model of a Spanish Facility." *Environmental Science & Technology* 48(24): 14103–14111.

Zarfl, C., A. Lumsdon, J. Berlekamp, L. Tydecks, and K. Tockner. 2015. "A Global Boom in Hydropower Dam Construction." *Aquatic Sciences* 77(1): 161–170.

Zezza, A., and L. Tasciotti. 2010. "Urban Agriculture, Poverty, and Food Security: Empirical Evidence from a Sample of Developing Countries." *Food Policy* 35:265–273.

Zhaoa, Z., and R. Kaestnerb. 2010. "Effects of Urban Sprawl on Obesity." *Journal of Health Economics* 29:779–787.

Zhou, Y., N. Li, W. Wenxiang, W. Jidong, and S. Peijun. 2014. "Local Spatial and Temporal Factors Influencing Population and Societal Vulnerability to Natural Disasters." *Risk Analysis* 34(4): 614–639.

Zwart, H. 1997. "What Is an Animal? A Philosophical Reflection on the Possibility of a Moral Relationship with Animals." *Environmental Values* 6:377–392.

# Index

Abject poverty, 26
Adaptation
    climate change and, 29, 39, 162–163
    genetically engineered (GE) food and, 39
    vulnerable vs. affluent and, 29, 39
Advertisement
    company taxes and, 285
    consumption and, 283–285
    directed at children, 277, 284–285
    regulation as solution, 284–285
    statistics on, 277
Aeroponics, 132
Agriculture
    arable land as limiting factor, 99, 119
    confined animal-feeding operations (CAFOs),
        160, 166–167
    ecosystem services and, 75
    farmers/climate change views and, 162–163
    global nutrition/shifting diets, 168, 169–170
        (tables), 171
    greenhouse gas emissions statistics/sources, 160,
        164
    industrial agriculture/community impacts,
        166–168
    Iowa farm products (1920–2012), 161 (table)
    mechanical revolution/effects, 159–160, 161
        (table)
    nitrogen pollution and, 164, 214
    organic agriculture and biodiversity, 68
    structure of agriculture, 159
    survey on public knowledge, 277
    treadmills of, 171–173
    US government subsidies, 160, 162, 162 (fig.)
    vertical farming, 132–133
    waste production, 160
    *See also food issues*; Water and agriculture
Agriculture/soil
    depletion/exhaustion (mid 1800s), 8, 213–214

disconnecting people from land/soil nutrient
    cycle, 2
erosion, 165–166
fertilizer beginnings/consequences, 214
Agriculture solutions
    agroecology/benefits, 173–175
    peasant-based movements, 175–177, 175
        (photo), 179
    rainbow evolutions, 173
    urban agriculture, 85–86, 179–180, 179
        (photo)
    *See also* Agrobiodiversity
Agrobiodiversity
    food security and, 85
    intellectual property rights/patents and, 84, 84
        (photo), 85
    open source seeds and, 84, 84 (photo)
    urban agriculture and, 85–86
Agroecology/benefits, 173–175
American buffalo, 70 (photo)
Anaerobic decomposition, 47
Annan, Kofi, 173
Ants and ecosystem roles, 70
Apolitical ecology, 223
Arable land, 118–119
Aristotle, 285
Aswan Dam, 89
Atmosphere
    changes over time/consequences, 21
    ecosystem services and, 76
Automobiles *See* Transportation/cars
Ayres, Robert, 262

Banana cultivars/Panama disease, 172
Bangladesh and climate change/refugees, 30
Batek people and nature, 278–279
Bees services/decline, 75
Beetle, Alan, 78

Behavior change
    high schools example, Fort Collins, Colorado,
        293
    pro-environmental behavior, 292–293
    social norms and, 293
Bekoff, Marc, 70
*Ben Adair, United States of America and the Klamath
    Indian Tribe v. (1983)*, 92
Berlin, Isaiah, 223–224, 268
Beyond Coal, Sierra Club, 33
Biochar, 41
Biocultural diversity, 76–77
Biodiversity
    benefits, 67–68, 220
    climate change and, 68, 71 (table)
    definitions, 72–75
    grazing animals example, 73–75
    habitat fragmentation and, 142, 144
    humans as component and, 74–75, 76, 80–83, 86
    organic agriculture and, 68
    patents and, 78, 79, 85
    species extinction/rates, 68, 70, 72, 77, 142
    species numbers, 68
    threats, 68, 71 (table), 75
    Three Gorges Dam and, 184
    tragedy of the commodity, 72
    *See also* Conservation
Biodiversity hot spots, 73
Biodiversity threats/loss solutions
    agrobiodiversity conservation, 83–86
    community conservation, 80–83, 81 (table)
Biofortification, 171
Biohazards and wastes, 52, 59
Biological species concept, 73
Biopiracy, 77–79
Bioprospecting, 78
Birthrates defined, 113
*Board of Education of Topeka, Brown v. (1954)*, 296
Bombay Natural History Society, 73–75
Bonding social capital, 145
Boserup, Ester/effect, 131
Bottled water, 93–95, 94 (table)
*Bowling Alone* (Putman), 144
Bretton Woods Institutions/creation, 96
Bridging social capital, 145
*Brief History of Neoliberalism, A* (Harvey), 223
*Brown v. Board of Education of Topeka (1954)*, 296
Bt binjal eggplant biopiracy example, 79
Bullard, Robert, 257–258
Bush, George W., 235, 237
Butani, Shahlini, 84 (photo)
Buycotts/carrotmob, 288, 289
Buyer power, 58

Calabresi, Guido, 232
Cap and trade, 39–40
*Capital* (Marx), 214
Capitalism
    globalization and, 214–215
    social/biological linkages and, 217

Capitalism contradictions
    environmental crisis (mid 1800s), 214–215
    metabolic rift, 8, 213–214, 215
    overproduction/underproduction and, 215–216
    treadmill of production and, 8, 212–213
Car sharing, 286
Carbon credits, 40
Carbon dioxide
    earth's early atmosphere and, 21
    *See also* Greenhouse gases
Carbon dioxide emissions
    carbon intensity, 208
    decoupling and, 212
    fossil fuels and, 20, 35, 41, 138
    population growth and, 115, 117 (table), 118
    relative vs. absolute efficiency and, 208–209
    sources, 20, 138
    statistics on, 20, 35, 138
    top countries, 209
    in United States (1980–2006), 210 (fig.)
    *See also* Climate change; Greenhouse effect;
        Greenhouse gases; Pollution; *specific sources*
Carbon dioxide removal
    geoengineering/ocean fertilization, 39
    sequestering, 41, 47, 241
Carbon Disclosure Project, 37–38
Carbon intensity
    climate change goals and, 209 (fig.)
    definition/description, 208
Carbon markets, 39–40
Carbon Mitigation Initiative, 36
Carbon offsets, 40–42
Carbon sinks
    climate change solutions and, 35–36
    definition/description, 35–36
    economic growth and, 8
    landfills and, 47
Carbon tax
    consumer behavior and, 199
    definition/description, 39
    disincentivize fossil fuel and, 199
    vulnerable vs. affluent, 39
    World Environment Day, Australia and, 221
        (photo)
Carbonfund, 41
Carrotmob, 289
Cars. *See* Transportation/cars
Carson, Rachel, 1, 247
Carter, Jimmy, 194
Children in less developed countries
    malnutrition and, 168
    water fetching time and, 98–99
Christie, Chris, 40
Cities
    sewage and Thames River, 8, 214
    traditional, commuter, automobile diagrams,
        136–137, 136 (fig.)
    *See also* Megacities; Transportation
Clausen, Rebecca, 72
"Clean coal," 186

Climate change
    adaptation and, 30, 39, 162–163
    apolitical ecology and, 223
    biodiversity, 68
    children, women, elderly, 27–28, 28 (fig.), 29,
        30
    definition/descriptions, 19, 28, 31 (photo)
    environmental racism and, 257 (photo), 260
    food security and, 25–26
    governance and, 235, 237
    grapes/wine industry and, 27
    habitat fragmentation/wildlife corridors, 142,
        144
    polar bears and, 229
    risky sites and, 25
    vulnerable vs. affluent, 21, 22 (fig.), 23–28, 24
        (table), 28 (fig.), 29–32, 280
    *See also* Coal; Energy; Greenhouse effect;
        Greenhouse gases; Water and climate
        change
Climate change refugees
    conflict and, 30–31
    definition, 29
    gender and, 30
    overview, 28–31
    poor vs. affluent, 29–30
Climate change solutions
    behavioral changes/household energy
        consumption, 32–33, 34 (table)
    carbon markets/offsets, 39–42
    coal use/energy source changes and, 33, 35
    consequences of delaying and, 36, 37 (fig.)
    costs of action vs. inaction, 32
    environmental movements, 32
    geoengineering, 38–39
    green building, 36–38
    mitigation, 31–32, 39, 162–163
    reducing social distance/improving
        understanding, 275
    stabilization triangle/wedges and, 35–36, 35
        (fig.), 37 (fig.)
Climate change/urban areas
    health impacts and, 24 (table)
    heat island effect and, 23–24, 23 (fig.)
    informal settlements and, 23
    overview, 21–25, 22 (fig.), 23 (fig.), 24 (table)
    responsibility/vulnerability and, 22 (fig.)
Climate change views
    ambivalence vs. indifference, 281–282
    awareness/predictors of awareness, 275–276
    blame-shifting and, 280
    complexity, 279–282
    conservatives/environmental skepticism and,
        280–281
    lack of control and, 282
    Norway study, 279, 280
    politics and, 275, 280–281
    religion and, 281
    role strain and, 282
    scientists vs. public, 19, 20

Clinton, Bill, 232, 268–269
Close Loop Fund, 53
Coal
    carbon-capture technology and, 186, 187
    carbon tax and, 199
    "clean coal," 186
    computer data centers and, 189
    ecological footprint/climate change and,
        186–187, 188
    mountaintop removal mining, 188
    plants off-line time and, 198
    strip-mining, 186–187
    uses/statistics on, 33, 184, 185 (photo)
    *See also* Fossil fuels
*Coal Question, The* (Jevons), 207
Coase, Ronald, 222
Coase theorem, 222
Cochrane, Willard, 171
Collective coverage (waste management)
    definition/description, 58
    slum/nonslum households, 59 (table)
"Collector's item" and waste, 48
Colony collapse disorder, 75
Commodity chain, 49
Community capitals framework, 267, 267 (table)
Community conservation
    citizen involvement/decision making, 81 (table)
    overview, 80–83, 81 (table)
    participatory forest management, Kenya, 83
    socioecological benefits summary, 82
    Tanzania example (woodland reserves), 81–83
Community severance, 146
Conservation
    agrobiodiversity, 83–86
    ex situ/in situ models, 76–77
    history, 80
    maps power and, 74
    removing people from protected areas and,
        73–75, 80–82
    species concept and, 72–73
    species selection and, 70
    *See also* Biodiversity; Community conservation
Conservative think tanks (CTT) and environmental
        skepticism, 280–281
Conspicuous consumption, 254
Consumption
    advertisement and, 283–285
    collaborative consumption as solution, 285–288
    ecological harm, 262, 264, 283, 284
    economic postgrowth solutions and, 262,
        263–264
    mechanisms linked to, 254–255
    "postindustrial"/"postpollution" economies and,
        264
    recreation/vacations and, 264
    sharing economy and trust, 288
    sociology of, 254–255
    storage/costs and, 287
    work-spend cycle, 263–264
Contingent valuation, 290

Convention on Biological Diversity (CBD)
  biopiracy and, 78, 79
  origins/goals, 38
  United States and, 38
Coriolis Effect, 46
Cornucopian view, 131–132
Costa Rica and HPI, 265
Countermovement, 280
Crutzen, Paul, 38
Cuba and HDI, 265, 266 (fig.)
Cultural hot spots, 77

Daly, Herman, 247, 261
Dams/diversions, 89–90, 91, 184, 236, 236 (photo)
  *See also specific dams*
Daylighting/South Korea example, 152, 152 (photo)
Dead zones, 163–164
Death causes by age, globally, 141 (table)
*Death of Nature, The* (Merchant), 277–278
Decoupling, 211–212
Deforestation
  effects, 68, 107
  in FTT, 219
Delucchi, Mark, 149
Democracy
  environmental concern and, 292
  famines and, 120–121
Demographic inertia, 127–128
Demographic transition model, 122–124, 123 (fig.)
Denial types, 279–280
Desalinization, 103
Dewey, John, 295
Dickens, Peter, 217
Dietz, Thomas, 32, 238
Diminishing marginal utility, 249–250, 252, 265
Disability-adjusted life-years (DALYs), 142
Discounting/"tyranny of the present," 233–235
Disease and climate change, 28
Disease vectors, 67
Down-cycling, 64
*Dumping in Dixie* (Bullard), 257–258
Dunlap, Riley, 12

E-waste. *See* Waste/e-waste
Earth Summit, Rio de Janeiro (1992), 78, 280
Ecofeminism, 277–278
Ecocide, 259
Ecological footprint, 2–3
  *See also specific issues*
Ecological species concept, 73
Economic growth
  alleviating poverty myth and, 250, 251
  average per capita income/happiness
    relationship, 250, 250 (fig.)
  diminishing marginal utility and, 249–250, 252, 265
  Economic Freedom Score/HLYs relationship,
    251, 251 (fig.)
  environmental degradation and, 8, 211, 212–218,
    247, 248

  as good for the environment myth, 216–218, 218
    (fig.)
  with income inequality and, 248
  life expectancy/GDP per capita, 249, 249 (fig.)
  limitations of, 247, 249–250, 252, 261–262
  "postindustrial"/"postpollution" economies and
    consumption, 264
  uneconomic growth, 247, 248
  *See also* Consumption; Employment; Inequality
    of wealth
Economic postgrowth solutions
  community capitals framework, 267, 267 (table)
  consumption decrease and, 262, 263–264
  failing growth economy vs. economy indifferent
    to growth, 262–263
  growth/employment link changes and, 262
  Happy Planet Index (HPI), 266
  Human Development Index (HDI), 265–266,
    266 (fig.)
  leisure/recreation and, 263, 264
  modeled Canadian economic stabilization/
    benefits, 264–265
  postgrowth society, 261–266
  Sen's theory of justice and, 266, 268
  shorter work week and, 263–264, 265
  tax changes and, 263
Economic sustainability, 80
Economism, 258
Ecosystem concept, 73
Ecosystem services
  definition/description, 68, 69, 69 (fig.)
  overview, 75–79
  values, 68, 75
Effective speed, transportation, 139
Efficiency, relative vs. absolute, 208–209
Efficiency shifting, 209
Ehrlich, Paul, 114
Electric vehicles, 38
Elwha River dam/salmon, 236, 236 (photo)
Embodied energy, 47
Employment
  current/future numbers and, 262
  growth/employment link changes, 262
  Kellogg/Great Depression and, 263
  shorter work week and, 263–264, 265
  World War II and, 263
  *See also* Economic growth
Endangered Species Act, US (1973), 229, 243
Endemism, 73
Energy
  car's mpg/gpm and, 196–197, 197 (fig.)
  compact fluorescent bulbs vs. incandescent bulb
    and, 195, 208
  public perception vs. reality on use/savings,
    195–197, 196 (fig.)
  sources/statistics overview, 183–186
  Three Gorges Dam and, 184
  top consumers, 183
  use by sector, 195

See also Climate change; *specific sources/types*;
    Transportation
Energy intensity, 207–208
Energy solutions
    carbon tax and, 199
    household efficiency and, 199–200
    public education and, 195–197, 196 (fig.), 199
    renewable energy and, 183–184, 193–194,
        197–199
    sacrifice/curtailment vs. efficiency, 194–195
    social norms and, 200
    subsidies and, 200
    See also Climate change solutions
Engels, F., 215, 216
Environment Programme, UN, 25–26, 60–61, 74,
    76, 243
*Environment, The: From Surplus to Scarcity*
    (Schnaiberg), 212
Environmental concern
    definition, 288–289
    democracy and, 292
    globalization of, 288–292
    Inglehart/postmaterialism thesis and, 289–290,
        291
    poor and, 289–292
Environmental issues
    complexity of, 11–12
    individualism and, 2–4
    poor people and, 3
    social sciences and, 4–7
    social world/material world, 5–7, 5 (fig.), 7 (fig.)
    solutions and, 2–4, 11–12
    views of, 1–2
    See also *specific issues*
Environmental justice
    evidence of improvement, 268–269
    Sen's theory of justice and, 268
Environmental justice definition/description, 256
Environmental Kuznets Curve/flaws, 216–217, 218,
    218 (fig.), 220
Environmental movement beginnings, 280
Environmental racism
    Cape Town, South Africa, 260
    climate change and, 257 (photo), 260
    definition/description, 256–257
    history of term, 257
    increase in, 258
    international/global injustice, 258, 260
    marginalized people and, 258, 259, 260, 268, 269
    Metales plant, Tijuana, Mexico, 269
    research findings, 257–258
    waste/e-waste and, 60, 61, 217–218, 232
Environmental skepticism, 280–281
Environmental sustainability, 80
*EPA, Massachusetts v.* (2007), 235
*Essay on Population* (Malthus), 119
Ethane/ethylene and fracking, 191
Ethiopia, family planning, 128
Ex situ conservation, 76–77

Exponential growth, 113
Extended producer responsibility (EPR), 63–65
Externality, 199, 221
Extrinsic values, 283–284

Fair trade, 224, 225 (photo), 226
False negatives (Type II error), 60
False positives (Type I error), 60
Family planning programs, 125, 128
    See also One-child policy, China
Federal Prison Industries, 52–53
*Ferguson, Plessy v. (1899)*, 296
Fermentation, 47
Fertilizer
    nitrogen pollution/effects, 164, 214
    treadmill of, 172–173
Fish and Wildlife Service, USS, 229
Fish In Fish Out (FIFO) ratio, 165
Fisheries
    ecosystem services and, 76
    technology/fish decline and, 215
Fishman, Elliot, 147
Food and Agriculture Organization, United Nations,
    25, 26, 121, 160
Food and population issues
    arable land, 118–119
    democracy and, 120–121
    famines, 120–121
    food insecurity/hunger causes, 120, 180
    non-human animal populations and, 121
    overview, 117–118
    vertical farming, 132–133
Food production
    affording food and, 179, 180
    aquaculture, 165, 215
    overview, 180
    treadmills of, 165
    as unsustainable, 214
    See also Agriculture
Food security
    biodiversity/agrobiodiversity, 75, 83, 85, 86
    climate change and, 25–26, 75
    pollinators and, 75
    population issues and, 117, 121
    See also Agriculture
Food sovereignty
    dominant models vs. food sovereignty models,
        178 (table)
    in Ecuador, 177
    La Via Campesina and, 177
    World Forum on Food Sovereignty and, 177, 179
Food system defined, 163
Food waste
    buy-one-get-one (BOGO) free promotions, 58
    buyer power and, 58
    cosmetic standards and, 57
    culture and, 56–57
    description/statistics, 46, 54, 56–58, 56 (fig.)
    France's measures to reduce, 54, 56

Food waste (*continued*)
  livestock food and, 58, 63
  market concentration and, 57–58
  Pay As You Feel (PAYF) cafés, 63
  per capita by regions, 56 (fig.)
  solutions, 62–63
  United Kingdom House of Lord study, 54, 56
  US Food Administration advice (1917), 57 (fig.)
Footprint shifting, 49
*Forbes*, 285
Ford, Henry, 255
Forest Transition Theory (FTT) and flaws, 219, 219
    (fig.)
Forests
  carbon dioxide removal and, 41, 241
  discounting/forest management, 234
  ecosystem services and, 75–76
Fossil fuels
  carbon dioxide emissions and, 20, 35, 41, 138
  energy/statistics, 185, 198
  externalities and, 199
  IT/computers and, 189
  statistics, 185
  *See also* Climate change; *specific types*
Foster, John Bellamy, 212
Foucauldian governance, 223
Foucault, Michel, 223
Fracking
  cracking/crackers, 191
  description, 189, 190 (photo)
  environmental/public health harm and, 188,
      189–191, 294 (photo)
  greenhouse gas emissions/climate change and,
      188, 189–190
  local control and, 192
  natural gas/plastic manufacturing and, 191
  preemption and, 192
  shale gas and, 187–188, 189–190
  social movement/water contamination, 294
      (photo)
  water contamination, 189–190, 294 (photo)
  *See also* Fossil fuels
Framework Convention on Climate Change, UN, 252
Framing processes, 294
"Free" parking/costs, 149, 155, 157
Friedman, Tom, 226
Fuel concept, 7, 9
Full irrigation, 163

Genetically engineered (GE) food, 39
Geoengineering, 38–39
Gille, Zsuzsa, 56
Global warming. *See* Climate change
Goldman, Irwin, 84
Goldschmidt, Walter, 166
Governance
  assuming worst of people and, 235, 237, 239, 252
  central government, privatization, common-
      property regime example/outcomes, 238
  climate change/emission reduction, 235, 237

common-property vs. open-access regimes, 238
dams/cost-benefit analyses, 236
discounting/"tyranny of the present," 233–235
Funtowicz/Ravetz "postnormal" science model,
    231, 231 (fig.)
global environmental problems and, 229–230
Pareto optimality standard, 232
regulation changes and, 243
welfare economics/cost-benefit analysis and
    flaws, 230, 232–233, 234, 235, 236, 237, 239,
    252, 258
Governance solutions
  climate change example/future generations,
      242–243
  common-property resource governance and,
      239–240, 285
  discounting reform, 240, 242–243
  precautionary principle, 243–245
  REDD, 241, 241 (photo)
Green building
  attitudes of those using, 36
  built urban environment and, 37–38
  climate change and, 36–38
Green revolution, 168, 173
Greenhouse effect
  description, 19–21
  *See also* Greenhouse gases
Greenhouse gases
  agriculture and, 160, 164
  cars and, 135, 138
  definition/description, 19, 20
  emissions sources/statistics, 20, 21
  fracking and, 188
  *Massachusetts v. EPA* (2007) and, 235
  population growth/carbon dioxide emissions
      growth and, 115, 117 (table), 118
  sinks, 35–36
  suburbs vs. cities and, 130
  *See also* Greenhouse effect; *specific gases*; *specific sources*
Growth. *See* Economic growth

Habitat fragmentation, 142, 144
Happy Life Years (HLYs)
  definition/description, 251
  Economic Freedom Score relationship, 251, 251
      (fig.)
Happy Planet Index (HPI), 266
Hardin, Garret, 237–238, 239
Harvey, David, 95, 223
"Health of the Planet" survey, 290
Heat island effect, 23–24, 23 (fig.)
Heinzerling, Lisa, 232–233
Heritage Farm, Iowa, 85
Home Depot/service area example, 153
Hoover Dam/Lake Mead, 89
Hughes, Thomas, 7
Human Development Index (HDI), 265–266, 266
      (fig.)
Hume, David, 278

Hurricanes, 30, 31 (photo)
Hydraulic fracking. *See* Fracking
Hydroponics, 132
Hypoxia, 163–164, 165

Implicatory denial, 279–280
In situ conservation, 76, 77
Index of Economic Freedom
    definition/description, 251
    HLYs relationship, 251, 251 (fig.)
Indigenous knowledge, 78
Indonesia and climate change/refugees, 30
Inequality of wealth
    changes in/statistics, 248, 261, 262
    consumption and, 284
    empathy gap, 276
    equality and cooperation, 252
    equality and innovation, 252, 254, 261
    equality benefits, 252, 254, 261
    foreign aid spending relationship, 252, 253 (fig.)
    health/social problems relationship, 252, 253
        (fig.)
    level of reward and, 261
    social distance and, 276
    solutions overview, 260–261
    treadmill of production and, 212–213
    welfare economics/Pareto optimality standard
        and, 230, 232–233
    *See also* Economic growth; Environmental
        racism
Informal settlements, 23
Inglehart, Ronald, 289–290, 291
Intergovernmental Panel on Climate Change (IPCC),
    25–26
International Monetary Fund (IMF), 95, 96
Intrinsic values, 283
"Inverted quarantine" concept, 94–95
Irrigation efficiency, 163
"Is-ought problem," 278
Islandization, 142

Japan's decreasing population, 124
Jefferson, Thomas, 240
Jevons paradox, 207, 208
Jevons, William Stanley, 207
Joseph, Sam, 63
*Journal of Health and Social Behavior*, 217

Kellogg, W. K., 263
Kelly, Kevin, 285, 286
Keoladeo National Park, India, 73–75
Kerala, India socioeconomic development, 126, 126
    (table)
Keynes, John Maynard, 262
Klamath people, 92
Kloppenburg, Jack, 84
Kyoto Protocol, 40, 252
Kysar, Douglas, 233, 234

La Via Campesina, 175–177, 175 (photo)

Landfills
    as carbon sink/sequestering and, 47
    climate change and, 47
    materials in, 44
    methane and, 47
    in other countries, 45, 48 (fig.)
    *See also* Waste
Landless Workers' Movement (MST), 176
Leggett, Jeremy, 244
Liberalism vs. neoliberalism, 95, 223
Liebig, Justus von, 213
Life-cycle analysis (LCA)
    description, 49
    disposable-paper cup, foam cup, ceramic cup,
        49–51, 50 (fig.)
    product selection and, 51
*Life Earth Global Warming Survival Handbook, The*,
    194–195
Life expectancy/GDP per capita, 249, 249 (fig.)
Lifestyle and consumption, 254
Lindhqvist, Thomas, 64
Literal denial, 279
Litman, Todd, 150
Longo, Stefano, 72
Low-elevation coastal zones (LECZ), 25
Lower Elwha Klallam Tribe, 236

Madison, James, 240
Mahbub ul Haq, 265
Malaria, 28
Malthus, Thomas, 119, 131
Mannheim's socialization hypothesis, 289
Market concentration, 57–58
Market environmentalism, 95
Markets and sustainability/fairness
    capitalism and, 211, 212–214
    continuing economic growth/environmental
        degradation and, 211, 212–218
    current system problems overview, 207–210
    decoupling and, 211–212
    Environmental Kuznets Curve/flaws, 216–217,
        218, 218 (fig.), 220
    fishing/technology example, 215
    free markets/enterprise meanings, 223–224
    globalization of environment and, 216
    natural capital/depreciation, 210–211, 212, 213
    Pollution Haven Hypothesis (PHH) and flaws,
        217–218
    poor/affluent and environmental degradation,
        216
    public goods and, 220–221
    treadmill of production/effects, 8, 212–214, 215
    world-systems approach, 218, 220
    *See also* Capitalism contradictions; Economic
        growth
Markets and sustainability/fairness solutions
    fair vs. free trade, 223–227, 225 (photo)
    solidarity purchasing groups/GAS example, 226
    total cost accounting, 220–222, 221 (photo)
Marx, Karl, 8, 213, 214, 215, 216, 217

Maslow's hierarchy of human needs, 289
*Massachusetts v. EPA* (2007), 235
Maternal mortality ratio, 128
Mather, Alexander, 219
Mechanical revolution, agriculture, 159–160, 161
    (table)
Megacities, 100, 117, 120 (table), 129–130, 133
Memory banks, 85
Menominee and nature, 279
Metabolic rift/thesis, 8, 213–214, 215
Methane
    carbon dioxide comparison/greenhouse gas
        effect, 47
    earth's early atmosphere and, 21
    fracking and, 188, 189–190
    as greenhouse gas, 20, 21, 47
    landfills and, 47
    *See also* Greenhouse gases
Micro-watershed councils, Mexico and Guatemala,
    107
Micronutrient malnutrition, 168
Mill, John Stuart, 261–262, 264
*Millennium Ecosystem Assessment*, 248
Mishan, Ezra, 283
Mitigation and climate change, 32–33, 39, 162–163
Mobile Bay Jubilee, 165
Mobile phones as waste/statistics, 47
Momentum concept, 7, 9
Monocultures, 171, 172
Moore, Patrick, 191–192
Mountaintop removal mining, 188
Municipal solid waste (MSW) management
    alternatives/solutions, 62–63
    in European Union, 48 (table)
    history, 44, 45 (photo)
    in other countries, 45
    transfer stations and, 62
    *See also* Food waste

Native Americans and ecocide, 259
Natural capital, 210–211
Naturalistic fallacy, 278
*Nature*, 68, 123
Nature
    differing ethnic groups relationships to, 278–279
    ecofeminism/feminizing of, 8, 277–278
    people losing knowledge of, 279
    religion and attitudes, 8
    roots of attitudes, 8
    worldviews of, 8, 277
Nazarea, Virginia, 77
Neo-Malthusians, 119
Neoliberalism
    definition/descriptions, 95, 223
    liberalism vs., 95, 223
Nestlé and waters in Canada, 106
Netting, Robert, 239
Neumayer, Eric, 234
New Environmental Paradigm (NEP), 290, 291 (table)
Nigeria and HPI, 266

Nitrogen pollution, 164, 214
Nongovernmental organizations (NGOs), 107
Nonpoint-source pollution, 102
Norgaard, K., 279, 280
Normal accidents, 194
*Normal Accidents* (Perrow), 194
North Pacific Gyre, 46
Nuclear power plants/energy
    expense, 193
    Fukushima Daiichi nuclear plant disaster, 194
    greenhouse gas emissions and, 191–193, 193
        (fig.)
    life-cycle analyses, 192–193, 193 (fig.)
    risks, 193, 194
    use statistics, 184–185
    waste storage facility/Native Americans, 259
Nuclear weapons becoming "uninvented," 77

Ocean fertilization, geoengineering, 39
O'Connor, James, 216
Oil reserves statistics, 185
Oil spill and penguins, 260
One-child policy, China, 113–114, 125 (fig.)
Open Source Seed Initiative (2014), 84
Open source seeds, 84, 84 (photo)
Organic system, 173
Ostrom, Elinor, 239, 240, 285, 296

Pareto optimality standard, 232
Patent laws and biopiracy, 78
Pay-as-you drive auto insurance, 154–155
Peanut biopiracy example, 78–79
"Peasant" term, 176
Peer-to-peer (P2P) renting, 286
Perrow, Charles, 194
Pesticides
    agriculture/water and, 99–100, 99 (table)
    insect pollinators and, 75
    treadmill of, 172
Peterson, Anna, 296
Phylogenetic species concept, 73
Pigou, Arthur Cecil, 221
Pigovian taxes/criticism, 221–222
Planned obsolescence and consumption, 255, 256
    (photo)
Plastic
    fracking and, 191
    as waste/in ocean, 46
*Plessy v. Ferguson (1899)*, 296
Point-source pollution, 102
Polar bears and climate change, 229
Political opportunity approach, 295
Pollinators ecosystem services, 75
Pollution
    affluent vs. less affluent nations and, 220
    China and, 143, 143 (photo), 183, 229–230
    climate change/water and, 102
    definitions/descriptions, 48–49
    EKC/flaws and, 216–217, 218 (fig.)
    environmental racism and, 256–258, 258, 260

"is-ought problem," 278
odor pollution, 48–49, 214
trans-Pacific transportation of, 229–230
*See also* Greenhouse gases
Pollution Haven Hypothesis (PHH) and flaws,
    217–218
Polycultures, 173
Popper, Karl, 244
Population issues
    affluent vs. poor and, 114–115, 116, 117 (table),
        118, 127, 130
    automobiles/biofuels and, 121–122
    China's one-child policy/population and,
        113–114, 125 (fig.)
    demographic inertia, 127–128
    demographic modeling/future world
        populations, 128, 129 (fig.)
    description/overview, 113–114
    ecological footprint/differences, 114, 115, 116,
        117 (table), 118, 127
    exponential growth concept, 113
    fertility rates, 115
    food and, 117–121
    gross domestic product (GDP), 125, 127
    household numbers per country, 130–131
    IPAT model/STIRPAT model, 116
    life expectancy and, 115
    poor people as "underused resources," 132
    population mobility/relocation and, 123–124
    population statistics, 114–115
    pronatal social norms, 122
    *See also* Urban sprawl
Population issues solutions
    cities and, 128–130
    countries with decreasing populations and, 122,
        123 (fig.), 124
    demographic transition model, 122–124, 123
        (fig.)
    family planning programs, 125, 128
    improving lives of poor, 132
    population increase and, 131–132
    socioeconomic development/fertility rates and,
        124–128
Porter Hypothesis, 226–227
Postmaterialism thesis, 289–290
"Postnormal" science model, 231, 231 (fig.)
Pragmatism
    pragmatic environmentalism overview, 295–296
    pragmatic solutions, 2, 12–13, 295–296
Precautionary principle vs. traditional risk
    assessment, 243–245
Pro-environmental behavior, 292–293
*Proceedings of the National Academy of Sciences*, 178,
    189–190
Pronatal social norms, 122
Public health
    scientists vs. activists value judgments, 60
    urban poor and social/biological links, 217
    *See also specific issues*
Putnam, Robert, 144

Rain forests ecosystem services, 73, 76
Reagan, Ronald, 194
Real Junk Food Project, 63
Rebound effect, 207, 208
Recycling
    behavior of people and, 10–11
    businesses using recycled material/problems
        and, 53
    changes in material recycled and, 53
    costs to recyclers, 10–11
    down-cycling vs., 64
    e-waste/prisoners and, 52–53
    ecological gains and, 51, 53
    economics of, 52
    extended producer responsibility (EPR), 63–65
    landfilling costs vs., 52
    LCAS and, 51–52
    not consuming vs., 53–54
    plastics/resin and, 53, 54, 55 (table)
    rates by locations, 51, 54
    social justice/worker health risks, 52–53
    three Rs of environmentalism and, 2, 53–54
    trends, 53
Reducing Emissions from Deforestation and Forest
    Degradation (REDD), 241
Rees, William, 222
Reforestation, 41, 219
Regional Greenhouse Gas Initiative (RGGI), 40
Renewable energy
    electrification and, 197
    energy solutions and, 183–184, 193–194, 197–200
    incentivizing, 199
    research and development, 199
    the sun/solar power and, 183–184, 193–194, 198
    wind power/turbines and, 198
    windmills/bird fatalities and, 198
Resource mobilization framework, 295
Role strain, 282
Roosevelt, Franklin, 263
*Rubbish Theory* (Thompson), 48

Salinization defined, 102
Salish people and nature, 279
Salmon
    as commodity, 72
    Elwha River dam and, 236, 236 (photo)
Schnaiberg, Allan, 212
Schor, Juliet, 263–264, 265
*Science*, 8, 68
Scott, H. Lee, 261
"Scrap" and waste, 48
Seed Savers Exchange (SSE), 85
Seed treadmill, 173
Self-identity and consumption, 254
Sen, Amartya
    China/population issues, 113–114
    food/famine and, 120–121, 180
    Human Development Index, 265
    on Pareto optimality standard, 232
    theory of justice/capabilities, 266, 267, 268, 269

Sequestering, 41, 47, 241
Seri and nature, 279
*Shopping Our Way to Safety* (Szasz), 94
*Silent Spring* (Carson), 1, 247
Simon, Julian, 131–132
Smith, Adam, 63, 213
Sneath, David, 238
Social capital, 144, 145
Social comparison/competition and consumption, 254, 283, 284
Social constructivism, 4
Social distance
    climate change attitudes and, 275
    description/examples, 276
Social movements
    framing processes/types, 294, 295
    overview, 293–295, 294 (photo)
Social norms, 200
Social sustainability, 80
Socioeconomic development, Kerala, India, 126, 126 (table)
Sociological ambivalence, 282
Sociological drivers overview, 8
Sociological imagination, 5
Sociological momentum, 7
Sociotechnical systems and consumption, 255
Socolow, Robert, 36
Solidarity purchasing groups/GAS example, 226
Solutions
    changing views/behavior, 284, 292–293
    complexity of, 220
    consumer-based solutions/problems, 94–95, 223
    sacrifice and, 3, 11, 194–195, 290–291
    *See also* Environmental concern; Pragmatism; Social movements; *specific issues*
Space mirrors, geoengineering, 39
Specialization and consumption, 255
Species problem, 72–73
Spence, Michael, 285
Street hierarchy, 151, 153, 157
Strip-mining, 186–187
Structure of agriculture, 159
Stuart, Diana, 6
Stuart, Tristram, 57
Summers, Lawrence, 232
Surface water and climate change, 102
Sustainability definitions/descriptions, 80
Sutherland, Rory, 283
Sweet potato farmers study, Philippines, 77
Szasz, Andrew, 94

Tea biopiracy example, 79
Technological momentum, 7, 9
Terminator technology, 85
Three Gorges Dam, 184
*Time* magazine, 72
Traditional Knowledge Data Libraries (TKDLs), 78
Tragedy of the commodity, 72
"Tragedy of the Commons, The" (Hardin) and criticism, 237–238, 239

Transportation
    energy efficiency by transportation types, 148 (table)
    policy and value judgments, 150
    US cars vs. Netherlands bikes, 9, 10 (photo)
    US history, 9
Transportation/cars
    biodiversity/habitat fragmentation, 142, 144
    biofuels, 121–122
    car numbers, 137
    car peak and, 155
    community disengagement and, 144–146
    congestion, 137, 138, 150, 151, 153, 155, 156
    costs of owning/operating, 137–138, 139, 149–150
    effective speed, 139
    electric vehicles, 38
    "free" parking/costs, 149, 155, 157
    fundamental law of highway congestion, 151, 153
    high-occupancy vehicle (HOV) lanes and, 151
    miles driven by age/gender, 137, 137 (table)
    momentum/"choice" in US and, 9, 10, 135–136
    mpg/gpm, 196–197, 197 (fig.)
    urban/community patterns and, 135–136, 136 (fig.)
    US history, 9
Transportation/cars and public health
    air pollution, 135, 138, 139, 140 (table)
    fatalities/injuries, 137, 140, 140 (table), 141 (table)
    fatalities/injuries risks, 137
    heart disease and traffic/aircraft noise, 140, 142
    obesity/overweight issues and, 138, 140, 140 (table)
    vulnerable road users, 140
    *See also* Transportation solutions
Transportation solutions
    bike-share programs, 149
    car insurance changes, 154–155
    changing street hierarchy to interconnectivity, 151, 153, 157
    congestion charge, London, 156
    dense/intermodal cities and, 146–147, 147 (fig.), 149
    disincentivizing the car, 154–157
    gas tax and, 154
    public transit movements, 156
    slowing down benefits, 151, 153
    street widths and, 153–154
    urban density/energy consumption, 147 (fig.)
Treadmill of production/effects, 8, 212–214, 215
Treadmills of agriculture, 171–173
TrustCloud, 288
Type I error (false positives), 60
Type II error (false negatives), 60

"Ultimate resource," 131
Uneconomic growth, 247, 248
United Church of Christ (UCC) environmental racism study, 257

*United States of America and the Klamath Indian Tribe v. Ben Adair (1983)*, 92
Urban density
    description/examples, 116–117, 130
    urban sprawl vs., 117, 130, 132
Urban sprawl
    cars and, 136 (fig.), 137
    description, 116–117, 119 (photo), 130
    public health issues and, 138, 140
    urban density vs., 117, 130, 132

Veblen, Thorstein, 254
Vernon, Luke, 54
*Vertical Farm, The* (Despommier), 133
Vertical farming, 132–133
Vickrey, William, 154
Vietnam and HPI, 266
Virtual water
    agricultural imports/exports and, 99
    by commodities, 93 (table)
    definition/types, 89
Volatile organic compounds, 117
Vulnerable road users, 140

Wallich, Henry, 264
Walmart CEO payment/comparisons, 261
Walsh, Conor, 63
Warr, Benjamin, 262
Waste
    composting facilities/health risks and, 60
    energy waste/life cycle analysis, 49–51, 50 (fig.)
    environmental racism and, 257–258, 260, 268, 269
    Great Pacific Garbage Patch, 46
    landfills/climate change and, 47
    Metales plant, Tijuana, Mexico example, 269
    nuclear waste/Native Americans, 259
    public health and, 58–60, 59 (table), 61
    solid waste generation by region/world, 47 (table)
    statistics on amounts, 45
    views of, 44
    *See also* Food waste; Municipal solid waste (MSW); Recycling
Waste/e-waste
    environmental racism and, 60, 61, 217–218, 232
    extended producer responsibility (EPR), 63–65
    increase, 46–47, 60–62
Waste regimes, 56
Waste solutions
    consumers and, 63–64
    e-waste/extended producer responsibility (EPR), 63–65
    food waste, 62–63
    MSW management alternatives, 62–63
Water
    bottled water, 93–95, 94 (table)
    California drought, 89 (photo), 103
    China's problems summary, 91
    city/rural demands and, 100

commodity water footprints, 89
contamination from fracking, 189–190, 294 (photo)
countries/statistics, 88–89, 90 (table), 92 (table)
dams/diversions and, 89–90, 91, 184, 236, 236 (photo)
disease and, 91
economics and, 88, 90–91, 104–105
ecosystem services and, 76
floods and, 91–92
investment in water infrastructure/returns, 90–91
relocation of people and, 91, 184
runoff/surface and, 91, 93 (table), 102
sector uses/statistics, 88
terms used for scarcity levels, 88
US Bureau of Reclamation and, 95–96, 97
watersheds development/consequences, 91
*See also* Virtual water
Water and agriculture
    amount used, 88
    hypoxia and, 163–164, 165
    irrigation/yields and, 163, 164 (fig.)
    overview, 99–100
    pesticides problems/costs and, 99–100, 99 (table)
    water use by products/nutritional value, 100, 101 (table)
Water and climate change
    drought and, 102
    floods and, 90, 102, 107
    pollution increase and, 102
    problems summary, 90, 100, 102
    soil erosion and, 90
Water footprint
    by country/statistics, 88–89, 92 (table)
    definition, 88
Water issues solutions
    changing how we view water, 103–106
    community management systems/problems, 107–108
    complexity/overview, 102–103
    pricing issues, 105
    responsibility and, 104–105
    water as right/value, 103–106, 105 (photo)
    water governance and, 106–108
Water pollution
    in China, 91
    climate change and, 102
    fertilizers and, 164, 214
    nonpoint-source pollution, 102
    point-source pollution, 102
    *See also* Water and agriculture
Water privatization
    affluent vs. poor, 95, 96–98
    description/overview, 95–99
    in India, 98
    International Monetary Fund (IMF) and, 95, 96
    La Paz, Bolivia example, 97
    problems, 95–97
    World Bank and, 95, 96–97

Welfare economics
    definition/description, 230, 258
    economism and, 258
    flaws of, 230, 232–233, 234, 235, 237, 239, 240, 252
    sustainability concept and, 240
Wellington Water Watchers, Canada, 106
Wetlands ecosystem services, 73
White, Lynn, Jr., 8
Whitehead, Alfred North, 277
Wildlife corridors, 142, 144
Wilson, Edward O., 68
Wine industry and climate change, 27
*Wired*, 285, 286
Wolf's two-year journey, 142
Women in less developed countries
    climate change effects, 27–28, 28 (fig.)
    fuel/firewood and, 27, 29, 30

    role, 27
    water fetching time and, 98–99
Work-spend cycle, 263–264
World Bank
    inequality and, 232
    origins/role, 96
    water privatization and, 95, 96–97
    "water scarce" definition/China, 91
Worldview
    definition, 277
    of nature, 8, 277
    privileged worldview, 8, 281
Wynne, Brian, 245

Xin Chung, 288

York, Richard, 6, 116, 209, 214, 290

CPSIA information can be obtained at www.ICGtesting.com
Printed in the USA
LVOW09s0801060716

495055LV00001B/1/P